MW01055211

To Evan with love, special thanks to Brian, Brad, Jill, John
and Judith for believing in me.

THE GIRL WHO LOVED ELTON JOHN
AND THE LITTLE BOY ON THE MOON

©2021 Tina Jenkins

print ISBN: 978-1-09839-410-3
ebook ISBN: 978-1-09839-411-0

THE GIRL WHO LOVED

ELTON JOHN AND

THE LITTLE BOY

ON THE MOON

A Memoir by

Tina Jenkins

PROLOGUE

"Nothing can dim the light that shines from within."
Maya Angelou

This is the story of how I became what I call a "Shiner." It is the story of how I found out who I really was and why I was put here on this place we all call Earth. It is my hope that my story will help others to make it through this journey we all call life. If reading this helps just one person to shine as bright as the sun itself, then telling my story was well worth the effort.

We are all are born into this world, usually with no memory of where we have been before our birth. I was different. I was born with a few memories of a place that I remember as my home, my true home. It looks like the Earth we are living on today, but everything there is in a state of perfection.

I remember being consciously connected to every animal that had ever been created. Even the grass and trees moved and were alive with life at its highest perfection.

If I wanted to eat an apple, all I had to do was think that thought and the apple would be in my hand.

In this perfect world, I remember my favorite hang-out place was by a huge thundering waterfall spilling into a lush, large lagoon that fed into an endless-looking ocean where I enjoyed swimming regularly.

I had a male black panther who was my friend who sat at the water's edge keeping me company. I also have memory flashes of riding on the panther's back through a verdant jungle at top speed. I can still remember what it feels like to be on his back feeling the strength of the cat's muscles beneath me as its legs raced through the jungle.

The panther and I had a close conscious and mindful connection of love and mutual respect.

There were also two angels helping me plan my up-coming life on Earth. I can still remember the excitement and enthusiasm I felt because I was going to the world of physical life and death. I recall watching souls on Earth live their lives as they bought clothes, married and had children. I watched them experiencing lives of great joy, and of wrenching pain not knowing that the whole experience they were living was pre-planned as a learning experience for the betterment of their souls.

I viewed the world of physical life and death as a learning ground, where a soul started out in pre-school, then graduated upon completion of college. A soul was born, lived and learned life lessons, died then reincarnated again and again until it no longer had any lessons to learn in the world of physical life and death.

Then each time a soul reincarnated and mastered its lessons the soul itself would shine brighter until it shined as bright as the sun itself.

I was like a racehorse, ready to break out of the gate to run my race on this place called Earth. I was so excited to be born and could hardly wait to experience all this for myself.

My next memory was of being acutely aware of being in my mother's womb, while still being consciously connected to my real home. I remember experiencing a floating feeling of drifting and sleeping, drifting in and out consciously between the two places. I remember feeling my mother's physical discomfort and emotions while being pregnant, and the cigarette smoke that swirled around me as she smoked as I slept in her womb.

Then suddenly one day I left that womb and was crying because now I felt disconnected from that world of perfection, alone and naked.

My journey had begun.

CHAPTER 1

I was born Maya Claire Johnson on June 9, 1961, at 10:28 p.m. in Los Angeles, CA, the City of Angels. I had dark brown eyes and dark brown hair and looked like a tan Creole baby. I was the result of what my father would later describe as a night of love in the backseat of his brand-new ice blue Chevrolet.

My Daddy, Clarence Johnson, who was 21 when I was conceived, worked part-time at the post office while attending Los Angeles City College as an art major. My mother was 17 and a senior in high school. They were in love and had been dating a year when my mother purposely became pregnant with me. At the time, my father was unaware that my mother had become pregnant on purpose.

Edwina Meilleur, who became my mother, was from a large strict Catholic Creole family that had moved from New Orleans, LA to Los Angeles when she was 12 years old.

Before moving from New Orleans, she had been hit by a car and suffered a serious head injury and now had a metal plate in her head. Aunt Chloe, her oldest sister, told me years later that my mother's personality was never the same after that accident.

Mother had been raised going to Catholic school until her mother and my grandmother Valentine Meilleur could no longer afford the tuition. That is when mother and her siblings had no choice but to attend public schools in Los Angeles.

Grandmother was horrified when mother started dating my father, because my father was older and out of high school. She was most upset that he was not Catholic and had been raised in the Baptist Church as the son of a Baptist minister who preached sermons on Sundays.

My grandmother, whom I called Ma-Ma, looked white, but in fact was a beautiful petite Creole woman with light brown, almost blonde hair, and brown eyes. Her daughter, Edwina, my mother was one of six children: three sisters and two brothers.

Her father, Bob Smith, affectionately called Pa-Pa, was Native American and white, and was a quiet thin man with dark graying fine hair that he kept neatly cut above his ears.

Ma-Ma and Pa-Pa loved each other totally and completely. I can still hear her voice calling for him from the kitchen while Pa-Pa sat in his chair with his legs crossed in front of the television set smoking a cigarette after eating a bowl of Ma-Ma's seafood gumbo.

My mother, Edwina, had full, long dark hair down her back; cream colored skin, big, bewitching dark brown eyes, full lips and had a dark beauty mark on the right side of her chin. She stood all of 5'3" and had what my father called, "a bombshell body."

CHAPTER 2

Clarence Johnson, my father, had a huge overwhelming family. Daddy's father, Franklin Johnson, came from a family of traveling Baptist Evangelists in Selma, AL. My father told me that grandfather's entire family had to leave Selma in the middle of the night to avoid being killed by a group of white supremacists.

Grandfather, at 17, was attacked by a white boy in town and beat the crap out of him as he defended himself. Daddy said that in the deep south back then in the 40's and 50's you could be lynched, tied to a car and dragged until dead or get your home burned down if you stood up to a white person.

My grandfather's family escaped that night to Indianapolis, Indiana where my great-grandfather Fred Johnson, a traveling evangelist, died from a heart attack while preaching a sermon in church on a Sunday morning.

One day I overheard Daddy telling mother that he had little faith in the Baptist Church. He insisted that he had witnessed too much wrong-doing in the churches to trust any preacher other than my grandfather. He further explained that he grew up watching church people committing adultery Saturday night then showing up to church Sunday morning; speaking in tongues as if nothing had happened. He also said that he knew a preacher who would drink from a hidden liquor flask before preaching his sermon.

Despite that, Daddy loved and trusted Dr. William Hornaday from The Church of Religious Science on 6th and Berendo Street in Los Angeles. My whole family belonged to that church, and I had been going since I was an infant.

Science of Mind is a philosophy based on the teachings of Dr. Ernest Holmes, who wrote the book "The Science of Mind." This philosophy is based on the Holy Bible and focuses on teaching you to do the things that Jesus did when he walked the Earth. Daddy called it, "making wine out of water."

Every Sunday my father's family would go to Washington Memorial Baptist Church in South Central Los Angeles to hear my grandfather preach.

I was just a little kid, but the minute I heard and saw the choir singing, people screaming, and getting happy with the Lord by dancing or falling to the floor in the church isle, I wanted to dance and have fun in the isle too. I would run out into the isle and start screaming and dancing. Then Grandmother Johnson would come after me and pull me back into the church pew. That did not matter since each Sunday I would do it again because it was such fun it was worth getting into trouble over.

After that service we would all go hear Dr. Hornaday give a lecture on positive thinking and the divine mind. Then afterwards the entire family would go to the International House of Pancakes for a feast, with lots of laughing and joking. Occasionally, Daddy would talk mother into going with us, which always made me happy, since my mother had a strained relationship with Daddy's family.

Many years later, Daddy told me that my mother was so beautiful that he knew without a doubt that any children he had with her would be just as beautiful, and how proud he had been to marry her, because he loved her.

Daddy dropped out of college and started working fulltime at the post office, to support us. Neither family approved of the marriage, and it was obvious to me at that young age that Daddy's side of the family thought my mother was crazy.

My grandparents wanted my father to finish college. Ma-Ma would have preferred that her daughter marry a Catholic, but since mother was pregnant with me at the time, she was happy just to see Daddy step up and do the right thing. The last thing she wanted was for one of her daughters to be an unwed mother. So, both families tolerated the marriage all because of me.

Daddy was one of 13 children. Because grandfather was old fashioned and did not believe in birth control, so by the time grandmother put her foot down and refused to have more babies, she had given birth to 11 girls and 2 boys.

Grandfather Johnson also did not believe in women driving cars or girls dating until they were 18, there were no sleepovers or parties outside his home. His mission was to make sure that all his children went to college on scholarships, and to ensure the girls were all virgins when they married.

This is the family I was born into.

My parents started out their marriage by sharing a two-bedroom apartment in Los Angeles with Daddy's best friend, Bernard King, who had recently married a Mexican woman and had a baby.

Sharing the apartment turned out to be a catastrophe for everyone. When Bernard and my father were not working, the party train they both rode before marriage continued right on down the track. The two would leave to have a drink on Friday night and not return home until Sunday morning drunk and high on marijuana.

My mother, who did not smoke marijuana, told me later in life that it pissed her off because she knew that his parents had raised him to know better.

CHAPTER 3

This was the beginning of my mother's life-long hatred for Bernard King. Because of the plate in her head, mommy could be unpredictable when she got mad. She was not the type of woman to put up with this type of behavior from her husband. She later told me that she and Daddy began to fight and argue like cats and dogs. Finally, they were asked to leave the apartment building for making such a constant disturbance. I was seven months old at the time and my father had no money saved to rent another apartment for us to live in.

My Aunt Marie, Daddy's oldest sister, had a one-bedroom apartment and took us in. She gave up her bedroom for us to sleep in while she slept on the sofa in the living room. Years later, she told me that sometimes she would come home from school and work for the day and notice that I seemed to be getting sick all the time. One day she came home early and found me alone in the apartment crying in my crib with a bottle of curdled milk and a soiled diaper.

She said my mother was nowhere in sight and later she learned that mother had gone down to the apartment building laundry room.

Aunt Marie drove me to the emergency room where I was admitted to the hospital, diagnosed with malnutrition, and had to be fed intravenously for two days. Aunt Marie then realized that my mother had not been taking proper care of me while she and my father were at work and school.

The hospital called the Child Protective Services, and mother and father were forced to attend counseling. At this point, mother's strange behavior had shown my father's family what she could do when she was angry.

Aunt Marie later told me that mother had used me to get back at my father for running the streets all the time with Bernard King. She figured that she could hurt him by hurting me.

My parents then moved from Marie's apartment to San Bernardino, CA into a three-bedroom house with cheaper rent because it was outside the city.

Before I could walk, I knew that something was not quite right about my mother; it seemed like there was something missing emotionally, as though a light was turned off in her head. I sensed the emotion of love coming from everyone else around me, but with my mother that was blocked out and missing.

I remember going to my Uncle Franklin's wedding and watching my mother lay down in the middle of the street when everyone came outside the church to throw rice at Uncle Franklin and his new bride. When seeing this my uncle yelled, "Quick someone hand me my car keys so I can run over this crazy bitch."

Mommy also had gotten into the habit of trying to make Daddy think she had killed herself if she did not get her way by leaving a suicide note then hiding to watch him freak-out.

It was at this point that my brother Dennis was born.

Father was no longer working at the post office and was now a sign painter because it paid more money. This made him happy because he had been an artist ever since he could hold a pencil in his hand. He doodled cartoon characters on almost everything he came across, so working as a sign painter brought him closer to what he really liked to do.

CHAPTER 4

My brother Dennis had chocolate brown skin and dark brown curly hair with big, dark brown eyes. A few of Daddy's sisters made jokes saying that the mailman had visited mother while Daddy was at work. That statement always confused me because I never saw the mailman visit my mother. He always put the mail in the mailbox and left. I just figured that Dennis looked like the Johnson side of the family.

From the moment I saw Dennis he was my best friend. We were a team from the first day my parents brought him home from the hospital. By then mother had gotten better at being a mom. I would watch her as she changed Dennis's diaper, and I would think to myself how handsome he was. Sometimes when my mother was not looking, I would dip my finger into Dennis's baby food to taste it.

When I was five years old and Dennis was three, our sister Stephanie was born. Stephanie looked like mother's side of the family, with a light golden skin tone and flaming, blonde hair with natural streaks through it.

Dennis and I welcomed her into our world enthusiastically; we loved her and did our best not to hurt her when we played "jump on the bed and fall down" with her. We did our best to protect her from the flies in the back yard during the summer months while she played in her play pen. Her skin tone was so fair that she got sunburned if mommy left her out in the sun for too long without sunblock on.

Stephanie was quiet by nature, by the time she was four years old she could be found sitting alone in a corner drawing just like Daddy. She was the only one of us who inherited Daddy's art talent and her hands were even shaped like his. If Stephanie ran out of paper to draw on, she would just draw on our cement front walkway with colored chalk. Or she would draw on the wall in the hallway of our house, which always got her in trouble with mommy. If that child could draw, she was at peace.

During this time, my parents bought their first home in Pomona, a suburb outside Los Angeles. Dennis and I happily spent our days playing outside in the hot California sun. We were partners in everything, and we always made these fun filled days for ourselves out of nothing. We would do things like find a bunch of ants in the backyard and herd them to go in whatever direction we wanted. After we were finished playing with them, we would play God by washing them away with the water hose. Or we would swing on the swing set that Daddy bought us for Christmas and put in the backyard. We had bike races with our training bikes up and down the driveway.

Dennis and I were always in the dirt or climbing trees in the front yard and doing things that mother claimed only boys did. I just thought that it was normal for me to do the same things boys did; I mean no one ever told me I could not so why not.

Dennis and I loved playing with our electric race car track complete with "Hot Wheels" racing cars, that we had asked Santa for in our letter to the North Pole.

Daddy said that each parent had to turn in a report card to Santa on how good the kid had been that year. He also told us about Santa's workshop, and how he worked all year round with his elves to make toys. He even took us to the post office with him to mail our Christmas toy list so Santa would know what to bring us.

CHAPTER 5

By the time I was six years old my mother was pregnant again with my sister Helen. I watched her stomach grow bigger and bigger as the months passed.

One day Dennis and I woke up from our nap before Stephanie. We decided to climb the big tree in the front yard and sit in it. While Dennis and I were sitting on a big branch sharing a chocolate chip cookie that I had stashed in my shirt pocket from lunch, we saw two white men in suits approach our front door and ring the bell.

We listened as the men told my mother that they were from some place called the health department and they needed to talk to her and Daddy. Mother invited them in asked,

"What's this about?"

as she shut the screen door behind them.

Dennis and I quickly climbed down the tree and rushed into the house curious to learn what these men wanted.

Once inside, I heard one of the men tell mother that they had treated a woman for a venereal disease, and that my father's name was on her list of sexual partners. Then they informed her that he was most likely infected as well.

Not understanding what venereal disease meant, Dennis and I watched mother's knees start to buckle and weaken as she stood in the middle of the living room facing the men. The men rushed forward and caught her before she hit the floor and helped her to the couch. One man asked if she wanted a glass of water.

"I'll get it for her." I said and ran into the kitchen. I worried about my mother as I quickly filled the glass. Not wanting to spill any water, I walked slowly back into the living room and handed the glass to my mother who was crying and holding her pregnant stomach, while the men tried their best to calm her.

After telling her that she had to see her doctor as soon as possible and get tested, one of the men handed her his business card and told her to have my father give him a call when he got home. Dennis and I watched as the men left and mother sat there on the sofa with her head in her hands crying. After a few minutes she got up and walked into the kitchen and called Ma-Ma.

Still crying, she told my grandmother how the men from the health department had shown up at the front door and what they told her, adding,

"He put our unborn child at risk! A venereal disease can cause the baby to be born with birth defects."

I wondered what a birth defect was, but I knew that disease meant that you were sick. All I knew was that whatever Daddy had done, it was serious. I had never seen my mother so mad and broken down before.

That afternoon when Daddy came home from work, mother was waiting for him in the living room chain smoking. She gave him the health departments business card and told him that the men had come to tell them that they had to be tested for a venereal disease. Mother paused for a moment and touched her pregnant stomach, before shouting,

"Last weekend you took off to go bowling with Bernard King and you stayed gone for the entire weekend! My educated guess is you did this last weekend with Bernard king you dirty bastard!"

Mother screamed, yelled and cried all at the same time as Daddy yelled right back at her and they fought for hours throughout the night!

My siblings and I sat huddled in a corner on the hallway floor holding one another so frightened we could hardly breathe. Stephanie was afraid and crying, but Dennis was too tough to cry, and I could not cry because I was the oldest and felt I had to protect my sister and brother.

We were all petrified as we watched mother pick up a lamp and throw it at Daddy's head; then she hit him in the back with an ashtray, as he ran into the kitchen trying to get away from her.

Mother ran to the coat closet by the front door and grabbed a pre-packed suitcase, opened the front door and threw it out on the front porch, where she loudly proclaimed, "Get the fuck out of my life!"

Desperate to get out of the situation, my father rushed out of the front door, grabbed the suitcase, and quickly got into his car.

My sisters and I stood at the front door and watched our father pull out of the driveway as our mother yelled, for all to hear, "Since you call your mother every day, go live with her, you fucking mama's boy!"

CHAPTER 6

A few weeks went by, and it seemed like I would never see my father again, I was wondering when he would be coming home. Time seemed to drag on without my father, then one day he just pulled into the driveway, and just like that he was home again; my mother had forgiven him.

It was a happy time for our family, Daddy was dancing around the kitchen again singing *"Earth Angel"* to my mother as he tried to teach her how to cook. Daddy would tell her,

"You're good at many things Edwina, but cooking isn't one of them."

A month later my baby sister Sara Helen was born. She was named Sara after Daddy's mother.

Sara Helen looked just like my mother, and you could tell that she was madly in love with the baby; always kissing and holding her. My mother was totally attentive to the new baby.

Every other weekend Daddy would drive us to Los Angeles to visit the relatives. We would roll down the highway with Daddy singing to the Four Tops, James Brown, or Smokey Robinson and the Miracles. Daddy would start dancing in his seat while driving, and mommy would get mad at him because he was not giving his full attention to the road.

When Daddy was not singing to the radio, he was complaining to mommy about the "Bill Man" taking all his money as soon as he got it.

We usually went to Grandmother and Grandfather Johnson's house first, where we were fought over by all our aunts. They would squabble over who was going to brush our hair and dress us. They even fought over whose bed we would sleep in! The aunts played games with us like Dodge Ball, Red Light Green Light, and Hide and Go Seek on the front lawn at Grandmothers big old house on Bronson Street.

My Aunts would put on talent shows in the house acting out musicals like, *"Frankie and Johnny"* or *"Camelot."* Sometimes we would go on big family picnics at the beach or the park. Grandfather and Daddy would load a grill into Grandfather's old 1950s station wagon. Sometimes Grandfather would let me and a few of my aunts stick our feet out the back of the station wagon tail gate while he drove down Pacific Coast Highway to the beach.

The family outings and the Sunday dinners at my grandparents were always happy times because we were all together.

Whenever we went to visit mother's side of the family Father would sometimes say bad things about Ma-Ma while he was driving us there. He would complain about Ma-Ma sitting in the front of the bus with the whites while the blacks were forced to sit in the back during segregation.

"That woman is just as black as I am," he said.

Then he would glance into the back of the car and tell us kids, "If you have one drop of black blood in you, you're black. I do not care how light your skin tone is or how straight your hair is, or how white your mother's side of the family looks. All of you are still black because your roots come from a slave plantation just like mine, so always remember that and be proud of it."

Personally, I did not care about being black or white. I just cared about eating a bowl of Ma-Ma's seafood gumbo. We had a relative in New Orleans who owned a grocery store and sent Ma-Ma special Cajun spices and ingredients for gumbo regularly through the mail. Mother had already told me Ma-Ma had a fresh pot of gumbo on the stove and I could not wait to eat some.

One day mother and I went with Ma-Ma to visit my great-grandparents, and she said that my Great-Grandfather, AKA, Gampy was suffering from cancer. I was six years old, and it was the first time I had ever been around someone who was about to die. I was taken to see him in a back bedroom so small that it reminded me of a closet.

It smelled like death all around him, and I wondered if anyone else could smell it, because it was so strong and awful. It looked to me like he was being eaten alive from within; I could sense the disease spreading throughout his body. I could also tell that he was in a lot of pain and suffering. His hair was all gone, even his eye lashes and eyebrows were missing. He looked pale and thin; I could see the pain and fear in his eyes as he lay there helpless in the bed looking up at me and my mother.

I bent down and kissed him on the forehead and could see on the TV screen in my mind that he already had one foot out of this world and would soon let go completely. His gradual separation from this world had started and I could see the layers of his life being peeled away and falling from him, until finally there would only be his soul left. Standing alone with no Earthly attachments, he would then be free from the pain that he was in.

Looking around the room I saw four angels against the wall. They reminded me of *"Casper the Friendly Ghost"*, a cartoon I watched on TV, and they were shining like the sun in the sky. Next to them, I saw a man and a woman waiting to take Gampy's hand and I knew they were his parents, my great-great-grandparents, next to them a strange door was open in the corner of the room. I couldn't quite see what was on the other side of that door, but I knew he would soon rise out of that sick body and walk through that open door with them.

A few weeks later, Gampy died.

I wanted to go to his funeral, but mother refused, offering no explanation. She would go alone, and that was that. Later Daddy told me that a lot of relatives from New Orleans would be coming out for the service, and that my skin was too dark to be accepted as family by them.

Puzzled by Daddy's explanation and wondering what dark skin had to do with anything, I went into the bathroom and looked at myself in the mirror. I closely examined my skin tone, I decided that I liked it; it was pretty to me. Looking myself in the eye, I concluded that; something was wrong those "relatives" because my skin tone was perfectly fine, as far as I was concerned. Shrugging at myself, I went outside to ride my bike and did not give it another thought.

Soon afterward I overheard Daddy telling mother that Grandfather Johnson got a phone call from the police in Salt Lake City, Utah. He told her that my Uncle Franklin had gone down there and been arrested at a hotel for supposedly not paying the bill and he was caught sleeping with a white girl in the hotel room.

"It's 1967," Daddy said angrily. "The hotel probably set him up because of the girl Franklin should know better than to go down there and mess with a white girl in a place like Utah."

Later that day my father and grandfather left California and drove to Utah to get Uncle Franklin out of jail and bring him home.

CHAPTER 7

Not long after that his wife packed up their kids and left him. I over-heard the aunts gossiping about it one day at Grandmother's house. Uncle Franklin's wife left him because she was tired of his running around with other women, drinking and smoking marijuana. When she left no one knew where she disappeared to because she wanted nothing from my uncle but her freedom.

My aunts said that Uncle Franklin gave new meaning to the song *"Papa was a Rolling Stone."* My uncle basically did what he wanted to do, and frequently his brother, my father, was partying right along with him.

It made me sad to know that my cousins would not be around the family, especially at Christmas time. This meant that they would be missing out on all the presents at grandmother's house. They would miss out on the big, full tree that our grandparents would always put up in the living room with bright, colorful decorations and lights throughout on it.

Christmas was a big thing in my father's family. The aunts would put on a Christmas show every year and come down the stairs singing *"1-2-3"* by Len Berry with a full dance routine. Then we would sing all the Christmas carols together, and every year grandfather would not allow anyone to touch the roasted duck until he had cut it and taken the first plate. It was always exciting.

One Christmas dinner my grandfather strangled my Aunt Barbara's mynah bird "Tweedy" at the dinner table when he got out of his cage and walked through Grandfather's mashed potatoes!

And now my cousins would no longer be part of all of this.

CHAPTER 8

I did not like it when bad things happened. I wanted everything to be a happy occasion filled with excitement and surprises, yet I was learning that life did not always turn out that way. That is when I promised myself that I would be always in control of my own life and happiness. No matter what happened, I would do my best to make choices that made me feel happy just like Dr. Hornaday talked about in church. Maybe this way I could prevent bad things from happening to me.

Life went on. My mother would make us lunch then Dennis and I would put on our swimsuits and fill up the big trash can with water from the hose in the back yard. We would pretend that we were swimming in the ocean and in our minds, we really were swimming in the ocean. This was one of the many things that I loved about my brother, who could escape into the land of make believe with me.

Daddy always told us to visualize what we wanted in life, and it would eventually come true. Dennis and I did that together. We would take turns holding the water hose over each other's head, so we could get that "wave crashing over your head" effect. Those trash can "waves" cooled us off for hours on end on those hot days. As the day turned into late afternoon, Dennis and I rode our banana-seat bicycles with the fringe hanging from the handlebars up and down the driveway and sidewalk in the little cul-de-sac where we lived.

Mother would be playing music on the record player loud enough for everyone to hear outside. She would listen to Blues, Jazz, Soul and Zydeco. If music was not blasting from our house, then one of the neighbors had it blasting from theirs. Mother would always have a blanket spread out on the front lawn for herself and Helen to sit on as she sat drinking RC Cola and smoking cigarettes as we played.

Our house was one of a string of homes built after World War II they all pretty much had the same style: one story homes at affordable prices because they were originally built for soldiers returning home from the war.

There was a white family that lived next door to us that my father liked; in fact, they were the only white people who lived on our street.

The Logans had a son in high school named Joe, who was a tall gentle giant to me only because I was so little compared to him. Joe had a blonde crew cut, blue eyes and said "groovy" and "out of sight" all the time. His parents, Mr. And Mrs. Logan were always so nice to the families on our street that I figured God had sent them to show Daddy that not all white people were bad.

Joe would give me and Dennis horseback rides on the front lawn almost every time he saw us out front playing. Joe was the coolest teenager I had ever met and reminded me of the Ricky Nelson guy on *"The Ozzie and Harriet Show"* that my mother watched on TV.

Dennis and I wanted him to be our big brother, especially when the Oscar Meyer Wiener truck, Helms Donut truck or the ice cream man showed up on our street. Joe always bought us treats from the trucks if he was around.

Then one day the fun with Joe ended when he received what my father referred to as the "The Greetings Letter" from someone called "Uncle Sam."

I asked my father who Uncle Sam was, and he told me it was just another word for the government. I heard them all talking out on the front lawn one Saturday afternoon as Joe and his father were telling my father and a few other neighbors about Joe being drafted into the Army.

My father told them that Uncle Sam had sent him a greetings letter as well, but he got out of going. Daddy said that there was no way in hell he was going to Vietnam to be killed by "Charlie." I heard Joe tell him that he wanted to go and fight for his country because he felt that it was his duty as an American.

My father asked him if he knew what he was really going over there to fight for? Then he spun his theory about how the government was somehow making money off the war, and how tons of young men were being slaughtered in a war that we could not win.

Joe told my father that he was prepared to take his chances.

I still remember the day that Joe left for the Army like it was yesterday. We all went outside on the sidewalk with his parents and friends to say our goodbyes and to see him off.

His mother had tears running down her cheeks and everyone was telling Joe that they would pray for his safety.

Joe hugged me, my brother and sister's goodbye and told us not to worry about him; that he would be back home in no time to give us horseback rides again. Joe and his father got into his father's car and drove away while his mother and girlfriend held on to one another crying on the sidewalk.

After that day, Joe came home to visit once while on leave. I was half-way through first grade when I saw him again. Dennis and I were excited to see him, but Joe was no longer his happy playful self. I was just a little girl, but it seemed to me that Joe was dead inside. Like someone had turned his happy light off inside his heart forever. There was now a permanent look of horror and complete devastation in his eyes, like he had seen one ghost too many.

I could tell that not only was he dead inside, but he was also in a state of shock, as though the real Joe had curled up into a ball in a small corner of his mind and he was never coming back again. Dennis and I were looking at a robot who was never coming outside to play with us again.

Every time Dennis and I knocked on his door to visit, his mother would always say that Joe was resting in his room. I did not see his friends or girlfriend coming and going like before. No loud rock music came from his bedroom window now, just silence. Joe's days of playing with Dennis and me on the lawn were now gone forever, and I blamed the Vietnam war.

CHAPTER 9

I began to watch the news on TV with Daddy about the war so I could see the actual film footage of "Charlie" trying to kill American soldiers. Even at my young age, I understood that my friend Joe was one of those American soldiers whom I saw on TV getting shot at. As I watched the war on the news with Daddy every night, I began to fully understand what it was that took my friend's complete personality away. I understood why the real Joe had gone to sleep in a corner of his mind.

Joe went back to Vietnam, and the following Christmas, I knocked on the Logan's front door to see if Joe were coming home for the holidays so I could make him a gift in school. I was going to make him a good luck necklace to wear around his neck so "Charlie" could not kill him.

His mother answered the door, and when I asked her about Joe she burst into tears. Mr. Logan came to the door and hugged her; he told her to go into the other room while he explained things to me.

Mr. Logan then looked at me and said, "Joe won't be coming home for Christmas. He was killed in Vietnam. I thought your parents would have told you and your brother by now."

I felt numb and heartbroken as tears began to run down my cheeks.

"Mr. Logan, I'm so sorry that Joe has died. I'm really going to miss him."

As I walked home, I thought how messed up it was that a nice guy like Joe had to go back to heaven early. I went to my bedroom and cried because now Joe would never get married to his girlfriend and have kids, and Joe was never going to grow old and have grandkids like my grandparents. I would never see his beautiful smile again or hear him laugh.

Crying, suddenly, I began to picture the good times we had together on the movie screen in my mind. I saw the real Joe smiling and happy, tanning in his backyard with his girlfriend on deck chairs again. He was playing his groovy rock music on the record player loud enough to be heard at my house.

I saw him giving Dennis and me, horseback rides on the lawn and playing ball with us. I suddenly knew that Joe was happy and okay.

Then I realized that this was the way he wanted me to remember him: happy and smiling as I heard a gentle voice inside me say. "I have Joe and all his pain is gone; he is well."

I knew it was the voice of God without a doubt. "Remember him this way" the voice said.

Mother interrupted everything by walking into my bedroom to tell me that dinner was ready. She saw me crying and asked what was wrong. I told her that Joe's father told me that Joe was dead.

"How come no one told me and Dennis?" I asked.

She replied, "Your father and I thought you kids were too young to understand, and there's nothing you can do about it anyway. He's with God and the angels now so stop crying and come eat your dinner while it's hot."

When I got to the table I saw to my disappointment, that she had made beef tongue for dinner. I hated beef tongue because the meat was so tough, and it had been cut out of some poor cow's mouth. Every time I looked at the tongue just lying there on the platter, I could see that cow in a pasture eating from the ground with that tongue.

She always tried to make me eat the beef tongue, and I always refused. Then she would make me sit at the dinner table with the plate in front of me thinking I would eat it if I sat there long enough, but I never did. I would sit there until it was time to go to bed if I had to. But on this night my mother told me that I did not have to eat the beef tongue, and I knew she had mercy on me because of Joe.

Now I realized that bad things could happen to you no matter how hard you tried to keep it from your doorstep; things like Joe being killed. I thought to myself that the world of physical life and death was a dangerous place to be, because now I knew that pure evil existed in the world.

Before I saw the war on TV, I had no knowledge of evil at all. Everything was innocent, like watching the crazy *"Banana Splits"* TV show at the dining room table while eating my bowl of Wheaties cereal in the morning and being excited when I found a toy in the box.

Now I looked at the world differently and knew that I would have to make all the right life decisions for myself in order to survive.

It was 1967 and I was six years old when my father started working a new job as a truck driver for Filbert Carrier Trucking Company. I remember how happy he was because he was in something called a "union" and he had to pay something called "union dues." This was the first time I saw my father happy and willing to pay for something.

Daddy would sit at the dinner table at night and tell mother how he and the few other blacks that worked for the trucking company were hired only to fill a legal racial quota, and that one of his supervisors was trying to set him up to be fired by making up stuff such as my father being late getting to a delivery destination.

After that conversation, I watched him begin to keep his own records to guard against being set up. Every evening at the dinner table I would listen to him fill Mother in on what had happened to him at work that day.

Daddy had a little red book that he took with him that he called "The Daily Reminder," and proudly proclaimed he had been using them since he was 13 years old. He would write down all his truck run times along with everything else he did that day in that little red book, as well as how much money he spent that day and what he spent it on.

He could open that red book and tell you the last time he gave us kids money for the Oscar Meyer weenie truck or the Helms donut truck.

Because of racism, the three black men, Terry Mouton, Julian Colbert and my father, stuck together at work and outside of work.

Julian Colbert became my uncle Julian because he eventually married my Aunt Chloe after her marriage to my Uncle John ended. They were always at our house with my favorite cousins Elliott, Samuel and Joshua for barbecues and drinking, especially when Cassius Clay's boxing matches were on TV.

Daddy would get so excited when Cassius Clay got in a good punch, that he would jump around the television set screaming,

"Go head on and knock him out."

Sometimes he would knock the lamp over by accident in his excitement.

I sat on the floor watching Cassius Clay, who I viewed as a brave man spouting intimidating words to his opponent before he even entered the ring. I really loved it when he did his fancy foot work dance and announced how pretty he was. But the thing I liked most about Cassius Clay was when he told you that he was going to beat the crap out of you in the ring, he totally did beat your butt with a smile on his face.

Daddy called it, "The psychological butt kicking before the physical one put you in the hospital."

Cassius Clay was a man of his word all right, and even as a young child I respected that. He stood up for the rights of all men; and every time I looked at him, I saw a ray of light around him. He had what I called, "The Shine" on him.

His spirit would shine like the sun in the sky on a hot summer's day because he was at his best, at the top of his game.

I could see that when a person was at their best physically and mentally, they did shine bright like the sun, and Cassius Clay embodied that. The courage and strength this man had was something I wanted to see in myself.

Because of his example, I knew that I could stand up and fight for what I believed in at home (like not eating beef tongue or liver for the rest of my life). I knew my father was inspired by him too, because he continued to fight against discrimination at work.

CHAPTER 10

A t this point Daddy was taking a tape recorder to work with him to gather evidence of racial discrimination on his job.

I would sit and listen with mother each night to the recordings of my father's white co-workers saying horrible things to my father like,

"Hey nigger, go load those boxes over there onto the truck."

One man even called him a jungle bunny.

My heart hurt for Daddy because not only was the Bill Man running after him all the time, but he had to go to work every day and be degraded for the color of his skin.

I made it my mission to ask God every night before I went to sleep to make the men at my father's job be nice to him. I always asked God to stop the Bill Man from taking his money, then my father could live happily ever after like the prince and princess in my "Sleeping Beauty" book.

After dinner, each night we would all go into the family room which my mother referred to as the den, to watch TV as a family. My favorite shows were *"Gunsmoke," "Mr. Ed the Talking Horse"* and *"Family Affair."*

Stephanie looked so much like the main character on "Family Affair," a little girl named "Buffy," that Grandfather Johnson started calling her Buffy and that was Stephanie's new name as far as he was concerned, and he called her that until the day he died.

My mother always had to have her cigarettes, which she often made me light on the kitchen stove for her. My father had his after-dinner drink, and sometimes he would go outside to the side of our house to smoke a cigarette that Mommy called Mary Jane, it smelled way different than the cigarettes Mommy smoked. She would always tell my father to stop smoking it before it killed his brain cells.

I can still remember the day Daddy brought home a big floor model color television set. It was the newest model and was his greatest pride and treasure along with his floor model stereo system. Because of the new television set, I hated it when my mother said the "bedtime" word. I wanted to stay up and watch more shows. I always had a hard time falling asleep; I would lie there in my bed listening to the crickets and heavy silence of the night while imagining things on the TV screen in my mind. I would see things like, me and my siblings having all the toys we could play with, and an endless supply of candy.

But most nights I would look out my bedroom window with my head still on my pillow and look at the bright stars high up in the sky. I had the perfect view because my bed was right in front of the only window in the room. I would admire the bright beautiful moon with the yellowish halo and somehow, I knew that God was there with the moon and the stars.

Not as a physical being but a presence that had a piece of itself in everything that it made. I not only knew this to be true but part of me remembered it and it all seemed so natural, like your next breath. I figured everyone remembered, but no one talked about it.

When I talked to God, I looked at the stars and the moon, believing that God heard me somehow. I would just lie there talking like God was my best friend sitting across the dinner table from me.

Sometimes as I lay there in the dark, I could see a group of Angels standing against the wall facing my bed. Just like the ones I saw at Gampy's house, they looked like *Casper the Friendly Ghost* on TV to me and shined brightly like the sun. They had no facial features, sex organs or clothes; just a person's form and an unusual brilliant, shining glow. I was not afraid of them, and somehow knew these beings were my friends, watching out for me and it seemed so natural that they were there behind the scenes of my life, and everyone else's lives on this Earth. I just assumed that everyone had a group of these special Angels surrounding and protecting them.

One night in bed as I lay there in total silence, I heard a voice from within me ask, "What would you rather have in your life, love or money?"

I thought about that for a minute. I knew everyone needed money, but somehow, I knew that love was more important, and decided to take the higher road. I answered back in thought saying, "I want love."

CHAPTER 11

One of the Angels, whom I named De-De because she felt like a female, even if she looked like *Casper the Friendly Ghost* with no sex organs. In my mind she was a female and sometimes she would take me flying after I had fallen to sleep at night. She would take my hand and I would get up out of my body, but my body would still be lying asleep on the bed. This seemed normal to me as well as I just stepped out of my shell of a body and felt free to fly. I could see a thin long cord attached to my body's belly button as I lay there on the bed. I knew on the other end of that cord was the real me, my very soul with no body but I was still conscious of being myself with a body.

It amazed me that my soul and body were attached to one another by a long, and what seemed to be endless umbilical cord that was not seen by the regular eye. I asked De-De what would happen if that cord were cut. She replied, telepathically, that if the cord were cut then I would not be able to get back into my physical body.

I loved going flying with De-De throughout the night having fun and seeing amazing, unusual sights. I would leave this place that we call Earth with De-De telling me not to let go of her hand as we ascended upwards in some sort of see-through protection tunnel. Up, up, up we went. I looked around me like I was looking out of a car window while driving on a busy highway at top speed, except this highway was going to another dimension.

Other spirits and entities appeared that I instinctively knew were bad because of the way they looked and made me feel, most of them looked like deformed nasty creatures. Strangely, they reminded me of a pile of dog poop in deformed shapes. I asked De-De what the nasty looking stuff out there beside us was?

De-De replied, "What you see is a mixture of disembodied spirits, demons, and souls that have refused the light." I stayed close to De-De, not wanting any of that stuff to touch me.

She went on to explain, "The distorted substance you see are cast off emotions like Jealousy, hatred, perversion and other negative emotions that have taken physical form; the light of God is not present there. This dimension is parallel to the one you live in, but it cannot touch you."

She explained further, "Souls on Earth are born protected from these things, but once you have stepped out of that protection and opened the door to that dimension, they would feed off the light God gave you. The demons and disembodied spirits try to take over the human body if invited in just to experience living in a body."

"I never want those things near me." I insisted.

"Then stop looking back and look straight ahead." she instructed me.

Following De-De's advice, I did what she said and looked ahead and that is when I saw the two ladders side by side. The light of God was shining brightly around the ladders, and they looked long and endless reaching from heaven to Earth. Working Angels in exquisite white robes were coming and going up and down the ladder, back and forth from heaven to Earth to help each soul on their path.

I knew this without asking De-De, and it was a welcome sight, and meant that we were not alone on Earth. We had angelic help that we could not see, so no man really walked alone.

CHAPTER 12

Then suddenly we were in time and space with the planets and stars all around us, and before I knew it, I was sitting on what seemed to be the moon floating on a cloud that dazzled with light in the middle of time and space. I could perceive another planet nearby, and I knew that it was called the "Red Planet." I could see a hot burning surface in my mind's eye that had a life form living underneath the surface. The word microorganism came to my mind even though I had no idea what that word meant. Then the answer came to me.

It was a life form in its early stages of creation, and I realized that God had done this on all the planets. All the planets and life forms were different but created from the same source. The planets that had no life forms on them yet were still in the creation stage like a baby being formed in a womb. A big explosion would happen in space and all the pieces which looked like big rocks to me, formed into planets.

It was like building a house from scratch; then after the house was built a life form was planted to evolve like a seed in the ground. Just like humans, each life form would grow to full realization of its maker eventually. The realization of all this was as natural as breathing. It was as if I had always known these things but had forgotten for a minute because I had been born to my parents.

I felt like I was one with everything in the universe because the same unseen force had created me and all of it.

Suddenly, I realized there was a little boy sitting in front of me. Even though we were there in spirit, I could still see him in his physical form from Earth and I knew that he could see mine.

A white boy, he had short blonde hair parted to one side of his head, a big strand of hair sticking straight up in the middle of his head just *like "Dennis the Menace"* on television, and a lot of freckles on his face.

He was there with his own angel friend that looked like De-De, and the two angels were making plans for our life on Earth together. While the little boy and I sat to the side of them playing Pat-a-Cake with one another, It felt as if I had known the little boy forever and we were best friends, like Dennis and I were. The connection between the two of us was strong as if we were part of one another, and together made one whole person. I knew that we were both the same age but had been born a few months apart.

We talked to each other using our thoughts instead of our mouths. Everything was consciousness to us, normal communication. We both knew that we would be married to each other one day when we grew up, and I knew without a doubt that he would knock on my door one day and take me away to live a life with him because he promised to. I realized that not only was this being communicated to us, but it was being programmed into our subconscious minds, to be tucked away until needed years later.

As always, the time came when we had to go back. Back into our bodies and back to our lives. We would hug one another goodbye, and as we hugged, I could feel his love for me, and he could feel mine for him. The bond between us could never be broken and I knew that the little boy on the moon and I would always be one person.

His angel would take his hand and De-De would take mine and within the blink of an eye we were gone from our special place on the moon and each other.

Suddenly I would be floating above my body above my bed, the cord that connected me to my body was pulling me back in faster than a thought.

Once I was back in my body, I would sit up in bed immediately, totally aware of the fact that I had been someplace else with my future husband. I could hardly wait to grow up and live my life with him and experience all our wonderful adventures together.

I looked out my bedroom window and saw that the sun was rising. I got up and went into the kitchen to make myself a bowl of cereal.

CHAPTER 13

It was Saturday morning and Daddy was already up and sitting at the kitchen table with his head bent down low. He had a stack of bills in front of him, and his red daily reminder book was open. He looked worried, and I could sense his stress and desperation over the bills.

"Don't worry Daddy. I prayed and asked God to give you more money so the Bill Man will leave you alone." I consoled him.

"That's good baby, I hope He heard you." Daddy replied.

Then I told him about the angel that took me flying the night before and how I had played Pat-a-Cake on the moon sitting on a cloud with my future husband, who was now my best friend.

"Good," My father said, "Now get yourself some cereal and watch cartoons while I finish going over these bills."

As I walked to the kitchen cupboard for my cereal, I knew that he did not believe that I went flying with the angel, but if Daddy did not believe me, then no one would.

When it happened again, I kept it to myself and did not even tell Dennis. Instead, I just made it a nightly habit to lie in bed every night and talk to God about everything on my mind including De-De taking me flying. Then I would always ask for Daddy to have plenty of money, to be happy and worry free. I would always tell God how good he was and how he made sure that me, my brother and two sisters awoke to a living room filled with toys on Christmas morning. How Daddy always sent money to Santa in the North Pole to help pay for toy supplies for us and children around the world; how he took us to the post office to mail our Christmas list to the North Pole and always looked so joyful as he watched us play with our new toys. Plus, there was all the great cooking he would do for our family since my mother's cooking was absolutely atrocious.

I always made sure to tell God all the good stuff about my father, so God could see that he deserved a break.

It really upset me to see my father unhappy, only because he was such a good and happy person, but most of all because he loved us. And I always had fun with my father singing in the car or dancing to James Brown, The Four Tops and other soul music in the living room in front of his big floor model stereo system on a summer's day.

When Daddy had a few drinks there was really joy, laughter and dancing in our home. He had a beautiful voice and would often sing songs like "Earth Angel", "In the Still of The Night" and "Unchained Melody" Doo-Wop style with a smile on his face and a drink in his hand. He told me that as a teenager he used to sing on a street corner with a group of guys.

I was eight years old and in the third grade when I finally understood why Daddy was always being pursued by the Bill Man. I was sitting on the floor in the hallway outside of my parent's bedroom door one Saturday afternoon waiting for him to come out.

I overheard my parents talking about some checks my mother had written that father said were bad. He kept telling mother that she had to stop "bouncing" checks and hiding it from him.

"I'm going to find out eventually when they garnish my paycheck like they did yesterday," he insisted.

Then the yelling and fighting started. I was only eight years old, but I knew that things were getting worse between them. The fights they had were more frequent and more intense. I realized that my mother did not have a conscience. I would often look into her dark brown eyes and see a blank stare instead of emotion. I wondered if anyone else could see that something was wrong with her. To me, this was dangerous to my father's well-being and happiness. In my mind, I felt I had to protect him as much as I could.

I decided that day to start spying on my mother, and every time she pulled out the check book, I would remind her that Daddy told her not to write checks.

CHAPTER 14

For the next few months, my mother did as my father asked and wrote no checks. Then one afternoon she took me and my sisters to the JC Penny department store and bought us matching overalls with daisies on them. I was excited about the pretty new clothes until the check book came out. That is when I reminded her that Daddy told her not to write checks.

"Just keep your mouth shut and stay in a child's place," Mother warned, as she signed the check.

When we returned home, I decided to sit on the front porch and wait for Daddy to pull in the driveway from work. I could not wait to tell him that she was writing checks again and fill him in on the afternoon's events. I figured I was doing them both a favor: Daddy would not get his paycheck garnished again and mother would not have to fight with him for causing the garnishment in the first place. It was all straightforward and simple in my mind.

As Daddy pulled into the driveway that afternoon, I ran to greet him as he got out of the car. I told him everything, then asked him if he wanted to see our new overalls.

"Not just now, sweetie; I'll see them after I talk with your mother."

When he and I went into the house, he was angry with my mother. He found her in the den watching *"Father Knows Best"* on TV; confronted her and demanded that she give him her check book.

They began to argue, then my mother got physical and broke a liquor bottle on his head. Blood ran down the side of Daddy's face, and he really lost his temper slapping her across the face. Then she picked up a chair and threw it at him.

I felt guilty and responsible for the fight. It dawned on me that none of this would be happening if I had kept my mouth shut.

Next thing I knew the police were at the front door saying one of the neighbors had called them reporting a domestic dispute.

Once they saw that my mother was safe, and my father was the one who had received the injuries, they asked him if he wanted to press charges against her, but he said no. The two police officers told him to go to a hospital and get his head stitched up, then left.

As the months went by my parents fought so often that the same two police officers would show up and started calling my parents by their first names instead of their last. Sometimes Daddy would leave the house until things had calmed down, and sometimes my mother would leave for Ma Ma's house with a suitcase for a week.

Their fights were always about my mother over spending or my father going out with Bernard King on Friday night and not coming home until Sunday.

I had a bad feeling about my mother spending money, so I continued to tell my father every time I saw her spending money. Then, when she became aware of what I was doing. That's when the beatings started.

I would tell my father about her spending money; they would fight about it, and as soon as my father was not around, my mother would make me take off all my clothes and run cold water in the tub. She would make me get in the tub to get my body wet then make me get out without drying off with a towel. She would then lead me into my bedroom and make me stand up against the wall while she whipped me with an extension cord naked and wet.

My mother would beat me until there were marks on my body, sometimes it would cut into my skin and bleed if she kept hitting me in the same spot too many times which she did intentionally. If I cried out or moved, the beating lasted longer. I trained myself not to move, cry or feel.

During these times, I could see the Angels in a circle around me protecting me from the pain. I figured the beating was worth it if Daddy got to keep his money.

CHAPTER 15

My mother always forced me to wear a dress to school the following day which was worse than the beating itself. The kids at school would see the extension cord marks on my legs and arms and then tease me. The feeling of humiliation and embarrassment was over whelming.

Sometimes I would cry as the other kids danced around me chanting, "You got a whipping; you got a whipping."

They would point at me and laugh at me like I was a freak. At home, Stephanie would laugh at me whenever I had marks on my butt and vagina. Because of this I began to hate my mother.

It was now a regular part of my life to see my parents love one another for a few months, then have a big fight which usually became physical. My mother would hit my father with something or cut him with a knife from the kitchen. My father would sometimes hit her back or try to restrain her while us kids huddled in a corner crying. I began to believe that when you were married that you and your husband yelled and got mad at one another regularly and sometimes someone got hit. Then you would kiss and make-up. This was just the way it was when you were married and in love.

By the time I was nine years old my mother was the one who left home; sometimes it was for a few weeks and sometimes it was longer. Since Daddy worked full time, he was unable to take care of us on his own so he would drive us to LA to stay with Grandmother and Grandfather Johnson until my mother returned.

My Aunt Marie would always pick me up from grandmother's house to stay at her new duplex with my Uncle Phillip, whom she had recently married. A handsome couple, my Aunt Marie looked like one of the magazine models on her wedding day, and her husband Phillip, was a smart, classy man with big dreams for his future. He was the epidemy of tall, dark and handsome. I was flower girl at their lavish wedding.

They loved me like I was their own child, because unfortunately, they were unable to have children of their own because of my aunt's medical condition. Staying with Marie and Phillip was like living in a fantasy world where every day was an adventure. For instance, they would take me to the movies to see, wonderful musicals like, "*The Sound of Music*," "Man Of La Mancha," and "*Oliver*," but "*Born Free*" was my absolute favorite movie. This was because of Elsa the lion and the relationship and love Elsa had for the married couple who raised her. When I grew up, I wanted to raise a wild animal too.

When Elsa was set free in the wild, I cried out of joy. I knew, somehow, that there was a place where all humans lived in peace and harmony with the animals and no animal was held captive. Everyday Aunt Marie let me play the "*Born Free*" soundtrack on her record player. I would listen over and over imagining that all animals were free to do as they pleased, myself included. I could hardly wait to grow up and have my own experiences, such as going out to dinner with friends and living by the ocean. To me, that was being free.

Marie and Phillip frequently took me to Bob's Big Boy Restaurant on Wilshire Blvd for the best hamburgers and milkshakes I had ever tasted. And if I still had room in my stomach, Uncle Phillip would order a banana split for my desert.

Marie bought me beautiful new clothes and brushed my hair while sitting at the mirrored vanity dressing table she had won on "*The Newlywed Game*," where she and Uncle Phillip had won prizes that included enough Broyhill furniture to fill every room in their three-bedroom duplex. Marie also made sure I had a bottle of "Mr. Bubbles" so I could take bubble baths, which made me feel so special.

Another exciting activity was helping Aunt Marie in the kitchen as she prepared gourmet meals. Whenever she made apple pie, she would make a little extra pie crust for me. Together, we would sprinkle cinnamon, nutmeg and sugar on the dough then bake it. It was our special thing to do together.

CHAPTER 16

Aunt Marie told me that she worked for the "Peace Corp" because she cared about other people and wanted to make a difference in their lives. While she worked, I went to grandmother's which was okay because I got to spend time with my brother and sisters.

Sometimes she would drop me off at the Public Library instead because they had a children's reading program twice a week, and I loved to read.

For me reading was an escape into a whole new world of imagination and adventure with the characters I was reading about, as if I were there. Sometimes the library had puppet shows and arts and crafts, complete with the glue that I loved to put on my fingertips then peel off after it dried.

The library also had the latest order forms for the Scholastic Book Club, where I was a proud member. I had just finished a book called, "The Island of The Blue Dolphins" By Scott O'Dell. It was my favorite because the main character was stranded on an Island in California with a wolf dog as her best friend. Because of that book, I decided to have a wolf dog as a pet when I grew up. I loved getting the Scholastic Books in the mail and loved the smell of new books. I always stacked my books neatly in my room and made sure my hands were washed and clean before reading them because I did not want dirt smudges on my pages. But the thing I loved most about the library was when a children's author would come and read their books out loud then sign your book afterwards.

When Aunt Marie was not working, we would sometimes drive down Pacific Coast Highway to the beach in her elegant green Porsche sports car. We would hold hands as she drove and sing songs from the radio like "American Pie" and "Wendy". Marie would buy me Copper-tone Suntan lotion and let me wear a bikini like the little girl in the Copper-tone TV commercial. We would spend the entire day at the beach collecting seashells, building sandcastles and playing in the waves.

In the evenings after dinner, Marie and Phillip would take me for a walk, or he would play card games with me like "Go Fish," "War" and "Old Maid." Every night they both tucked me into bed, Uncle Phillip would read me a book or make up a wonderful bedtime story of his own. His voice was like magic to me, and I felt warm and safe in my little twin bed. To me, being treated this way was special, because in my young mind only "*The Brady Bunch*" kids on TV lived this way.

I loved my aunt and uncle with all my heart and soul. Because of them I learned that you could be married without fighting and arguing all the time. I decided that I would have a marriage like theirs when I grew up, I now knew that I had a choice.

The little boy on the moon would find me one day, and we would go on adventures together in far-away places. We would be madly in love, hold hands and hug each other all the time. And we would be best friends forever just like Marie and Phillip.

My aunt and uncle dreamed of owning a big, beautiful home one day and always planned everything and worked toward it as a team. I remember the day they bought their first dark blue Mercedes-Benz; it was the most beautiful car I had ever seen. On weekends Uncle Philip could be found outside washing and waxing it.

After church on Sundays, we would often go to open houses in various up-scale areas around the city. Some of the homes we looked at were more beautiful than anything I could have ever dreamed of or imagined living in.

Uncle Phillip told me to always aim high and dream big. That is when I decided that I would have a beautiful home when I grew up, with a fireplace and hardwood floors. And in my driveway, I would have a jazzy red convertible sports car just like the man in the *"Get Smart"* TV show, as well as elegant furniture and gorgeous clothing to wear. This was all planned out in my mind.

CHAPTER 17

Marie and Phillip lived within walking distance of grandmother's house, so I was enrolled in the elementary school down the street from her house. My sisters and brother were enrolled there as well, so we were able to see one another at recess and lunch.

When my birthday came, and I turned eleven years old, Marie and Phillip decided to give me a birthday party. Marie even gave me pretty birthday party invitations to hand out at school to my friends. I invited the few friends I had made at school and all Daddy's family was there, but not my mother. We played games like pin the tail on the donkey and musical chairs. I got a lot of gifts, one of which was a promise from Marie that I could take ballet lessons.

But before I could go to my first lesson, my parents reconciled, and mommy moved back into our house in Pomona. I did not want to return home with my parents since I was happy living with Marie and Phillip. I was also going to miss my new friends, especially this funny kid named Barry Fallon and some kids that sang in a group called the "Sylvers." All the girls at my school had a crush on Foster Sylvers, the lead singer. We all walked to and from school together in a group.

Each day we walked past a local LA radio station to and from school. After school, each day one of the disk jockeys would be leaving the station after his shift and we would mess with his head by screaming and acting like we wanted his autograph, we really gave him the star treatment. It was funny to see this old blonde dude blushing and grinning ear to ear as he signed his autograph on our notebooks. Once I even faked a faint when I asked to just touch him by shaking his hand. That really boosted his ego.

Moving back to Pomona with my parents would end my new life, Foster Silvers had promised to let me watch his band rehearse. I was also going to miss Barry Fallon who had such an interest in money that he brought his Monopoly game to class once a week for us to play with.

I also looked up to my teacher Miss Johnston, who was nice and drove a cherry red Volkswagen Bug convertible with a black rag top. I loved her car and told God in my prayers that I wanted one when I grew up. I felt safe, happy and spoiled living with Marie and Phillip, and I wanted everything to stay the way it was.

But a week later, Aunt Marie was packing my things, promising me that she would pick me up every free weekend she had so I could spend the night at her place.

When my father showed up to take me home that afternoon, I could see my mother sitting in the car from Marie and Phillip's living room window. I knew she stayed in the car because she and Aunt Marie had developed a strong dislike for one another.

Aunt Marie thought mother was unfit to raise kids, and my mother resented being judged. Everyone on my father's side of the family believed my mother was totally crazy and capable of doing anything.

When Daddy took me down to the car, mother got out and hugged me. It felt strange because she hardly ever hugged me or displayed affection toward me.

Then we went to grandmother's house to pick up my brother and two sisters. They were all happy to see our mother and to be going home. To me, it meant life was back to no more special breakfasts of scrambled eggs and bacon with cantaloupe every morning at Aunt Marie's. I was now back to cold milk and a box of Wheaties cereal, with the occasional toy in the box as a consolation.

After moving back home, I prayed to God every night for a miracle to happen so I could live with Aunt Marie and Uncle Phillip permanently. Through their example I knew that dreams really did come true.

CHAPTER 18

This time when my parents reconciled, mother started selling Avon Cosmetics for extra money. My father had purchased a 1950's "taxicab" for her to get around in from a former taxicab driver. It even still had the meter in it!

My mother would pack us kids into her car after school and we would all go deliver her Avon orders to her customers. Sometimes she would give me lipstick samples to play dress up with.

For a while, everything went well. My mother was doing her best to stay out of trouble and be nice to everyone. When I asked to be signed up for the "Girl Scouts," she paid the fees, and bought my uniform which I kept neatly in my closet with my black and white Buster Brown oxfords.

Being a Girl Scout was a big deal that was important to me, and I loved it. I went to regular meetings with the other girls on trips and enjoyed the group activities. I liked being part of a group because everyone contributed, did their part and together we were a whole force. I could hardly wait to earn awards. " In my mind, a girl had really hit the big time when she became a "Girl Scout."

Unfortunately, my peaceful existence was short lived and interrupted just as I was getting used to living with my parents again.

One Saturday night my parents got dressed up: mommy in one of her fancy dresses, jewelry and full make-up. Her hair, which she had bleached blonde, was parted on the side and hanging in a perfect finger wave. She was beautiful. Daddy had on his three-piece suit and a gold medallion around his neck, rings on his fingers and his fancy hat on his head.

They hired the babysitter who always made out with her boyfriend in my parent's bed after they left and gave us candy to keep our mouths shut.

This night my parents were meeting some friends for drinks at a night club. I sat on my parent's bed as I watched Daddy look at himself in the bedroom mirror, and say,

"I look sharp as a tack. Sharp as a mosquito's nose."

Then he did a little dance and took another sip from his liquor glass.

We kids watched TV, after they left, while the babysitter pretended to study with her boyfriend in my parent's bedroom. All of us went to bed after watching a few hours of television, but in the middle of the night we were awakened by the sound of our parents yelling at one other.

No one had checked the mailbox that day, so my father took in the mail when they returned from the night club. He opened a letter from the bank saying my mother had bounced a few checks to Avon.

"You spent the customer's money instead of turning it in to Avon? What's wrong with you?" Daddy yelled. "Don't you realize we have to pay this off? You could go to jail for writing bad checks!"

My father was seriously pissed off.

My sisters and brother got into bed with me out of fear. The four of us just lay there in my twin bed together as our parents fought for what seemed like hours. They spent the following week not speaking to each other as Daddy slept on the sofa in the living room, while mother slept alone in the bedroom.

I would go to school each day and watch the other girls wishing I were them because I figured they had parents like Marie and Phillip at home. They also had cool clothes to wear and nice haircuts. Everything seemed perfect for them. They would bring their home lunches that had the fancy sandwiches in them, and always had good stuff in their lunch bags like potato chips, Twinkies and Coca-Cola in the little glass bottle. I on the other hand ate whatever the cafeteria served on the menu that day because my mother had signed us up for the school lunch program.

Every time I handed the cashier my lunch ticket, I was angry. As I ate my lunch at the table, I would watch the other kids and wonder what their home life was like. Did their parents fight all the time like mine? Did they get tucked into bed each night along with a bedtime story? To me, it looked like most of the kids at school had the perfect life. I figured it would never be that way for me until I grew up and made my life that way on my own.

I was still waiting for the little boy on the moon to marry me, then take me away for a life of adventure. Until then, I would have to be patient and control the things in my life that I could. Like keeping my books, toys and clothing in perfect order the way I liked them in my bedroom.

CHAPTER 19

Christmas Day came and as usual my brother Dennis and my two sisters and I got enough toys to make the living room look like toy land. My father made his usual special Christmas breakfast for everyone before driving us all up to Los Angeles for Christmas dinner and more gifts with both sides of the family. I was looking forward to hearing Grandmother Johnson play the piano, and Dennis was going to sing "It's A Small World After All" with me on back-up. I was going to sing "Where Is Love" from the "Oliver" movie.

I was excited because Aunt Melinda's husband Dan Peterson, just out of the Air Force, and now a reporter for the Los Angeles Times, was going to record us singing on reel-to-reel tape and take pictures of everyone.

After the photoshoot, Daddy was taking us to Ma-Ma's house for a few hours. As usual I could hardly wait to eat a big bowl of her seafood gumbo along with her Christmas turkey. But by the end of the day, I was under punishment.

Everything went well at Grandmother Johnson's house, and when we got to Ma-Ma's house all my favorite cousins were there: Elliott, Samuel, Joshua, Lonnie and Ned.

After we had eaten, Ma-Ma let us out into the backyard to play. I suggested that we all go peek into our Uncle Billy's garage apartment window. This was not the first time we had watched my uncle through his window. Sometimes he would smoke "Mary Jane" cigarettes like my father and listen to rock music on his stereo. If his girlfriend were there, they would sometimes kiss for long periods of time on his bed. But today he was just lying on his bed alone listening to rock music.

Bored after 10 minutes with no interesting events to watch in Uncle Billy's room, I suggested to everyone that we sneak into Ma-Ma's bedroom to play with Pa-Pa's teeth. After sneaking into the bedroom, I took the little box that Pa-Pa kept his teeth in from his top nightstand drawer. He wore fake teeth every day in his mouth, but for some reason he kept the real ones that had fallen out of his mouth in a little box.

I always wondered why he kept them. To us the teeth were a source of entertainment because we played "cowboys and Indians" or "GI Joe" with them. I was just getting the battle lines set up on the floor with Ma-Ma's bobby pins when she opened the bedroom door and caught us in the act! She started praying out loud for Mother Mary and all the Saints in heaven to give her strength. Then she yelled for our mothers to come get us as she pushed us out of her bedroom.

My mother angrily informed me that I had to stay in my room for two days. Then we were forced to stay in the living room where we could be watched. That was not so bad because Uncle Victor, Ma-Ma's brother, was there. He was always fun and was what my father referred to as a "player," but mother called him a "pimp."

Uncle Victor, a handsome Creole man with olive skin and straight black hair that hung straight to his shoulders, he looked like a handsome Spanish pirate to me. He was flashy and always dressed in fancy three-piece suits with diamond rings on his fingers and gold chains around his neck.

No one in the family ever talked about where Uncle Victor's income came from, but to hear my mother tell it he was a street hustling drug dealer who pimped out women. He drove a big fancy Cadillac that my father admired and wore a Fedora hat that had a feather on the side. He would tell me that I was going to be a fox when I grew up, kiss my cheek and give me a silver dollar just for being pretty.

I asked him why he dressed in fancy suits, and he told me that he was a business and a ladies' man which required him to always look good.

Occasionally Uncle Victor would invite Daddy to go out night clubbing with him and mother would stop them because she knew that Daddy would stay out all night with him.

CHAPTER 20

A few months after Christmas, I was sitting on the front porch watching Dennis do wheelies on his bike out front when the mailman came and handed me the mail. My mother had instructed me to always bring the mail straight to her, but this day I ran into the house and saw Daddy first and gave it to him instead. I was on my way back outside when I heard him yell out her name.

"Edwina, how the hell did we get three months behind on the house payment?"

Oh my God I thought to myself, here we go again. Stephanie and I sat on the front porch listening to them argue while Dennis continued to ride his bike out front unaware that mother had not paid for the roof over our heads.

I could hear my father yelling, "Why are we three months behind? We do not have the money to get caught up on these past due payments. We're going to lose our home because of you!"

Later that night I overheard Daddy talking to my grandfather on the phone asking to borrow the money he needed to keep our home. Then I heard him say "thanks anyway, I know you and mother would give it to me if you had it." As he hung up the phone, my mother walked into the room, and they started fighting again.

Since the last reconciliation, my mother had stabbed my father and threw a pot of boiling water on his hands. We had been in and out of the emergency room getting him medical attention. This time she threw a side table at him.

The police showed up as usual and gave my mother the option to leave the house or go to jail this time for hurting my father.

I stood on the front porch with Dennis and watched our mother pull out of the driveway in her taxicab car, unaware that it would be almost a year before my siblings, and I would see her again. Four weeks later the bank repossessed our home.

CHAPTER 21

The day my father moved us into a two-bedroom apartment a few blocks outside South-Central Los Angeles, he looked beaten down and defeated. We now lived in a street-gang filled area near Exposition Blvd in Watts and my father was not happy about losing his home.

I was forced to quit being a Girl Scout and change schools again. None of us were happy about the situation. Most of the kids that lived in our new apartment building were streetwise and had no wish to be a Brownie or a Girl Scout. I saw food stamps for the first time in that apartment building because most of the people who lived there received them. I was grateful that Daddy had a good job as a truck driver and paid cash for our food.

The girls who lived in the building were constantly touching me and my sister's hair, which was down our backs at this point. They claimed we had the good hair like the white girls. I did not understand why they thought our hair was so great, because hair was hair. I decided I had no choice but to adapt to my new environment.

This was the first time that mother had left us for such a long period of time, and I was getting used to her not being around again. This time my father figured Dennis and I were old enough to help with Stephanie and Helen while he worked, so we were not sent to live with relatives this time.

That was the year I began to realize how much I had been exposed to at such a young age. I was in the fourth grade, and I felt like an adult already, although all I really wanted was to be a "Girl Scout." But there was no time or money for the "Girl Scouts" now. Now I had to wake up and get my two younger sisters up cleaned and dressed for school. Then Dennis and I would get the cereal and milk out on the table and turn the TV on for the "Gigantor" and "Speed Racer" cartoons before school. At the end of "Speed Racer" we knew it was time to start walking to school if we were going to get there on time. Dennis and I each had a key for our apartment on a chain around our necks so we would not lose them.

Daddy would drop Helen off at grandmother's house before work. He had enrolled her in kindergarten at the elementary school down the street from grandmother's house. Then grandmother would take care of her until Daddy returned from work.

Dennis and I worked like a team and took care of the two younger ones together. I was happy Dennis was there to help me as it made the responsibility for Stephanie and Helen easier.

Dennis seemed a lot wiser than his years. It was as if an adult was in a child's body, and he was so smart that he always made straight A's in school without trying. He got a B+ once and became upset.

When boys at school would pull our hair and run, Dennis would chase them down on the playground and sock them until they cried like a wimp, or a teacher made him stop.

Dennis was crazy about Michael Jackson. He would practice singing and dancing like him on a regular basis. Dirt bike racing had been replaced with Jackson Five albums, with a hairbrush as a microphone by the stereo. He always made Stephanie and I sing back up while he played the role of Michael Jackson.

As we walked to school each day we saw drug addicts for the first time, who had been high and running the streets all night; a few homeless people pushing shopping carts with everything they owned in them, and you always saw a hooker coming home from a hard night's work.

CHAPTER 22

Dennis and I held Stephanie's hand until we arrived at school, because she was afraid of the strange people she was seeing on the way. I remember making a mental note to myself that I was never going to end up running the streets at night like the people I was seeing.

Once we got home from school each day, my father would always call to make sure we had arrived home safely. We were not allowed to go outside to play until he came home from work. We were supposed to do our homework first, then do chores like washing dishes and cleaning up the rest of our little apartment.

Daddy would come home every evening at five to make our dinner. He would make us help so we would know how to cook for ourselves. He always had some Al Green or Stylistics playing on his turn table so we could all sing as we cooked.

He was such a good cook and would make us a big pot of his special spaghetti with red kidney beans in it. He would brag that it was good enough to open his own spaghetti house.

"I can see it now." he would say, "Clarence's Spaghetti House in lights."

He would make us delicious pot roast that was so tender it would melt in your mouth, telling us not to fill up on meat and to eat more rice and vegetables, because he always wanted leftovers for the following night. He taught us that cooking enough for leftovers saved money on your grocery bill.

On Saturdays when my father was off from work, he would take us to the movies on Hollywood Boulevard to see the latest release. We saw all the Clint Eastwood movies. From a young age I was a fan of Clint's. I would imagine that my husband was cool like the characters Clint Eastwood played in *"A Fist Full of Dollars," "For A Few Dollars More"* and my favorite *"The Good, the Bad and the Ugly."* They were all Italian "spaghetti westerns" where Clint Eastwood kicked butt against corrupt law enforcement and greedy rich men in a soft-spoken way. And he always got the money, the girl and left a trail of dead men in the end.

I loved it when the good guy won. Daddy would joke and say, "Clint Eastwood walked into town broke, but in the end rode off on a horse, with the gold and the option of taking a woman with him."

We also saw all the new black written and produced films that were now making a market for themselves in the film industry. I loved Pam Grier movies and "Coffee" was my favorite.

After we saw a movie called "Shaft" we were all hooked on the soundtrack. Then my father started wearing long sideburns on his face like John Shaft and got his Afro cut in the same style. Some guys in those movies had huge Afros that moved when they walked. They fought crime, prostitution and drugs in their communities, which was always being brought in by some rich white dude, who was referred to as "The Man."

Whenever we saw the black films, Daddy usually took us to the Baldwin Hills Theater. Daddy said it was his contribution to the black community. My father said they were really trying to build up the Baldwin Hills area, which was nicknamed "The Jungle." He felt it was his duty as a black man to support it.

The Baldwin Hills Theater was old, built in 1949. Whenever I walked into that theater, I could see flashes of the past in living color as I stood in line for popcorn. People dressed in 1950's clothing enjoyed socializing in the lobby during intermission.

And every time we went to the Wiltern Theater on Wilshire Boulevard, built in 1931, I could imagine the building's glory days when girls dressed in smart uniforms sold cigarettes and cigars from a tray, while the male ushers wore military style jackets with matching pants and little hats. It was all very alluring.

I felt excitement and nostalgia for old buildings that held memories in the structure itself of everything that had happened in them. Instinctively I knew that this was the explanation for what I was seeing; not ghosts, but a film clip of a past memory that the building held. Then the movie clips would end, and I would be back in the present, standing in line for popcorn.

We were still going to church on Sundays and then to Grandmother and Grandfather Johnson's house for Sunday dinner. I would sometimes see the Angels standing up against the wall at church and I always saw a white light glowing around Dr. Hornaday's body as he preached and walked around shaking hands after church. There was something special about Dr. Hornaday; I felt an electric current of energy go through my hand every time he shook it.

I was no longer in the Sunday School classes in the back building, but now sitting in the adult church next to Daddy. Before service we all sang "Open My Eyes That I May See." Then Dr. Hornaday, whom we all called "Dr. Bill," would begin the lesson. I was learning how to visualize what I wanted in life, and how to mold my future the way I wanted it to be. I knew at the time I was being supplied with survival tools that I could use for the rest of my life.

Dr. Bill would read a verse from the Bible, then lecture on how to apply that principle to your everyday life as Jesus did when he walked the Earth. It was all exciting: God was real and was my friend, along with the Angels, so no one had to convince me to believe in God. If it had not been for Dr. Bill and his church, I would have believed I was crazy.

My father would always take us downstairs to the church bookstore after the service. Sometimes he would let me pick out a book to buy. I loved reading a book called "The Quiet Mind" by John Earl Coleman, as well as "The Science of Mind" by Ernest Holmes.

My father and I had just about every book that the bookstore sold on mastering the mind. We always shared the books; Daddy would read them first since he paid for them. After he finished, I received the book. Our spiritual library helped us both cope with daily challenges.

We would also go to positive thinking lectures during the week at the Wilshire Ebell Theater on Wilshire Blvd near Perino's, my favorite old Hollywood restaurant. Every time we passed by that restaurant, the little movie screen in my mind would flash past events like dinners after glamorous red carpet movie events with legendary stars like Joan Crawford, Natalie Wood, and Bette Davis along with a ton of other actors at the very top of their game at the time. Actors, producers, screen writers, studio heads, all spending time in the building having dinner, lunch or making a movie deal over drinks all part of Hollywood's Golden Age. I wanted to go myself when I grew up.

CHAPTER 23

We lived this way for almost a year with Daddy taking care of us and doing the best that he could by himself. My sisters, brother and I knew without a doubt that we would always be able to depend on him and we loved him for that.

Then one night, Daddy came home from work and told Dennis and me to warm up the leftover meat loaf in the oven and feed everyone.

"I'm going out to meet your mother," he told us. "And I need you to watch the other kids for a few hours. I'm going to talk her into coming back home with me."

After missing in action for almost a year, he finally heard from her. He told us she had been working in a night club to support herself. Part of me wanted her to come back so we could be a family again; but the other part of me wondered how long it would be before she was beating on me with that extension cord again.

As Dennis and I prepared dinner, I wondered if mother had changed since she had been away, and if she still looked the same as when we last saw her. The part of me that missed her wondered if she missed me too.

After my father left to go talk with her, we ate our dinner then watched TV. A few hours later right after we had taken our baths and put on our pajamas, my parents walked through the front door together.

We all ran to her at the same time, screaming, "Mommy you're back!"

As we all hugged her, it was one of the few times I can remember my mother kissing and hugging me back and it felt good. It felt like my mother absolutely loved and missed us. She acted totally happy to be back home with us and it no longer mattered that we had lost our home or who was to blame; what mattered was we were all together again.

CHAPTER 24

Time passed and it felt like we were a normal happy family in our dumpy two-bedroom apartment, in a rough neighborhood. Mother stayed home and helped us get ready for school and got the cereal and milk out on the table for us. She attempted to cook a good meal, cleaned and then watched her soap operas: *"General Hospital," "One Life to Live"* and *"Dark Shadows."*

It felt familiar walking in from school with my sisters and brother to find mother sitting in her chair with a bottle of RC Cola and her pack of Virginia Slims cigarettes that she still had me light for her on the stove whenever she ran out of matches.

Every now and then out of curiosity, I was still taking puffs from her cigarette as I lit it, but never inhaled. I just took the smoke in and blew it out as fast as I could. I made sure not to get caught. My mother was so unpredictable you never knew what she would do in any situation. I had long ago accepted the fact that she was never going to tuck me into bed at night, or even read to me. I realized she felt pain and disappointment, but for some reason she was incapable of having compassion for the pain that others carried.

By now, I was old enough to understand that my mother had no conscience, and she could not help it. She was just trying to survive the best way she knew how, and I accepted that. I knew in her own way she loved us kids and her husband.

I would rush and do my homework so I could watch the *"Dark Shadows"* soap with her. It had a main character named Barnabas Collins, an unwilling vampire who lived on a large estate in an ancient mansion called "Collinwood." Everything about the show, including the story lines, the music, the clothes and talented actors, appealed to me. It was something that my mother and I enjoyed watching and talking about together.

One afternoon after we had arrived home from school, my mother took us to see a larger apartment with three bedrooms. The apartment was in the heart of the "Jungle" near the Baldwin Hills movie theater. She said we needed the space, and this new place had a swimming pool in the apartment complex.

Dennis and I were sold on the new apartment the minute we saw the heated swimming pool. No more trash can "swimming" for us, we would now be able to swim in a real pool every day after school and on weekends.

My mother took my father to see the apartment the following day and he approved of the place so a few weeks later we moved in.

In the new apartment the three girls shared a bedroom and Dennis had a room. My parents took the master bedroom that had a built-in bathroom. I liked this apartment building better than the one we had just left. It looked like no one had any interest in chasing me and my sisters with hairbrushes trying to brush our hair.

CHAPTER 25

My mother enrolled us into our new school, and each day we would walk past a certain corner on the way where a gang called the "Crips" sold their drugs. One afternoon one of the Crips stopped me and told me that I was going to be a fox when I grew up. I did not know what to say so I just kept walking holding tight to Stephanie's hand, thinking to myself,

"Why did that guy just tell me I was going to be an animal when I grew up?" I turned around and asked Dennis.

"Because you're as ugly as an animal," he replied.

Every now and then another gang called the "Bloods" would show up on the boarder of our neighborhood. The Crips would yell out "Crips" and the Bloods would scream "Bloods" from the other side of the street. Occasionally, you would see a Crips and Bloods knife fight on the way home from school.

Strangely enough, we did not feel any danger from the Crips. They may have been selling drugs, drinking and listening to loud music in their low rider cars on the street corner, but they never messed with anyone who lived in the neighborhood. If anything, they protected us. It was their 'hood and territory and everyone who lived there understood that.

Back then I could play outside without fear of being shot in a drive-by shooting; unfortunately, the same cannot be said of the "Jungle" today.

Early one morning we were all awakened from our sleep by the Earth shaking. Next thing I knew Daddy was in my bedroom yelling "Earthquake " while telling all us kids to get out of bed.

By the time we got into the hallway my mother was running into the dining room with Helen in her arms and Stephanie by her side. As we all ran past a window, I saw the swimming pool moving and the water splashing from side to side.

I heard Daddy yell, "Get under the table!"

We all huddled under the dining room table together as dishes fell to the kitchen floor and broke. What little life I had lived so far flashed before my eyes, and I wondered if we would make it out of the apartment alive. Then, as quickly as it started, the Earthquake stopped. It was 1971 and I had never experienced an Earthquake before.

My father said, "Don't move, just stay where you are in case there's an aftershock."

We stayed under the table for a while until we started hearing the other building tenants outside. We all went outside and saw all the tenants talking to one another about the Earthquake, and I heard someone yell,

"The power is out!"

One guy came out of his apartment with a transistor radio that ran on batteries and turned it on. According to the radio announcer, California had just experienced a 6.6 Earthquake. He said that all schools were closed for the day, which was great for all the kids!

Everyone was afraid that another Earthquake would hit, and they were nervous about going back into their apartments.

I was still amazed by seeing the water in the swimming pool swaying back and forth during the Earthquake. I walked over to the pool to make sure it was okay, looking for cracks on the bottom and saw none.

Dennis walked up to me and asked, "Why are you looking at the pool like that?"

I replied, "I was just looking to make sure there are no cracks on the bottom; thank God the pool is okay,"

"Makes me think of that TV commercial for margarine where the woman says, Don't mess with Mother Nature?" Dennis said.

I nodded in the affirmative saying, "Yeah."

"Well, I guess Mother Nature got mad this morning." He smirked.

"She must not be mad at us, because she left us the pool and at least we can go swimming all day because school is closed." I observed.

Mother called us to come inside and help her clean up the mess from the Earthquake. After cleaning we had our breakfast, then Dennis and I headed straight for the pool where we raced each other doing the breaststroke and swam all day as if the Earthquake had never happened.

CHAPTER 26

A few weeks later one of Daddy's friends died, and he was asked to be a pallbearer at the funeral. Daddy went to the funeral on a Friday morning and was gone all weekend.

At 4 a.m. Sunday mother woke me up. She told me to hurry and get dressed without waking anyone, then to meet her in the kitchen. I was confused at first, then I remembered that she had been pissed off all weekend because my father did not come home or call.

When I walked into the kitchen, it was obvious she had been up all night, chain smoking waiting for him to come home or call. At this point she was livid, but she also looked hurt like her heart had been broken. She took a butcher knife out of the kitchen drawer and put it in her purse, as I watched in fear.

"Where are we were going?" I asked in my frightened tiny little girl voice.

"We're going to look for your father," she said with that flat, dead emotionless look in her eye. That meant she was out for blood.

We got into her car, leaving my siblings at home alone sleeping. I knew there was no doubt that if or when she found her husband, my father, she would certainly use that knife. About 15 minutes later, she pulled over and parked the car in some neighborhood I had never been to before. We got out and walked around with her telling me to look for his car.

"You know what the car looks like! Help me find it!" She said frantically as we walked down a dark alley looking for his car.

The night sky was disappearing as the colors of morning sunrise flared across the sky. This was the first time I had seen a sunrise. The vivid colors made me want to get up earlier to see future sunrises. But I was also sad that seeing this sunrise probably meant a tragic outcome for my family.

Praying silently for God to stop my mother from finding my father while she had that knife in her pocket, I beseeched him to protect us from her anger.

I vividly remembered the time she put a knife to my throat for telling Daddy she had written a check, and as she held the knife to my throat, she told me that she had brought me into this world and that she could take me out of it. Then she made me drink hot sauce for talking about her business.

Thankfully, God answered my prayer when my mother said, "We better get back to the car; the other kids will be up soon."

Back at our apartment, my sisters and brother were up already. Dennis had everything under control and had given Stephanie and Helen cereal as they watched "The Archies" cartoon.

"Where were you guys?" He demanded.

"I had an errand to run and took your sister with me," my mother answered.

Not wanting to make her any madder than she already was, I got myself a bowl of cereal and sat down at the table to eat it as if nothing had happened. I kept thinking as I ate that since my father was absent there would be no church that morning and that was disappointing.

CHAPTER 27

L ater that afternoon my father finally appeared. I could tell that he had been drinking and he looked raggedy. As mother started cussing and calling him names, he kept telling her that he wanted to go to bed so he could get up for work the next morning. She discovered where he had been all weekend, and that is when the fighting started as she threw anything within reach at him.

Stephanie and Helen cried as we watched our mother go to the kitchen to get a knife to cut our father; he hit her and knocked the knife out of her hand. She escaped into their bedroom crying and started putting her clothes into a suitcase, as she shouted:

"I'm leaving your ass for good this time and I'm taking my kids with me!"

"You're not taking my kids anywhere. Don't even try it!" Daddy said.

The fight ended on the steps outside our front door when mother tried to hit him one more time before leaving. Instead, he pushed her away from him, and when he pushed, she accidentally fell down the stairs.

I stood there and watched in horror as she slid down the stairs on her back, while her hand still gripped her suitcase. I was relieved when she got up, and I could tell from the look on Daddy's face that he was horrified too.

She looked up at him and said, "You chicken shit motherfucker, go fuck yourself because you will never be with me again."

A few months later she filed for divorce and asked for custody of us kids. Somehow, she had managed to rent an apartment a few blocks away from where we were living. She applied for welfare, and had my father served with legal papers that allowed her to take custody of us.

As she packed our stuff in boxes, she told him that she had fought with him for the last time, and maybe paying child support would stop him from drinking and partying out in the streets all the time.

A few minutes later my Uncles Jimmy and Billy showed up with a pick-up truck. I knew they were there not only to move our stuff, but to make sure that my parents did not physically kill one another.

My uncles liked my father but did not say a word to him, as they walked into the apartment and started loading up our beds, sofa, TV, dining room table, dishes and anything else mother felt she needed. Before she forced me into the car with her, I ran to my father and hugged him, pleading to live with him.

I heard my mother scream, "Well, you can't live with him. You must live with me. you can see him on the weekends."

My father hugged me tightly and said, "I'll come get you this weekend. Don't worry; everything will be alright."

But inside, I felt that everything would not be alright. As Daddy hugged and kissed me, my sisters and brother goodbye, I knew that they did not want to leave him either. He stood there looking like a broken man with his head down and his hands in his pockets. I stood there facing him with tears rolling down my cheeks as he turned around and walked back into the now empty apartment. We got into our mother's car and drove to our new apartment with our uncles following behind us with their truck that held our furniture.

CHAPTER 28

Within a few weeks, Daddy was coming by our apartment trying to convince my mother to get back together with him. But she had no intention of ever returning to him. Instead, she was fixated on a 19-year-old named Maxwell Rogers, who lived in the apartment building next door with his parents.

I hated and despised Maxwell from our first meeting. He was a dark-skinned 19-year-old black guy with an uneven, scraggly Afro hairdo that he always had an Afro pick sticking out from. What I hated the most about his appearance was his nose; it reminded me of a big balloon except it had two large openings at the end that allowed you to see all the dried-up boogers packed in it.

The other reason I hated him was the fact that he was not my father.

My mother was a beautiful woman who kept her nose clean, and I just did not understand the attraction between the two of them. Somehow, they met, started talking, one thing led to another and next thing I knew Maxwell was coming over to our apartment every day. I was friends with his younger sister Stephanie and knew from talking with her that Maxwell had no job and was hoping to make it big in the music business. He played bass in some soul band that rehearsed in his bedroom at his mother's apartment. You could hear them from the sidewalk every time they rehearsed, and not only did their music suck but none of them had any talent.

I could not believe that my mother, who still looked awesome, was going over there to watch this fool rehearse. I kept thinking that she should have been looking for a job instead of watching Maxwell's feeble attempts to play bass.

Then Maxwell started coming over to our apartment late at night after mother put us to bed. Dennis and I would sneak into the hallway and peek around the corner into the living room where she had jazz music playing on the stereo and candles lit to create a romantic atmosphere. She had on one of her sexy dresses and a ton of make-up and, for some strange reason, an Afro wig like she was Pam Grier. Why was she wearing a wig when her own natural hair was so beautiful? It was like she was trying to be someone else.

Sometimes Dennis, my sisters and I would just lie there in our beds at night listening to Maxwell having sex with our mother; we could not help but overhear them. The noises they made were not only strange to us, but funny. I would lie there wondering how my mother was able to have sex with all that make-up on and an Afro wig without it all coming off in the process. Of course, I really did not know any details about having sex. I just knew I was not supposed to be doing it. And judging from what I had seen in the movies, it seemed to me that your make-up would be smudged, and your wig would somehow come off.

A few months later my siblings and I walked in from school to find that Maxwell had moved in with us. This was a dark day for the four of us. Dennis and I were so upset that this lazy-assed punk had moved in that we stayed in our room all afternoon and listened to our Jackson Five records just to avoid him.

When Daddy picked us up to spend the weekend with him, Dennis and I gave him a full report about Maxwell moving into our apartment. We told him about the sex, the wig, everything. I overheard him talking to mother over the phone that weekend while we were at his apartment. He told her that he did not agree with her taking up with some young unemployed punk in front of his kids.

It was sad because I could tell that he still loved her and wanted to get back together, but she hated him.

CHAPTER 29

Since Maxwell had moved in mother was now always in full make-up and well-dressed. She would vacuum the living room to one of her favorite songs, *"Mr. Magic"* by Grover Washington Jr., while dancing at the same time. I could not believe she was dressing up for this fool every day. I kept thinking that she should have been dressing up for my father, not this loser. At least, my father had a paying job and was good looking. But this Maxwell guy was so ugly it left an imprint upon my young mind of devastation and total disbelief that my mother even looked at him twice. It looked like all she cared about was Maxwell and getting our child support check from my father.

My father would have me run in the child support check and give it to her when he picked us up on the weekends, while he waited in the car. He always did his best to show us a good time on the weekends. We would sleep over at his little one bedroom furnished apartment on Ardmore Street near downtown Los Angeles. He would take us bowling at Midtown Bowl where he bowled in a league. We would go to the movies, church and Sunday dinner at grandmothers. Then at night we would spend hours listening to his Soul and Jazz album collection while we all cooked together as a family like we used to.

Sometimes my father would tell us that his "money was funny" or "money was too tight to mention." This meant he was low on cash. On those weekends, he would take us to Griffith Park or the beach when the weather was good. Or he would take us with him to visit the new Cadillac he was visualizing for himself at the Lou Elders Cadillac dealership on Wilshire Blvd. He would visit the car, which sat on the showroom floor without a dime in his pocket, telling us it was his dream car and how it was already his.

After that, my father would put us in the backseat and sit behind the wheel soaking in that fragrant new car smell of the leather and the feel of the seat beneath him as if the car were already his. He visited that Cadillac for months. One morning while we were sleeping over at his apartment, we all awakened to the sound of his car starting up outside his bedroom window. The apartment windows faced the parking garage, and we could hear and see everything that went on out there from the window.

When my father looked out the window and saw someone sitting inside his car, he ran outside in his underwear to stop the guy sitting in it from stealing it. By the time my sisters, Dennis and I reached the front door, he was running down the street barefoot in his underwear chasing after his car.

After the car had turned the corner and was out of sight, my father stood there in his underwear for a minute then came back inside mad as hell and called the police. He filled out a police report and a few weeks later the police found his car stripped and abandoned on the side of a road in Riverside, CA.

The insurance company gave Daddy a check to buy a new car. That meant my father's dream came true, he took that check, along with his savings, immediately to Lou Elders Cadillac dealership. He gave them a huge down payment on that brand new 1972 canary yellow, top of the line, fully loaded Cadillac, with a built-in eight-track tape player. It was the same car that he had been visiting and visualizing as his every week. Then my father bought himself a canary yellow three-piece suit and hat to match the car.

Excited, my sisters and I watched as he got his hair slicked back in a hairstyle he called, "The sweet Jesus," a hairstyle he had admired on an actor named Billy Dee Williams in the movie "Lady Sings the Blues. He had been letting his hair grow for some time so he could also wear it that way.

CHAPTER 30

When we went to church that following Sunday, everyone in the family gathered in the church parking lot after the service to see my father's new canary yellow Cadillac.

My father drew a crowd around him as he told everyone the story of how he had visualized himself owning and enjoying the car every morning before he got out of bed, and every night before he went to sleep.

"You have to be able to smell the leather and that new car smell," he instructed.

"Then go touch it, claim it as yours, sit in it and get the feel of the car. I thought it was a tragedy when my car was stolen, but when I got that insurance check in my hand, I knew my dream car had manifested," he told everyone.

"The Lord works in mysterious ways," Grandfather said.

Then Grandmother told him that the car was nice, but he looked like a pimp with the matching suit and hat.

That is when I spoke up, "The police thought so too, because they pulled Daddy over on the way to church this morning. The cop didn't even know we were in the back seat until he walked up to the car."

"Serves you right," Grandmother scolded him, "You need to at least take that hat off. It's shameful to show up at church looking like a pimp."

"This is my *"Superfly"* suit," Daddy told her with a grin on his face.

"I look sharp as a tack," he said adjusting his hat.

"You look like a fool," his mother still insisted, then turned around and walked to her car saying she was going home to start Sunday dinner.

Daddy told the truth about how he got the new car. He had done an experiment to see if everything we had been reading and learning at church and in those books really worked. He even told me when he started the experiment.

But I agreed with my grandmother about the suit and hat. Daddy needed to burn that entire outfit and put it out of its misery!

At first, he was sad when mother left him; I could see that he loved and missed her. But now the sadness was gone, and he was happier than I had ever seen him with my mother. He had a new life now, and his whole outlook on life had changed as he was having the time of his life being single and driving his new Cadillac.

It was such a joy for me to sit in the front seat next to him as we listened to the *"Superfly"* soundtrack and the Delfonics on his new eight-track. I hated going back home to my mother's apartment after having fun with my father during the weekends.

I wanted to live with Daddy fulltime because life with Maxwell and my mother was depressing. Now the creep was running around mother's apartment giving us orders, telling us what to do like he was our father or something. And when I complained to mother about it, she told me that I had to obey.

I could not believe that she really expected me to listen to him. He was an unemployed fool living off my mother's welfare check and our child support payment checks. Also, since he moved in, I noticed that our food supply did not last as long. I was watching this whole situation like a hawk.

There were some days when there was nothing to cook, so Dennis and I would make peanut butter and syrup sandwiches for the four of us to eat.

It seemed to me that if mother had not been cooking expensive steaks and fat hamburgers for Maxwell to eat with our child support money, we kids would still be eating Campbell's soup for lunch with a tuna sandwich like the old days.

One day after she went to the store Maxwell told me to take out the trash. I looked him in the eye and told him that he had no right to tell me, my brother or sisters what to do.

"It's not like you're paying bills; my mother and father are. You are jobless; you are just living off us, while you have sex with my mother. You are even driving her car like it is yours. My father bought that car. Take the trash out yourself," I yelled at him as I turned around and ran into my room, thinking, "screw this freak."

When mother came home, she slapped me in the face for smarting off to Maxwell and I could not go outside for a week. She was going to beat me with the extension cord, but I objected and claimed I was too old to beat. I was so mad I could not even cry about the injustice of it all. This situation was so wrong, and I knew it. I was old enough to know that real men did not lie around living off their girlfriend's child support and welfare checks.

As far as I was concerned, they both needed to get a job, but it became obvious to me that neither one of them intended to work. In my reasoning, I wondered why they did not understand that something was very wrong with the way they lived.

The two of them ate gourmet meals, while we kids ate cans of chili with cheese melted on top, or slim priced hot dogs with chili. On bad days it was peanut butter and syrup sandwiches. I missed my father's leftovers and the fact that I ate well when I was with him. With my mother it was the cheapest things you could buy with food stamps, while she and Maxwell spent our child support money on themselves.

When I complained, she told us kids that if we talked about anything going on in her household, she would beat us. So, we dared not ask anyone for help. A month later, while we were at my fathers for our weekend visit, mother and Maxwell drove to Las Vegas and got married.

Daddy was especially upset about the whole thing, as were my brother, sisters and me. Even Maxwell's parents were against them getting married. His mother thought my mother was too old for him, and she just flat out did not like my mother.

It was a sad day when we all found out they had gotten married. I went to my room thinking, "now I'm stuck living with this butthole in my life."

I had hoped and silently prayed that Maxwell would get bored with her and dump her for a younger woman. Then things got even worse when my mother and Maxwell started getting behind in the rent. Three months after they got married, we were evicted from our apartment for non-payment of rent. This was the beginning of a period where we would move numerous times after being evicted from every dump we moved into.

At one point we had no choice but to move in with one of my mother's girlfriend's where Maxwell and mother slept in her spare bedroom while we slept on the floor in her friend's living room with only blankets for bedding.

Mother put all our stuff in storage and then lost it all when she got behind in the payments. All my books, toys, our furniture, and most of our clothes were just gone. One Saturday afternoon she and Maxwell left to go run an errand. Dennis and I were bored and ended up in the bedroom that mother and Maxwell were sharing. We started jumping on the bed to see how many times we could touch the ceiling with our hands.

That is when we both saw a tiny hand-gun fall on the carpeted floor on the side of the bed. I stopped jumping on the bed and picked up the gun from the floor and held it. Dennis and I both stood there looking at it while we tried to figure out if it were real or not.

"It's a fake. It has got to be. Why would they have a real gun. It looks like a toy." I told Dennis.

Then I pointed the gun at my brother ready to pull the trigger, when I heard a loud voice from inside me say, "Point the gun away from Dennis; it's not his time yet."

I pointed the gun away from him and aimed at the wall behind him just as the gun went off with a loud popping noise. I quickly realized that the gun was real. And I had almost killed my brother with it!

Mother and Maxwell had just returned and heard the shot. They came running into the bedroom and saw what I had done. Maxwell yanked the gun out of my hand and put it up on the closet shelf, then he beat me with the extension cord while mother watched. When he was finished, she told me that if I complained to my father or any family members that she would kill me. This was the beginning of my deep-seated hatred for the two of them; a hatred that just intensified over time.

CHAPTER 31

A few months later mother got into an argument with her friend over money, and we were told to move out. My mother moved us into a little motel on Western Blvd, where we had two bedrooms, a front room and a bathroom. One bedroom had a large, king-sized bed, while the other had two small twin beds. Mother and Maxwell took the larger bedroom with the king-sized bed, and we were given the room with the twin beds.

As usual, the three sisters shared a bed and Dennis slept in the other. There was no kitchen, and the only television was in the adult's room.

Since we had no icebox to keep milk in for our morning cereal, we kept the milk on the windowsill in our room and tried to keep it cold for as long as we could. We would go to the corner liquor store with food stamps to buy a small container of milk which had to be used each day before it spoiled.

It was summer vacation, but I found myself wishing that school were still in session just so I could eat a free lunch in the cafeteria. We were surviving off peanut butter and syrup sandwiches, warm Kool-aide made with tap water, and canned goods for our meals.

Finally, mother bought a small hot plate so we could cook our cans of Chef Boy-ah-Dee ravioli, or Campbell's soup in the bathroom. Every now and then we got lucky, and she would buy us a can of Spam to make sandwiches with.

I was angry and hated my mother and Maxwell. The two of them had turned our lives into a living hell. They dined sumptuously on Kentucky Fried Chicken, hamburgers and Maxwell had a daily supply of RC Cola while we kids had the hot plate food in the bathroom.

One night I prayed to God and asked for a Suzy Q snack cake by Hostess, I was so hungry. Two days later Dennis and I were playing on the sidewalk outside the motel room. I looked down on the sidewalk and saw a bright shiny quarter on the ground at my feet. I picked up the quarter, looked up at the sky and said, "thank you God."

I looked at Dennis and said, "let's go to the liquor store on the corner and buy a Suzy Q to share."

We ran to the corner store and bought the Suzy Q and took it back to the motel room where I split it four ways so Stephanie and Helen could have some too. I was happy that day because I had a little bit of heaven in my mouth, and I thought it was totally cool of God to answer my prayer for the Suzy Q. Now if only He would answer the rest of my prayers, I would have it made in life, I thought to myself.

Our father was still picking us up on the weekends and we were still forbidden to tell him or anyone else what was really going on. Mother was able to hide the fact that we were living in a motel from him by using Ma-Ma's house for the pick-up and drop off destination. We would go to his apartment and eat everything in his kitchen. He thought we were going through a growing stage or something, totally unaware that we were trying to get as much food in our bodies as we could to help get us through the following week.

CHAPTER 32

After living in the motel for four months, Maxwell finally got a job as a security guard after realizing that he was never going to make any money in the music business. At last, we moved out of the motel and into a two-bedroom apartment on Normandy Ave. near Wilshire Blvd. and not far from my father's apartment. In fact, I could walk there in 20 minutes. I was not thrilled about sharing a bedroom with my sisters again, but the apartment building had a swimming pool that Dennis and I could not wait to swim in.

We came in from a swim one afternoon, and for some reason, mother was in a bad mood. She decided that our hair was too long, and she was sick and tired of combing out the knots and decided to solve the problem by cutting off all our hair.

One by one she called us into her bedroom and cut our hair so short that it no longer went down our backs or even touched our shoulders. As she cut my hair, I cried and begged her not to; but she acted like she did not hear me and kept cutting. I loved my hair so much and now it was gone. I felt naked without it and violated. After she finished cutting my hair, I picked my long wavy locks up off the floor and took my hair to the bedroom. I wrapped a rubber band around my hair and put it on the shelf in the closet. I was not yet ready to let go of my hair, so I kept it.

As time went by, I would take my hair down every night before I went to bed and run my fingers through it. The first few nights I cried quietly into my pillow so my sisters, who were sleeping at the bottom of the bed, would not hear me. I kept that hair until it dried up and my mother forced me to throw it in the trash.

Months later we were still living with no furniture. All we had were a few twin mattresses on the floor that mother had picked up used somewhere. And a black and white TV set that sat on the living room floor with a metal coat hanger sticking out of it as an antenna to get a clear picture.

We were still hungry all the time, so we started stealing from the supermarket. I had gotten so skinny that everyone on my father's side of the family started calling me "Bones." We did not have any pots and pans, so Dennis and I got creative and used metal ice trays from the freezer to cook in. We always did our store runs when Maxwell and mother were gone from the apartment. Otherwise, we would have to explain where we got the food from. Occasionally Dennis would steal us a box of his favorite Neapolitan Ice Cream Sandwiches for dessert. We saw kids on TV commercials with snacks and Oscar Meyer hot dogs, and we were wishing for the good old days in Pomona when we had plenty of food to eat and our parents were still together.

Dennis and I figured we were good at stealing from the store without getting caught. We always took Stephanie and Helen with us because who would suspect four little kids of stealing Mac & Cheese? Candy yes, but not Mac and Cheese. One afternoon after we had stolen two boxes, we were walking back to the apartment and had to cross a large high traffic intersection. The traffic light turned green, and as we began crossing the street, I noticed a big truck coming toward us at full speed and I realized it was going to run through the light.

It was so close that there was no time to move away from it before it would hit us. The only thing I could think to do was to grab everyone's hand and try to shield them from the impact of the truck with my body. I heard Dennis and Stephanie scream as they saw the truck bearing down on us.

Suddenly I saw a big, tall Angel who looked like a bird man because of its big wings. It was glowing like a light bulb in front of the truck with its arms outstretched towards the truck making the truck stop before it could hit us. Then as fast as the Angel appeared, it was gone. I looked up and saw that the truck's bumper was just inches away from us. All four of us should have been dead.

I looked at Dennis and said, "Did you see that Angel stop the truck?"

"No" he replied, "what are you talking about?"

It quickly became obvious to me that I was the only one who saw the Angel stop that truck. And if I tried to tell people no one would believe me they would just think I was crazy.

Suddenly, the truck driver and other people were asking us if we were okay, we were in the middle of a small crowd of people without a scratch on us.

The truck driver kept telling everyone that he did not mean to run the light, and he asked us if we were okay. I told him that we were fine. Dennis and I were afraid that someone would call the police, and then we would get busted with the stolen Mac & Cheese. So, we got out of there as fast as we could.

CHAPTER 33

I lay in bed that night thinking about the Angel I saw stop the truck. It dawned on me that God was watching out for us even though I could not see Him, He was always there; I could feel him.

"Please God, don't let Maxwell and my mother ruin our lives. Help us! We don't have anyone else." I prayed.

At first, I got no answer, but then as I lay there the realization hit me that God knew everything that was going on with me, my sisters and brother. For some reason I did not yet understand, He was allowing this suffering to happen instead of getting us out of the mess.

As my thought ended, God answered with His thought. "I allow this because you are gaining survival tools through this experience to be used later in life. I have my hand on you protecting you."

"That is why the Angel appeared to stop the truck from hitting us," I thought to myself: God sent the Angel. Okay that makes sense. I have a safety net here on Earth. You just could not see it with the naked eye. You just had to recognize that it caught you when you fell and know that it was God that saved your butt in the end.

By now I knew that no one in the world had the power to take my hopes and dreams away from me or my inner happiness. I also knew that I never had to be afraid of someone killing me in life because God had my back.

I lay there a while longer and asked God to hurry up and make me a grown up, so I could travel all the time with the little boy on the moon. I fell asleep visualizing my unlimited future with him. In this dream, we were traveling and exploring the world together in perfect harmony.

CHAPTER 34

A week later we got busted stealing Mac & Cheese from the supermarket. Some man in plain clothes stopped us at the front door as we were trying to walk out of the supermarket with it.

He told Dennis and me to hand over the boxes of Mac & Cheese we had just taken. Then he took us into a back room and shut the door. Stephanie was scared and started crying, not knowing what was going to happen to us. Then another man came into the room and told us that he was the store manager. He asked us why we were stealing Mac & Cheese.

I told him we were only taking it because we were hungry, and how we were too young to get jobs to pay for it.

"Don't you get food at home?" The manager asked.

"We get food with food stamps, but it's not enough and my stepfather says he doesn't want to feed someone else's kids, so we took the food because we were hungry." I answered.

Dennis asked if he was going to call the cops on us.

"Not this time," The man said. "It would be different if you did this just to get candy, but you took Mac & Cheese, so I believe you when you say you were just hungry. But I am warning you: I better not catch you stealing again, or I will call the police."

Then he told us that we could keep the boxes of Mac & Cheese, and he took a $10 dollar bill out of his pocket and gave it to me.

"You can go pick out some meat to go with that Mac & Cheese," he said.

"Thanks Mister. I promise we won't steal anymore," I assured him.

He let us out of the little back room, and we headed straight for the meat department where we bought hamburger meat to go with our Mac & Cheese. After we paid a couple of dollars for the hamburger meat, we still had seven dollars and some change left. Dennis and I figured we had better save it for emergency Mac & Cheese since we could not steal it anymore.

That money lasted us for a few weeks, then out of the blue, Daddy started giving each of us five dollars apiece each weekend for pocket money. What a blessing! My heart knew that the God I could not see, but felt, had my back because now I could buy food instead of stealing it.

CHAPTER 35

Summer ended and it was time to check into yet another school. My Mother enrolled us into a Elementary School, which was two blocks down the street from our apartment building. I was going into the sixth grade as a12-year-old and thought I was hot shit because of it.

I liked my new school, which was a big, sprawling reddish-brown brick building that looked like it was at least 200 hundred years old. I loved old buildings because when I stood in them, I could see the memories that they held. It was like seeing history on a movie screen in your mind. Sometimes before going into the building for school in the morning, I would just stand on the sidewalk in front of it as the movie started in my mind as I saw flashes of the past: nuns teaching in the building long ago, and students in school uniforms walking to and from class. Generation after generation of students, some in uniform and some dressed in 1950s clothing.

The memories were so vivid to me in this building, I wondered if I was going crazy. So, one day I asked my teacher if the building used to be a church before it was a school. She told me that it had been a Catholic girl's school some years before. Now that I was sure that what I was seeing was real and not some kind of hallucination, I walked to and from class feeling fortunate to be a student in a building that had been used for nothing but the education of so many people.

The first month of school I met two boys that I kind of had a crush on. They were brothers DeWayne and Jeffery Jones. DeWayne and Jeffery were cool boys to play tetherball with during recess. They were two gorgeous black guys with big Afro's that reminded me of Michael Jackson's. DeWayne was my age and in the same grade as I was. Jeffery was a year younger and a grade below us. I never told either of them how I felt; I kept that information to myself. Their father, Mark Jones, was one of the few black TV news reporters in Los Angeles. Soon we were recess friends playing ball, but sometimes we would talk about dumb stuff on the school yard.

I made other friends who liked me so much that they wanted to come over to my house after school to hang out. I lied and told them that my mother worked and did not allow people in the apartment when she was not home. I was too ashamed to bring friends home. Since Maxwell had become a security guard, he now loved guns and owned a .357 Magnum that he was in the habit of leaving on the living room floor loaded like it was a pack of cigarettes or something.

CHAPTER 36

It was bad enough that my sisters, brother and I had to walk past that gun every day, but to have my friends be subjected to it was just too embarrassing. Plus, I was also ashamed because we had no furniture, and I would not even be able to offer my friends a chair to sit on. I decided it was best to lie and keep all school relationships at school.

One day the lie about mother working came true. She got a job as a caregiver working from 3 p.m.-10:30 p.m. at a nursing home. She was even talking about going back to school to get a RN nursing degree. Her car had broken down and was too expensive to repair, so she sold it and took the bus to work. Her bus would pull up at the bus stop at 11:10 each night. Since she was afraid to walk home from the bus stop by herself at night, Dennis and I would have to walk to the bus stop on Wilshire Blvd. and Normandy to walk home with her. Meanwhile, Maxwell lay around smoking and watching TV.

I felt that he should have been the one to meet her at the bus stop. That was part of being someone's husband, I thought to myself. It was insane to me that she put up with Maxwell and his crap.

He never once walked her home from that bus stop, and yet she kissed his butt and worshiped the ground he walked on. Why either of them thought it was safe for two young kids to be out late at night alone, waiting at a bus stop on a busy street like Wilshire Blvd., was a mystery to me.

Sometimes while she worked, Maxwell would make Dennis come into their bedroom to watch TV with him. I would always ask him afterwards what happened in there with him and Maxwell.

"Maxwell wants someone to watch TV with and he gives me soda pop and chips," Dennis said.

I hated him so much that no amount of soda pop and chips could get me to spend time with him. In fact, I was waiting for him to die and go to hell where he belonged, and I wanted him to take that gun with him.

When school ended for summer vacation, I was sad. Maxwell went to his security guard job at midnight, but we were stuck with him and his stupid gun during the day. It made me mad that he had the gun and bullets just laying around all the time because it was dangerous, and I had a bad feeling about it. I kept asking my mother to make him keep the gun away from us, but she told me to mind my own business and refused to do anything about it.

I spent the summer tanning by the pool with my transistor radio, channel surfing until I found a song I liked. I had no suntan lotion, so I used baby oil. We kids would spend hours at that pool just to avoid being in the house with Maxwell.

One afternoon I was sitting on the steps in the front of our apartment building reading the latest copies of "Right on" and "Tiger Beat" magazine. That is where I read that my friends that I used to walk to and from school with when I lived with Marie and Phillip, "The Sylvers," had a hit record that was playing on the radio all the time. Both magazines had articles about them.

My reading was suddenly interrupted by a cute boy standing in front of me who introduced himself as Micky Tyler. I noticed how good looking he was. He was Creole like me, tall muscular, with dark brown eyes and hair that fell in loose curls around his face.

"Hi, I live with my family down the street, and I saw you around the neighborhood and wondered who you were." Micky said.

"Hi yourself, my name is Maya." I replied smiling.

After that we started talking about music and the Catholic high school he attended, and how much he loved playing basketball on the high school team.

Micky was 16 and I had just turned 13, but the age difference did not seem to matter as we talked with one another with ease and became fast friends. At first, we would just sit together on my building steps talking about all the things we had in common like books and movies. Until one day we were walking back from the corner store, sodas in hand, when he asked me if I would be his girlfriend.

I was totally surprised and did not see that coming because he was in high school. I immediately thought about the little boy on the moon, and I knew that the Micky was not him. Besides, I wondered to myself, would it be wrong of me to date other people until he showed up in my life? It could take years for him to show up in my life. And I was excited that a boy liked me enough to even ask me to be his girlfriend. He was nice, well mannered, and cute so I said yes.

A month had passed before he tried to kiss me down in the dimly lit parking garage under my apartment building. I confided all the details of my relationship with Micky to Dennis, who soon after betrayed my trust by telling mother.

CHAPTER 37

My mother was not thrilled with the idea of me having a boyfriend at age 13. She told me to stay away from him, and that I was too "fast" for my age.

"That boy is too old for you, and you are too young to be anyone's girlfriend." She informed me.

But I had to have boyfriends in order to meet the little boy on the moon, I reasoned to myself. So, I totally disregarded what my mother said and went behind her back and dated him. If you call it a date sitting outside my apartment building, walking to the liquor store, or playing basketball in the school yard at the elementary school I had just graduated from.

When mother was not home, I would sneak out of the apartment and meet Micky outside. We would go on walks holding hands, then at the end of each little walk he would give me a quick kiss on the lips. I was nervous the first time he French kissed me, because he was older and knew what he was doing and I on the other hand had no idea what I was doing. Then it progressed to him holding me tight after he kissed me, then whispering in my ear that he loved me.

I knew that I was not in love with Micky and never would be, but I was not about to lie and pretend that I loved him. He was just a cute boy to me; someone to pass the time with. Not the "Little Boy on The Moon," my future husband.

That is why I never said "I love you" back to Micky. I just said, "that's so sweet of you to say that."

By the end of summer, I had outgrown my attraction for Micky. One afternoon after a walk, the poor guy kissed me goodbye, and my skin crawled just having his lips on mine. The feeling of attraction I had for him all summer was just gone, and it was not coming back.

A few days later I got up enough nerve to tell him that the romantic part of our relationship was over. I told him that the last thing I wanted to do was hurt his feelings, but I could not be his girlfriend anymore.

The hurt look in his eyes made me feel like I was a bad person. Then he said, "I thought you loved me; what can I do to make you love me again?"

"You can't" I said, "I just don't have those feelings for you. I don't know why, but I just don't."

I left out the part about my never having had those feelings for him to begin with, because I did not want to hurt his feelings any more than I already had.

"Can we just be friends?" I asked.

He looked at me with anger in his eyes and voice and said, "I never want to speak to you again,"

And he walked away.

"Wow," I thought. "I did not see that coming!" I felt bad for him because the last thing I wanted to do was hurt his feelings. I knew there was nothing I could do, and maybe it was better this way. If I had remained friends with him being attracted to me, it would have been an uncomfortable situation.

Later that night in bed, I filled Dennis in on the breakup details. "I never promised him a rose garden of love," I said. "He's the one who started saying that he loved me. I swear I never told him that I loved him back. And I feel guilty even though I did my best not to lead him on."

I explained further. "For some reason, he just assumed I loved him back. I am just going into the seventh grade in the fall, and I could tell that he was going to want sex eventually. I am not ready for that. I am still trying to deal with the fact that I have a period every month with painful cramps hitting my kneecaps. Sex is the last thing on my mind."

"He'll meet someone else his own age and she'll love him back," I told Dennis.

"How do you know?" He asked.

"I just do," I replied wisely. "Now I understand why mother said I was too young to have a boyfriend. This is one of the rare occasions that I agree with her."

CHAPTER 38

Soon after that Maxwell lost his job. I was certain mother knew the reason, but she was not talking about it.

Now we had to put up with him lying around the apartment all day and night watching TV, as he cleaned his gun while chain smoking Benson & Hedges cigarettes. Even more disgusting, he walked around the apartment all day in his boxer shorts, which showed a lot more of him than I wanted to see.

Soon after Maxwell lost his job we were evicted once again for nonpayment of rent, and we were forced to move into a lower rent neighborhood.

Mother tried to make light of the situation by saying we were now moving into a larger apartment. She found a three-bedroom apartment in Culver City on Bedford Street. As we pulled up in front of our new apartment building in Uncle Jimmy's truck, I thought to myself, "another bad neighborhood." It was a horrible looking apartment building with a play area that had a broken-down swing set and an old merry-go round sitting in a pile of dirt where there used to be grass.

And there was not a swimming pool in sight.

There were a few girls hanging out in front of the building about my age, but I also saw a few drug dealers hanging around in front of the building. A customer would pull up in front of the building, and the drug dealer would run up to the car and exchange drugs for money. Right out in the open, while young children played hop-scotch on the sidewalk.

I had been looking forward to going to junior high school before we moved and had my heart set on going to John Burroughs Junior High with the friends, I had made in the sixth grade. Now I was in the school district for Louis Pasteur Junior High where I knew no one. It had such a bad reputation for gang activity that I was no longer looking forward to being a junior high school student. Now I just wanted to turn 18 as fast as I could so I could make my own decisions.

A few days before I started school, my Uncle Billy died. I overheard my mother saying that Billy had taken a few hits of acid with his girlfriend and was driving in his car while high. The police pulled him over and Billy pulled a shotgun on the police. They shot him five times and he died on the operating table.

Ma-Ma was so grief stricken her beautiful face looked like it had aged 50 years over night. I was not allowed to go to my uncle's funeral, which really upset me, because I loved him and wanted to tell him goodbye.

All I could do was cry and grieve alone for him in my bedroom. A few weeks after the funeral, Ma-Ma came by the apartment and gave me my Uncle Billy's flute and two Rock and Roll albums that belonged to him.

One of the albums was by a man named Elton John entitled "Elton John." The other was by a group called the "Who" entitled "Who's Next." She also gave me a little portable turntable he had with built in speakers. I listened to those two albums for hours that day in honor of my uncle. And I thought about all the times we listened to music together in his room, and how wonderful it was to just be around Uncle Billy. As I listened to each track, I fell in love with both albums. But Elton John was my favorite, and I wanted more Rock and Roll albums to listen to by him. His voice reminded me of Angels singing. I could tell that Elton John had music build within his very soul. His lyrics and his piano playing was phenomenal. When he sang " Your Song" it felt like it had been written for me. And the song "Sixty Years on" blew my mind with all the beautiful string arrangements. The man was a musical genius as well as drop dead gorgeous to me. I loved music but from that day forward Elton John was my musical love.

I started school at Louis Pasteur Junior High and hated it immediately.

Since my grandmother gave me Uncle Billy's flute, I decided to take a beginning winds class. I was excited to learn how to read music and play the flute properly so I could be a musician like Elton John and play all of his songs. And I figured it would be the perfect escape from my home life; perhaps I could even be a musician when I grew up because I loved music so much. It was the one and only thing that I looked forward to in school.

After a few months of living in the new apartment Maxwell showed no signs of looking for a job. He just slept, ate better food then us and played with his gun.

While mother worked at night, he was still taking Dennis into the bedroom he shared with my mother to watch TV with the door shut. When I asked him again why he was watching TV with Maxwell at night, he would say "he makes me watch TV with him and he gives me chips and soda." It was always the same answer, and something did not seem right about it to me.

Maxwell was also getting bolder with his gun. He was now opening the front door late at night and shooting up toward the sky. He knew he could get away with it in that neighborhood since it was not unusual to hear a gun go off around there. Then it escalated to him shooting at the walls in the apartment. There were random bullet holes in the living room wall and in mother's bedroom.

One night I went into her bedroom to ask her a question. She was knitting while sitting up in bed. I watched Maxwell pick up his gun, and for no reason at all, he just pointed it at her and shot at her just missing her head by inches.

I stood there in shock because not only was Maxwell crazy, but her reaction to the whole thing just floored me. She did not blink an eye when he shot at her; she did not even look up from her knitting. She just acted like nothing had happened, like it was normal behavior.

I wanted to shake her and say, "A bullet just went over your head barely missing it, what the hell is wrong with you?"

But all I could do was stand there in utter disbelief that she was this crazy. I was just a kid, but I had enough common sense to know that this was a dangerous situation for all of us.

I went to my bedroom, looked out the window up toward the sky and asked God to protect me, my brother and sisters from Maxwell. I knew that telling my father was no good because she told me that she would kill me if I spoke to other people about what went on in her home. But deep down in my gut I had a bad feeling about that gun that would not go away.

Within months things got even worse. After school, Maxwell would be at the front door pretending to be a cop. He would kneel on one knee like a cop with his gun in hand pointed right at us and yelling, "freeze." Then he would break out laughing at the look of fear on our faces as we just stood there, wondering if it was safe to move yet.

He did this so often over a period of months that it became common place to us. Maxwell would shoot at us and miss on purpose, then we would walk into the apartment as if nothing had happened. We had become used to the fact that he was a dangerous nut case whose behavior was never going to be normal.

CHAPTER 39

If someone had asked me how many times Maxwell had pointed that gun loaded and unloaded at us and pulled the trigger, I would not be able to give an accurate count. Because it had become a daily thing and he was firing that gun at least twice a day. He had tons of True Detective and gun magazines lying around. At this point not only did I hate Maxwell, but I hated my mother's guts as well for allowing this freak of nature that looked like a human being to shoot at her own children.

As far as I was concerned, I did not have a mother.

One night I had a nightmare, that Maxwell killed one of us kids. When I awoke, I could not remember which one of us he had killed, but I remembered that he did kill one of us with that gun. I got out of bed and got the diary I had started keeping and began to write down what I could remember about the dream.

I also wrote that my mother was to unfit to be a parent and that she and Maxwell were both insane. I used that diary to say everything I wanted to say out loud but could not.

After thinking about the dream all day in school, I decided to wait until Maxwell was not in the same room and attempt to talk some sense into my mother. After school that day, I found her alone in the kitchen cooking dinner before she had to go to work. I just came right out and told her that I had dreamed the night before that Maxwell had shot and killed one of us kids.

I hoped that would make her realize the danger she was putting us all in, and by some miracle, she would snap out of it, and kick Maxwell with his damn gun out on the street where he belonged. But unfortunately, the conversation ended with my mother slapping me in the face, then putting me under punishment.

I had to stay in my room for three months and could only come out for school and the weekends with my father because it was court ordered. I could use the bathroom, but all my meals had to be eaten in my room because she claimed that she wanted to see my face as little as possible.

Unbelievable! I was in trouble for trying to prevent her freak of a husband from killing one of us kids. I tried to convince myself that the dream I had meant nothing, that it was just a dream that would not come to pass.

I spent the time in my room practicing my flute using the beginning woodwinds book, as well as listening to the two albums that belonged to Uncle Billy. I spent hours listening to those albums repeatedly.

My parents had not exposed me to a lot of Rock & Roll. They always played Soul music, Jazz, or the Blues. I liked the music my parents played, but this Rock music was just mind blowing to me.

At this point, I was even more totally and completely in love with Elton John's music. I may have been locked in my bedroom but I had Elton John to keep me busy. He was the best piano player I had ever heard in my life, and now I was hooked on the violins in his song arrangements. I loved the sound of the violin because it reminded me of the angels and the beauty of their wings brushing together.

I would listen to Elton's album, close my eyes and escape into another world as I visualized his lyrics attempting to fully understand the meaning of the song. Because of him I was determined to study music, play the flute and be a real musician just like him. This kept me out of the streets and trouble.

After I had learned how to finger all the notes on my flute, I started trying to figure out the notes to the songs on the Elton John album. I really had no idea what I was doing, but I would get a sheet of notebook paper and a pencil then sound out the notes to the songs on my flute. Within a few weeks, I had gotten good, I was proud of myself and felt a sense of accomplishment.

Then one night, I dreamed again that Maxwell shot and killed one of us kids. When I woke up, I still could not remember which one of us it was. I knew that I had to try to prevent this from happening, but how? I had already tried talking to mother to no avail.

The only choice I had now was to tell my father when he picked us up on the weekend.

CHAPTER 40

I knew he would call her about the dream, and she would beat the hell out of me, but it would be worth it if no one got killed.

Then I realized that it could be my own death I was dreaming about. That would make sense because I hated Maxwell and he knew it. Maybe I told him to go to hell to his face, and then he shot me for it. I wrote the dream down again in my diary, and how I was planning to tell my father so he could get us out of there. I wrote how much I hated my mother and Maxwell for putting us through this mess.

That night while I was in the bathtub, Dennis went snooping around in my stuff and found my diary. He read what I had written about mother and Maxwell, then showed it to her. By the time I had finished with my bath, mother had read it and was seriously pissed off. As I walked out of the bathroom, she called me into the kitchen and confronted me with my diary in her hand.

"Your brother found this and gave it to me!" She screamed. "Why did you write such horrible things about me in this diary?"

"What was I supposed to do?" I asked. "If I tell anyone outside of this house what really goes on in here, I get beat or put in my room, so I write what I think in my diary. And everything I wrote is true. I have dreamed twice that Maxwell killed one of us kids with his gun, and it is dangerous for him to shoot at us when we walk in from school, and to leave the gun lying around loaded. Somebody has to be the voice of reason in this nut house." I said. "I want to live with my father, not some nut case that shoots at everyone in the house every day."

She slapped me in the face, then grabbed a paper grocery bag, and rushed past me to my bedroom. She grabbed what few clothes I had and threw them into the bag, then she told me to get out of her house.

"You can go live with your father right now!" she yelled. Then she went back into the kitchen and called a taxicab service.

As I grabbed my flute and book bag, I heard her giving the taxi service the address to Grandmother and Grandfather Johnson's house on Orange Drive. I heard her telling them that my grandparents would pay for the cab fare when the driver dropped me off.

I felt so hurt and betrayed by what Dennis had done, that I could not see past my own anger. I looked at Dennis and told him that I hated his guts, and that he was a turn coat.

"I thought we would always stick together. I thought we were a team. I can't believe you read my diary then gave it to mother!"

Dennis said nothing; just stood there looking at me.

Once I arrived at my grandparent's house, with the taxi driver by my side wanting payment, my grandparents were in total shock and disbelief that my mother had just kicked me out, then put me in a taxicab that they had to pay for. They paid the driver and took me inside the house.

When grandfather asked me what happened, I told them both the whole story about Maxwell and his gun. I now no longer had to be afraid of what my mother or Maxwell would do to me for telling on them. So, I told my grandparents everything.

After I finished it felt like a huge weight had been lifted off me just to finally be able to tell someone. I told my grandparents that I knew for sure that Maxwell was going to kill one of us kids if someone did not do something about that gun.

Grandfather immediately called Daddy at work and filled him in on the situation. Then my grandmother called a few of my aunts and told them what my mother had done. Within an hour the news had spread throughout the entire family, like a wildfire burning dry brush in the forest.

Grandmother fed me and tried to make me feel better. She and grand-father told me that everything was going to be alright. I wanted to believe them, but unfortunately, I could not shake the feeling that something horrible was going to happen with gun-wielding Maxwell.

CHAPTER 41

That evening when Daddy got off from work, he came to grandmother's house to pick me up. I was now going to be living with him in his one-bedroom apartment in the Wilshire District. I was excited because I had always preferred living with him rather than mother. Best of all, I would no longer have to attend Louis Pasteur Junior High and could now go to John Burroughs Junior High with my friends from elementary school.

I thanked God for making my dreams come true.

At Daddy's apartment, I told him about Maxwell living off our child support checks, and everything else that had been going on in that dysfunctional household. He called mother and told her that she had to make Maxwell remove the gun from the apartment immediately or he would take her to court for full custody of us kids.

They argued for a few minutes, then she hung up on him. He looked at me with a worried look on his face and said, "I'm going to call my lawyer in the morning."

And that was the end of it. We made tacos for dinner, and I slept on the sofa.

The next morning, he dropped me at grandmother's house before he went to work. She made me scrambled eggs and bacon and I had breakfast with my grandparents.

After breakfast, grandmother drove me to Louis Pasteur Junior High to check me out of school and get my records, then drove me to John Burroughs to enroll me in school there.

The official name of the school was John Burroughs Middle School. It was a distinctive red brick building built in 1924 and named after a man who had significant accomplishments in life. John Burroughs had been a teacher, published writer, and a treasury clerk in Washington D.C., and studied animals. I considered the school an antique and a higher institution of learning. All the best teaching tools went to public schools like John Burroughs first.

In my mind it was the closest I would get to a free education that equaled that of the private schools, and all my friends were going there.

The school was surrounded by elegant large homes that only people with a lot of money could afford. A lot of well-off Jewish kids and kids whose parents were actors went to John Burroughs. But it also had a good amount of Mexican and black kids like me whose parents made under $50,000 dollars a year.

The minute grandmother and I walked up the front steps of the school and walked into the building, I knew I was home. I followed her into the office where she enrolled me. I was given a guidance counselor who helped me choose the classes I needed.

Before grandmother left, she gave me strict instructions to walk straight to her house after school was out.

By the end of the school day, I was reunited with eight of my friends from elementary school, and I had homework from three classes already. None of the new kids I met were stuck up. Nobody cared if your parents were rich, famous, or poor. Everyone was treated as an equal; race and class were left outside the school doors. Even the popular ninth grade girls with their expensive "Gucci" bags were nice to everyone.

There was even a 13-year-old boy who believed that babies, including himself, were born in a cabbage patch.

"The souls are dropped down into the cabbage patch from heaven," he said. He claimed his mother had given him this information, and that it was factual. Everyone in school called him "Cabbage Patch Boy" instead of Eric Wasserman, his real name.

I happily walked to grandmother's house after school where she had a sandwich waiting for me. Then she made me get my lessons done, which was her terminology for homework.

When grandfather got home from the used furniture store he owned and saw me doing my homework, he said that he was proud of me.

The thinkers are the rulers of the world, while fools catch hell. I can tell you are not a fool because you're doing your homework," he added.

He always had great words of wisdom to speak that I figured was on account of his preaching. Sometimes he paid me to clean out the used refrigerators at his furniture store on the weekends. I saved all my money to buy sheet music and Elton John albums.

CHAPTER 42

Along with picking up my brother and sisters on the weekends, this was my new life. Mother claimed that she made Maxwell get rid of his gun, and my siblings said they had not seen it lying around the house. I figured Daddy had the whole thing under control.

I was still mad at Dennis for taking my diary and giving it to mother, so we were barely on speaking terms. I had been living with Daddy for about a month when he had a Friday off, and told me I could skip school. He decided that we were going to Marine Land, an oceanarium located on the Palos Verdes Peninsula. He invited his girlfriend Jenny, a Filipina woman, he met at the Midtown Bowling Alley.

After we picked Jenny up, we headed out toward the ocean in Daddy's Cadillac while listening to his new Marvin Gaye eight-track.

Once at Marine Land, I was having so much fun that I felt like a normal kid for once. Having Jenny with us did not bother me because at least she acted like a sane human being, unlike Maxwell who was totally mentally unbalanced.

After spending a fun filled day at Marine Land, we dropped Jenny off at her house and drove back to our apartment.

Daddy and I started making a pot of his famous spaghetti because we were picking my brother and sisters up the following morning. I was chopping onions in the kitchen when the phone rang. He went into the living room to answer it. That is when I heard him let out a strange scream.

I was immediately alarmed because I had never heard him scream before. I rushed into the living room and saw Daddy drop to his knees crying on the carpeted floor. I could hear my grandfather's voice calling my father's name through the telephone receiver as it lay on the floor beside him.

"Daddy, what's wrong?" I asked with a sick feeling forming in the pit of my stomach.

He did not answer; he just kept crying out loud like a baby.

As I picked up the telephone receiver to ask grandfather what had happened, I heard Daddy scream, "I'm getting my shotgun out of the closet and I'm going to kill that son of a bitch."

I asked grandfather what happened? That is when my world came crashing in on me as he told me that Maxwell had shot and killed Dennis!

Tears ran down my cheeks as I realized my worst fears and dreams materialized. As the shock washed over me, grandfather's voice seemed far away as he told me that Ma-Ma had called my grandmother from the police station where Maxwell was in police custody.

CHAPTER 43

It did not seem real. In fact, it seemed unreal that my brother was dead at age 11. I felt numb, angry and devastated all at the same time, and my grandfather's voice seemed very distant.

In a monotone voice, I asked him if he knew what happened. He said that he did not have any details yet; all he knew was Maxwell shot Dennis and he was dead. Then he told me that I had been right about Maxwell killing one of us.

My father walked back into the living room with a shot gun that I never knew he had.

He took the telephone receiver from me with tears running down his cheeks and began talking to grandfather again. He walked into his bedroom with the phone, crying. After a while he started talking again. I could tell that grandfather was trying to calm my father down and comfort him.

I sat on the sofa crying thinking that it should have been me that he killed, not Dennis. I felt like I was the oldest, I should have been there to protect him and take that bullet instead of him.

Why shoot Dennis? I thought Maxwell liked him. I was the one he hated with a purple passion. I also felt guilty because the last thing I said to Dennis was how much I hated him, and how I would never forgive him for taking my diary. The diary issue seemed so stupid and childish now. The last month I had barely spoken to him. He was my best friend and he died thinking that I hated him, when he was my hero and the best brother anyone could ever have. This is what messed with my mind the most. I did not even get the chance to tell him goodbye.

Where was God while all of this was going on? Why didn't he send an angel to stop Maxwell from killing Dennis, like he did the day the truck almost hit us?

I could overhear my father in the bedroom telling grandfather that he was going to shoot and kill Maxwell. I could tell from my father's side of the conversation that grandfather was trying to talk some sense into him.

In the bedroom I saw Daddy on his knees with the telephone receiver in his hand, crying. The shot gun was on the carpet next to him.

I had never seen him this broken before, and my heart hurt for him and my brother all at the same time. I guess grandfather finally talked him into putting the shot gun away, because I watched him put it back into a bag that zipped up then place it on the shelf in his closet. Daddy talked to grandfather for a few minutes longer then hung up the phone.

Then he laid down on his bed and cried with great racking sobs as though his heart would never be whole again.

Not knowing what to do next, I went back into the living room, sat on the sofa and cried my heart out for my brother. I wanted my brother back, but he was not coming back. It was so messed up! Then something hit me; maybe Dennis had saved my life on some unconscious level. Maybe it had been fate, that mother had kicked me out of the house when she did.

I knew if I had been there, I would have been the one that Maxwell killed because I always stood in front of my brother and sisters whenever he pulled his gun on us.

Then I heard the telephone ringing again and my father's voice from his bedroom. After a few minutes, I figured out that he was talking to Ma-Ma and crying at the same time. After he hung up the phone, he walked into the living room and sat on the sofa next to me. He told me that Ma-Ma had identified Dennis's body. Then he was silent for a moment as he just stared into space with tears rolling down his cheeks. He looked as if he had aged 100 years.

Then he told me, "Your grandmother just told me what happened to your brother. It is painfully obvious that your mother lied when she told me that Maxwell had locked his gun up. Because now your brother is dead."

"What happened to him?" I asked.

"Dennis was watching cartoons with Stephanie in your mother's bedroom when Maxwell walked in and shot him. Your grandmother said Maxwell told the police that he overheard Dennis tell Stephanie that he was going to hide Maxwell's gun. The son-of-a bitch claims that he went into the room to take the gun from Dennis, but when he handed it to Maxell it accidentally went off and killed him."

He paused for a moment and continued, "I don't believe that shit for a minute. I believe Maxwell gunned him down in cold blood."

"So, is that the story mother and Maxwell are giving the police?" I asked my father. "I know without a doubt that he murdered Dennis. Daddy, I know he did." I sobbed in anguish.

"The bad news is, no one knows where Stephanie is, and the police are looking for her." My father said.

"What if he killed Stephanie too and stashed her body somewhere?" I sobbed.

Daddy replied, "Your mother told Ma-Ma and the police that the last time she saw Stephanie was when Maxwell's sister showed up and took her out of the bedroom before the police showed up. Ma-Ma told me that Maxwell called his sister, and your mother called Ma-Ma before they even called the police."

"Where are mother and Helen now?" I asked.

"Your mother and Helen are at the police station with Ma-Ma and your Aunt Chloe. I am going to drop you off at your grandmother's house and go down to the police station with your grandfather to see what they are doing to find Stephanie. Then I am going to see your brother at the morgue. Get your coat on and get ready to go," he said as he walked into the bathroom to wash his face.

CHAPTER 44

Daddy dropped me off at grandmother's house where grandfather got into Daddy's car and the two of them went to the police station.

Grandmother cried as she hugged me and told me everything was going to be okay, and how Dennis was now in heaven. But I did not want him to be in heaven; I wanted him here with me. Grandmother tried to make me eat some dinner, but I had no appetite.

Then my father's sisters started showing up. Everyone was crying and in a state of disbelief that Dennis was dead at age 11. They were saying things like how they wished Maxwell and my mother had killed each other instead.

I kept thinking to myself that I had warned them about that gun and my dream, and no one checked that the gun was gone, or called the police to make sure we were safe. No one protected us, and now everyone was shocked? They just took my mother's word when she said the gun was no longer around the kids. I felt that someone should have checked to make sure she was not lying, but no one did and as a result my brother was dead.

Daddy and grandfather came back from the police station with Stephanie and Helen. All the aunts gathered around them, happy and relieved that they were unhurt.

I was so happy to see my sisters alive and breathing that when I hugged them both I did not want to let go. Stephanie looked like she was in a trance, or something, and would not answer when you spoke to her. When I asked Daddy why Stephanie was not answering me, he told me that she was in shock.

"On Monday morning I have an appointment with the Child Protective Services to get her some psychiatric help and get temporary custody of the three of you until a court makes it permanent. They opened an investigation into your mother and Maxwell for neglect and child endangerment," Daddy told everyone.

Grandmother took my two sisters into the kitchen and tried to feed them dinner, but they were not hungry either.

I sat in the living room with the rest of the family while Daddy and grandfather told us what information they had from the police. Apparently, Maxwell said he had his gun on the nightstand in the master bedroom. According to my mother, the television in the living room had stopped working, so Stephanie and Dennis were watching cartoons in her room.

Maxwell was in the living room when he overheard Dennis say he was going to hide the gun so Maxwell could not leave it laying around anymore.

Then Maxwell went into the bedroom and told Dennis to give him the gun, and when he handed it to Maxwell, it accidentally went off.

"That's his version of the story," Daddy said bitterly. And then continued with the account.

"After the shooting, your mother and Maxwell tried to hide Stephanie at Maxwell's sister's apartment so she couldn't tell the police what she saw. The police picked Stephanie up at Maxwell's sister's apartment and took her down to the police station and questioned her.

Stephanie told the police that when Dennis handed Maxwell that gun, Maxwell stood there, pointed it at him and shot him. She also said that Dennis laid there in her arms telling her to run, with blood bubbles coming out of his mouth. Then Maxwell pointed the gun at her so there would not be any witnesses; she tried to run away, that is when he shot at her and missed.

Edwina heard the gun shots from the bathroom where she was giving Helen a bath and went to see what was going on. Edwina walking into that bedroom when she did saved Stephanie's life, because Maxwell was about to shoot at her again.

Instead of calling the police, Edwina called her mother. When she arrived with Chloe, the police had not been called yet and they found Edwina trying to dig old bullets out of the bullet holes in the living room wall with a knitting needle before the police got there.

Chloe was the one who actually called the police, and since Stephanie was the only witness, Maxwell called his sister before anyone showed up at the apartment and had her take Stephanie to her apartment before the police could talk to her.

Stephanie told the police that Maxwell's sister put her in the bathtub and washed Dennis's blood off her. Then she held Stephanie's head under water telling her that she better not tell anyone what she had seen in the bedroom, or she would be killed too.

By the time the police showed up at her apartment, she had Stephanie dressed in the fresh clothes mother had sent with her, sitting at the table in front of an uneaten sandwich." Daddy said shaking his head.

CHAPTER 45

Daddy said that Stephanie was so traumatized and afraid that they would kill her if she talked, that Social Services had to call in a child psychiatrist to get even this much information from her.

He continued to tell the entire family that when the police arrived at the apartment with an ambulance, Dennis was lying dead in the back seat of a neighbor's car. Edwina claimed that they were trying to take him to a hospital, but he was already dead.

The police arrested Maxwell and detained my mother for questioning. This was all the information my father had at this point.

We stayed at my grandparent's house for a few more hours grieving with the family. Then we went back to Daddy's apartment, where he gave us the bedroom to share while he slept in the living room on the sofa.

Grandmother had offered to put us up at her house for a while, but Daddy said he wanted all his kids under his roof from now on. I could tell that he was afraid to let us out of his sight.

The following days were surreal as I watched my father and grandfather make the funeral arrangements for Dennis. They were waiting for the medical examiner to finish with his autopsy so his body could be sent to the funeral home. At one point, I saw Daddy break down crying in my grandfather's arms saying, "I can't believe I outlived my own child."

A few days later, Dennis's body was transferred to the funeral home, and my father got a copy of the autopsy report. When I asked, he allowed me to read it. It said that Dennis had been shot with a .357 Magnum, and that the bullet hit his rib cage and his rib cage crushed his heart. It also said that he lived for two and a half minutes after being shot. There was no gun powder residue on his hands, so he did not shoot himself.

Daddy had been waiting for this information because Maxwell and mother were saying that Dennis had shot himself, and that Stephanie's account of what happened should be disregarded because she was only eight years old and confused.

In other words, she was calling Stephanie a delusional nut case. My mother was claiming that she saw the whole thing from the hallway. I could not believe she was defending Maxwell and lying for him.

Daddy said she had gotten an attorney for Maxwell because the police had charged him with murder. I personally would have filed for divorce and left his ugly butt sitting in jail. Then, to add salt to the wound, mother was staying with Maxwell's family while he was in jail. The whole thing disgusted me.

Who covers for the guy who murdered your kid? I just could not understand that. I tried talking to God about it, got no answer. I realize now that I was too angry to hear God's answer.

Two weeks later, Dennis's funeral services were held. My mother's side of the family showed up, but she was not allowed to attend the service or to see us kids at all. Daddy had worked with Social Services and gotten emergency papers filed to keep her away from us.

He and grandmother bought Dennis a handsome dark blue suit, with a powder blue bow tie and a pair of black leather Buster Brown shoes. I went with Daddy and grandmother to drop his burial clothes off so I could put my favorite charm necklace around his neck so he would know how much I loved him. This way something, I loved would be around his neck forever protecting him.

I wished I could put a box of Metropolitan ice cream sandwiches and a Michael Jackson album in the little blue coffin with white satin lining my father had chosen for him. I knew those were Dennis's favorite things, but I realized that it was impossible. I was hoping he knew I was not mad at him anymore; that the whole fight was a stupid mistake on my part.

The day of the funeral, everyone except Stephanie and Helen walked past his open coffin to say their final goodbyes.

As I looked down into his open casket, I thought about how he was just a little boy, and how he always made straight A's in school without even trying, not to mention his amazing bravery on the playground, whenever someone picked on me, how he would beat them up. He was the best fighter

I had ever seen. We would never again ride bikes together or sing to the Jackson Five records with hairbrushes as microphones.

But the thing I was going to miss most was his big spirit, and the fact that he was different from anyone I had ever met or would meet again. I cried as I bent down to hug and kiss him goodbye. He felt stiff as a board and cold as my lips kissed his cheek. His face and body looked swollen and stiff from the embalming fluid.

Then I noticed some type of liquid running down his forehead, as if he were perspiring. That is when I realized that my brother was no longer in that body, it was only a shell that he left behind. His body felt and looked like an empty box now that his soul had departed from it.

Since "Ben" by Michael Jackson was his favorite song, Daddy had Aunt Shelby sing that song at his funeral service.

As relatives got up and spoke about my brother's life, told stories about funny things he had done, it all seemed like a blur of faces and meaningless words to me. All I could see was how much I wanted my brother back and how guilty I felt because I had not been there to take that bullet for him.

I do not remember how much time had passed before I was put into a limo and driven to Forest Lawn Cemetery to lower his casket into the ground. At first, I thought about him being trapped underneath all that dirt in his coffin. Then once again I reminded myself that Dennis was not in that casket. It is only his shell I kept telling myself repeatedly.

Anger and deep hatred for Maxwell and my mother raged through me. I hated them for taking Dennis away from me and vowed to never forgive them. I was also angry with my father and his family because I had told them about Maxwell and that gun, and no one called the police. Maybe if someone had, Dennis would still be alive.

No one rescued us, and once again I wondered where God was in all of this and why all this was happening. I was 13 now and I realized that day, that the only thing I could depend on fully was myself and God because my family had let me down.

After the funeral everyone went back to grandmother's house to eat and tell stories about Dennis. I went into my grandparent's den and sat on the big sofa in there among all the books that they had in the built-in bookshelves on the wall.

I liked sitting in that room because of the books and grandmother kept her piano in there. She had a photo of Jesus Christ walking up to a door and knocking on it. I often liked to sit there away from everyone else and examine that picture while trying to figure out why Jesus was knocking on that door. Whose door, was it? What was the true meaning of that picture? I did not know much about Jesus besides what I heard in church. I only knew about God because a part of me remembered God, and the fact that I could feel God around me but was unable to see His physical form.

So, the Jesus thing was kind of a mystery to me. I had learned about miracles He had performed on Earth in Sunday school and how some evil people had killed him by crucifixion. But that was all I knew.

The picture was extra profound to me that day as I sat in the room staring at it and I wondered if Dennis was with Jesus at that very moment.

Later that day while helping grandmother wash dishes, I asked her the meaning of the picture. She told me that Jesus knocks on the door of every man's soul, but it is up to you if you want to let Him in.

"Is Jesus going to knock on my door one day?" I asked her.

"Do you want Him to?" She replied.

"Yes, I do. He and God have some explaining to do about Dennis," I said belligerently.

"Your brother is in heaven now and he's safe. Just concentrate on doing the right thing in your life and getting good marks in school," Grandmother advised wisely.

CHAPTER 46

A few weeks later, we moved from Daddy's one bedroom apartment to a big three-bedroom duplex on Detroit Street near Wilshire Blvd. I was happy to be moving into a larger place, and my father was giving me my own bedroom. It was a five-minute walk from grandmother's house, and 20 minutes from John Burroughs Junior High.

He also asked our permission to marry Jenny. We were okay with it because Jenny was nice to us and acted like she had some common sense. She wore cool clothes and never acted like she was my mother. It was more like she was my father's girlfriend, but our friend at the same time. She had a full-time job at some factory, working her butt off instead of spending Daddy's money.

After he popped the question and she said yes, they dropped us off at grandmother's one weekend and drove to Las Vegas where they got married.

When they returned, Jenny moved her stuff in, and we all started a new life together. Jenny started taking care of my sister Helen who was only eight years old and entering the third grade in the fall. She helped grandmother get Stephanie, who barely spoke anymore, to her therapy sessions. Jenny did her best to help Daddy out with us.

Whenever Stephanie did attempt to speak, it was with great effort and a stutter. She now no longer drew pictures or smiled. Stephanie also had to go to a special school that had psychiatrists as teachers. She had something the psychiatrists called a mental block and could no longer count or even spell her name. Everything she had learned in school over the years had been washed away with the shooting. All she could see in her mind was Dennis with bubbles of blood coming out of his mouth as he tried to tell her to run with his last breath.

Stephanie had regular nightmares about the shooting. Every time I looked at her, I could see that a movie of that shooting played repeatedly in her young mind. Now she was at kindergarten level in school and had to start all over again, all because of Maxwell.

I hated him so much that I wanted to kill him with the same gun he killed my brother Dennis with.

Soon I figured out the only thing I could do to help Stephanie feel better was to act normal. I would do stuff with her and act like nothing had happened. I started bringing her into my bedroom, where I would play my Elton John and Jackson Five records while she sat on my bed. And when I went outside to sit on the step of our duplex, I would take her with me. Anything to make her forget and feel like it was a normal day. Helen and I were in therapy as well, but ours was different from Stephanie's.

Living with our new stepmother turned out to be a piece of cake. You could tell that she was doing her best not to control us, and her interactions with us were always pleasant. The most important thing she did right was not to discipline us. Jenny never hit or yelled at us, she minded her own business and let Daddy tell us what to do.

On the weekends when she was not working or driving one of us kids to a psychiatrist appointment, Jenny would hang out at her mother's house in Hollywood and would often take us with her. Her family was always roasting a pig in their back yard and having big family parties filled with different Filipino dishes. They were always speaking the Tagalog language, and I would just sit there at the table trying to figure out what they were saying while stuffing my face with roasted pork and my favorite, a dish they called "Pancit."

I became friends with Jenny's little sister, named Kathy and her little brother Mike, who were both close to my age, so we got along well. Jenny's mother, whom I called Miss Ebro, was a nice woman who warmly welcomed me and my sisters into their family. It was a welcome change from the life we had lived with our mother and Maxwell.

CHAPTER 47

When the day came for Maxwell's first court hearing, my whole family was angry because his lawyer got his charges reduced to manslaughter and child endangerment. I kept thinking this happened because mother had lied to cover up for him. I wanted to go to the court hearing, and at first father was okay with it. Then my grandparents intervened and told my father that I was too young to be exposed to all of that.

I protested that I had been exposed to him shooting at me every day, so why not allow me to see him go to jail? I had been waiting a long time to see Maxwell get what was coming to him. I wanted to see him look scared like Dennis probably did when he shot him, and Stephanie, when he tried to kill her to cover his tracks.

Stephanie was allowed to go because she was the star witness for the prosecution. She was so afraid that mother and Maxwell would find a way to kill her if she told on them, that the psychiatrists really had to work hard to get her to a point to where, if they cleared the court room, she would feel safe enough to tell the judge what happened that day.

Every time my father and Stephanie came home from the courthouse, I would grill him for information. After going to court a couple of times, he came home one day even more angry about the situation than usual.

When I asked him my usual questions about what happened in court that day, he told me that my mother was pregnant with Maxwell's baby.

"It must have happened before he killed your brother because he's been locked up since the shooting," My father said. "This punk killed my son in cold blood, and now he's having a baby of his own," My father said in disbelief.

"Then your mother gets on the witness stand and contradicts everything your sister told the judge. Your mother claims that she was standing in the hallway, about to walk into the bedroom after bathing Helen, and saw the whole thing.

How she heard Maxwell tell Dennis to hand him the gun, and when he did, it accidentally went off. She also claimed that Stephanie had always been slow in the brain, confused and did not know what she was talking about.

So, basically your mother is trying to say that your brother shot himself and that Stephanie does not know what she is talking about. "He said.

I was disgusted and speechless. Bad enough, my mother defends Maxwell in court, but the biggest slap in the face was walking into that court room carrying his child while Dennis lay dead in Forest Lawn Cemetery.

With tears in my eyes, I looked upward at the ceiling and thought to myself,

"Where are you God?"

"Life sure can kick you in the ass sometimes,"

My father said sounding defeated.

Then he hugged me and told me to go help Jenny make dinner in the kitchen while he called my grandmother.

After a month of going to court the trial ended with Maxwell getting convicted of manslaughter and child endangerment because my mother's conscience finally surfaced. She recanted her previous testimony and said she now was not clear on all the details. Apparently, she cried and told the district attorney maybe everything did not happen exactly as she remembered.

Based on that, Maxwell was sentenced to 8 to 25 years in Chino State Pen.

I told my father, "I hope Maxwell and my mother rotted in hell together."

"Yes, I agree, but at least the bastard was convicted." He said.

My father's family was exhausted with grief but relieved at the outcome, even though it did not bring Dennis back.

A few months later, my father was granted permanent custody of me and my sisters. A judge had stripped our mother of all parental rights; she was not even allowed weekend visitation with us. Her choice to stay married to Maxwell also cost her all her family as well as her kids.

Her mother, sisters and brother refused to have any further contact with her. She was cut off from the family; no one wanted anything to do with her but Maxwell and his family. She had gone to far this time.

My mother and Maxwell's mother always hated each other; now I found solace in the irony that not only was she knocked up with his kid, but she had to deal with his family while he was locked up.

CHAPTER 48

Stephanie continued to get better and was finally at a point where she could spell her name again. She was now at a second-grade level in the special education school, but we were encouraged because if she was able to spell her name again, then maybe she could relearn everything else. Although she was still waking up in the middle of the night with nightmares, we kept telling her she was safe and after a while they stopped coming so often.

One night I went to bed and had a dream that I was in an art museum looking at some art on the walls. As I turned a corner in the museum instead of there being more art to look at, I was suddenly in a room with nothing but a closet door in it. At first the door was closed, but then it opened, and Dennis walked out. We ran to each other, so overjoyed to be with one another again that I began to cry tears of joy as we stood there in a long loving embrace.

Then, Dennis looked at me and smiled just the way he used to when he was alive. He also looked like himself when he was alive; dressed the same too: a pair of shorts and tee-shirt with sneakers. He was dressed in play clothes just like it was another day on Earth.

As we looked at one another smiling, I told him that I really was not mad at him and how sorry I was for fighting with him in the first place, and how much I really loved him.

"I know you really love me. I love you too." Dennis assured me. "I am here so you can see that I am alright, and to tell you not to be mad at Maxwell for killing me. I was not meant to live past the age of 11. It was planned this way before I was born. Maxwell was only used as a tool to bring about my passing, and you shouldn't be mad at him."

"Is it fun where you're living now?" I asked in wonder.

Dennis smiled at me with a gleam in his eyes and said, "I get to eat all the Metropolitan ice cream I want here. Plus, I am with Uncle Jimmy and the rest of our family, and I saw Joe, and he is okay too. I like it better here. It is so much fun, you just do not remember how beautiful our real home is. When you finish your life, you will come home too, and I will be waiting for you with the rest of the family."

Still smiling Dennis went on, "Everything will be okay, so do not worry about me anymore because I am happy. Just remember that I went back home and that I will always be watching out for you from here." He promised.

Then Dennis hugged me again and we kissed each other on the cheek.

"I have to go back now, but I will love you always and don't forget to forgive Maxwell and mother." He said.

Then he pulled away from me and turned around and walked back into the closet he had walked out of, and the door shut by itself behind him. I awoke suddenly and sat up in bed, my eyes fixed on my closed bedroom door. There was a bright ball of energy the size of a grapefruit just floating there in mid-air in front of my door.

I knew without thinking that this was my brother's spirit floating there in the air and I was amazed at how beautiful the colors were.

I had never seen anything like it before, but I knew that it was my brother. Then suddenly the ball of energy went through my bedroom door.I jumped out of bed and opened the door to follow him just in time to see his spirit one last time as he lingered in the hallway for just a moment then took off like a rocket.

I stood there in the hallway for a moment thinking, "he's gone," then went back into my bedroom, got back into bed knowing that I had just been with Dennis. I also now knew it was okay to live my life without feeling guilty for being alive.

As I lay there in bed thinking about everything he said. The hardest thing was going to be forgiving Maxwell and mother, I just did not know how to do that. My brother knew my habit of holding a grudge would not serve me well in life. As usual, Dennis had my back even in death.

CHAPTER 49

I now also knew that my scattered memories of being someplace else before being here on Earth were real memories. Dennis had just given me proof that there was another reality besides this one, another world or dimension that looked like this one but was better.

I remembered it as being sheer perfection with beautiful waterfalls and oceans that were a pure brilliant blue and sparkled like diamonds. Every species of marine life that had ever lived in the ocean was there, and all of them were peaceful and nonviolent. All Nature was in a state of perfection and balance there. I thought about some of the dreams I had over the years about playing in a beautiful forest, where all the animals and I were one in consciousness. And I would never forget my friend the big black panther. I missed walking through the jungle with him and relaxing by the sparkling pool of water with the huge water fall that had sparks of light dancing upon it.

The panther and I had a deep mutual respect as true friends. I remembered riding on the panther's back at top speed through the jungle, feeling totally free. I could feel the power and strength of this magnificent animal as I sat upon its back. In my dreams, instead of talking, we could read each other's thoughts. The animals had no urge to eat you, everything there coexisted peacefully. The grass, the flowers and trees were alive and at their height of perfection.

It was a beautiful place where if you wanted to eat an apple, all you had to do was think that thought and it manifested. It reminded me of a story I learned in Sunday school about Jesus who had gone to a wedding where the wine had run out. He took plain water and made it into wine. He thought the thought and the water manifested into wine. In this verdant, peaceful world you could manifest things into the physical by just thinking the thought.

Then I understood what Dennis meant when he said he could eat all the Metropolitan ice cream he wanted. There was no hunger, sadness or ill will in the world he was living in only love, kindness, joy and the knowledge that you were connected to everything around you.

Dennis was right; there was no need to worry about him any longer because he was safe at home, his real home.

By now I was wondering why we were even here on Earth to begin with where bad things happened; people lied and killed without hesitation. Was this place some sort of school or testing ground to prepare a soul to live in a perfect world? Was this thing we call God testing our reactions in certain situations? Why was it that most people had no memory of where they came from before they were born? Why did I remember? I had a lot of questions and I wanted answers.

All I knew for sure was that if I was not crazy, and this place really existed, I had better learn how to forgive my mother and Maxwell if I wanted to live there again. Because hatred and not forgiving people had no existence there.

I got out of bed to get a glass of water from the kitchen, and as I stood by the kitchen window drinking it, I watched the sunrise and thought, this is the dawn of a new day for you. It felt as if a huge weight had been lifted off my shoulders. I was now free to be a kid and live my life, and I knew that in spirit my brother would always be with me.

CHAPTER 50

When my father and everyone else in the house woke up, I told them about Dennis coming to visit me. But no one took me seriously except Stephanie. She stuttered as she told me that she often dreamed that she and Dennis were playing together, "And he is always wearing his regular play clothes." She said.

"He always tells me that he's okay and not to worry about him. He also said I'm going to get better with talking and remembering stuff in school." Stephanie told us, confirming my account.

During Sunday dinner after church that weekend, I told everyone in the family about seeing Dennis and everything he said to me. Everyone looked at me like I was nuts or grieving too hard, or both.

Aunt Mary told me later in the kitchen that Dennis had come to her in a dream as well. "I was feeling guilty because the last time he was at my apartment he was begging me not to send him back to your mother's place." She confided. Then Mary, whispered, "He told me that Maxwell had been doing things that made him feel uncomfortable behind closed doors, sexual things."

Mary looked up at me, and with a tear rolling down her cheek said, "I sent him back to those killers, and I never told anyone. I was too afraid of Maxwell and your mother."

"I know you are telling the truth because Dennis told me not to worry about him too. He told me not to feel guilty about his passing because he wasn't meant to live past the age of 11." I said. Looking Mary in the eye I continued, "don't feel guilty, listen to what Dennis said to you in that dream."

We hugged each other for a moment, and I said, "I love you Aunt Mary."

"I love you too pretty girl." Mary replied.

CHAPTER 51

As the weeks turned into months, we all began to heal and adjust to our new life as a family without Dennis. I loved living with my father and Jenny because they really did their best to take good care of us.

I liked living in our 1950's Spanish style duplex because of the hardwood floors and the Spanish architecture. For once, I was not ashamed of where I lived, and could have friends over for the first time. When it was my turn to wash the dishes, Daddy would let me plug in a transistor radio so I could rock out in the kitchen to the KLOS radio station.

He would walk into the kitchen, hear me listening to it, and say that Rock and Roll was stolen from the black man. Then he would shake his head whenever I broke out into a dance, like this girl is crazy.

My Father also bought me a used color TV set with a little TV stand on wheels from grandfather's furniture store for my bedroom. I felt like a real teenager with my record player and color TV in my room.

I loved watching a TV show called "Happy Days" because I thought the music from the 1950's was really cool, and the clothes were a work of art to me. Then I would watch "Love American Style" and "Room 222." Sometimes on the weekends I would watch the beach movies with "Gidget" and "Moon Doggy" wishing I were "Gidget" being serenaded on the beach by "The Little Boy on The Moon."

By then, I also had every Elton John poster that I could get my hands on taped to my ceiling and walls. So the minute I opened my eyes in the morning, I saw Elton's beautiful face.

Our family had become friends with the Payton family who lived upstairs from us, and I became friends with the two girls, Bridget and Naomi, who were around my age. Miss Payton was a divorced hairstylist raising her daughters on her own.

Stephanie and I would go up to their place on the weekends and watch "Soul Train" with them in their living room. Bridget and I would practice doing the dances we saw the "Soul Train Dancers" doing. Then she would do my hair in some ridiculous hair style with her mother's hair supplies.

One Saturday afternoon I thought I died and went to heaven. Elton John preformed, *"Bennie and the Jets"* on "Soul Train." It was a big thing because everyone was saying that Elton John had crossed over from Rock stations to Soul. Black record stores everywhere were selling out of *"Benny and the Jets"* 45's like crazy. For Elton to perform on "Soul Train," on his own personal piano on stage was a major event for me.

Janis and Brenda started laughing at me when they saw the tears of joy running down my cheeks as I watched Elton sing and play the piano. I did not care if they laughed since I felt lucky just to witness the beauty of Elton John's fingers playing notes on those piano keys.

"He's so gorgeous! Look at the gap between his teeth and his English accent is to die for. Even his body is perfect," I told Bridget and Naomi.

They both looked at me like I had taken leave of my senses, but I did not care. Elton was my guy; he was the Beethoven of Rock and Roll to me, and I loved him.

I had read a magazine article that said Elton John was gay and coming out of the closet. I did not care, I still had fantasies about going to England once I grew up to marry him if the "Little Boy on The Moon" did not keep his word and show up to marry me first. I figured once Elton met me, he would change his mind about being gay.

A little Jewish girl named Sofia Steinberg who lived four doors down also became my friend. We were the same age, in the same grade, and in the same biology class at school.

Down the street, a block away in the opposite direction lived Barry Fallon who always had a funny joke to tell. He was my friend from Wilshire Crest Elementary school when I lived with Marie and Phillip. All of us walked to John Burroughs together every day in a group, all the while running our mouths. I always had my transistor radio on and loaded with fresh batteries just in case an Elton John song came on. We all thought we were hot shit because we were in Junior High school.

I also befriended Jake and Peggy, a white married couple, that lived in the duplex next to ours. They were this cool hippie couple that often allowed me to hang out in their living room where I would listen to their Rock and Roll collection on their expensive stainless steel stereo system for hours.

They had all the albums that I could not afford to buy for myself. Because of them, I knew the difference between a cheap sounding stereo system and a good one. Their living room and dining room windows faced my bedroom window, so I could see and hear everything that went on over there. I would often sit by my window watching them have dinner parties complete with music, wine and the laughter of good friends. I daydreamed that one day me and my husband would have a cool place to live in with lots of great friends to invite over for dinner.

CHAPTER 52

When I turned 14 years old Daddy started letting me go places on the bus by myself, but I always had to be home before dark, and all my chores had to be done. He always had to know exactly where I was going, and if I was going to meet anyone once I got there. Sometimes, he would take things too far by saying weird stuff like, "girls need supervision at all times so unplanned pregnancies don't happen."

Despite telling him that I was not interested in having sex with anybody, the "supervision" continued.

"I don't even have a boyfriend." I told him.

"And I'm not stupid enough to have a baby I can't support. Besides, I have plans for my life, and having a baby before the age of 20 isn't what I want."

It still took a lot of talking to convince him that all I wanted to do was go look at albums and musical instruments I could not afford, just like he did with his Cadillac.

He must have believed me, because he started letting me go out into the world on my own. I would take the bus to a record store on Melrose Blvd. called, "Aaron's Records and Tapes." I wanted to work there so badly. They always had free posters by the front door for new album releases. I would take what I wanted for my bedroom then go look at all the albums I was going to buy once I could afford them, and I had a list.

Aarons also sold used Levi jeans and vintage blue jean skirts among other things, so I would try stuff on just to see how I looked in it. Then I would walk down the street to a place called the "Guitar Center" on the corner of Fairfax and Melrose across the street from Fairfax High School. The musicians hung out in there, and sometimes you could walk in and hear a guitar or bass player jamming, often on a guitar they could not afford to buy. People who were saving up money for an instrument were there to visit it and dream a little dream of owning it. That is what I liked about hanging out there; I was among other dreamers who believed anything was possible.

You could be an unknown musician today, and a star tomorrow with your big break around the corner. The energy in that place was electric! I was always the kid standing in the corner just watching the boys play, trying to figure out how a flute could do what they were doing on the guitar.

Then I would catch the bus back home before dark, thinking to myself what a great afternoon it had been. Sometimes after dinner we would all sit in the living room together as a family and listen to a radio show called "Mystery Theater." It was 30 minutes of murder and intrigue with great sound effects and talented actors that I loved and always looked forward to in the evenings. My father told us that "Mystery Theater" was from the "Golden Age" of radio. Before people had TV sets, radio was the big thing for entertainment. "That's why it seems so real," he told us.

My father and I also listened to the radio in the mornings while he was getting ready for work and I for school. Daddy would have the radio on full blast for the morning lecture, so everyone in the house could hear. We would listen to "This Thing Called Life" with Dr. Ernest Holmes that Daddy said was an exploration of the world's great wisdom designed to provide tools for improving your life in health, business, relationships and enhanced spirituality.

The program always started with this beautiful song, *"Oh, what a beautiful morning."* I loved the words to the song, especially the part that said, "I've got a wonderful feeling everything's going my way." After hearing that song every morning before school, I would leave home to start my day believing I could do anything I set my mind to.

CHAPTER 53

As Sofia Steinberg and I walked to school together every day with our little group, we started getting close. We began to hang out a lot at each other's houses on the weekends and after school. Sofia was a small-boned girl like me, with beautiful long brown hair that had a slight wave to it and flawless olive skin. Sofia was a little hippie girl, with her sunglasses and what she called her "Janis Joplin" floppy hat. I thought she was so cool, for a variety of reasons. She walked to school bare footed in a long-tie-dyed hippie skirt, or a pair of faded bell bottom blue jeans and a halter top and no bra. Sometimes she would draw the "Peace" sign right above her belly button with a black marker. I loved the fact that Sofia was wild and free.

She always snuck out of her house at night while her mother was sleeping, and the next day she always had a wild story to tell about what she did. Sofia would meet some guitar or bass player late at night. And all the guys she messed around with were older like 16 and 17, and few were Jewish.

Her mother would have hit the roof if she had known what Sofia doing. It was 1975 and I did not know anybody my age, except Sofia, who was having sex. She had gone down to Planned Parenthood for birth control without her mother's knowledge. I figured if she was smart enough to guard against unwanted pregnancy, then she must know what she is doing.

Frequently, Sofia would come to my bedroom window and fill me in on all the details late at night after her dates. Sometimes Bridget would hang her head out of her window as well to hear about Sofia's latest adventure.

This time She was in love with a guy named Joe Freeze who went to Fairfax High School and played bass in a band that had just preformed at some little club on the Sunset Strip.

"He looks just like Edgar Winter from "The Edgar Winter Group. I just love Edgar Winter," Sofia said.

"So, you're in love with him because he is an Albino?" I asked.

"His pale skin and hair are a turn on," she replied."

Then she told us how she had snuck out of the house, caught the bus to the club where she got in for free because she was with the band. After watching him preform, they had sex on the grass at La Brea Tar Pits Park near the pond.

Since I had no sexual experience of my own, I had come to depend upon her adventures, and a copy of Cosmopolitan magazine for information. Every now and then I would walk into a liquor store and read an article on the subject in "Playboy" magazine. Otherwise, I really did not know much.

One night I decided to sneak out of my bedroom window. I had asked my father earlier if I could spend the night at Sofia's, but he said no because I had church in the morning. So, I told him I was going to bed early and stuffed pillows under the blankets in the shape of a body.

Since he hardly ever came into my room after I had gone to bed, I figured I was safe. When I arrived at Sofia's house, her mother had already left for a date with her boyfriend. Another girl from school named Sally Jones was already there when I arrived. The three of us planned to listen to "Dr. Demento" and "Wolf Man Jack" on the radio. Then KLOS was going to play David Bowie's new album "Young Americans."

Since KLOS always played the new album releases before the store release date, it was a chance to see if the album was any good before you spent your money on it.

We all loved David Bowie's album *"Ziggy Stardust and the Spiders from Mars,"* and all agreed it was a work of art. Sally and I had a whole routine to the song, "Rock and Roll Suicide." We would act the lyrics out while singing, even putting a Sherman cigarette in our mouths when Bowie says, "time takes a cigarette and puts it in your mouth." It was all very entertaining. David Bowie was dressed in a cool looking suit, had his hair slicked back and was calling himself "The Thin white Duke."

After hearing the new album on the radio and loving it, we all agreed it was worth spending money on. I decided not to push my luck with the sneaking out routine and returned home right after we had finished talking about the new album. The last thing I needed was for my father to know that I was leaving the house without permission. I had better things to do then to sit in the house under punishment. When I got back into my bedroom through the window, my room looked just as I had left it. I had gotten away with it!

That Monday after school, Daddy gave me permission to go to Aaron's Records and Tapes on the bus with Sofia and Sally. All three of us were going to buy our album copies of "David Bowie's" new release together. It was important to me to get my albums on release day because you were getting the first pressing. Then we were going to the Fred Segal store so Sally could buy an expensive pair of jeans.

When Daddy came home from work that evening, Sofia and I had the album opened and playing on the turntable, and to my surprise he listened to "Bowie" with us and liked the song *Fame.*

CHAPTER 54

A few weeks later, my father's opinion of Sofia being okay for me to hang out with started to change. We had gone to church and Sunday dinner at my grandparent's house. While we were gone, Sofia went into my bedroom through the window, which was now getting a lot of use, because she wanted to borrow one of my tops.

On the way home in the car, I asked my father for an advance on my allowance, so I could buy sheet music and a copy of Elton John's "*Goodbye Yellow Brick Road*" album.

He asked if I had cleaned my room, like he had told me to do. I told him yes, it was clean, so when we got home, he walked into my room to double check that it was. When he opened my closet door, there was Sofia, naked from the waist up and just pulling my top over her head.

Daddy shut the closet door fast, looked at me and demanded, "why is Sofia in your closet half naked?"

I did not want him to know that I was using my window as a source of coming and going. So, I lied and told him that I had given her my house key earlier so she could borrow a top to wear. Sofia came out of the closet with the top on and said,

"Sorry Mr. Johnson." Sofia said looking embarrassed.

"Okay it's time for you to go home now." Daddy said.

"Sure thing." She agreed.

I followed her to the front door and let her out, relieved. My father fell for it and my secret was safe!

CHAPTER 55

One of my passions was collecting 1950's style clothing after being influenced from watching too many episodes of "Happy Days." I remembered seeing my aunts wear those clothes when I was young. Now I thought that poodle skirts were cool and had started going to the thrift stores looking for them in my size. I would buy them and wear them to school, with red lipstick and a ponytail. I even had a copy of Bill Haley and The Comets singing *"Rock Around the Clock"* on a 45 single.

I had learned from watching "Happy Days " that being a teenager in the 50s had been fun, and I felt I had missed out by being born too late to enjoy that era. So why not live that out anyway, I thought. As Dr. Hornaday always said in church, "No one is stopping you but yourself."

The Women's Movement was starting, and I was interested in female empowerment. I was impressed with Gloria Steinem, Jane Fonda and Helen Reddy singing *"I Am Woman."* Every time I heard that song, I felt empowered and proud to be a girl.

A few of the girls at school had decided to extend the Women's Movement to our school and challenge the school dress code. We all stopped wearing our bras to school in protest. I had no business going without a bra because I was a 36D cup and my breasts bounced when I walked, and I had gained 20 pounds from Daddy and Jenny cooking fattening meals.

I suggested that we burn our bras in the 9th grade lunch court during lunch period, but Sofia said that we would be facing suspension from school for starting a fire on school grounds. I also decided that walking around school with no shoes was okay, and my right as a human being.

There was this thing I had going on with my feet and the Earth. I loved feeling the Earth and the ground under my feet, and it made me feel connected with it for some reason.

When I showed up in Mrs. Tessier's English class barefoot, she always made a point to tell me to put my shoes on. I would refuse, then I would walk to the back of the classroom and sit on the floor instead of my desk to protest the school dress code. I called it a "sit-in."

I figured if strange Mr. Becker, my history teacher, could teach a class with a Barbie doll he called "Baby" sitting on the top of his desk in a toy Volkswagen Bug Convertible and dressed in the latest fashion, then I could dress the way I wanted at school.

Mr. Becker claimed that "Baby" was human. None of us students knew for sure if he was truly crazy, or just putting on a show for us. But each day he would update all his students on "Baby's" recent adventures. "Baby" always had a fun filled week-end and seemed to drive her Volkswagen Convertible Bug to Las Vegas quite regularly. Also, the Volkswagen Convertible Bug that "Baby" drove was my dream car. I often wondered why Mr. Becker was teaching history in a school, instead of living in a mental institution.

My "sit-ins" always ended with my teacher sending me to the principal's office. Grandmother would be called, and I would be told to put my shoes back on. Because of the "sit-ins," all the kids in school now knew me and wanted to be my friend. I was suddenly friends with everybody, and the feeling of being liked and accepted by my school mates was cool. No one cared what I looked like or what color I was, the kids at school liked me for who I was.

One day a smart assed new boy pointed at me and yelled "whale on the beach" while I was shooting hoops at nutrition. I weighed 140 pounds at 5 feet tall, and I was proud of it. My weight gain did not bother me at all since I had been skinny all my life and I finally had some meat on my bones. In my mind beauty came in all shapes sizes and colors.

I was just about to tell the little punk to go to hell when a skinny tall blonde-haired boy I had seen around school, came to my defense.

He walked up to the bully and said, "You have two choices, walk away now or get your ass kicked."

The kid decided to go with choice number one and walked away.

"Thanks" I said, "but I was just about to tell him the same thing myself."

"It pisses me off when I see buttholes like him messing with people because of the way they look." He said. "My little sister is in the 6th grade, and she comes home from school crying because of being called a fat pig at school."

"Well, this is the first time it's ever happened to me," I said. And thanked him for standing up for me, and we started shooting hoops together.

"You're the girl that refused to wear shoes and a bra. My name is Steth Romberg." He said. We did the handshake and continued shooting hoops.

When the end of nutrition bell rang, Seth picked up my books and walked me to class. From that day on Seth and I were friends and he started hanging out with me and my little group of friends.

Seth was a 9th grader and could have eaten in the 9th grade lunch court, but he chose to hang out with us at lunch. Seth and my friend Barry, who was the only drag queen in our school, really hit it off. Barry was black and proud to be the first out in the open drag queen in our Junior High school.

He came to school dressed in tight Jordache blue jeans, and a rabbit fur jacket and a ton of "Lip Smackers" lip gloss on. None of the teachers or kids at school treated him any differently than anyone else. He even used the girl's bathroom.

In Los Angeles we saw drag queens on the street every day, so to have one in school was natural to us.

Barry was one of the Hollywood Street kids, meaning he lived in Hollywood and his mother was a drug addict who did not care what he did. He told us stories about the hookers turning tricks on Hollywood Blvd. On Friday and Saturday nights just to feed themselves. But he loved going to school and was a straight "A" student, and he never missed a day of school unless he was ill.

I respected Barry and valued our friendship because he had been dealt a rough hand in life like me. He was a survivor, we had that in common, and he was funny and tons of fun to be around. Barry showed up to school every day no matter what was going on in his personal life. To me that meant he was rising above his unfortunate circumstances.

We also shared clothes and a deep love for "Elton John." He introduced me to a girl named Felicia Sanders who also started hanging with our little group at school. Felicia was a red headed freckle faced Jewish girl who was always taking risks like selling pot at school until she got busted. She always pushed her parents to the limit. My father always let me sleep over her house because her family was Jewish. When Daddy met her parents and saw how religious they were, he figured I was safe from drugs and boys under their roof because he had no knowledge of her drug bust.

Felicia and I had a list of rock concerts from "Rolling Stone" magazine that we were planning on attending together. We had just scored tickets for the Alice Cooper "Welcome to My Nightmare" concert at the Los Angeles Forum and Seth was going with us. And that pass October we enjoyed Elton John at Dodger Stadium where I wrote "I love you "Elton" on my butt in black magic marker then mooned him. I was right up front near the stage so I could see Elton perfectly, he put on the best show I had ever seen, and he was even more beautiful in person.

The whole "Welcome to My Nightmare" album was a Rock and Roll play about a little boy named "Steven" who I thought was mentally insane. Plus, Vincent Price, the king of horror movies had a cameo appearance in it. Daddy was okay with me going, since "Welcome to My Nightmare" had aired on television, and he had already watched what I was going to see in our living room. Since I was only 14, he made me take my sister Stephanie with me, and pay for her concert ticket.

On concert day Felicia's mother drove us to the Forum, dropped us off, and said to call her from a phone booth to be picked up right after the concert ended. All the seats were filled, so the place was really packed. Seth had gotten there hours earlier. I looked around us and saw a lot of people doing drugs and drinking; you could smell pot being smoked everywhere. Some guy sitting in a chair next to me with no shirt on, offered me a beer out of the cooler he had with him.

I said no thanks; I had never drunk beer before, and I had no wish to try it. I had grown up seeing my father drinking when he was married to my mother. I remembered how it always got him into trouble, so I was going to play it smart and avoid trouble.

When Alice Cooper came on stage the whole crowd went crazy as he opened with the song *"Welcome to My Nightmare."* Then when Vincent Price came on stage to do the *"black Widow"* song I was truly blown away that I was there in person to witness such a work of art.

When the concert was over and we were leaving the Forum, Seth held my hand. I could not believe that I was at a rock concert and a boy was holding my hand like we were on a date.

CHAPTER 56

The following week, Seth and I were walking to class, and stopped at my wall locker so I could get a book. That is when Seth asked me if I would be his girlfriend. I was thrilled and excited, my first junior high school romance.

"Yes, I'll be your girlfriend," I said immediately.

He gave me a quick peck on the cheek and said it is official then. We continued to walk to class together, but this time we were holding hands. I was not necessarily attracted to Seth in a physical sense; it was more like he was my buddy that I could do things with and have fun. We enjoyed reading magazines together, both loved clothes and liked to shoot hoops together.

How cool was it having a boyfriend and being known as a couple around school! After that at school Seth and I walked around with our arms around each another. He would also carry my books while walking me to class, then plant a quick kiss on my cheek. I was happy that he hardly ever tried to tongue kiss me, and that is one of the reasons I agreed to be his girlfriend. He also was not trying to get me in a corner alone to feel me up. I was a little hesitant about the act of tongue kissing. The last boyfriend proved to me that boys could have bad breath, and bad breath to me meant germs and bacteria in your saliva. When someone put their tongue in your mouth you were swapping saliva with them.

In my mind, I needed your mouth to be clean and germ free in order, to put my tongue in there. I always had chewing gun with me to keep my mouth clean for my self-preservation, aware that not all others did.

Seth usually called me each evening to say goodnight. Whenever Daddy answered the phone and asked why a boy was calling me, I told him that Seth was part of a study group at school that I was in. I figured the word "study" would prevent him from suspecting the truth. Daddy not only forbade me to have a boyfriend, but he claimed I was never getting married either!

One Saturday Daddy gave me permission to take the bus and shop for blue jeans with Sofia Steinberg. We both lied to our parents about going shopping together. In truth, Sofia was meeting Joe Freeze and I was catching the bus to Seth's house. Then we were going to eat falafels at the Middle Eastern food stand on Fairfax, followed by trying on jeans at Fred Segal's that we could not afford. Then it was on to Aaron's Records and Tapes on Melrose Blvd to buy a pair of blue jeans that I could afford.

Sofia and I walked to the corner of Wilshire and Detroit Street together, then parted ways. I got on the bus headed for the Fairfax district where Seth lived right off Fairfax and Third Street near the Farmer's Market. I got off the bus on Fairfax and started walking up a few blocks to Third Street, which was primarily a Jewish neighborhood. As I walked past the shops, most of the people I passed on the street were dressed in Orthodox Jewish attire. I saw a lot of Orthodox Jews wearing black hats with side locks hanging, dressed in black suits with white shirts.

They all looked so holy and sacred to me. They had their own shops and businesses with Jewish products in them, including special foods and supplies to uphold their traditions started long ago and still being honored.

I wondered how many of them were Holocaust survivors or had family members who were. I had learned about Hitler in history class and the horror that he had inflicted upon Jews. I could not even begin to imagine the pain and sadness they had been through, and yet they still believed in God. It was amazing to me. In my mind there was something uniquely special about this. I had great respect for their ability to survive all the horrors of the war and everything else the world had thrown at them.

I thought about how Jesus Christ was born into the Jewish religion, and in the "Ten Commandments" movie the hand of God parted the Red Sea so they could escape the ruler of Egypt. I had appreciation and respect for all that I saw as I walked to Seth's house.

When I arrived at Seth's house and knocked on the door, he opened it with his eight-year-old sister standing next to him. He invited me in as his sister yelled out, "Mommy Seth just let a black girl in the house."

Wow!! I thought to myself, this is uncomfortable.

Then his grandmother, who was sitting in a chair in the living room said, "Seth why can't you bring a nice Jewish girl home?"

His mother came out of the kitchen, looked at me, then politely said, "hello," ignoring what his little sister and grandmother had just said.

Seth grabbed his backpack and we got out of there fast. While walking to the bus stop Seth apologized to me for his sister and his grandmother's reaction to my race. He explained to me that his grandmother was a holocaust survivor and had been in a concentration camp. She believed that Jews should only date and marry other Jews.

"Do you believe that too?" I asked.

"If I did, I wouldn't have asked you to be my girlfriend." He said.

"Well, my father thinks that all Rock and Roll was stolen by the white man, and some of my family members have said some bad stuff about white people, but I figured I would judge people by the way they treat me not by their religion or race." I said.

"That's the way I feel about it." Seth replied.

After putting that behind us, we had a great time that day.

CHAPTER 57

Seth and I had a trouble-free relationship for the entire school year, until a week before school was due to let out for summer vacation. Seth came to school and told me that he wanted to talk to me alone at lunch.

Then he told me that he had concluded that he was gay and broke up with me.

I was shocked. I did not see that coming!

I looked at him and said. "You're joking right?"

"No, I'm as serious as a heart attack." He said, "I have been attracted to boys ever since I can remember. I was slightly attracted to you, but I had to face the fact that it was not a sexual attraction, but I am attracted to Freddy Mercury from Queen. In fact, I have fantasized about having myself gift wrapped in a big box and delivered to his hotel room when he comes to town for a concert."

"That's funny," I laughed "because I am not sexually attracted to you either, but I'm definitely not gay. I just loved your personality I guess."

After confessing his true feelings to me I totally understood where he was coming from. That is why he never tried to tongue kiss me or tried to go to second base. Girls were not his thing. At least he was being honest and up front about the situation, so I was not angry or hurt. In fact, I wished him well and since he was graduating and going on to Fairfax High, it was for the best. Besides, I was still waiting for the little boy on the moon to find me so anybody else I dated would be practice until I met him.

On the last day of school, I was eating a sweet roll during nutrition with Barry, Seth, Sofia and Felicia. Suddenly I saw my destiny walk right past me in the form of this beautiful blonde-haired boy with ice blue eyes. The minute I saw him not only was it love at first sight for me, but I knew that he was going to be my husband one day. And as crazy as it sounds, I remembered being married to him before the very moment I set eyes on him. Deja Vu hit me like a ton of bricks.

Felicia interrupted my thoughts by saying, "don't you hear me talking to you, what's wrong with you? Why are you just staring off into space?"

I turned to Felicia and said, "See that guy over there?"

"Yeah, what about him?" She asked.

"I'm going to marry him one day," I told her.

Felicia got a disgusted look on her face and said, "Gross! He's Nick Papalikis and I have biology class with him."

"Do you know him." I asked?

"Not really, I just see him in class. He is not particularly good looking, so I never pay any attention to him. He's pretty quiet, but I do know that he and his brother Steve hang out with the 18th street gang." She said.

"He's a gang member?" I asked surprised.

"Not yet, I know Steve's girlfriend Sue Ann and she told me that the two of them are hoping to be jumped in. Right now, they're just hanging out with them." She elaborated.

"Yeah, but isn't the 18th street gang all Hispanic?" I asked.

"Mostly, but I've seen a few white boys get in," she said.

I looked at him across the school yard and thought, this guy has long blonde hair to his shoulders. He looked more like a surfer boy to me then a wannabe gang member.

"You're either crazy or you have bad taste in men," Felicia complained.

"To me he looks like an angel. He's the most beautiful boy I've ever seen," I explained.

The bell rang ending our last nutrition for the school year, and as I watched Nick Papalikis walk into the school building I looked up to the sky and silently told God: "That's him God, that's the little boy on the moon. I remember him and he seems so familiar to me. He looks a little different from when we were little, but it must be him because I fell in love the moment, I saw him. Please God, let me marry him when I grow up,"

I prayed. Then I heard God's voice from within me say, "He's going to some dark places in life, and I don't want you going there with him."

"I don't care," I told God. "This is love at first sight and my soul remembers him, I will help him to stay out of dark places."

That is when God told me. "He must experience these dark places because his soul must learn compassion for the poor, the drunk and the drug addict that sleeps on the street. Your soul already embodies this compassion, but his does not. He believes that he is better than the man who lives in the gutter."

"Well, can I be with him for a little while until he goes to the dark places? Why would you let me play with him as a kid, have me waiting for him to marry me, then tell me I cannot be with him? What's up with that?" I asked God. I got no answer.

CHAPTER 58

I sat in my last class that day trying to figure out what God meant when He said that Nick was going to some dark places in life. If Nick were the little boy on the moon, why would God tell me he had a dark future? Maybe God was going to let his soul learn its lessons early in life, then by the time we were adults Nick would be ready for me?

I also wondered if I was crazy in the head like my mother or if God really was talking to me. I did not hear His voice very often, but I sure did talk to God every day anyway. I figured He could hear me because he made me.

The only thing I knew for sure was I fell hard for Nick Papalikis the moment I set eyes on him. I figured I had two more years at John Burroughs to get acquainted with him. I stood in front of the school building after school that day, and watched Nick walk out of sight with his brother and six Hispanic gang members. I could hardly wait for school to start again in September.

But for now, I had the entire summer vacation to figure out how I was going to get Nick Papalikis to remember me and fall for me.

School let out on Friday and by Tuesday afternoon I had obtained a summer job as a birthday present to myself. I had just turned 15 and was ready to be a working woman just like Mary Tyler Moore on the "Mary Tyler Moore Show." I even had a 45 record of the theme song, which I played that morning while getting dressed.

It was my first real job working for the "Congress of Racial Equality" (CORE). I was proud of my new job and feeling pretty grown up because I would be making a difference in the community and earning money at the same time. It was a win-win situation for me. I had to be at work by 9 a.m. Monday through Friday and would catch the bus to headquarters, then hop into a work van with 10 other people. We were dropped off in different areas around the city where we would go door to door collecting donations for Core.

Then the money would go to fund various low-income programs for underprivileged children around the city. The pay was commission only, but I did not care because I believed in myself and my own ability to earn a paycheck.

From my first day on the job, I made money. I would knock on doors and tell the truth, no sales gimmicks or manipulations as I asked each person if they wanted to support programs for youth then explained each program so they would know where their donation was going. Afterward, at home, I visualized having the highest donation scores in my group each night before sleeping and every morning before starting my day.

Just as my father and Dr. Hornaday taught me, the visualization was working. Within two weeks, I had a $300 paycheck to prove it, and my boss was quite impressed.

Daddy always scrutinized my paycheck to make certain no one was cheating me, he took me to his bank to cash it through his account, and then took 15 percent of my earnings for rent!

"Now that you're working, you should pay rent and contribute to the household," he explained.

This made me mad because I had plans for my money, and felt that as a teenager, I should be able to keep all my money.

"I need all my money because I have expenses," I reasoned with him.

"What expenses?" Daddy asked.

"Well, I have to buy records, sheet music, make-up, clothes and a rabbit with a cage." I said.

"You need to be able to take care of yourself in this world. That is why I am making you pay rent." He replied.

"But none of my friends have to pay rent, their parents pay for everything and give them money whenever they ask." I replied.

"Well, that's them and this is you." He said.

What a cheap butthole! I remembered Aunt Carol, his sister, telling me how he had paid her twenty-five cents a day when she was little to do all his household chores. My father had a reputation for being so cheap that he could squeeze a buffalo off a nickel. I once watched him go back into a supermarket over two cents because the cashier had short-changed him.

It was obvious that he did everything in his power to keep the money he earned, so why expect any less from me?

There was no choice but to pay the rent.

I worked my butt off that summer and by the end of July I had $1800 saved. I quit my job at Core a month before school started so I could go on a camping trip to Yosemite Falls with Felicia and her family and tan on the beach. Felicia and I attempted to climb Yosemite Falls, the lower waterfall, that summer.

We were at a quarter point of the 320-foot climb, when we ran into some climbers who told us that two people had fallen to their deaths trying to climb the falls that week. After hearing that, we decided that climbing up to a waterfall was not worth our lives, so we turned around and went back to camp.

I quickly found out that I was not a camping girl at all. The mosquitoes were a pain in the butt, and when you sprayed the repellent spray on your skin it felt sticky and smelled. The flies were aggressive and seemed to never leave you alone. Swatting flies away with my hands, I told them that I was not a pile of shit they could sit on.

Our last night there I had an encounter with a bear in the middle of the night. I left the tent to use the restroom and when I came out of the stall a medium sized bear was in the corner of the bathroom standing near a stall just looking at me. Thank God the bear was not blocking the doorway so I ran out of the bathroom, scared out of my mind, I ran back to the tent and zipped it up as fast as I could.

The main event of the trip happened when we got back to LA, and Felicia's parents were driving me home. A Mercedes-Benz ran a red light and hit their car. My neck was sore when I got out of the car but otherwise, I was okay.

Once the police and an ambulance showed up at the scene, a neck brace was immediately put on my neck. I was put into the ambulance and driven to the emergency room. Felicia and her parents were fine and stayed at the scene of the accident with the police.

When Daddy showed up at the hospital, the doctor told him that I had something called whiplash and should wear the neck brace for at least a week. I also had to go to a chiropractor for therapy. He drove me home and the next morning when I got up my neck was not sore. I felt fine enough to do something constructive like lay out in the backyard and get a suntan. I put on my swimsuit and went into the kitchen for a bowl of cereal before laying out. Daddy was already at the table eating hot links and scrambled eggs.

"Where do you think you're going and where's your neck brace?" He demanded.

"I don't need it any longer; my neck feels fine." I said annoyed.

"It doesn't matter You have an insurance claim." He said.

"What's that?" I asked.

"It means the insurance company is going to cut you a check because you were injured in the accident. If your neck does not hurt anymore, then you need to pretend it hurts. The insurance company is going to pay for you to go to a chiropractor for therapy on your neck. Then, after a month, the insurance company will cut you a settlement check."

"So, I have to pretend it still hurts?" I asked.

"Only for a little while," he said. "Now remember, don't walk around without that neck brace on and definitely don't leave the house without it on. You never know if someone from the insurance company is watching."

So, I did as he told me and when I went for my chiropractor appointments, I pretended like my neck still hurt. The heat pads they put on my neck felt good and so did the back-rubbing machine they put me on. Despite that, my gut instinct told me that even the chiropractor was in on the scam. I felt like I was doing something dishonest and was tired of wearing that blasted neck brace.

I asked my father that evening if what we were doing was wrong? That is when Daddy explained to me how much he hated insurance companies.

"They're crooks" he said, "They take your money every month but never give any of it back to you if you are accident and ticket free. They just pocket the money and get richer; so, this just evens things out. So, no, you're not doing anything wrong; just taking some money back from a band of legalized thieves."

After three weeks of going to therapy, the doctor said I was good to go and released me from his care a week before school started.

Everything happened just the way Daddy said it would: I received an insurance check for $1500 and felt rich for the first time in my life as Daddy drove me down to Bank of America to cash the check.

As the teller counted out my money, I thought I had died and gone to heaven. Combined with the money I had saved up from my job at Core, I now secretly had over $3000 saved at only15-years old.

CHAPTER 59

That afternoon I talked my father into driving me to a pet store where I bought a bunny rabbit, a cage and all the supplies. It was a boy and I named him, "Elton Hercules John," after one of my favorite people in the world. My rabbit was snow white, and cute. My goal was to train Elton to sleep with me like a dog would, and to just chill and listen to music or watch TV with me.

Once I got Elton home and settled in my bedroom, Daddy told me I had to keep Elton in my room and he had to be in his cage, and the minute he saw rabbit shit in the house Elton would be history.

That night I removed Elton from his cage and put him on my bed to sleep and watch TV with me. I put a towel under him in case he used the restroom. I lay there with my rabbit watching television until I fell asleep. The following day I awoke to rabbit shit and piss all over my bedroom floor and decided that Elton would not be sleeping with me anymore unless his cage was on my bed.

After I cleaned up the mess, I left to meet up with Sofia and Felicia to take the bus to go shopping for school clothes. I felt like a kid in a candy store as I bought myself designer blue jeans, new shoes and a bunch of new tops. We then went to the May Company department store where I bought make-up and some hair products that my Daddy was too cheap to buy for me. He thought it was okay to buy school clothes from Ralphs supermarket, while the only thing I wanted from there was food.

I had lost 12 pounds over the summer from all the walking door to door for Core, and I was giving myself a complete makeover before school started. After buying two new pairs of platform shoes, I planned on keeping my shoes on this school year.

On my last day of summer vacation, I took the bus out to Santa Monica Beach by myself. As I lay there on my beach towel drifting off to sleep in the sun, I heard God speak to me in the silence. He told me that what I had done with the insurance company was stealing and dishonest.

"Don't do that again," The voice said.

My first thought was, I knew from the beginning that what I was doing was wrong because it felt wrong. Then I told God I was sorry and that I would never do that again.

"I don't want you corrupting yourself," said the voice and was gone.

I lay there on the beach feeling disgusted with myself. It did not matter that Daddy had pretty much forced me to do it; I felt bad because I had disappointed God.

I remembered what Dr. Hornaday said in one of his lectures: "Recognize that you messed up; correct the behavior and move on because to dwell upon it is a waste of good energy."

CHAPTER 60

The first day of school came and I was excited. I had my new clothes on, my hair was cut in a perfect short, feathered hair style thanks to Bridget's mom Miss Payton.

When I arrived at school I purposely looked around for Nick in the gym where everyone was lined up to choose their classes. When I spotted him, he was dressed in a pair of brown cords, a white t-shirt and a pair of tan Wallabee shoes, his hair was even longer than the last time I saw him.

"His clothes suck, but he's still the most beautiful boy I've ever seen," I remember thinking.

It was time to move my plan into action. I was a girl on a mission. My game plan was to get him to be my friend first, and then he would see what a cool girl I was and return my feelings. I walked over to the line he was standing in and stood behind him, then I bumped into him on purpose and claimed it was a mistake when he turned around.

He said, "Hey, your sit-in girl!"

"Yeah, that's me live and in person. That was last year's project this year I have got something else in mind." I said. Then I apologized for being clumsy and bumping into him and said. "Hi, I'm Maya."

After he told me his name, I started up a conversation by asking what classes he was taking. He showed me his schedule and I saw that we had no classes together. I was taking band, orchestra, choir and a beginner's class for writing music. Then I had biology and math, while Nick had all the regular subjects such as science, history and wood shop. But we did have the same nutrition and lunch time.

His turn came up in line, he said. "See you later."

I thought, "you can count on that."

Each day I went to school, I made it a point to look for Nick at lunch and nutrition time. If I saw him in the hall between classes, I always made it a point to say hello to him. I still wondered why he felt so familiar to me. It was weird.

In the meantime, I was determined to live my teenage years to the fullest. When I got old, I did not want to look back on it all and say to myself, I wish I had done this or that.

CHAPTER 61

Since Daddy still would not let me go out at night, I was forced to use my bedroom window to sneak in and out of the house.

Sofia and I would go hear the live bands play in Hollywood. At one point she was dating a 21-year-old man who was working the door at the Starwood Night Club. We always got our underaged butts into that place with no problems.

And if it were not the Starwood we went to, it was some other club where she knew someone who would let us in a side door. Not only did I love going to the Strip at night and watching the bands play live, but it was also fun to watch people act like fools after drinking too much or doing too much coke in the bathroom.

The people who did the Quaalude's were totally stupid. Word around school was that guys gave them to you to get you in the sack with them. It was normal to walk into the Starwood bathroom and see people snorting coke or having sex in a stall. The place was out of control, and no one seemed to care what went on there.

I went to enjoy the music and felt that I was a musician in the making and wanted to live the life of one, so that meant checking out the music scene even if everyone around you was messed up on something.

Someone once said, "youth is wasted on the young," and I had no intention of wasting my youth by getting into coke, heroin, or pills. I could barely handle taking more than four Midol for menstrual cramps in one day. Plus, life was complicated enough, and I wanted to experience as much of it as I could without missing a thing.

Although I was doing well in my music classes, I really had no interest in classes like biology, where the teacher was forcing me to dissect a frog. I found the frog dissection disgusting. The last thing I wanted to do was cut a frog open and then be tested on the names of its body parts, but I did what I had to do to make passing grades in my non-music classes.

This way I could get into college and keep grandmother and Daddy off my back about grades. I figured I was going to play for the Los Angeles Philharmonic after college or play with a group that did movie soundtracks. I had fallen in love with elevator music. The radio station I listened to called it easy listening music. I liked it because it was all instrumental and relaxing.

Playing my flute could be used as a form of singing; like playing a song with no words, but the notes you played spoke volumes. In my opinion that was why classical music had survived for so long because the music told a story.

Times were good and I was loving my life since it seemed that the bad times were a distant memory. I still thought about Dennis at least once a day, but now felt peace about his passing. I also knew he was watching over me.

As the school year progressed, I had begun to establish a good friendship with Nick Papalikis. Every time I spoke with this guy, I could sense he had low self-esteem and was a follower not a leader. And as I got to know him, I understood why he was following his older brother into gang life.

Sometimes when he was talking to me, I could see into him, the real Nick. He was weak-minded, but pretended to be self-confident, and I saw his fear of being a coward and how he was trying to conquer that by getting himself involved with this gang situation. He had such a low opinion of himself, that he had no idea that he was even good looking.

Nick never had any money for a sweet roll at nutrition, so I always offered to buy him one. He told me that his parents gave him cash at the beginning of each school week for food from the cafeteria, but he always spent it on pot.

I asked him about his family. He said he had two sisters and two brothers and that his parents were still together. He still had no attraction for me beyond friendship, but I was optimistic for the future.

Nick showed up to school one day with a black eye and bruises on his body, and I assumed he had gotten himself jumped into the gang.

Seeing the bruises, I thought how stupid the whole gang thing was: you get beat up just to hang around with a group of people. And since gang members were usually doing things that landed them in jail, it really was not worth it to me.

One Saturday afternoon Sofia Steinberg showed up at my bedroom window and climbed in as usual. She sat on my bed and started crying. I asked her what was wrong.

She said that she had been hitch hiking to Venice Beach that morning when a guy picked her up and raped her.

"He looked normal enough, but then he started going in the wrong direction." She said crying. "When I said something about it, he pulled a gun on me."

"Oh my God." I said.

"Then he took me to some abandoned building in Watts and raped me, and when he was finished, he just dumped me out of the car by the train tracks near Exposition Blvd in Watts." She cried.

I was shocked and did not know how to react or what to say to her, the only thing I could think to do was put my arms around her to console her.

"Have you called the police or told your mom?" I asked.

"No, and I don't plan on telling my mother or the police. I just want to forget it ever happened to me. I am never going to hitchhike again. I have learned my lesson. And now I have to get checked out and make sure that asshole didn't give me a venereal disease." She said between sobs,

Then she asked me if I would go to Planned Parenthood with her the following day.

"Sure, I'll go with you. Maybe you should spend the night here with me and I will tell my father that you are sleeping over. We can stay in my room then you will not have to deal with your mom. I will tell my dad that we are going to eat dinner in my room and watch television. That way we can be alone to deal with this." I told her.

That night as we lay in my bed together, I held my friend as she cried herself to sleep.

The next day we caught the bus to Planned Parenthood where Sofia got checked out, but still refused to tell anyone but me what had happened to her. She literally swore me to secrecy, and I could tell that all she wanted to do was forget it ever happened to her.

Within a month, Sofia seemed to be back to her old self, just like it had never happened. But we both knew in the back of our minds that it did happen, and the two of us would carry that secret between us forever.

Because of Sofia's rape and trigger-happy Maxwell, I now had a distrust of guys over 18. I figured I would be safe from rape if I stuck to catching the bus and hanging out with kids in my own age group.

I also decided that I was going to enjoy being a teenager and not grow up so fast by getting VD or having sex. I just wanted to experience new things like rock concerts and have fun with my friends.

I spent the next year and a half concentrating on studying music and making as much money as I could to go shopping. Unfortunately, I found my rabbit dead in the cage one Saturday morning. I had a service for him in my back yard a few hours later. I played "Funeral for A Friend" by Elton John at his service.

The day I graduated from John Burroughs Middle School, everyone in my family was there. Daddy and everyone in the family was proud of me. My guidance counselor, along with the principal, were happy to see me graduate as well, because of my refusal to abide by the school dress code.

They viewed me as a political disruption to the school rules.

Until I came along, they were used to students being sent to the office for fighting or skipping class. In parting, the principal said that he hoped I was able to put that much energy into something constructive one day. Despite that statement, I sensed that many teachers would also miss the excitement of having me around; because I knew I was going to miss them as well.

CHAPTER 62

Three days after graduation was my 16th birthday, and Daddy threw me a big birthday party at a restaurant. He rented a banquet room and charged all the guests $10 to help pay the bill. He invited all the family, even my mother's relatives, who still had no contact with her.

All my friends were invited, including Nick who unfortunately was unable to attend. Even without Nick there it was a good party where I got many birthday cards with money and lots of presents. I thought it is times like this when coming from a big family pays off, because I made out like a bandit.

I was excited about being 16 and looking forward to spending my summer tanning on the beach and working. I had a job working for a vitamin store on Wilshire Blvd called "Great Earth," where I was hired as a stock girl to unpack boxes of vitamins, price them and stock them on the shelves in the back room. I had hoped to get promoted to cashier, but that never happened.

That entire summer I worked from eight a.m. until two p.m. Monday through Friday. I spent the rest of my time on the beach tanning and swimming. I even bought a monthly bus pass so I could hop on the bus right after work and go directly to the beach for a few hours during the week and all day on Saturdays.

By the end of August, I felt important and grown up, because I had a job and was going into high school. I bought some stylish school clothes over the summer and had beautiful, tanned skin.

Meanwhile, Daddy was delusional about my going to Los Angeles High School although we were not even in that school district. He was talking about getting me a permit and busing me there every day. He claimed they had more black students attending that school, and several of my aunts had gone there. He went into a long, involved story about how he was one of the first black students to attend an all-white high school, and how he was treated differently because of the color of his skin.

Daddy said his history teacher was teaching the class about President Lincoln freeing the slaves, when the white boy sitting behind him tapped him on the shoulder laughing and said, "I bet you're glad that Lincoln freed you." Daddy turned around and punched that boy in the face right there in class.

I told Daddy that was a different time, and these days no one in school treated me differently because of my race.

"It's not like that in school anymore." I said.

"All my black, Japanese, Chinese, Russian, Jewish and white friends are going to Fairfax. Besides, do I need to remind you that my mother, your ex-wife, is not fully black, and neither is your mother. Plus, you married a Filipino woman, so why would you even care?" I asked him. Then I told him, "Fairfax High is a school of many nations and I want to be a part of it."

I fought to go to Fairfax High with Nick and all my other friends as fiercely as if I were in war on a battlefield. I was determined not to let my father mess up my game plan for high school. I knew it was time to call in the big guns—Grandmother!

I called and told Grandmother everything about the school's marching band, the orchestra, and how great their classes were, and how I had planned on going to UCLA from there. The minute I mentioned college, grandmother approved and agreed to talk to Daddy. She backed me up by telling Daddy that Fairfax was one of the best public schools in the city, he agreed to let me go.

Thank God for Grandmother I thought because Daddy was living in a dream world. There was no way in hell I was going to Los Angeles High School.

I was ready for the first day of high school at Fairfax! At 16 I could now have a boyfriend and go on a date without hiding it. I kept hoping my first date would be with Nick, but until that happened, I was excited to join the marching band and orchestra and could hardly wait to wear the marching band uniform with the big hat, during halftime on the football field.

Lots of actor's and entertainer's kids went to Fairfax: Fats Domino's son was on the football team; Tina Turner had two sons there, and A famous retired football player had a son there who walked up to me on the first day to introduce himself dropping his father's name. Like I was supposed to be impressed or something.

He told me that I was as fine as aged wine and asked me if I wanted to take a taxi-cab after school up to his house in the Hollywood Hills that he shared with his father. I thanked him for the invitation, then lied and said I had a jealous boyfriend so he would not ask me again.

Then he approached Sofia who was standing right next to me and asked her the same question. She turned him down flat as well.

"Well," he said, "if you lovely ladies change your minds, let me know."

Then he tipped his hat and did a bow in front of us and walked away. Sofia and I looked at one another and started laughing.

"Can you believe he's trying to get laid by dropping his father's name?" I smirked.

"He's probably targeting 10th graders because he thought somebody would be impressed." Sofia chuckled.

"Little does he know; my Aunt Carol knows his father and plays tennis with him." I informed Sofia.

"Could be it's working for him; you never know." She said.

Then she told me that Tito and Jackie of The Jackson Five went to Fairfax for a few weeks when they first moved to California from Gary, Indiana.

"The word around school is Tito Jackson crashed his car into one of the trees in front of school, and he even met his wife here at Fairfax." She said.

"Are you serious? My brother Dennis would have gone berserk if he had lived long enough to be a student here. He idolized Michael Jackson." I said.

"Well, they were students here. I guess too many fans were making it impossible for them to attend public school so after two weeks they checked out."

"Just think Sofia, we could be sitting in the same chair in class that one of the Jacksons sat in." I speculated. "I can't wait to tell my father when I get home." I told her.

You can also mention, "Carol Lombard, Herb Alpert, Ricardo Montalban, Mickey Rooney, David Arquette, Al Franken, Timothy Hutton, Phil Spector and Jack Kemp among other famous people went here as well." She informed me.

"Wow! I feel totally lucky to be a student here." I said.

CHAPTER 63

I had no classes with Nick but was happy to see that he was out of his "I want to be an 18th Street gang member" stage of life. He had wised up and joined the track team and taken up pole vaulting instead. He still had luxurious long blonde hair, but now it was in a feathered cut around his face. His acne had cleared up over the summer, and I thought to myself how handsome he was.

Since I had no classes with him, I decided to start running on the school track after school a few days a week. I always made sure the track team was out there as well whenever I ran. I wanted him to see me run. I wanted him to see that we had something in common. I was a girl on a mission knowing I only had three more years of school with him and had to get him to see how great I was by then.

I saw my former boyfriend Seth in the hallway one morning and nearly fell out in shock. That boy had really come out of the closet since our days together at John Burroughs. He had grown his blonde hair out extremely long to the middle of his back and had the whole Farrah Fawcett Majors from "Charlie's Angels" hair-cut style going on. He was not only in full make-up, but also full drag queen mode. Seth was a totally different person from the boy who had carried my books for a year. He was overjoyed to see me and gave me a big hug. He told me how happy he was that we could hang out at school again, and how he had already taken Barry under his wing and introduced him to every gay kid in school.

My first few months at Fairfax were exciting. I met a bunch of cool new friends plus I still had my old ones from elementary and junior high school. I was going to school with kids from all over the world and that was educational itself.

I met a boy in history class who looked black but had a thick accent. I asked him where he was from and was shocked when he said Israel. The guy had coarse hair and was wearing a big Afro.

"I had no idea they had black people in Israel." I said.

"I'm not black, I'm a Jew." He said.

"Well why do you look black?" I asked him.

He explained he was a full-blooded Jew born in Israel, with no European blood in his family blood line. Therefore, his skin tone was darker, and his hair was course as a result. I wondered to myself if this was what Jesus Christ looked like when he was walking the Earth.

Subsequently, I met this delightfully cute blonde-haired girl named Sandie Paulsen, and we sat next to each other in marching band and orchestra. We both played the flute and bonded while playing a duet of the "Mash" theme. Sandie's younger sister Kelly also went to Fairfax, and both were extremely intelligent straight "A" students without even trying.

Kelly was only 15 and had a 26-year-old boyfriend who owned a home in the San Fernando Valley. Her mom liked the guy and had no problem with Kelly dating him.

It was Sandie who introduced me to Tommy Chong's two daughters, Robbie and Rae Dawn Chong who also attended Fairfax. They were both cool girls because they acted normal considering who their father was. You would never have known that their father had made movies like "Up in Smoke." The two of them were serious and studious, nice girls.

They were both also drop dead gorgeous with long curly hair that fell down their backs. Seeing the two of them made me look at myself differently because, they were mixed race like me. Their father was Chinese and Scots-Irish while their mother was African-Canadian and Cherokee. Looking at them was like looking at myself in the mirror.

Since I had the same type of look that they had, I felt like I had finally fit into a racial category and was not the only one of mixed-race descent. Sandie knew them because she had lived next door to them when she lived up in the canyon above Hollywood.

Sandie and I fast became close friends. She was so smart and politically minded who would not want to hang out with her. Every time she walked into the band room the guys would all gaze like they were in a trance at her huge breasts stuffed inside a tight-fitting T-shirt, and her skinny butt in tight blue jeans. None of them knew the extent of her intelligence, they just saw her body when they interacted with her. Sandie was also on the gymnastics team with a great athletic build from doing gymnastics for years.

CHAPTER 64

Sandie's mother was a litigation attorney whom I liked and had a ton of respect for and her accomplishments. She had worked as a waitress at night while going to law school during the day, along with balancing the job of being a single mother. Now she was married to a successful investment banker. Sandie never talked much about her real father except to say that he lived in New York, and she rarely saw or spoke with him.

Spending the night over Sandie's house was awesome because she had one of those cool moms that let her kids do pretty much as they pleased. Sandie, her sister Kelly and I would discuss Middle Eastern politics, Socialism, Communism and The Palestinians fight for land, along with the history of American politics.

Their mother had raised them to be well informed on all political viewpoints and subjects. Their mom was the only parent that I knew who insisted that her two daughters stay home from school to watch the Watergate hearings on television.

Almost every discussion in that household had something to do with politics. I felt honored when Sandie gave me a collector's anti-Nixon T-shirt from Nixon's presidential campaign. It had a big picture of Nixon's face on it, with a Tricky Dick cartoon nose that was long and curled up in the air. And on the back of the shirt it read, "Beat Dick." It was the coolest T-shirt I had ever owned beside my Elton John shirts.

When we were not talking about world events we would listen to the Beatles "white Album" or "Abby Road" together on the record player in Sandie's bedroom or go for a midnight swim in her apartment building swimming pool, then the sauna before going to bed.

Since her apartment building was two blocks away from Sunset Blvd, the three of us would sometimes walk to nightclubs on the Sunset Strip to hear bands play.

We also went to all night parties in the Valley at Kelly's boyfriend's house out in the San Fernando Valley where there was always plenty of acid, pot and coke in punch bowls on her boyfriend's coffee table in the living room. Although I did not drink alcohol or do drugs, every now and then I would take a hit of pot but that was it. I never bought the stuff myself, I figured I had enough problems just dealing with myself daily without adding addiction to the mix.

I liked feeling in control of myself. When you did hard drugs, you gave up control of yourself to the drug. The drugs made me feel a little uncomfortable. I kept thinking, what if a neighbor called the police about the loud rock music playing? They could raid the place and take me to jail for being in the wrong place at the wrong time. Then my father would know I lied to him about sleeping at Sandie's because no way would he let me go to an all-night party in the Valley where drugs and drinking were rampant. Thank God those parties never got busted, I would have been grounded until I was 18!

Sandie and Kelly loved tanning on the beach like I did. Sandie always insisted on going to Malibu Beach so she could sneak on to a private beach some rich person owned. This way she could remove her bikini top on the beach without people looking at her. Sandie was irritated when guys would look at her physical appearance and ignore her intelligence. That is why she liked to have an older boyfriend because she claimed that older men could hold a conversation with her on just about any subject instead of looking at her tits.

The thing I loved most about Sandie was the fact that tons of guys wanted to go out with her, but she turned them all down. If a guy did not stimulate her on an intellectual level, then he had nothing to offer her in a relationship but sex. And to hear her tell it, it was a rarity to even find a guy who was knowledgeable enough about sex to please her.

The only prospect I had for a boyfriend was Kenneth Bates, a 13-year-old genius who had skipped a few grades to high school. We were in marching band and orchestra together. His father was an actor on a TV show with an actor named Perry King for whom I had the hots.

When we met it was love at first sight for Kenneth who was a cute little dark haired Jewish boy who looked like a singer, I liked named Cat Stevens. But Kenneth was three years younger and three inches shorter than I was.

He started following me around school with his camera snapping pictures of me whenever he could. I would come out of the bathroom at school and there he was waiting for that "Maya walking out of the bathroom" camera shot. He had shots of me eating lunch, walking to class, and playing my flute in class.

The boy was just obsessed with me; anything I did at school Kenneth Bates had a photo of it. One day, when the poor thing honestly thought my eyelashes were naturally long, I tried to help him snap out of it by taking my tube of black mascara out of my purse and showing it to him.

"This is why my lashes look so long; I applied make-up on them." I said.

He still insisted that I was his perfect idea of a woman, while I insisted that he was crazy.

One morning I opened the front door at home to go to school and was shocked to see Kenneth standing on my doorstep waiting for me. And he had that damn camera with him.

"Now I have a photo of you first thing in the morning." He said. As he snapped a picture of me.

As my father stood behind me chuckling, I wanted to tell him that nothing was funny about this situation, but I held my tongue.

"Kenneth what the hell are you doing at my house at 7 a.m.?"

"I wanted to surprise you. I have bagels with cream cheese and a ride to school. My father is waiting out front in the car!" He said enthusiastically.

"Did it ever occur to you to call someone first instead of dropping by unannounced?" I asked him.

"Then it wouldn't have been a surprise." He replied.

"Oh my God." I thought to myself.

"Look Kenneth, I told you before that we are never going to be anything but friends; you are just too young for me, and I don't want to lead you on by accepting the ride to school." I said.

"I know you said I was too young, but that's just my age; on an intellectual level we are the same age." He said, with faltering enthusiasm.

Wow! I thought, this kid is lovesick. With a great reluctance I accepted the ride to school because he already had his dad sitting out front.

When I got in the backseat, Kenneth served me my bagel with cream cheese, which I ate as his father drove us to school like he was a chauffeur. It was kind of scary to think of what Kenneth might be doing with all the photos he took of me. I truly felt sorry for him because I was pretty much in the same circumstance with Nick, except I was not stalking the guy.

The only photo I had of Nick was the one in the school yearbook, and I would never show up at his house without being invited first. In fact, I did not even know where Nick lived or his phone number. I did not want it unless he himself gave it to me.

A week later Kenneth approached me excitedly and said,

"My dad got an autographed photo of Perry King for you, but you have to come over to my house and have dinner with me so I can give it to you."

Kenneth had this worshipful look in his eyes, and once again I felt sorry for him.

"Alright, I'll come over, but you better understand that this is not a date. You are just my friend giving me a photo of Perry King. That's all Kenneth and I'm serious." I sternly told him.

"I know we're just friends." He said looking somewhat dejected.

A week later Kenneth and his father picked me up and took me to their house for dinner. Once we arrived at their house, he gave me the autographed photo of Perry King which had my name on it. It was a promotional photo for the TV series he was currently in: "The Captains and the Kings."

I would have preferred a photo of him in the movie "The Lords of Flatbush," but I was happy with the gift.

Kenneth then took me to his room to show me a new keyboard his dad had bought him. When he opened the bedroom door all I could see were photos of me blown up to poster size all over his walls and ceiling. Now I knew what he was doing with all the photos he had taken of me.

I ate the dinner he had cooked for me as fast as I could, then asked to be driven home. Seeing the posters of myself on his wall made me nervous about spending any more time there than necessary.

When Kenneth walked me to my door, I told him that he was not allowed to take any more pictures of me.

"Otherwise, we can't hang out together anymore because it's not healthy for you. Besides, it scares the shit out of me so its friends or nothing. That's all I can offer you." I said.

He agreed and walked away with his head hung low. When we returned to school Kenneth still hung out with us, but he kept his camera away from me.

CHAPTER 65

One afternoon during lunch Sandie, Kenneth and I were sitting on the front lawn with our instruments practicing for a classical concert our orchestra was having in the Rotunda that evening, when a beautiful thin dark, skinned girl with long French braids down to her butt approached us with her lunch. I immediately recognized her from my "Roots" class.

Fairfax had created the class so students could study Alex Haley's novel "Roots." She asked if she could sit down and listen to us play.

"Sure" I said, "cop a squat."

"My name is Sally Hudson." She said.

We introduced ourselves and I went back to practicing. She ate her lunch while listening to us.

After we finished practicing, we all talked for a while, and I immediately liked Sally's funny intelligent personality. She started sitting with us during lunch, and we started sitting next to each other in "Roots" class.

As I got to know her, I admired her bold and daring personality; this girl had no limits on anything. She was lucky enough to live like an adult in an apartment in Hollywood with her sister Mary, who was a senior at Fairfax.

Their mother Frances paid the rent and bought groceries because they were still in high school, while she lived in a beautiful home high up in the Hollywood Hills with a Russian film producer she had married and had a son with.

I thought Sally was lucky and wished my father would rent me an apartment in Hollywood and buy my groceries while I went through high school.

Occasionally I would take the bus to Sally's apartment to visit. Sometimes her mother would be there putting groceries in the refrigerator for her and Mary.

Her mom, whom I really liked, was not only super cool but she had also been a Playboy Bunny back in the day and had worked at one of the clubs when they first opened. Frances was a true inspiration: strong and knew what she wanted out of life. She also managed to keep a Playboy Bunny body into her 50s. She still had an extremely voluptuous body with a tiny waistline and a shapely butt. She wore long French braids down her back like Sally and smoked pot.

She would tell us stories about all the movie stars she had dated during her early days in Hollywood while puffing on her joint. She told us a story about a dinner party at a famous actor's house that was mind blowing.

Sally seemed to be following in her mother's footsteps when it came to dating guys in the movie business. She was madly in love with a young actor who had played Jesus Christ in the musical stage play of "Jesus Christ Superstar."

She talked about him constantly and how great he was. The minute she saw him it was love at first sight. She introduced herself to him at a Hollywood nightclub, spent the night with him and came back believing that he walked on water.

After she had been sleeping with him on and off for about four months, she claimed that not only was he the best lover in the world, but she was madly in love with him. She wanted him to stop dating other girls and see her exclusively. He, however, did not want a girlfriend; he wanted to remain romantically unattached, according to Sally.

One Saturday night I spent the night at her apartment, just so I could go to some nightclub where the guy was meeting her. I wanted to see this guy for myself. After Sally introduced me to him at the club, I understood why she was so crazy about him. He had a warm funny personality, good looking with dark hair and sexy oozed from his pores.

After he and Sally danced for a while, he started dancing with other women. It was like they all wanted a piece of this guy, any little piece they could get.

I warned Sally on the way back to her apartment that night that the writing was on the wall and that she had better read it because this was a young actor who wanted to stay single.

"You know this guy is not going to ask you to move in with him or say, 'I love You.' So, I wouldn't get all emotionally invested in him if I were you." I advised.

By now, Sally was so far gone on him that she continued to call him to set up meetings at different nightclubs, until finally he told her that he only wanted to be friends.

Sally came to school heart broken and told Sofia, Sandie and I the details of the breakup. I told her it was not a break-up but more like a six-month hook-up that he ended.

"I tried to warn you so don't be too heart broken." I reminded her.

Meanwhile, I did my best to be a supportive friend by telling her that one day some guy was going to buy her a big diamond ring and marry her. I did not know how I knew that, but I did. I suggested that maybe she should go out with someone in school.

"There are tons of good-looking guys right here from all over the world getting their sexy-on speaking different languages." I said.

"The guys here at school are too immature for me. I want him," Sally cried.

Then end of lunch bell rang and we all went to class. I said a little prayer for Sally and asked God to help her to stay away from young actors.

CHAPTER 66

I loved school but unfortunately my grades in all my non-music classes never reflected that. I still had big dreams of playing in a major orchestra and, after seeing the movie "Rocky" with Sandie, I knew I wanted to play in an orchestra for movie soundtracks. Bill Conti did the music for "Rocky" and to me it was a masterpiece.

As each song on the soundtrack told the story of "Rocky," the movement and emotion of the songs brought tears to my eyes. To play flute in Bill Conti or James Horner's orchestra would be a realized dream, I had no interest in classes other than music and drama.

Daddy and grandmother would be called to school for the parent teacher conference and told that I had the ability to make better grades than the C average I was pulling in their classes. Miss Tisdale, my writing and speech teacher, told Daddy that not only was I a talented writer but a good speaker as well.

I tried to retain the information I was receiving in my other classes, but the subjects were just so boring. I tried hard to pull a B in some of those boring classes because Daddy and grandmother were not thrilled with my school performance. I told my father that he should be grateful that I even went to class, because there were kids at school who were always outside the school instead of in it.

"At least I show up to class." I told him.

CHAPTER 67

By the time I was a senior at Fairfax High my sister Stephanie stopped going to the special educational private school she had been attending for years. Daddy then enrolled her in Fairfax High with me. She was still in special education classes at Fairfax, and she still spoke with a stutter, but she had advanced enough over the years finally to attend a regular public school.

Every now and then some asshole kid would tease her in the school hall by calling her retarded, make fun of her stutter and the fact that she was in special ed classes.

That is when I would step up and threaten to open a can of whip ass on them if they ever messed with my sister again. It did not matter if I had been friendly with that person before; if you messed with my sister all bets were off.

I made sure that Stephanie hung out with me and my friends at nutrition and lunch, I wanted her to feel like everybody else and fit in. Sometimes during lunch Stephanie, Sandie and I would sit on the lawn near the cafeteria to listen to music.

There was an outdoor stage for special announcements and students to perform. It was usually Mike's band playing Rock music. Mike was head trumpeter in marching band and orchestra and played Bass guitar, Guitar, Trumpet and Piano . He was the best musician in band and orchestra and could jam the shit out of "The Theme from Shaft." He was in a rock band the Red Hot Chili Peppers with three other students.

On this day they were up there rocking out some serious hardcore rock song that they had written. All of them were dressed like rockers, one had his hair cut in a Mohawk dyed different colors and had a piece of lunch meat hanging as an earring from his ear. They were cool. With their cigarettes and creative clothing.

A lot of Fairfax High students smoked cigarettes during lunch. We had an open campus for the cigarettes and even a little smoking area.

The school principal always complained over the loudspeaker about phone calls from surrounding homeowners who groused about students littering on the lawns as they smoked cigarettes. I would occasionally see a few of the boys from the band smoking on someone's lawn. So, I always thought about them whenever the principal complained over the loud speaker about the smoking off campus.

CHAPTER 68

I had been talking to God about setting me up with a well-paying part-time job. I had been approved for the student work program. You could get out of school at 1:00 every day if you had a job for at least six hours a day.

Searching for jobs on the help wanted board in the hallway outside the main office, I eventually found a job as a lab assistant for a small gynecology lab. Of course, I had no experience, but they hired me anyway. Various doctor's offices around Los Angeles sent their Pap Smear slides to this lab on Wilshire Blvd.

I was trained to operate a machine that had different colored dye solution in it. I would place the Pap Smear slides into the machine and flip the switch on. The machine would spin around fast, and the dye solution would cover the slides. When the machine stopped the slide would turn a certain color if you had cervical cancer. I had to look at each slide and write down the results on a form. Then I had to send the slides back to the doctor's office with the results.

I liked both the job and my boss Mr. Smith, and my hours were good. I worked from 2 p.m. until 7 p.m. Monday through Friday, unless I had a football game or an orchestra concert to perform in at school.

After work I would catch the bus home and do homework until 11 at night. Weekends were free to lay on the beach or go out with friends.

My boss said not to tell anyone outside of work that I was working with the Pap Smear slides. I figured you had to have a college degree to do what I was doing, and maybe he could get shut down if anyone found out. So, I concentrated on my job and everything Dr. Smith was teaching me because there was no room for mistakes. If I messed up on those slides and got the results wrong, someone could die of cancer. I was proud of myself. The job made me feel grown-up and intelligent and it paid well.

Things were going well for me, and I was overly optimistic about my future. The only thing missing from my life was Nick Papalikis as my boyfriend. I had tried everything over the years to get him to see me in a romantic light: I ran every morning before school to make my body firm and healthy looking, I bought healthy food to eat instead of junk which was now my lifestyle. I had my wardrobe together and I had my hair cut in a shoulder length feathered style that was popular.

In my opinion I looked good.

I still prayed for God to work out some miracle where Nick would return my feelings. As far as I knew he had never had a girlfriend, only because none of the girls at school gave him a second thought. And every time I told one of my girlfriends how beautiful I thought he was, they would say I had bad taste in men.

I was the only girl in school who had a physical attraction for him, so I figured I stood a chance because there was no competition for his affection.

One Saturday morning while taking out the trash, the bag burst before I could get it in the trash can. As I was picking it up, this cute guy approached me and started helping me pick up the trash.

He said his name was John Gall and he had just moved across the street with his mother from white Plains, NY. He was gorgeous and was my age with long blonde curly hair, a great body and looked just like Robert Plant from Led Zeppelin. He was also a musician like me, played the guitar and had his own band.

We started hanging out together for little jam sessions, just for the fun of it. I would hang out at his house whenever my father was not home and watch the band rehearse for gigs. John's favorite band was Cheap Trick, and he was constantly trying to play their songs with his band.

One afternoon, after the band had finished rehearsal, John and I were alone in his room when he kissed me. I was surprised because I had no idea that he was even attracted to me. He was a good kisser and did not have bad breath which was refreshing. I could hardly believe my luck. This guy liked me.

After that first kiss, we started seeing one another all the time; for 10 or 15 minutes each morning before school. He was a senior at Dorsey High School. I asked why he was attending a school out of our district? He told me that he had met "Blaze," his bass player, during the summer before school started. Blaze and most of his friends attended Dorsey High, so he got a permit to attend school there.

Soon John started acting like he was my boyfriend, and even took me on a date to see Cheap Trick perform live at a club on the Strip.

When I introduced him to my father, he disliked John immediately.

I figured Daddy hated him because he was trying to date me. I thanked God that my father and stepmother had joined a bowling league and went bowling three nights a week because this allowed me to spend time with John behind my father's back.

Sometimes we would make out on his bed, but mostly we just played our instruments together. Or we would listen to music on his turntable while playing backgammon.

When I introduced him to my girlfriends, they were all shocked that a guy who looked like Robert Plant's twin brother was stuck on me. They just did not see it coming; hell, neither did I. All my girlfriends thought he was fine as hell, and for the first time in my life I was the girl with the good-looking boyfriend that the other girls wanted to be with.

Whenever his band played a gig in some club in Hollywood, Sandie, Sally and I would stand in the front row cheering him on and dancing. After the show we always went backstage to meet up with John and his friends. There were always groupie girls drunk or high on something hitting on John and the other band members. They would invite John to parties, slip him their phone number and occasionally attempt to kiss him.

He would put his arm around me and say, "I have a girlfriend."

Whenever John had his mother's car for the day, he would sometimes skip a few classes and show up at Fairfax during lunch and buy me fried rice from Helen's Restaurant across the street from school. He always held my hand or had his arm around me, so all my friends at school knew that we were together.

I really cared for him, but was not in love, in fact every time he kissed me, I wished it were Nick. As the school year progressed, I ended up in a health class studying sex education with Nick.

To my surprise we were becoming closer as friends, and suddenly he was asking me if I wanted to hang out with him at lunch. He knew that I was dating John, and for some strange reason Nick did not like him when I introduced them.

One morning Nick showed up at school in a white 1970s Ford Mustang that his father had just handed down to him. So, we started driving up to Bronson Park to Batman and Robin's cave with Nick blasting music by Pink Floyd or Led Zeppelin in his car. We called it the Batman and Robin cave because rumor around school was it was the cave that was used in the original TV show with Adam West as Batman and Julie Newmar as Cat Woman. At the beginning and ending of each show the Bat Mobile would come speeding out of that cave. There were thousands of signatures all over the walls inside the cave, including mine. It was traditional to write your name on the wall if you went in there.

There were usually beer cans left by someone who was partying there late at night, so you had to watch your step when you went in.

Nick and his friends liked to smoke pot in the cave during lunch, then we would rush back to school in his Mustang for our next class. Sometimes we would get a falafel, a Middle Eastern fritter, from across the street from school; I usually paid because Nick had no after school job and was always broke. I was surprised when he told me that he had never had a job, not even during summer vacation. His father, an architect, paid for everything. Nick said that it was impossible for him to be on the track team, go to school and work.

"There's no time for a job." He said.

Nick also told me that his father filled up the Mustang's gas tank once a week, paid his car insurance and gave him a weekly allowance which he promptly spent on pot instead of the food for which it was intended.

Wow, I thought if my father did all that for me, I would have been taking advantage of that situation by not spending all my money on pot, or wasting my time just hanging out drinking beer and getting my head bad all the time. I would have been collecting the fat allowance money and working.

Also, I noticed that he had plenty free time, to run track, go to school, and work a part time job if he really wanted to. It seemed to me that the kids who had it easy sometimes took it all for granted, and I saw that as a hand- icap for a healthy adult life. He was clueless about organizing his time and would often fake being sick just to get out of taking a test at school because he partied the night before instead of studying. This showed me that he would most likely have problems facing tough situations in life.

Despite those character flaws, it did not seem to change the way I felt about him; he was still the most beautiful guy I had ever laid eyes on.

On days, that John would show up to take me to lunch I told Nick the truth, that I could not hang out with him because I had a date with my boyfriend.

After a while, I started to suspect that Nick was getting a little jealous of my relationship with John. Nick started inviting me to watch him at his track meets, although I usually did not have time because of work and John.

CHAPTER 69

Sandie, Sally and Sofia were always complaining that I never had time to go out with them any longer. What none of them understood about me was I knew what it was like to be so hungry that you had to steal Mac and Cheese to survive. None of them knew what it was like to live in a motel and have someone like Maxwell shoot at you every day.

I totally understood how someone could immigrate from a country with little opportunity to the United States without a dime to their names and end up a millionaire within 10 years. If you started with nothing then you had nothing to lose if you chased after your dreams, but you had everything to gain.

Many years ago, I had made up my mind that I was going to have a good, "I've got my shit together" adult life. I was 17 and calculated that I had less than a year at home, then I could move out, get my own apartment and begin living my dream life as an adult.

My attitude was that my friends would just have to settle for the time I could spend with them.

Friday afternoon I was sitting in health class next to Nick when he asked if I wanted to go see a movie Saturday. I had plans with Sandie and Kelly to sleep over their house Saturday night, then go eat breakfast at Schwab's Pharmacy on Sunset Blvd that Sunday morning.

We loved it because it was an old Hollywood landmark, the food was cheap and rumor around town was that aspiring actress Lana Turner had been discovered by director Melvyn LeRoy while at the soda counter. We always sat there hoping one of us was sitting in the same exact seat that she sat in.

I cancelled my sleepover at Sandie's and had Nick pick me up at my friend Linda's house so Daddy would not embarrass me by interrogating him.

When he picked me up, I asked him what movie he wanted to see.

"You can choose the movie." He suggested.

"Let's go see that new horror movie "Phantasm." I replied.

I had waited years in agony for this guy to notice me and the fact that he wanted to go to a movie with me meant that something had changed in the way he looked at me. I wore my Sassoon blue jeans and my Blondie T-shirt that I had purchased in a night club on the strip while watching the band perform live. I considered it my lucky T-shirt because Debra Harry, the lead singer, was a bad ass strong woman and I felt empowered when I wore it.

Nick picked me up looking freshly showered with the strong smell of Flex shampoo coming from his hair, which I loved. When we approached his car, he opened the car door for me.

First, we drove out to Point Dune in Malibu, parked, then walked to this big rock overlooking the ocean and sat on it. Nick pulled a joint out of his pocket and lit it. As he sat smoking pot, there was an uncomfortable silence between us.

"Is anything wrong? You're awfully quiet." I asked.

"No everything's fine." He said.

I attempted to break the silence by telling him about the new song John and his band were working on, and how cool it was.

"I don't want to hear about your boyfriend's band." He said.

"Well, why not?" I replied.

"Because I can't stand the guy." He said in a raised voice.

"Are you attracted to me or something? " I asked. "Because you've been acting a little weird lately."

We had another long moment of silence and then he said, "Yeah, I'm attracted to you, but you keep talking about John and his stupid band."

That is when I leaned over and kissed him. The moment I had been waiting for was finally here, and as mad as it sounds, I heard an angel ring a bell as I kissed him. And I wondered if this was what happened in heaven whenever a wish came true for someone on Earth.

I could tell that he was inexperienced at kissing because he was so bad at it; I literally had to show him how to kiss me. After we kissed, we looked into each other's eyes for a moment.

Then he said, "I don't play in a rock band, but you should break-up with that boyfriend of yours and start going out with me."

My head was spinning because all of this was happening so fast.

"Sure, I can do that." I said.

"I like sitting here with you watching the ocean," he said as he put his arm around me.

"So do I," I replied.

He looked at his watch and said, "We better get going if we're going to make that movie on time."

As we drove to the theater I was in a state of bliss and kept thinking how cool God was for answering my prayers for this guy to return my feelings.

When we got to the theater, he paid my way and bought me popcorn. When we sat in our seats, he put his arm around me and kept it there throughout the whole film. As we sat there watching the movie, I knew that I had to call John as soon as I got back home and break up with him.

After the movie, Nick drove me home and we sat outside kissing in his car for at least 15 minutes.

After he had driven off, I rushed upstairs to call Sandie and Kelly to tell them the good news. They both thought I was crazy for dumping John for Nick. They told me that Nick had no redeeming qualities and was not even into the same things I was.

"But I love him and he's the one I want to be with," I protested.

They both continued to tell me I was nuts.

Afterwards I tried to call John to break-up with him, but no one answered his phone. I figured he was out with Blaze somewhere. I figured it would be better to tell him in person anyway; only a butthole would break-up with someone over the phone.

It was late so I got ready for bed with my head in the clouds. It is a miracle I thought; a real dream come true.

The next morning, I went out to breakfast at Schwab's with Sandy and Kelly. They spent most of their time telling me I was making a mistake, and how they had gotten used to going to see John's band play and how much they liked him and the music.

"It's a shame. He was really nice to you." Sandie wailed.

"Well, you have my permission to date him yourself because he's about to be back on the market," I joked.

"Did you think I was going to date him forever? Everything ends eventually and right now I want to be with someone else." I added.

"I guess you have a point there." Sandie admitted.

"Remember I thought you were nuts when you broke up with Santiago from Ecuador, who was drop dead-let me-just-look-at-you-gorgeous. Everyone at school wanted to date him, and you dumped him after three months."

"Did I ever tell you that he cried when I broke up with him?" Sandie asked.

"He was a sensitive guy," I said.

"Yeah, I know, that's why we're no longer together." She concluded.

Sandie drove me home and the next morning I got up and walked across the street to talk to John.

After breaking the news to him, he wasted no time letting me know that he was not happy about being dumped for someone else. He was so hurt and pissed off that he did not even want to be friends.

As I walked back across the street, I wondered why guys got so pissed off when you told them the truth.

Was I supposed to pretend that I felt one way when I did not? Whatever happened to the good breakup? I just did not understand all the male drama where relationships were concerned.

I was so happy about being with Nick that I decided to put the unpleasantness out of my mind. If John did not want to be friends, that was okay.

Nick and I started meeting in the school parking lot every morning before school, just to kiss one another good morning. He would show up in his track team jacket looking handsome. He would kiss me then walk me to class while holding my hand.

When the kids at school saw us walking down the hallways together hand in hand, they did a double take.

Now we were officially a couple, and I was ecstatic because I knew that God had heard my prayers and answered them.

CHAPTER 70

I had waited years for the little boy on the moon and looked for him in every guy I met. I started to believe that perhaps my dreams of leaving my body and playing Pat-a-Cake with him on what looked like the moon were only childhood dreams that would never become a reality.

Suddenly, now with Nick I felt a strange familiarity with him, as though I knew him from another time and place where he was my husband. For me it was love at first sight and he was the only guy I had ever met that I loved.

Every time he held me in his arms or kissed me, I felt safe and at home with him. Therefore, I accepted him despite his short comings. I figured if you really loved someone you would help guide them in the right direction if they went off track, and I believed that I could protect him from the dark places in life.

Nick started calling me on the telephone every night just to say good-night, and he was romantic, which surprised me. He would say corny things to me such as "your eyes are like limpid pools; your teeth are like a string of pearls and your hair outshines the moon beams."

His two nicknames for me were "Kitten and "Monkey." The "Kitten" name I understood, and it reminded me of Eartha Kitt as Cat Woman, but the "Monkey" name did not make any sense to me.

The first time Nick took me home to meet his family his sister Sadie said, "You're that fat girl from junior high school that Nick called "fat Maya.""

Shocked and a little hurt I replied, "Well, I'm not fat now."

Embarrassed, Nick told his sister to shut up. Then he introduced me to his older brother Kyle who was a talented artist. Some rich guy his father worked for was sponsoring him and paying him a salary just to create art all day.

His mother Dorothy was a housewife, while his father worked. Both his parents were from Iowa and had met in college where they fell in love. They lived in a lovely two-story house near the Wilshire District.

I thought Nick was lucky to have had a normal childhood with two parents who loved one another and their children.

We now had a standing date every Saturday night. I would catch the bus over to his house, where he would have pizza waiting for me.

Nick and some of his friends were putting a 360 cubic inch engine into his Mustang. At first, I thought he was lucky because his father was shelling out money for this project like it grew on trees. Then as I stood in Nick's back yard one day watching them work on the car, I started getting visions on the TV screen in my mind about the failure of his car project.

His father was throwing his money away, because Nick and his auto shop buddies from school lacked the knowledge, experience and tools to professionally install a 360 cubic inch engine.

As I looked at the car, I could see something called timing going wrong on the engine and various other problems I could not name. It was just going to be a real mess and the death of the car. He should have just left the car as it was instead of trying to turn it into some type of hot rod.

I also knew if I told him, he would not take me seriously, because I knew nothing about cars, and it would scare the shit out of him if he knew that I could see and know things that other people did not. People were often afraid of what they did not understand.

CHAPTER 71

I considered my little gift as a tool for me to use so I could navigate my way through life without getting into tons of trouble. I never investigated other people's lives on purpose; that was an invasion of their privacy, and in my opinion, a misuse of a gift.

Although I did use it to get jobs and clothes with since I could visualize what I wanted on the TV screen in my mind. I would see the light of God there empowering it, then I would add a strong belief that it was going to come to pass then push it from my mind into my physical world. Sometimes it would take weeks, even months to manifest into my physical world. But it always came to pass if it was God's will, always.

Sometimes I could not help picking up information on stuff like Nick's little car project from that little TV screen in my brain.

Throughout the years I had done my best to be just like everybody else and fit in, and I had achieved that. So, I decided not to warn him.

One Saturday night I arrived at Nick's, to find that he had cleaned his bedroom and wanted to eat the pizza in there instead of the kitchen table or the garage while he worked on the car.

After we had eaten the last piece, Nick locked his bedroom door and started making out with me, and before I knew it our clothes were off. As he kissed every inch of my body, I realized that he had planned the whole thing out. His parents were at the gym and going out to dinner afterwards. His brother and sister were gone as well. We had the whole house to ourselves, and Nick was taking full advantage of it.

At this moment I was grateful that I was on the pill. My father had taken me to the emergency room a year prior for bad menstrual cramps. The pain would start at my knees and go up to my lower back and stomach, and I was bleeding past a seven-day period. I would just lie in bed in pain throwing up into a small trash can by my bed.

The doctor put me on the pill, and it helped stop me from bleeding past seven days. Now it was going to come in handy for another reason. This was the moment I had been dreaming about for so long and now it was finally happening. Unfortunately for me, it was over before it had really started because Nick reached climax before he even entered the gate. Then he immediately fell asleep with his head between my breasts.

I wondered if I should take this as a compliment. Was I so wonderful that he could not control himself? Unsure, I decided not to say anything about it to him.

Since the last thing I wanted to do was embarrass the poor guy. I figured the next time would be better, so I just lay there happy to have him in my arms.

He awoke a half hour later and we took a shower together before putting our clothes back on. When his parents returned home, he borrowed his mother's car and drove me home.

CHAPTER 72

A s our senior year flew by, Nick and I spent all our free time together and were now saying that we loved each other. I attended all his track meets and cheered him on. Even if he failed to come in first place all the time, I was still proud of him.

When prom night came, I finally got up enough nerve to introduce Nick to Daddy for the first time. For some unknown reason he hated Nick on first sight. He pulled me to the side and told me that Nick reminded him of a wet chicken.

"I don't like him." He said,

"Well, I like him and he's here to take me to the Prom so don't chase him away. "I replied.

I walked back into the living room thinking, I am almost 18 years old, and my father is not going to tell me at this point who I can date.

Nick and I drove out to the beach first before going to the prom, but we never made it to the prom. We ended up making love in the back of his brother-in-laws van. We just stayed there at the beach star gazing, embraced in each other's arms until I had to go home. I was so in love with this guy that I did not care about missing the prom, or the money I spent on my dress that only Nick saw.

All I cared about was being with him even though his love making skills still had not improved. It was always over in 10 minutes. I agonized over whether I should show him what to do, but I was afraid it would crush his ego. The love that I felt for him in my heart bypassed the sex; he could have been in a wheelchair with no function in his sexual organs at all and I still would have chosen to be with him.

CHAPTER 73

A few weeks later Nick claimed he was finished putting the new engine in his Mustang. He anxiously picked me up from work in it on Friday night. As he drove me home, I knew something was mechanically wrong with the car due to the sound and feel of the car.

Then the TV screen in my mind clicked on and I could see oil leaking from a car part underneath the hood and problems with something called timing and seals. There was also something wrong with the carburetor. The car sounded loud and souped up; you could hear it coming from a block away.

Nick thought it was all good and was proud of himself, until the car broke down as he was driving me home. He had only been driving the car for a day before it completely broke down. He learned later that he had blown the engine because it had not been put together properly.

He walked to a phone booth, called his father and a tow truck, then called a taxicab to take me home.

When I got home, I was 30 minutes past my curfew. Daddy was so pissed off that he started yelling at me the minute I came in the front door. I explained to him what happened, but he hated Nick so much that it did not matter. He told me I could not see Nick while I was living under his roof.

That was the final straw for me. My mind just snapped, and I thought to myself that the minute school is out, I am moving. I had always planned on moving out and had been looking forward to it. I still had my "Mary Tyler Moore" fantasy of being the independent cute girl who was making it on her own.

Now I was as determined as Bilbo Baggins on a quest in the Hobbit book I had just finished reading. I was on a mission. I had a little under half a year left before school would be out and I would be able to work full time and leave my father's house.

Instead of buying clothes and records, I was now going to have to start saving my money to get my own place. Meanwhile, I would just sneak and see Nick anyway. This was my game plan.

Grandfather always said, "The thinkers are the rulers of the world while fools catch hell." And "Never argue with a fool; just do what needs to be done."

And what needed to be done was for me to be free to live my life as I wanted.

But all that changed two weeks later when the Department of Social Services decided to interfere with our lives. My father and stepmother Jenny went to the bowling alley to bowl in their weekly bowling league, and I was looking after Helen and Stephanie. My parents had been gone about 20 minutes when the doorbell rang. I answered the door and found the police standing there with a woman who told me that she was from the Child Protective Services. She said that my sisters and I had to go with her.

"Why do we have to go with you?" I asked.

"Our office received a complaint from your mother that you and your sisters are living in an unfit cockroach infested environment," she said.

"My mother? She lost custody of us years ago for allowing my step-father to kill my brother. She does not even have our phone number or our address. As you can see, we do not have bugs, our living environment is clean, and our home is fit. You really need to talk to my father and stepmother about this because we're not going anywhere with you." I said.

"Well, we still have to investigate each complaint and until that's done you need to get your coats on and come with us." She said.

"Can I call my father at the bowling alley or my grandparents?" I asked.

"No, you need to get your coats now," the official insisted.

I got our coats out of the coat closet, gave Stephanie hers and began putting Helen's coat on her. Then one of the cops just grabbed her from me the second I had that coat on her and began taking her out the front door. Poor Helen was kicking and screaming calling for me and Stephanie to help her, she even bit the cop on his shoulder to try and get away from him.

It broke my heart to see my little sister kicking and screaming my name completely petrified, and not understanding why she was being taken away by an unfeeling cop.

The social worker physically restrained me as I tried to go after my sister, as the other cop grabbed Stephanie and she began to cry. My two sisters were taken away in separate police cars, and I was driven to a temporary foster home in a van the social worker was driving. The whole car ride I was thinking that Daddy was going to freak out once he got home from the bowling alley and found us all missing.

I had no idea where I was when we arrived an hour and a half later at a house in a residential neighborhood. The house had bars on the outside of all the windows and the front door. The social worker rang the doorbell, and I was tempted to make a run for it before I was trapped inside those bars. But as I looked around me, I thought where would you go? You do not even know where you are thanks to the lack of windows in the back of the van.

An elderly white woman about 60, opened the front door and welcomed us into the house and introduced herself as Mrs. Johnson. She asked me if I wanted a sandwich even though it was quite late now.

I looked at her and said, "I don't have an appetite."

As I stood there in a state of shock I felt like a trapped animal in a cage. My parents, my family and my life seemed extremely far away at that moment. I was also worried about my sisters; this was the first time in my life that I did not know where they were or who had them.

The social worker left, and Mrs. Johnson told me the rules and showed me around the house where all the doors had key locks on them, even the bedrooms. In addition, the telephones had locks on them so you could not dial out.

Mrs. Johnson took me to my bedroom which had two twin beds and two dressers in it. There was a girl already asleep in one of the beds. Mrs. Johnson gave me a nightgown to wear and told me she would see me at 7 a.m. for breakfast.

As I heard the lock turning in the door as she locked me in that bedroom I thought, "God please help me and my sisters out of this mess."

I put on the night gown she gave me and got into bed and lay there wondering how my mother even found us, and how she was able to pull this off after being court ordered to have no contact with us at all.

My father and stepmother were not unfit. That was just bizarre. Daddy was a pain in the ass when he tried to control my social life, but he was a good father and Jenny kept our home neat and clean.

That is why it was simply wrong that Social Services could just remove us from our home and uproot us from the life we had, including school.

What were Nick and my friends going to think when they found out I was gone? How was I going to tell them that I had been in a foster home? All I could do was lie there and ask God to help us.

I spent two agonizing weeks in that foster home without going to school. Within that two-week period, Daddy and my grandparents had hired a lawyer and went to court to fight for our release. Stephanie had been placed in Juvenile Hall and Helen had been placed in a foster home.

We were all traumatized after that experience, and I was doing my best not to be mad at Stephanie. It turned out that our mother had somehow got our phone number and had been talking to Stephanie on the phone for some months without anyone knowing.

The lies about our home being unfit came from my mother trying to get revenge on my father for taking her kids away. She also did not like the fact that Jenny was raising her kids. Stephanie knew better than to have any contact with her. I had tried throughout the years to make her understand that any contact with our mother was like playing with a rattlesnake.

When I finally returned to school, I lied to Nick and all my friends that my great-grandmother had died in New Orleans, and I had to go to the funeral with my family. I was too embarrassed to tell anyone the truth; then I would have had to explain about my brother being killed and the reason that I was not allowed to see my biological mother. So, I lied and did my best to play catch up on my studies.

After school that day I went back to my job and explained to my boss why I had been absent for two weeks. He understood, but it was too late; he had already hired someone else. It was pretty messed up that I had to find another job just because my mother made up a bunch of lies.

Fortunately, within a week I found another job at Time Life Books in Santa Monica selling books over the phone. The pay was commission only, which was fine with me because I knew I could earn a paycheck. I knew I was good at sales because of my previous success when I worked at Core.

I spent all my free time sneaking around with my boyfriend. It was embarrassing to me that I had to sneak to see Nick. Why couldn't Daddy just treat him with respect and accept that we were together?

The whole thing was nuts. He believed that Nick could not be trusted although there was no basis in fact for that opinion. I just kept my mouth shut, saved my money and counted the days until freedom.

CHAPTER 74

My first month at Time Life Books, I was already number one in sales. So far, I had made over $600 in commission. Who knew you could make that much money selling "The Wild West" series over the phone?

By now, graduation was eight weeks away and we were practicing "Pomp and Circumstance" and the "Star Spangled Banner" in band class for the ceremony. I was excited because our graduation ceremony was being held at The Greek Theater, one of the most celebrated venues in Southern California.

I would be playing my flute on the same stage where Elton John had played a concert. It was going to be memorable for me.

So far, I had managed to save $1500 toward my first apartment. I had it all planned out: I would wait until I had $2500 saved so I could have enough money in case of an emergency. I was hoping to find a small apartment near the beach in Santa Monica so I could attend Santa Monica Junior College at night and work during the day.

I still wanted to be a musician but did not have the balls to see it through and had decided to play it safe and go into the legal field instead because it paid well, and I would always have a job. Being a musician was wonderful but being a starving musician would be a nightmare.

All my friends had plans too: Barry Fallon changed his name to Brian Aster and had already begun a career as a comedian and was appearing on "The Tonight Show." His mother worked for CBS, just a 10-minute walk from our high school. Brian would walk to his mother's job every day after school and wait for her to get off from work so they could go home together.

Brian started telling jokes to some of the employees at CBS when one day Johnny Carson overheard him, thought he was funny and put him on the show. He got an agent and started wearing slacks and a suit jacket to school along with carrying a brief case around. He was going on to USC.

Sandie was going to Santa Monica Junior College with me. Sally had no plans to go to college and Sofia Steinberg, who had changed her name to Swann after a character in the rock concert movie "Phantom of the Paradise," was going to work at the Los Angeles Museum.

Everybody had a plan, and we were all filled with positive energy and ready to take on the world and make our mark in it.

CHAPTER 75

On graduation day my whole family was there to see me perform in the music program and walk across the stage to get my diploma. I had on my cap and gown and was excited but also sad at the same time.

I thought about all the performances I had participated in with the school band and how I had played Linus in "You're a Good Man Charlie Brown" in the school play. All the times I had walked those halls at school with my friends and all the good times we had together.

It was kind of sad to leave it all behind for something new, but I was excited for the new experiences I was going to have.

My Father was throwing me a combination graduation and birthday party at an Italian restaurant in Los Feliz near Griffith Park. After the ceremony everyone in my family hugged and congratulated me for making it through high school in one piece without getting pregnant, hooked on drugs or arrested. Then everybody headed over to the restaurant for my party.

I wished Nick could have attended but he was going out to dinner with his family, and my father would have never allowed him to be anywhere near me. No problem though because we had plans to meet up later after my party. I lied and told my Daddy that I was going out with Sandie, Sally, and Kelly to a disco dance club called OSKO'S on La Cienega Blvd. I even invited the three of them to my party to make the lie as truthful as possible.

After two hours of eating a lot of Italian food and birthday cake, I opened my presents and cards with the welcomed checks in them. Then I was ready to call Nick and get out of there. I called Nick from the phone booth in the restaurant to come get me. I told Daddy that I was leaving the restaurant with the girls in Sandie's car. When we walked out of that restaurant my friends got into Sandie's car and I got into Nick's car. I thought my plan had worked perfectly until I caught a glimpse of my father and Uncle Franklin walking out of the restaurant together. They saw me in the car with Nick as we drove past the front door.

Shit, I thought, now he knows I lied to him, and he will be absolutely pissed when I get home. I decided not to let the thought of how mad he was going to be mess up my graduation night. Hell, you only get one graduation night from high school.

That night a group of us sat on the beach out in Malibu with a bon fire going. There was beer, marshmallows roasting on the fire and pot going around. Since I was already in trouble, I decided to break curfew and stay out until 3 a.m.

When I returned home, my father was waiting for me, as expected, but I did not care anymore. I was through sneaking around.

The minute I closed the front door he came out of his bedroom and started yelling at me.

"You've been out with that wet chicken after I told you to stay away from him, and you are hours past your curfew!"

"I went to a graduation party at the beach with my friends and yes, I was there with my boyfriend." I yelled back.

"Well, you either follow the rules of my household and do what I tell you to do under my roof, or you can get out." He shouted.

"I think I'll just move out." I said.

Then I went to my bedroom and shut the door.

The next morning, I called Sally and told her that my father was driving me crazy, and I just could not take it anymore. She offered me the sofa in her Hollywood apartment to sleep on.

"You can just move in if you want and split the rent with me and Mary. Now that I am out of high school my mom is making me get a fulltime job so I can pay the rent and support myself since I refuse to go straight to college." She complained.

"I can do that for a little while and that would work out perfectly until I can afford my own apartment." I said.

Excited, I hung up the phone and knew I would still be able to go to school and work plus feed myself. I looked up at the ceiling and said, "Thank you, God, for helping me to move out."

A few days later when my father and Jenny left to go bowling, I sprang into action. I packed my clothes, took my album collection, but left everything else until I had my own apartment.

Sally picked me up in the used car that her mother had given her for graduation. As she helped me put my stuff into the back of her Pacer, my two sisters just stood there on the sidewalk watching us. Neither one of them wanted me to move out, and I kind of felt guilty about leaving them. But I knew I had to go; I had waited all my life so far for this moment.

I explained that once I was settled, they could come visit me and I would still be coming home to visit them. I gave Stephanie a note explaining to Daddy that I had moved out while he was gone because I knew that he would try to talk me out of it. I told him that I was moving in with Sally and not to worry.

As Sally and I took off in her car, I looked at my two sisters standing on the sidewalk waving goodbye to me. I kept looking at them until they were no longer in sight, because I knew that I would never live with my father and sisters again. I was finally leaving my childhood behind.

CHAPTER 76

Later that night I enjoyed my first night of freedom out on my own as an adult by going to a house party in Santa Monica. It was being held by a surfer boy named "Killer Joe" whom I had become friendly with at work. Before I caught the bus over to the party, I called Nick to let him know that I had moved in with Sally and why. I gave him her phone number and told him that he could reach me there from now on.

When I arrived at the party it was in full swing, Kashmir by Led Zeppelin was blasting from a turn table; people were drinking and smoking pot. I found Surfer Joe in a back bedroom talking to some guys who looked like total beach bums. Except I knew better. They were probably rich boys from the area who owned the best surf boards, wet suits and surfed everyday while mom and dad paid for everything.

You could tell by the condition of their skin and hair, that they had years of exposure to the sea water and sun on a regular basis. Joe offered me a beer, but I turned it down. I was still a non-drinker because of the horrible taste and the way it made some people act. I ended up dancing the night away with a few girls I met at the party.

At four in the morning one of the girls I met gave me a ride back to my Hollywood apartment. I put my bedding on the sofa and slept until two that afternoon.

I awoke to Sally telling me that Nick was on the phone for me. When I answered the phone, Nick was excited as he told me that he was happy I was now out on my own and we did not have to sneak around any longer.

Sally was already in the kitchen making a sandwich and coffee.

"Your Father called twice." She said.

"I'll call him back after I drink a cup of coffee." I said.

When I explained how happy Nick was about my freedom, she replied, "I'm happy that you are happy, but I don't like Nick or trust him."

"I really don't understand why you dislike him when he's never done anything negative to me." I said.

"No one likes him because you can do better. Nick needs a big tube of acne medicine and a job." Sally said.

"He's a good person. You just don't know him like I do." I said.

"Thank God for that." Sally said taking a bite of her sandwich. "I'm looking forward to you sharing the apartment with me and Mary, but I will never understand what you see in him, especially since he sucks in bed. I have no idea how you even deal with that situation." She continued, "That would drive me crazy. I keep hoping after being with him for a while that you come to your senses and dump his ugly ass."

"Sex isn't important to me. My love for him goes beyond sex," I explained.

"Okay" Sally said, "Let me know in six months how that's working out for ya."

I ignored her comment, drank my coffee and then went into the living room to call my father back. The conversation with him was just as unpleasant as I had expected it to be. He needed to realize that I was 18 and there was nothing that he could do about my moving out.

A few hours later I was thrilled when Nick arrived in his mother's Audi to pick me up for us to spend the day together. He had no car of his own because the engine in the Mustang was completely blown. He was now selling it for parts.

He took me to spend the day with his family and to enjoy the spaghetti dinner his mom had cooked. His mom made delicious sauce, but nothing compared to my father's. Everyone in his family was nice and warm towards me and did their best to make me feel welcome in their home.

Later that night Sally let me know that my father had called the apartment wanting to talk to me again.

"What did you tell him?" I asked.

"Don't worry, he doesn't know you were out with lover boy." She replied.

"Thanks, I just don't need that hassle right now." I told her.

After talking with Sally, I called Daddy back just to get it over with. I knew if I did not, he would just worry. I listened to him tell me why I needed to move back home. He told me that my stepmother Jenny was pregnant. I was shocked but happy for them. Perhaps now he would get another boy and stop focusing on running my life and personal business.

A few weeks later I called and told him that Nick and I were seriously involved. He exploded as I expected he would.

I explained that his parents had invited me to stay with them and I was considering it but had not decided yet. If I accepted the offer, Nick and I would be sleeping in separate bedrooms.

Then, in the coldest voice I had ever heard come out of my father's mouth, he told me that I was trading in my black family for a white one.

I told him that was not true; that all I wanted was to live on my own, and how he should be proud that I wanted to leave home at 18.

"You are making the biggest mistake of your life and will live to regret it. White boys like him don't marry black girls." He insisted. Then he hung up.

I was upset because he had never hung up the phone on me before. Well, this was it; he was just going to write me off because of Nick; the whole thing was insane.

CHAPTER 77

W hat was wrong with following your heart and trying to build a decent life for yourself? I searched my mind for an answer and decided that there was nothing wrong with what I was doing.

I had waited so long to be an independent adult ready to live life and live out my fantasies such as having an office job, going to work every day in my "Leggs" panty hose and high heels. I wanted to do something worthwhile and important with my life.

My plans included traveling, playing music and having a career that I could be happy with and a beach house so I could look out at the ocean and see God there every morning. The ocean reminded me of God because it looked vast and endless when you looked at. The motion of the large waves coming in and out crashing on to the shore was like watching God breathe to me. Being before the water gave me a certain peace of mind and it was a treat just to sit there and witness it all.

I wanted to be an adult, and I was not going to let anyone rob me of that. I knew in my heart that God was watching out for me, because I could feel some unseen force around me, and I knew whatever this force was had created me. That is why I was not afraid. Rather, I felt fearless and protected. I told myself that Daddy was just freaking out because I was the first to leave home. Eventually he would have to accept the fact that I was not a little girl anymore.

After letting him know I was in love with Nick and might move in with him, Daddy told all my aunts and grandparents who all insisted I was making a mistake; that Nick was not good enough for me. Everyone was afraid that he would get me pregnant, then not marry me, or marry me and ruin my life.

I understood that they did not want me to be a single mother, and I understood that they all believed that I should have applied to UCLA and studied music or law.

Grandfather Johnson told me, "I want you to have someone concrete that you can depend on in life."

Aunt Louise told me that pretty girls like me had the option of meeting and dating a doctor, or lawyer, with money. I thought she was telling me to date guys with money and live a loveless, messed up existence having sex and kids with some guy who really made my skin crawl.

Just be a trophy wife with a husband who would keep me on a shelf at the mansion and take me down every time he needed to show me off in public? For me, that would be a living hell. Aunt Louise said she detected little intelligence in Nick. She predicted he would never be anything special in life and had no backbone.

Finally, she said she did not want me to live in poverty with him and said love did not keep the lights on.

I refused to listen to a word anybody said to me. I loved Nick and believed in him. And one day we would prove them all wrong.

After hearing my family's views about my relationship with Nick, I asked God daily, while working fulltime at Time Life Books, for the perfect adult office job that had health insurance and benefits. I asked God to make sure that my job paid enough for me to live in Beverly Hills in my own apartment. That would make me happy and shut my family up.

I changed my work schedule to work on Saturdays so I could have a weekday off from Time Life Books. That way I could spend one day a week looking for the perfect office job. Before I went to sleep every night and morning, I asked God for the perfect office job. Then I visualized myself having that well paid office job, being dressed to kill in my career perfect clothes.

My weekly day off was spent walking up Wilshire Blvd filling out employment applications, dressed in L'eggs panty hose, dress shoes, and a smart looking cream colored suit I had purchased from The May Co. department store on the corner of Fairfax and Wilshire Blvd. I started on Wilshire Blvd in downtown Los Angeles, walking into every office building and filling out a job application. It did not matter to me if they were hiring or not, I just wanted one on file just in case something opened. I was leaving no stone unturned.

I was determined to get a high paying job in an office if it killed me. Failure was not an option. As I walked into each building asking for a job,

I knew in my heart that God was going to give me one. All I had to do was keep going until someone said yes.

Since getting more serious with Nick, for the first time in my life I had quit going to church, because he thought it was all bullshit. No one in his family went to church. No one in his family even talked about God or listened to any preaching on the radio like Daddy and I always had. I still believed in God and talked to Him every day, but I was trying to fit in with Nick and his lifestyle.

I figured I would continue talking to God on my own every day as I always had and knew that was what counted most. All I knew for sure was this God that I could not see with my eyes but could hear in my heart and head was real. So, I was not going to give up the invisible safety net that I depended on in life for anyone, no matter who they were.

A week later, I came home from work on Friday and found a telephone message from a woman named Kathy Smith from California Federal Savings and Loan. I rushed to the phone to return the call hoping it meant I had an interview and a job offer. I called, asked for Kathy and was told to come in for an interview the following Monday morning at nine. I excitedly told her I would be there and thanked her for the opportunity.

After I hung up the phone, I called my boss at Time Life and got permission to take Monday off from work. I was just so excited! A bank job was just the type of job I had been searching for to support myself with. I knew that God had already given me this job because I had asked Him for it.

Monday morning, I showed up for my job interview dressed in my suit, heels and panty hose. I was first given a math and spelling test by a woman in personnel. Then Kathy Hunt walked into the room and introduced herself as the manager of the Accounts Payable Department. She gave me a strong handshake and said she was happy to meet me.

During the interview she asked me tons of questions and told me that her department needed a new file /accounts payable clerk and that the job paid $750.00 a month with full benefits.

"I want to hire you; I was impressed by your answer to the question on the application why you thought the bank should hire you. You answered that you are a hard worker and even if you had no prior banking experience that you are willing to learn and you are trainable." Kathy said.

"Well, given the chance I would never let The Savings and Loan down, I'm a good employee and I've been working since I was 13." I replied.

"When can you start work here?" Kathy asked.

I told her that I would have to give my present employer at least a few days' notice.

"Okay. Let me get your test scores back and I will call you in the morning. If your scores are good enough then you've got this job."

I thanked her again for her time and the opportunity to even be considered for a position at California Federal Savings and Loan.

When I got home, I called Time Life Books to find out how much notice I had to give to quit. My boss told me that I did not have to give any notice; all I had to do was quit.

The following morning Kathy called to let me know that my scores were high and that I had the job. I explained that I checked with Time Life which did not require any notice for quitting.

"Great, then you can start day after tomorrow." She informed me.

"I would be happy to do that!" I replied.

"Good then I will see you at 8 a.m. sharp day after tomorrow." She said.

I hung up the phone and did a little victory dance while singing, "I got the job."

Later, at Nick's house, I told his family my good news. They hugged me and told me how proud they were of me. Then I called Daddy and told him too.

I spent the whole day in a state of complete bliss; I kept telling God how grateful I was that He had given me a real adult job.

Now I could move on to step number two of my plan which was my own apartment in Beverly Hills even if I had to get a roommate to help pay the rent. It had to be Beverly Hills or an upper scale neighborhood like that because of safety. In Beverly Hills if you called the police, they would be there within minutes. In South Central you could be waiting a while before the police showed up.

I was on cloud nine fantasizing how my first apartment would look and how happy I would be living in it.

After dinner that night Nico Papalikis, Nick's father, gave me a genuine leather brief case to take to work with me every day. My heart was truly touched that he thought enough of me to buy such a thoughtful gift for me on such short notice. To me it was a symbolic gift that meant "welcome to the world of being an adult."

Nico told me to keep up the good work, and how he wished his sons had the drive and determination that I had.

As I thanked him again, I realized that he was genuinely happy to see me succeed on my own. I liked and respected Nico because I knew that he had studied and worked hard to be a successful architect who was always impeccably dressed, drove a Mercedes-Benz and owned two Audi's. But most of all because Nico had dreams, ambitions and goals that he worked toward daily. He reminded me of my Uncle Phillip; they both had an air of real inner drive and determination about them.

I was a dreamer too, so I admired this quality in both my Uncle Phillip and Nico. So, it was a compliment to me for him to think highly of my accomplishments.

CHAPTER 78

On my first day of work at California Federal Savings and Loan, I took a moment to tell God thanks again. I dressed in the career clothes I had laid out the night before, ate a bowl of cereal and had a cup of coffee. Then I caught the Wilshire bus which let me off right in front of the building. After I had gotten off the bus 15 minutes early, I just stood there in front of the building for a moment taking it all in. I watched businessmen and women walking through the big double doors of the building with their briefcases.

They all looked so professional, and now I was one of them. I took a deep breath as I walked through those doors myself toward the elevators, and for the first time I truly felt like an adult. I got off the elevator on the fourth floor and walked down a long hallway looking for the door that said Accounts Payable Department.

Once I found it and walked in the door, the first thing I noticed was all the file cabinets that lined the walls. In the middle of the room were three rows of large desks each with a typewriter, adding machine and telephone. There were women sitting at each desk except one and I assumed the empty one was mine.

Kathy walked out of her office in front of the desks. She glanced at her watch and said, "Good, you're here five minutes early."

Then she introduced me to the four women who were starting work and the fact that I was the new file clerk.

"Let's welcome Maya to our team," Kathy said to them.

Everyone got up from their desks to introduce themselves and shake my hand as they welcomed me to the department. Kathy then told me that the empty desk was mine and to put my purse in a drawer and follow her. I did as she asked then followed her over to the file cabinets.

Kathy handed me a set of keys and explained that they were for the file cabinets.

"These file cabinets hold all the financial records for all 52 of our bank branches. Every morning when you come in, the first thing I want you to do is to unlock these cabinets. Before you leave the office at the end of each day, I want you to lock the cabinets. We have proof of payment for all our operational bills for the branches in there. Also, all employee travel expense vouchers are housed in there along with copies of each reimbursement payout.

So, you see how important it is that the cabinets are locked up at night. The keys are kept in a locked box in my office, so every morning you are to come into my office and get the keys from me.

If you need any supplies for your desk, there is a supply room around the corner. You will also be responsible for ordering all our office supplies. Finally, you must also go down to the third floor every afternoon after we have the batches of bills done for the day to print the checks. Now follow me." She said as she walked into her office.

Kathy unlocked a drawer and took out a small black metal lock box. She unlocked it and said,

"This is the bank president's signature plate for the blank checks and a roll of blank checks are in the drawer above. You are to take both down to the third floor every afternoon, give them to a technician who will print out the day's checks for you on a big printer with the signature on the bottom.

Then you will bring the signature plate back to me, and you take the checks to your desk to mail out.

Now don't feel overwhelmed because I am going to train you to do all this."

She explained.

"I'm not overwhelmed at all; I'm actually excited," I said.

"Good. Then let us get started," Kathy said.

As the day progressed, I got friendly with the other women who worked in my department. They included Nancy, a 29-year-old black woman from South Central Los Angeles and Kathy's best friend at work and outside of work.

Bernie was a big, heavy-set white woman in her 50s, with a disability that forced her to walk with a cane and wear special shoes. She seemed nice and offered me Mentos candy all day long.

There was Cindy, a skinny blonde in her 60s, who dressed in suits from the 1950s. You could tell that she bought the suits when they were new and in style, then kept wearing them. The thing that really threw me was that the suits looked as new as the day she had bought them. Her hair style and make-up were also from the 1950's. She reminded me of Kim Novak in an old Alfred Hitchcock movie.

Nicole was in her 50s and married with three kids. She and Nancy were neighbors and friends in South Central Los Angeles, Nancy was responsible for getting her the job at the bank. We were the accounts payable team that paid all the bills for California Federal's fifty-two different bank branches, and I was proud to be part of that.

CHAPTER 79

Within a few weeks I had not only been trained to do the checks, but also tasked with adding up invoices on my 10-key by touch machine and charging them to different cost accounts and balancing batch sheets.

I loved going to work every day so professionally dressed. Now when I watched the Mary Tyler Moore Show, I thought how lucky I was to be a young woman working in the world like Mary. All I needed now was my own apartment.

Apparently, my success influenced Nick because he started looking for an office job, and after a few weeks he found one as a mail room clerk at a law firm in downtown Los Angeles. He had to wear a suit to work every day, I thought that was an improvement on his past wardrobe choices.

Since this was his first job and he had no money of his own, his mother took him out and bought him some clothes to wear to work. Nick cleaned up nicely and I really liked the way he looked in a suit and tie.

We both had to be at work at the same time, so I met Nick the same time every morning and we had breakfast together.

I was elated that my dreams for my adult life were finally starting to realize. I felt like a wild horse that had been let out of a stable for the first time; I was young, fresh and alive inside and filled with wonder and excitement towards the world.

My whole life lay ahead of me, and I felt like I could do anything. I could shape it and mold it into whatever I wanted it to be. I was finally in control of my own life, and it felt good.

CHAPTER 80

By now Nick and I got into the nightly habit of coming home from work, eating dinner then watching television in his bed. I loved watching television in bed with Nick, who watched "Dallas" with me. At this point we had a little bet going on about who shot JR, the show's main character. We also enjoyed watching "Saturday Night Live" and loved Mr. Bill and Al Franken.

Frequently, I spent the night, supposedly in the guest room but.... We were quite comfortable with our routine. I even started saving for dishes, furniture and first and last month's rent for my planned apartment in Beverly Hills.

One day I was eating lunch in the cafeteria at work with a few co-workers, when one of the women sitting at the table started complaining about her husband and how she was about to file for divorce just because she was sick of looking at him. She was also looking for a place to live, she said that she wanted out of the marriage so badly that she was giving him everything, even the house.

She worked in another department and was new to California Federal like I was.

I told her that I was saving money for an apartment in Beverly Hills, and how I planned to find a roommate.

Paula Beck and I soon became fast friends and discovered that we shared the same birthday.

"We're both Geminis and how cool is that to meet someone who was born on the same day as you were. We have to be roommates!" She exclaimed.

I quickly agreed with her, better a co-worker than a total stranger.

Paula was a small attractive black woman and although she was 10 years older than I was, there was no age gap between us; we just hit it off from our first meeting.

We started eating lunch together in the cafeteria every day, and we were amazed at how similar we were in our likes and dislikes. Then we started hanging out together outside work. I introduced Paula to my other girlfriends, as well as Nick and his family.

I would have introduced her to my family, but I was still on the outs with them.

Paula and I were constantly on the lookout for the perfect apartment in Beverly Hills that we could afford. We quickly discovered that we could not afford the rent deep into Beverly Hills.

We discovered we could afford the rent in a neighborhood a few blocks within the beginning of Beverly Hills right off Robertson Blvd. That became the focus of our search as we concentrated on that area.

After looking for two months we finally found the perfect two-bedroom two-bathroom apartment one block inside Beverly Hills near Robertson Blvd. It had a tiny, cute balcony right off the living room, a kitchen and a large living room with a small built in bar area. The best part was it was in a security building, and you had to ring a buzzer and speak on an intercom to get in.

The building was owned by a Middle Eastern couple who lived in the first apartment downstairs on the first floor. We were impressed that all the tenants were professional people.

The rent was only $525 per month including utilities and we would each pay $262.50 per month. And we both could easily afford to live there without financial strain. We quickly filled out the rental application and gave the owner a check for the deposit, both hoping that would stop anyone else from getting the place while we waited for approval. Paula was not much for praying, so I prayed for both of us.

A few days later, while I was at work, I received a call from the owner saying we had been approved. I called Paula and gave her the good news.

"We can move in at the beginning of the month." I told her.

She was as thrilled as I was.

"You only have to suffer three more weeks living in the same house with your husband." I said.

"That three weeks can't come soon enough for me. He is begging me every day to stop the divorce, but I can't because I am no longer in love with him. The nicer he is to me the more I want to get away from him." She explained.

I sort of felt sorry for her husband because, according to her, she just woke up one morning and decided that she no longer wanted to be married to him after nine years. He had done nothing wrong and had tried to be a good husband to her, but she wanted out. It seemed harsh to me that you could marry someone, be in love and then just wake up one day thinking "I can't get away from this person fast enough."

When I went to Nick's home after work that evening, I told everyone about the apartment including calling my family. They were happy just to hear that I was moving in with a female and not Nick.

That night I stayed with Nick and as we were getting ready for bed, he told me that he wanted to move into my new apartment with me and how much he loved me and wanted to wake up with me every morning.

"Plus, I want to spend as much time as I can with you in case, I join the Army." He said.

"The Army! Why the hell would you want to do that?" I asked.

"I've been talking to a guy at work who has been in the Army as an Airborne paratrooper. It sounds cool. You should hear some of the stories he told me, I've been thinking about it for a while."

I had no idea why anyone would want to join the Army after what happened to Joe when I was a kid. War got people killed, and after living through the Vietnam War, I had little faith that soldiers came back the same if they came back at all. I thought Nick had gone crazy and I did not want him to go into the Army. I wanted him in LA with me.

My opinion was that he should stay home and go to college while working.

"I plan on going to college at night in the fall and we could go together. We could come up with a plan and live out our dreams while we make tons of money together." I suggested.

"Well, what if your dream is to go Airborne?" He asked.

"Then I can't stop you from doing what you really want to do." I said.

"If I do join, will you wait for me?" He asked.

"Sure, I will. I love you. I'll just spend the time you are gone working and going to school." I told him.

"I'm going to see a recruiter tomorrow on my lunch break and I'll have more information about the whole thing after I talk to him." He said.

"So, you're okay with me moving out with you?" He asked.

"Yeah sure. I just have to check with Paula. I'm sure she won't mind since it's a two-bedroom two-bath apartment." I said.

"Don't tell my parents anything about all of this yet, I want to tell them myself after I talk to the recruiter," he said.

The following day Nick called me after seeing the recruiter on his lunch break and told me that he had decided to join the Army.

That night at dinner he told his family that he had decided to join the Army and go Airborne. He told us all that he would be gone for four years; three years in Italy and then he would be stationed in the United States.

Everyone in his family told him he was crazy and thought it was a bad idea, except his father. He not only thought it was a good idea but said it might make a man out of him.

Nico got up from his chair and patted Nick on the back and told him that he was proud of him. But his mother was freaking out because she was afraid that a war would break out while Nick was in the Army.

I could tell that she felt the same fear I did; that Nick would die and never come back. I was thinking of Joe and what happened to him while Dorothy was thinking that her baby boy could possibly be killed.

Then, I realized that I would be out of college by the time he got back from serving his time in the Army. I wondered if he would meet someone else and forget about me. There was no question that I would have no problem waiting for him.

This would be the first big test for our relationship, and if he came back to me after four years then that would mean that he really loved me.

Later that night while we were lying in bed, I told Nick how afraid I was that his joining the Army would break us up.

He told me not to worry; that he had no intention of being with anyone else but me. And how we would talk on the phone and write one another all the time. He told me that he could come home for a month every year and that he would fly me over to Italy a couple of times a year.

"We can still be together, but joining the Army is something I have to do," He said.

I had no choice but to support him in his decision and wait for him to come back home in one piece.

The next day Nick gave his job notice that he was leaving and signed some papers with his recruiter that got him even closer to becoming property of the United States Armed Forces. Nick would be leaving for basic training and "Jump School" in a month. It was all happening so fast.

Then the day came when we moved into my new apartment with Paula. Dorothy allowed us to take Nick's bed and color TV set with us. Nick told me that he wanted me to sleep in his bed while he was gone so I could keep it warm for him. I bought an old family sofa for a $100 and along with the other household items I had purchased and saved we were set.

Paula had gotten her soon to be ex-husband to sign the legal separation papers that he really did not want to sign. Somehow, she also convinced him to help her move her things into the apartment as well. I felt sorry for him as he carried her boxes into the apartment, telling her the whole time about how much he loved her, and what a big mistake she was making by moving out of their home.

This poor man was just lovesick for her, but Paula wanted no part of it.

Paula said that she woke up one morning and realized that she was no longer in love with Barry, all she wanted was for him to share the car with her that they were both buying.

After Paula and I moved into the apartment, I found out that she had been seeing a younger man the whole time and was in love with him; only problem was he wanted to see other people. She told me that she met him six months prior in a Beverly Hills nightclub. Paula said that his uncle was a famous singer and he lived with him on his estate.

Once she divulged information about the guy she had been seeing, I suddenly understood why she was so anxious to shed her husband. She had now fallen for someone else and was laying the groundwork for a new relationship. Women could be treacherous when they wanted to be, and I saw the writing on the wall; this guy was not right for my friend, and I could see that she was headed for a train wreck. I tried to warn Paula by telling her that sometimes I could see things about people.

I could see this guy out there in the street night clubbing and sleeping with every attractive female who looked his way. Do not take it personally I warned her; the problem is that he is young and still in party mode. He will not be offering you the exclusive relationship that you crave from him. I strongly advise you to forget about him before he breaks your heart.

Paula refused to listen to me because the heart wants what the heart wants.

On the other hand, I was sad because Nick would be leaving soon, although part of me was excited because I was starting to live out my childhood dreams of having my first apartment. I was looking forward to life as a career woman in the big city, with a cute apartment and roommate until I was ready to move on to a new life experience.

Building and creating my own life really excited me because I had waited for so long to be in control of my life. I had a detailed list of the things I wanted in my life such as the type of clothing I wanted to wear, the type of home and furniture I wanted to own, even the type of cars I planned to own.

None of these goals or achievements had anything to do with impressing other people. I wanted these things for my own happiness and experience because I wanted to enjoy them while here on Earth.

I absolutely did not want to grow old and die, then sit amongst a group of angels looking at my life in retrospective regretting all the things I could have done while on Earth but did not. I also had a fear of being left behind; yet had no idea what I would be left behind from or by whom.

CHAPTER 81

I stood on my balcony the first night in my new apartment and looked at the moon and the stars, while Nick and Paula slept, as I talked with God. I thanked God for everything He had given me so far and told him how cool He was for spoiling me, by helping make my dreams a reality.

"God, I am going to make my future a good one and I know unlimited goodness is my future with you and the angels on my side. It's going to be one big adventure and because of you I have no fear." I prayed.

I looked up at the stars and thanked Him for allowing me to feel His presence even though I was unable to see Him; I had always known that He was there with me. I had learned a long time ago to keep the fact that I talked to God to myself because every time I tried to tell other people, they looked at me like I was weird.

It often amazed me how many people did not believe in what made them. I mean, breath came in and out of your nostrils 24 hours a day and that had to come from somewhere. I believed that creative force also created the solar system, other planets, life forms, animals, trees and oceans along with everything else. I knew that God was not human, but spirit, endless and vast beyond human comprehension and experience.

This was my memory and understanding of God as I looked out at the moon and stars to communicate with a being, I knew could hear me.

As the days passed, Nick started spending all his free time hanging out with his friends smoking pot and drinking. His childhood friend Glen Smith was the worst; when Nick was with him there was always heavy drinking and drug usage. In fact, Glen's father was a cocaine dealer who had previously served time in jail for dealing.

Nick and I started fighting about all the time he spent drinking with Glen. I told Nick that he should be spending time with me instead of partying with Glen, and if he wanted me to wait for him to get out of the Army, then he had better put in some quality time with me before he left town.

"Take me out to dinner and make a memory to remember me by while you're away." I prompted.

But still he went out with his friends. I would come home from work, and he would be gone already, returning home in the early morning hours drunk, stoned on pot and high off free cocaine, courtesy of Glen Smith.

I began to seriously wonder if Nick would ever love me the way I loved him. When was I going to be number one in his life?

Thoughts of "Is this guy really worth it all?" began forming. I was getting pretty pissed off about the whole thing and he knew it. So, he did try to be home to eat dinner with me for a few nights before he went out.

A big part of my heart longed for the little boy on the moon, while my common sense told me that I was holding on to a childhood dream that would never become real. If he were a reality, he would have found me by now. At least part of me remembered Nick the moment I set eyes on him at John Burroughs Junior High. It was still amazing to me that I remembered and loved him as my husband from another place and time and could not shake that memory.

But Nick was apparently not the little boy on the moon; if he were, he would have asked me to marry him by now, and he would never be friends with someone like Glen Smith.

The night before Nick was due to fly out for basic training, he really tried my patience by telling me that he would attend a going away party that Glen Smith was giving him.

"It's just us guys. Then I'll spend the night with my parents because my mom wants to spend time with me before I leave." He said.

I could not believe this guy did not have some romantic dinner planned, or a speech with a promise ring or something. After he walked out the door, I went to my room and cried. When I finished crying, I decided that as soon as Nick was gone, I would write him a letter and tell him that the relationship was not working.

There was no way I was waiting four years for a guy who treated me this way, and he claimed that he never wanted to get married. I would just have to get over him, love or no love.

I would start going out with my girlfriends and playing my flute again. I would start going to Hollywood again to watch the bands play. I would do all the things I used to do before I hooked up with Nick. God willing, I would meet and marry some wonderful man and we would live our lives as if it were a big adventure together. I was not going to settle for less, life was too short.

Then Nick surprised me that night and came back to the apartment after his party, to spend his last night with me instead of sleeping at his parent's house. As usual, after a night out with Glen Smith he was drunk and smelled like a liquor bottle.

He made love to me for 10 minutes then rolled over and went to sleep, as I lay next to him awake wondering if we were going to make it together.

The next morning Nick's parents picked us up from my apartment, to drive Nick to the Army recruiting station that he was due to leave from. He would be taken on a bus to the airport where he would fly to Fort Benning, GA for basic training and "jump school." He told everyone how he was looking forward to learning how to jump out of an airplane.

We were not allowed to go into the building with him when we got to the recruiting station on Wilshire Blvd. Nick had to say his goodbyes outside the building. A tear ran down my cheek as I kissed and hugged him goodbye, because I figured that I might be kissing him for the last time. I had taken the day off from work, so when his parents dropped me off at my apartment, I spent most of the day crying because I was in a failed relationship with someone I absolutely loved.

CHAPTER 82

Within a week a few of my aunts saw Nick's enlistment as an open door to get me away from him. My Aunts Carol and Louise started calling me trying to set me up on blind dates although I had not told anyone that I was planning to end my relationship with Nick. I kept that to myself until I got up enough nerve to write Nick.

Initially, I turned them down but when the girls at the office and Paula started telling me that Nick should have at least given me a promise ring or something before he left and would never marry me, I decided to listen.

My father told me I was a fool in waiting hoping for a wedding and a ring that was never coming.

"He doesn't have to marry you when he can get the milk for free without buying the cow." He told me.

"What does that mean?" I asked him.

"It means that he can live and sleep with you without marriage," he said.

"And the minute he gets you pregnant he'll be gone."

It really upset me because I knew that he was right. Nick never wanted to get married and I did. I was feeling low and lonely, especially at night when I would sit in my living room listening to my Elton John vinyl collection because I had always sought comfort in his music. Elton had a song for every mood a human being could be in.

Then I would look to the stars for my God to come and take my inner pain and disappointment away. The world seemed like such a big and lonely place for the first time in my life. And the thought of spending my life alone, or worse in a series of bad relationships, that were drama filled, was at times too much to bear. I just could not allow that to happen. I realized that my childhood had been jammed packed with enough drama to last a lifetime.

I was ready for the good stuff. I knew now that the choices I made, especially starting out in life, could affect the rest of my life. I realized that

I had to be focused and stick to my life plan and not get sidetracked by outside things that looked good and shiny. When in reality it was only just a box of shit wrapped up all pretty with a big bow on it. So, I continued to wish upon the brightest star in the sky asking God to send me my true, life partner and love to go through my life journey with. I told God that if the little boy on the moon was real then to help him find me and put a ring on my finger that looked like the oceans of heaven itself. That was what I asked God every night.

CHAPTER 83

I started spending more quality time with my sister Stephanie who would ride her ten-speed bike over to my apartment and spend the weekend with me. Nick's absence helped us spend more time together.

One Friday afternoon Aunt Louise called me at work and invited me out to dinner later that evening with her and one of her friends. I figured it would do me good to get out of the apartment and eat some delicious food for free. She told me to wear nice clothes and make-up because we were going to a steak house in Beverly Hills. I jokingly, asked her if I had to take a shower as well. I thought the comment was funny, but she did not.

That evening Aunt Louise picked me up and told me her friend was meeting us at the restaurant. When we arrived, the hostess showed us to our table, where an older man was waiting for us with a cocktail in his hand. As he stood to greet us, he shook my hand and introduced himself.

I wondered what my aunt could possibly have in common with someone who looked the same age as her father and my grandfather. He was so tall I had to look up when I spoke to him.

While we were eating steak and lobster, sports celebrities stopped by our table to say hello to him along with a few other people I had seen on television.

I found out over dinner that he was a retired basketball player I had heard about when I was a kid because of his cartoon on television that my siblings and I watched while we were growing up.

For someone who had experienced such success in life he had a gracious manner. You never would have known that he was famous by just talking with him.

After a parade of people came by the table to say hello, he turned his attention to me and Aunt Louise. I sat and listened while they talked about sports and business, trying to look interested while being bored senseless.

At one point Louise and I went to the bathroom together, and as we were washing our hands, she turned to me and said, "I want you with a guy who can afford to buy you a nice dinner at a restaurant like this one. Always remember that steak and lobster taste better than a fast-food hamburger."

I told her once again that I was not going to date some guy because of his bank balance.

"I don't want some guy kissing and touching me that I'm not in love with."

The following week Aunt Carol, who was an awesome tennis player, called and told me straight out that she was setting me up on a blind date. She told me about some guy named Andy, and how he was an up and coming 23-year-old tennis player.

At least he is in my age group, I thought.

"He lives in Los Angeles, but he's been in Europe for the past six months playing tennis."

She said she wanted to set us up on a blind date before he left town again.

I thought this is a chance to go out with someone else and find out if I could even be attracted to someone besides Nick. I told Carol to give him my phone number and said that he had better be good looking.

The next evening after I had returned home from work, Andy called. He sounded nice enough and said that my aunt had shown him a photo of me and how beautiful he thought I was.

"I would love to take you out to dinner and get to know you." He said.

I agreed to go out to dinner with him that Friday night in Westwood and gave him my address. I loved Westwood so this guy had already earned a brownie point with me.

That Friday night Andy showed up on time wearing expensive designer blue jeans and a nice shirt. Andy looked casual, chic and kind of cute. He was a young black guy, mixed like me. He had a handsome face and curly brown hair with cream colored skin, and his eyes were a light shade of blue. Andy was tall and had a beautifully built muscular body from playing tennis every day for years.

My Aunt Carol had the same type of muscular body that I had always admired. She had been playing tennis for over 20 years and had won many competitions and awards.

Just looking at a tennis player's body made me want to pick up a racket and play tennis just for the physical benefits.

I tried not to feel guilty about Nick as Andy opened the door to his BMW for me. We went to a lovely restaurant in Westwood where we talked with an easy flow about music and movies while eating. Andy told me jokes that I laughed at, and I realized that I was having fun and that he really was a nice guy.

Being honest, I told him about my relationship with Nick and how he wanted me to wait for him.

"Has he asked you to marry him?" Andy asked.

"No," I replied. "That's why I'm out with you; this is my first date with someone else."

Andy said that I was too young and beautiful to be waiting for some guy to come home from the Army who had not even put a ring on my finger. And if Nick had not done that before he left town, he never would.

"You should be enjoying yourself and meeting new people like me." He said with a grin.

After dinner we walked around Westwood which was alive with people going to movies, shops and restaurants. All the college students from UCLA were out in full force that night. And I was having fun just walking around on a warm night with someone holding my hand.

When Andy took me home, he tried to kiss me, but I turned my head just in time for him to hit my cheek rather than lips.

"It's a little too soon for me to be kissing someone else," I explained.

"I still have to break up with the guy." I told him.

"Well look," He said, "I'm going to keep your phone number so next time I'm in town we can go out again." .

"Sure, you can give me a call. That would be really nice. "I said.

We hugged goodbye and he was gone.

As I got into bed I thought about the date, and how weird and unfamiliar it felt to be out with someone other than Nick. I felt like I had just cheated on my boyfriend. I knew that I was going to be forced to write that break-up letter soon. I was waiting for Nick to write me a letter first with a return address.

I would tell him that I wanted to get married one day and have a family, and how he had made it clear that he was never going to get married. We just wanted different things.

The next morning Aunt Carol called to find out how the date went. I told her that Andy was nice and that I had enjoyed his company.

"Are you going to see him again?" Carol asked.

"He said that he would call me when he got back in town so we could go out again," I replied.

"He's going to England to play tennis." She said.

"Yeah, he told me about that over dinner, so don't worry. I think he's cute and nice so far." I assured her.

"Good, because you deserve better than Nick." She responded.

On that note I hurried and got off the phone, the last thing I wanted to hear was a Nick bashing from Aunt Carol.

I hung up the phone wishing that my family would stop saying negative things about him. I found this attitude from my Aunt Louise that all white people were not to be trusted enough to date disturbing. It was as if Martin Luther King Jr. had marched and died for nothing.

It was 1981 and I strongly believed in his "I Have a Dream" speech. Dr. King said that he wanted to see blacks and whites walk hand in hand together; for all races to have equal rights, and for men not to be judged by the color of their skin, but by the content of their character. I felt as if I were living this man's promise become reality.

I felt strongly that I was free to date and marry a white man if I wished without the risk of being put in jail for it. Or having the KKK burn my house down and kill me and my family.

My grandparents never once told me to judge a man by the color of his skin. And I never heard them tell my aunts or anyone else not to date or marry outside of their race. My grandmother was not a full-blooded black woman; she was mixed with Jewish and Native American.

I knew that racism still existed and yes, there was work to be done to wipe it out, but I was not going to think or believe as my aunt did. I had learned from my grandparent's example through the years that when it came to falling in love there was no color barrier.

CHAPTER 84

One week later I returned home from work to find my first letter from Nick in my mailbox. I was excited to hear what he had to say as I opened it. He had included a photo of himself with his head shaved, in uniform and had a tired drained look on his face. He looked different without his long hair, and I thought what a shame it was that it was all gone now.

I started reading the letter which was noticeably short. He told me how basic training was going and that he was not allowed a lot of free time to write letters, and he was not allowed to make phone calls yet, but he loved and missed me very much. Then at the bottom of the letter he wrote, "Wait for me." He had drawn a big heart at the bottom of the letter with an arrow going through it.

I put the letter on my nightstand and thought, now I have a return address to write him that break-up letter. I felt guilty about it, but everyone was right. Nick was never going to marry me, and he needed to understand that I was not going to just live with him forever.

The only problem was I was madly in love with the guy despite his short comings. Breaking up with him in a letter was not something I really wanted to do, but I knew that I had to because I could not give up on the hope of getting married. As I thought about it, I decided that it would be too cold to mail him a break-up letter while he was in basic training.

I would wait until he came home on leave and tell him in person. So, when I wrote him back, it was not a love letter but a short inspiring letter of support for him to make it through basic training. I mailed the letter and tried to get on with my life.

Hanging out with my girlfriends from high school again gave life normalcy and they were all happy to have me back in the fold again. I had not realized how much I had missed going out with them, or just hanging out by the pool or the beach. Being with Nick had taken all my free time, and I could see where I had changed my entire life to fit into his. It felt good to be back in my own skin again.

My roommate Paula introduced me to one of her girlfriends named Janet Smith. Janet was a young black girl who was a knockout in every way. She was an aspiring actress and model, and a real "Playboy" model who had posed nude for the magazine. Janet was just the nicest person; she was down to Earth and did not let her beauty and success change the person she really was inside. That is what I liked about her. Since she was normal and fun to be around Janet invited Paula and me to go to the Playboy Mansion with her for movie night.

She even encouraged me to start modeling. I had never considered it before because I was only 5'3" and models were usually tall. Janet said that I could do print work and TV commercials like she did. She suggested that I meet her agent at the Playboy Agency.

"You have a raw, natural exotic look about you and a killer body," she said.

I was flattered because I had never thought of myself as modeling material. I just thought I was okay looking.

"Are you really serious? Playboy would really have interest in a girl like me?" I asked.

"I have an appointment to see my agent next Monday. You should come with me and meet my agent, then we can go have lunch afterwards," Janet suggested.

"I'll have to get permission from my boss first to take the day off from work. If she gives me the time off, I'll go with you." I told her.

The next day I went to work and told Kathy and the girls in the office about Playboy. Kathy thought it was a good opportunity and gave me the day off. But as the days went by that week, I began to have second thoughts about the whole thing.

Could I really take all my clothes off in front of strangers and a camera? I was kind of body shy, and I started thinking about my grandparents and the fact that my grandfather preached at a church every Sunday morning.

What if someone showed my grandparents a magazine with me naked in it? I knew that they would be disappointed in me. And what would Nick think? All these thoughts kept running through my brain, and by Monday morning I was not so excited about Playboy anymore, but I still went.

That morning at 11 I met Janet outside the Playboy building on Sunset Blvd as planned. We walked into the building together both of us wearing platform heels, blue jeans and tight T-shirts. We got into the elevator and went up to her agent's office.

When we walked into the reception area, Janet said a friendly hello to the receptionist who said that Sandy was waiting for her in the office.

We walked into her agent's office where Janet introduced me to Sandy, and I was offered a seat while the two of them talked about a few jobs that Janet had coming up.

When they finished talking, Janet told Sandy that she brought me along because I had interest in modeling.

Sandy got up from her chair and walked over to me while asking me to stand up. She looked me over and told me that I was a pretty girl.

"What nationality are you?" She asked.

"I'm black." I replied.

"You don't look fully black; in fact, I am trying to figure out what you are mixed with which can be a problem when it comes to getting booked out for jobs. What are you mixed with?" she asked.

"I'm mixed with Creole from my mother's side of the family, which is French, Choctaw Indian tribe and black. My mother and her family are from New Orleans. My father is black, but his mother looks mixed like me because she is part Jewish, Native American and black." I responded.

"You are quite exotic looking and girls that have your type of look do well in Europe," she said.

"I may be able to work with you but I'm telling you now you're not going to get a lot of bookings like Janet. Here in Hollywood when they ask for a black girl, they want a black girl.

That blonde haired, blue eyed California girl look is really hot right now, and you definitely don't fit into that category," she said.

"But that's not what every California girl looks like; we come in all shapes, sizes and colors so what you're telling me is very unrealistic." I said.

"That may be true, but that does not change the fact that I get a ton of calls for girls who look like Christie Brinkley.

As I said before, you would do well in Europe. Let us see what you look like on camera. Playboy has a clothing line, and I could probably use you in a sportswear ad from time to time. I am going to call downstairs and book you an appointment for a test photo shoot to see how you photograph. If you look good on film then I will sign you." She said.

"Can I come in on a Saturday for that photo shoot?" I asked.

"Sure," she said, as she picked up the phone and called the Playboy photo studio downstairs.

I was relieved that she had not mentioned posing nude in the actual "Playboy" magazine. My father would have exploded.

When she hung up the phone, she told me that my photo shoot was set up for 1 p.m. that coming Saturday.

"Don't wear any make-up. We want you as natural as possible," she instructed.

I thanked Sandy for the opportunity then Janet and I left.

Outside, I thanked Janet again for everything she had done to make this happen for me. I was so excited that a Playboy agent thought I was pretty enough to model. Wow! That just amazed me!

After lunch, Janet and I went back to my apartment so she could hang out with Paula. The first thing I did was write Nick telling him everything about my visit to the Playboy Agency. I spent the rest of the night watching TV in bed and wishing Nick were there to hold me while telling myself to get over him.

When Saturday came, I got up and prayed to God that my photo shoot would go well. I was nervous about having my picture taken. What if the pictures turned out badly? Paula had arranged to have the car that she shared with her soon to be ex-husband for the weekend. The plan was she would drive me to the photo shoot and stay with me so I would not be alone.

When we arrived at the studio, I was taken into a small dressing room where a woman told me to remove my clothes and put on the robe, she handed me.

"Hey, I'm not here for the nude magazine. I am here for the sportswear catalog, so why do I have to take my clothes off? I thought you would have a swimsuit or something I could wear." I informed her.

"We still need to know how your body will photograph." She said.

"Don't worry. Only a few Playboy employees will see these photos. It's just a test shoot." She said in an assuring tone.

"Your body is too athletic to be a centerfold anyway, she's right to use you for the catalog. You are going to be okay. Do you like Joan Collins?"

"Yes, I love her; she's a great actress." I said.

"Well, she was here yesterday taking pictures, so think of it this way: you're in the same photo studio that Joan Collins was in yesterday." She said.

The thought of that did put a smile on my face.

"Just keep your mind relaxed and all you have to do is take direction from the photographer and try to look natural." She said.

She messed with my hair a little more then told me to take a deep breath and follow her.

I still felt naked and uncomfortable as I walked out into the studio. I was body shy and self-conscious. The photographer set me up under some lights and a back-drop. Then he told me to take my robe off and relax, as he turned on some music. The Rolling Stones were singing "(I can't get no) Satisfaction" as I dropped my robe. His assistant did some lighting adjustments and said, "look natural" as the photographer started taking pictures of me. He took pictures of me from every angle, including head shots and 30 minutes later it was over.

After picture time in the nude, Paula and I drove back to our apartment and had a late lunch of peanut butter and jelly sandwiches with milk.

Then we drove to Hollywood and saw a movie at Grauman's Chinese Theatre.

A week later Sandy called me from Playboy and said she had gotten my test shots back and wanted me to come in to discuss what she thought of them.

"I can come in after four." I asked.

"Yes, come in at 4:30 day after tomorrow."

"Okay I'll see you then," I said.

When I showed up for my appointment a few days later in my work clothes, Sandy looked at me and said, "You clean up well."

"Thanks, I have to dress this way for work." I told her.

"Well, you look very professional and business like," she said, and continued,

"When we build your portfolio, we need a photo of you dressed like that. You look like you could be in an eyewear or luggage ad dressed like that. You photograph well, and I have decided to sign you for Playboy Models. Now I am going to give you the phone number of one of our photographers to call. We have to get your portfolio started."

She then handed me a contract to read and sign. Then she explained to me she was my agent and all my work had to go through her. She also explained that the agency got a percentage of all the money I earned.

It took me a while to read the entire contract and sign it. After I had signed the contract, Sandy told me that she understood that I had to work for a living, but to be prepared to take off from work for auditions or work if I had a job booked.

"Always make sure to show up on time and be professional, and if you show up to a job high or hung over, I will drop you."

"No problem; I don't drink or do hard drugs."

"Okay," she said. "I guess we have covered everything. Call the photographer and when he shows me the photos, I'll have you come back in so we can decide which photos to use for your portfolio."

I got up and hugged her while telling her how grateful I was that she was willing to take a chance on me. I caught the bus home feeling so proud of myself since I was signed with "Playboy Models." All thanks to Janet, to whom I would always be grateful.

The following week I met one of the photographers on the list, on Saturday morning at Griffith Park. He had instructed me over the phone to bring a variety of clothing for different shots, in various outdoor locations. We drove to four different locations around Los Angeles including the beach for the photos.

The ones I liked the best were at the beach location, only because it was the closest to my true personality. I posed in a red and white striped bikini on roller skates that reminded me of the cover of Linda Ronstadt's "Living in the USA" album cover.

When I returned home, Sally called and asked if I wanted to go to some night club in Inglewood with her. I threw on some jeans and a pair of heels, and we hit the dance floor.

Afterwards we went to "Fat Burger" on La Cienega Blvd at 3 a.m. and ate chili cheeseburgers. By the time I went to bed I was happy, full and well worked out from dancing. Life was good and I was looking forward to the days ahead.

CHAPTER 85

A week later Uncle Phillip called and invited me to have lunch with him the following day on my lunch break.

"I'll buy you lunch at the restaurant across the street from your job," he said.

When I met with him the following day, he told me that he had a business opportunity for me.

"It's concerning our Real Estate company. I was wondering if you had access to the bank's foreclosure list."

"Why?" I asked.

"Because I want to buy up the homes before the bank can foreclose on them," he replied.

"I work in the Accounts Payable Department. I don't have access to that information."

"Well, do you know anyone who does?"

"My friend Tyrone works in that department," I replied.

"Would he be willing to take a little money in exchange for that list?" Uncle Phillip asked.

"I don't know but he has a crush on me. I'll talk to him and get back with you."

I responded.

As I ate my shrimp salad and Uncle Phillip ate his hamburger, it occurred to me for the first time that what he was asking me to do might be illegal, so I asked him if this was illegal, and he assured me that it was not.

"But the bank won't be happy if they find out, because I will be buying the foreclosed properties before the bank can foreclose on them, so you need to keep it quiet," he said. "I am offering you and your friend $200 each for every home I buy off the list."

I told him that I would talk to Tyrone and call when I had an answer.

When I got back to the office, I called Tyrone at his desk and asked him if he wanted to have a drink after work. He was surprised to hear from me because when we first met in the cafeteria, he had asked for my phone number, and I declined to give it to him. After telling him that I was living with my boyfriend he settled for my friendship at the lunch table in the cafeteria.

For this reason, I stressed that this would be a drink between two friends and nothing more.

"I'll even let you drive me home afterwards," I joked.

Tyrone quickly agreed and told me to meet him out front after work.

"I know just the spot to get a good Long Island iced tea," he said.

"Great! I'll see you after work." I told him.

After work I met Tyrone outside in front of the building as planned. He pulled up in front of the building in his new Datsun Nissan, I got in and we drove to a little bar he liked further down Wilshire Blvd not far from the bank.

After Tyrone had his Long Island iced tea in hand and me with my Diet Coke on ice, I explained my uncle's business proposition to him and asked him if he was interested.

"You do realize that is illegal? I could go to Federal prison if I got caught," He said.

"I asked my uncle the same question and he told me that the bank wouldn't like it if they found out; but he didn't say that you could go to prison!"

"Well, it's not like you're robbing cash from the vault downstairs but it's still against the law," he said taking a sip of his drink.

"Well, I'm going to call him when I get home and tell him no; I have no intention of going to jail over $200 for each house he buys off the list." I said.

"Wait a minute." Tyrone said. "He's willing to pay $200 for each house he buys?"

"That's what he offered." I replied.

"Well, that makes it worth my while." He said.

"I have easy access to that list of homes, and it would be nothing for me to print out an extra copy of that list and take it home with me."

I told him, "I don't want anything to do with it. I just signed with Playboy Models, and I do not have time to go to jail. I cannot even imagine having a police record. No amount of money is worth my freedom."

"Look, I can do this without getting caught since I print out that list anyway. All I need to do is give it to your uncle." Said Tyrone.

Tyrone smiled and said, "Now I have an excuse to come over to your apartment."

Once again, I reminded him that I had a boyfriend and that he had no reason to come to my apartment.

Before we left, Tyrone said, "If you were my girl, I would have at least put an engagement ring on your finger. Now, enough about your absent boyfriend, tell me about this Playboy thing you mentioned."

"It's not nude Tyrone. It's for the clothing line and the catalog, and please remember that we're never going to be anything but friends." I informed him.

After Tyrone dropped me off at my apartment, I thought to myself,

"What the hell am I getting myself into?"

I called Uncle Phillip before I went to bed and told him that Tyrone agreed to do it and that I would give Tyrone his number.

A few days later he picked up the first list, and within a week he had purchased 10 of those homes before they were foreclosed. Tyrone received his cash and no one at work suspected anything.

Since Tyrone now knew my uncle, I introduced him to Sally, and he started going dancing with us at the clubs. He even turned us on to a good ocean front club out in Long Beach. Tyrone would have a drink then dance the night away with me and Sally.

My favorite songs to dance to were David Bowie's "Let's Dance" and "Man-Eater" by Hall & Oates. It was fun: you could order food to eat at the club then sit on the beach to eat it; then go right back in and dance the meal off. I noticed that Tyrone and Sally were hitting it off. I had my fingers crossed that the two of them would get together and that would take the pressure off me since I needed Tyrone not to be attracted to me.

CHAPTER 86

A week later I was at Playboy looking at my photos with my agent and realized for the first time that I was a beautiful girl. I had never viewed myself in this light before. You see the same face in the mirror every morning and become accustomed to it.

All my life, until that point, I figured I was just okay looking. But now I was amazed how different I looked in my photos and liked it.

My agent and I chose the photos we wanted in my portfolio, and the head shot that would be my calling card with my information on it. Now all I needed was a booking.

When I got home, I found another letter from Nick in my mailbox. He wrote that he had graduated from basic training and was now entering "Jump School" where he would learn how to jump out of airplanes. Then he had to go to AIT school, after which the Army would allow him to come home on leave for a month before being shipped off to Italy, his permanent duty station.

My heart could hardly wait until he came home on leave to feel his arms around me once again. My common sense told my heart to calm down and not allow myself to be excited because I planned to end the relationship. I wondered how his parents were doing. I had only spoken to his mother a few times since he left town. I thought it was best not to even call them if I had no future with his family.

I had built a nice little life for myself and was happy, even if my heart still longed for Nick, I had to remember that he never wanted to get married.

As the months flew by, I got used to Nick not being around and was finding joy in just being an adult and making it on my own.

Then the day came when Nick was due to come home. I figured I would just sit him down and give him my prepared break up speech. Paula and I drove to LAX Airport to pick him up.

When Nick walked off the airplane he was in his uniform, looking handsome and fit. The minute he saw me he took me into his arms and gave me a long passionate kiss. It felt like time had stopped as we kissed one another.

Finally, Paula told us she had other things to do besides watching the two of us kiss forever.

We got into the back seat of Paula's car where we could barely keep our hands off one another in the back seat. She dropped us off in front of our apartment building then drove off to run some errands to give me and Nick some time alone.

From the moment I shut the front door he began to undress me as we stumbled into the bedroom embraced in a kiss. I thought my body was going to explode as he pushed me down on the bed and took his uniform off in front of me. As he took off my clothes and lay on top of me, I chickened out. I could not break up with him as I had planned. My heart belonged to him, and I wanted us to be together.

He made love to me for his usual 10 minutes, then he collapsed into a deep sleep for a few hours.

As I lay next to him, I watched him sleeping, disappointed that nothing had changed with him in the sex department. I had hoped that after going through basic training, including a daily workout, that he might have gained some staying power.

Not only did I wonder what was wrong with him, but I had no idea how to approach him about the subject. I was afraid I would wound his ego for life if I just told him straight out that he sucked in the sack. Then the thought that maybe he thought this was normal crossed my mind. I asked myself again, what would I do if Nick were paralyzed from the waist down. The answer was I would still love him and want to be with him.

So, I decided to keep faking it. Having a life partner was more important to me than sex. Now all he had to do was put a ring on my finger.

Nick missed me so much that he spent his first two days home with me in my apartment, which he kept referring to as our apartment. Then he was off with his friends drinking and smoking pot until the early morning hours again

I would come home from work, and he would be gone already, just like before. I kept telling myself that he would grow out of it and realize that the party was over, and that going into the Army was a good thing because it kept him away from his drugged-up drinking friends he chose to hang out with.

One night, he was at the apartment when I returned home from work. We were eating dinner together and talking about my modeling for Playboy. Nick told me how much he liked my photos when the phone rang. He got up from the table to answer it, then a minute later I heard him say,

"Who the fuck are you?"

His voice sounded angry and elevated. I got up from the table, walked over to him and asked who was on the phone.

He looked at me mad as hell and said, "some fucking guy saying he's back in town."

I took the telephone receiver from his hand realizing that Andy was on the phone. I covered the phone mouthpiece told Nick,

"It's just Andy, a tennis player my Aunt Carol tried to set me up with. Honestly, I had forgotten about him; that is how unimportant he is to me." I said.

The look on Nick's face was priceless and he was really pissed off. I, on the other hand, was unfazed because I knew I had been faithful, and I figured it might help him to realize that other men were attracted to me. Maybe he might step up his game and make an official commitment to me.

I got on the phone in front of Nick and said, "Hi Andy. Remember that boyfriend I was telling you about?"

"I remember," he said.

"Well, he's home, and judging from the look on his face right now I don't think he wants you calling me."

"Okay, I guess you decided to stay with him then."

"Yeah." I replied.

"Well, I wish you luck." He said.

I hung up the phone and told Nick the whole story about how I had planned on breaking up with him, and how my Aunt Carol had set me up with Andy. I said that I went to dinner with Andy but refused to let him kiss me.

"I went out with him to see if I could be attracted to someone else," I told him.

"I even told him about you, and he told me you were crazy for not putting a ring on my finger. Then he flew to London the next day to play tennis. He was calling to tell me he was back in LA."

Then I explained to him that I wanted to get married and have a kid one day, and how he never wanted to get married but expected me to wait for him to get out of the Army. I looked at him and said, "I don't think the relationship you want with me is the one I want with you. The least you could do is put a promise ring or something on my finger." I said.

There was nothing he could say because he knew I was right. After the phone call and my little speech Nick started worrying that someone might steal me away from him while he was gone. And he told me that as soon as he could afford it that he would buy me a ring.

Suddenly, overnight, Nick started spending less time drinking with his friends and more time with me. He also spent time with his family and tried to clean-up his act.

CHAPTER 87

When the day came for Nick to fly overseas to Italy, his parents picked him up from my apartment at 6 a.m. I was not going to the airport with them because I had to be to work by 8. We kissed goodbye at my front door, and he hugged me like he never wanted to let me go. He called me his little monkey and was gone again.

I went back to my routine of going to work, dancing at clubs on the weekends with Tyrone and Sally and on occasion Paula would tag along.

Also, I started getting calls from my agent Sandy to go on auditions a few times a month. A few were for TV commercials, and on one of the auditions I had to kiss another actor. It was not only uncomfortable, but the guy had bad breath and left spit on my lip. The other was a cattle-call for a movie, where I sat in a waiting room with at least 50 other girls, most of them drop dead gorgeous.

I had to do a cold read and had 20 minutes to memorize my audition lines. Once it was my turn to go into the audition room, I was nervous as hell as the casting agent told me to turn around. I suddenly knew why this was named a "cattle-call" because I felt like a piece of meat as three men and a woman checked my body out. Then I had to say my lines into a camera. I did not get either one of the jobs. On occasion I would go on an audition asking for a black girl only to be told that I was not black enough, or I was too exotic looking. It was all very frustrating.

Janet, on the other hand, was getting enough work to support herself because you knew Janet was black when you looked at her. At this point she was breaking into a new market called music videos and was in talks to be in a Michael Jackson video for his new album "Thriller." She had been chosen by Michael Jackson himself to be in a video for the title song "Thriller." She had already met with him and his people and passed the audition. I was quite happy for her and her success, since she was a beautiful girl with a good heart, and I believed she deserved every drop of success that came her way.

I really was starting to think that maybe going to college was what I was meant to do right now because getting quality work for a girl who looked like me seemed almost impossible.

Once Nick arrived at his new duty station in Italy, I started getting letters each week. I could see that he was really trying to make me happy. His letters were passionate and filled with details of his new life in the Army. He always ended each letter telling me how much he loved me and missed me, and at the bottom of each one he would write "wait for me."

He called me collect a few times a month, which always cost me a small fortune. Then he started writing about how homesick he was, which was odd to me. If I had the chance to live in Italy, I would be enjoying my surroundings, not complaining. He also mentioned his fears about some other guy stealing me away from him while he was gone. He wrote that his Army buddies saw my photo and told him that girls who looked like me did not stay single for long.

I assured him that I was not even thinking about seeing other guys because I was too busy trying to figure out how to fit college into my busy schedule. The only thing I thought about was buying myself a used car and had no thoughts about other men.

Then one day I came home from work and found my usual weekly letter from Nick in the mailbox. As I opened it, I was expecting to read the usual stuff he wrote about, but I quickly saw that this letter was different from the rest.

I was shocked to read that he was asking me to marry him! I could hardly believe what I was reading as he poured his heart out to me. He wrote that the thought of me being with someone else drove him wild; how he had come to realize that he wanted to spend the rest of his life with me as his wife.

I was so touched, that tears began to run down my cheeks. I rushed into the living room where Paula was sitting on the sofa eating one of her homemade cupcakes. I showed her my proposal letter and yelled out "I'm getting married."

After reading the letter Paula stood up and hugged me and told me how happy she was for me.

"I think I'm in shock because Nick told me that he never wanted to get married. Now look what has happened; it is a miracle from God. Thank you, God in heaven for making my dream come true,"

I exclaimed looking at the ceiling.

I was just on cloud nine as I called my father to give him the good news. I could hardly wait to tell him I was right, and he was wrong.

He was not at all thrilled with the news.

"I still don't trust him because he's an idiot."

As I called and told the rest of my family members over the next few days, none were happy for me. Everyone told me that I was making the biggest mistake of my life, and they all said that they did not trust Nick.

That Saturday Nick called me collect, and the first thing he asked me was if I got his letter. I told him that his letter had arrived three days ago.

"Are you really serious?" I asked him.

"As a heart attack," He went on to say that he had been thinking about it for a while, and how he had decided that he wanted to be with me forever, and how he wanted me to live in Italy with him as his wife.

"Do you want to do this when you come home on leave? "I asked.

"No, I don't want to wait that long, I want to get married as soon as possible."

He said that he wanted me to move to Italy and marry him there.

"Get here as soon as you can because I miss you," he said.

I asked if he had any money saved up to support this idea.

"Not right now, but I know that you do. I don't know how much you have saved, but if we start saving now, we can put our money together and do this." He explained.

"Italy is a long way from Los Angeles." I told him. "I have to quit my job, and Paula has to find another roommate. And you should make sure we have a place to live before I get there."

We talked for a few more minutes, before he told me he had to hang up because he had to be in formation in five minutes. We said our goodbyes and from that day on my life changed. Little did I know it would never be the same again.

CHAPTER 88

As the weeks passed, my entire family embarked on a mission to talk me out of moving to Italy and marrying Nick. They all believed I would be making the biggest mistake of my life. Aunt Louise even took me out to lunch to tell me so.

"Being a military wife is a poverty filled existence." She told me.

"Do you really want to live that type of life?" She asked.

"He only signed up for a few years not a whole lifetime," I told her.

"You watch, one day you will live to regret marrying this idiot." She said.

A chill went up my spine when she said that to me. I told her she was wrong about Nick. "Everyone said he would never marry me, and everyone was wrong." I said.

Meanwhile my father's hatred of Nick had reached new heights and now he was telling anyone who would listen that Nick was taking his first-born child away to a foreign country. He started coming over to my apartment every other day after work to tell me what a huge mistake I was making, and how afraid he was of what could happen to me in a foreign country with no family to fall back on.

I kept telling him that I was going to be alright, and that I would come home as often as I could. Then I reminded him that his parents did not want him to marry my mother, but he followed his heart.

"And look how that turned out: it ended in divorce and the death of my son." He said bitterly.

"Well, nothing bad is going to happen to me, and I'm not getting divorced." I said.

Sandy at Playboy was the only person who was happy for me. I asked her if she knew of an agency in Italy that I could sign with.

"You told me that I could get more work in Europe, and now that I am moving there, I might actually stand a chance of getting some print work or a commercial," I said to her.

"I'll contact a few agents I know in Milan and see what I can set up for you."

I had already given Paula and California Federal notice that I would be leaving, as I made it my mission in life to save every extra dime, I could get my hands on. I ate Top Ramen for dinner and Cream of Wheat for breakfast just to save money on food. I quit buying make-up and clothes. No more Frances Denny make-up for me, it was sad, but it had to be done.

A few weeks later Sandy called me at work to tell me that an agency in Milan, Italy wanted to sign me.

"They are called the Nicole Agency." She said.

"They liked your photos that I sent and want to use you for print ads. The agency is new, and they need a girl who looks like you."

I was thrilled now that I had some work lined up in Italy. She gave me the address and phone number for the agency and told me to call them as soon as I arrived in Italy.

I could hardly wait to leave work so I could go home and write Nick the good news. Things really seemed to be falling into place for me and it seemed as if all my dreams were coming true. Nick and I had been writing one another making plans for our future together, and I found that very romantic.

He seemed to be spending a lot of time training in Germany, and sometimes he would be gone for an entire month. Nick wrote that he did not like training in Germany because it snowed there, and he hated training in the snow.

He also told me that he had put in the paperwork to get permission from the Army to get married. He said the request was going up his chain of command for approval.

I could not believe we had to get permission from the Army to get married; I had never heard of such a thing. I really did not like the idea that the Army could tell Nick if he could get married or not. It was as if he were a little kid asking mom and dad for permission to go outside to play. I was not even around the Army yet, and I already disliked it.

CHAPTER 89

The weeks flew by fast as I ran around trying to get everything done such as applying for my first passport, buying my airline ticket, and moving all the stuff I was not taking with me into my grandparent's garage. I was shipping some albums to Nick's company in a box with some of my other things. I bought a backpack for my little cassette player and cassettes. Besides my clothes and shoes, that was all I could take with me.

My Grandmother was nice enough to give me an old traveling trunk from the 1950's and a few suitcases from the same time period which was very cool. I spent my last remaining few months in Los Angeles going out with all my friends and tanning on the beach whenever I was not working.

By the time I was due to leave, Paula still had not found another roommate, and I felt rather bad about that.

The morning I was due to fly out, my father drove me to the airport and insisted upon stopping at Kentucky Fried Chicken on the way. He said he wanted to buy me a bucket of chicken to eat on the airplane. I really did not want any chicken, but it dawned on me as I looked at the worried look on his face that he wanted to take care of me for the last time.

So, I went along with it and let him buy the chicken. Since he was late for everything but work, I told him that my plane left an hour earlier than it did. I then had some time to kill once we arrived at the airport, my father went inside with me and stayed until it was time for me to board the plane.

As I hugged and kissed him goodbye, I felt sorry for him because he looked sad. I told him not to worry about me, that I would call him as soon as I arrived in London. Then I boarded the plane feeling as if I were embarking upon a great adventure.

I got settled into my seat and took out my little battery-operated cassette player and headphones. I relaxed as Elton John begin to sing *"Daniel."*

As the plane took off, I felt no fear about moving to a foreign country at 19; it was the beginning of a great adventure as far as I was concerned. I looked out the window and said, "Goodbye LA, for now."

I decided to fly to London and take the train the rest of the way. I wanted to take the scenic route and see the countryside. The flight to London, England seemed like it took a lifetime, but I finally arrived.

The first thing I noticed was everyone had a heavy British accent, and I thought their accents were so cool. I felt like I had stepped back in time and into another world and I liked it. After collecting my luggage from the baggage claim area, I found a phone booth and called my father collect through the overseas operator to tell him I had arrived in London safely. Then I got a taxi outside the airport to take me to a train station where I was to take a train to a place called Dover where I would board something called a boat train. The boat train was going to take me across the English Channel, and from there I would take the train all the way to Italy.

When the taxi dropped me off in front of the station with my luggage, a uniformed train station porter rushed up to me asking if I needed any help.

"Yes, I do thanks." I said.

He took my luggage and loaded it on to a cart with wheels. I told him where I was going, and he took me to a ticket window to purchase my ticket for the boat train. Then he took me to the correct train platform to wait in line for boarding so I would not get lost in the station and miss my train. I thanked him for all his help and tipped him well.

As I boarded the boat train, I was excited about going across the English Channel for the first time. I thought to myself: this is beyond my wildest dreams.! I found a window seat and looked out at the choppy sea before me and wondered, what is underneath all that water. Were there sharks as well as old sunken ships from battles that had happened long ago? My imagination ran wild, and I felt like a child seeing the world for the first time.

But 20 minutes into the ride across the Channel, I suddenly began to feel dizzy and weak. My forehead began to drip beads of sweat, and my stomach felt nauseated as the boat train moved at full speed through the choppy waves of water. I did not know what was going on, but I knew it was not good.

A little old English lady who was sitting across from me realized what was going on. She handed me a sick bag that the boat train had near each seat. I got the bag open just in time to throw up into it. As I threw up, I could hear her telling me in a thick English accent that I was seasick.

I took my head out of the bag and wiped my mouth with a tissue from my purse.

"What does seasick mean?" I asked her.

Instead of answering me she reached into her purse and produced a small bottle of pills. She handed me two of them and told me to swallow them.

"It will make the nausea go away." She said.

I swallowed the pills and thanked her.

"Now just sit back and try to relax, the pills will take effect soon." She said.

As the pills began to take effect, I silently thanked God for the little old English lady coming to my rescue.

Now, instead of enjoying the boat train ride across the Channel, I could not wait to get off. I was relieved when the boat train reached land and I was able to get off although I still had a few hours before my next train was due to leave the station.

Exhausted and hungry, I collected my luggage and went into a little train station pub to eat and rest. I ordered a cup of Earl Grey tea and some fish and chips. The food and tea helped make me feel better and it tasted delicious, much better than the fish in America.

I remembered watching the movie "Oliver" when I was a kid, where the characters ordered fish and chips. Now, here I was in England eating real English fish and chips. I was excited as I sat back in my chair and just took in my surroundings. I observed everything that was going on around me and did not want to miss a thing.

The train station, which was huge and beautiful, had hundreds of people walking and rushing about. I observed the racial diversity of people standing in line to buy train tickets. There was even a line to buy different currencies right there at the station, although, so far, everyone was accepting American dollars and I had not been required to convert my money.

There were also people waiting for a train or getting off one, many of whom looked like businesspeople commuting back and forth from work. I liked the way the people dressed and looked, and I made up my mind right then and there that the English people were cool.

I sat there slowly drinking tea and observing my new surroundings until 30 minutes before my train was due to leave. Once I got to the area where all the trains were, I was mesmerized. Once again, I felt like I had walked back in history as if time stood still and nothing had changed. As I stood there, I felt its history which had seen troops from World Wars I and II, along with various other wars.

But the strangest thing was that it all felt so familiar to me, like I was coming home after being away for a long time. I felt totally comfortable in this environment, and for one quick moment I saw flashes on the movie screen in my mind of soldiers coming back from war to their waiting sweethearts wearing clothes from the 1918s and 1940s. I could see that the train station held many memories, and I was only seeing a small fraction of what it held.

My thoughts were interrupted when I heard a man's voice over a loudspeaker announcing the departing trains ready for boarding one of which was mine.

A porter approached me and asked if he could take my luggage to be put on the cargo car. I thanked him, handed him the cart I had my luggage on, then boarded the train.

The interior of the train was cool looking and reminded me of an old Alfred Hitchcock movie. Quite impressive, it had sleeping compartments and a dining car with a bar area. I felt like I was living out a dream that I never had, but God had surprised me with it anyway.

Trying to contain my excitement, I found my seat which was in a small compartment that seated four people and had four bunk beds which came out of the wall. I was sharing the compartment with three other girls around my age. They were all very friendly and introduced themselves. Everyone was dressed like hippies from the 60s.

They told me that they were on their way to Paris for a rock concert. Their accents were so cute that I found myself wishing I had a British accent. One of the girls had a boom box and put in a Rolling Stones cassette.

As Mick Jagger sang *"(I Aint Got No) Satisfaction,"* one of the girls pulled out a small flask with liquor in it and passed it around to everyone. When it came to me, "I said thanks, but I don't drink."

"Really, and why is that?" One girl asked.

"I just think it tastes really bad and I don't like the way it makes me feel." I replied.

"Well cheers then!" She drunkenly proclaimed and took another drink from the flask.

They asked me where I was from, and when I told them they all wanted to hear stories about growing up in Hollywood. They in turn told me about the club scene in London, and what it was like growing up there. When I said I was moving to Italy to model and get married, they all thought that was romantic.

After the flask had gone around a few times, one of the girls got up and started dancing and singing to the "Rolling Stones."

This was a real blast, me on a night train with three drunk English hippie girls on our way to Paris.

When we arrived in Paris a few hours later, my new friends wished me luck and got off the train. It was early evening and from what I saw from the train window Paris was beautiful. I took in the beauty of the lights of Paris and wished I could have gotten off the train with those girls. It would have been an awesome experience to attend a rock concert in Paris, but I did not have the time.

A few hours later I went to the dining car for some dinner. As I sat at a table in the dining car, I noticed that I was surrounded by people speaking different languages. Some were speaking German, French, Italian, and African languages. There were people from all over the world on that train, even white American Hari Krishna's.

As people around me ate and drank, I had a sandwich and observed my surroundings trying to preserve the experience in my memory bank forever and how it felt to be there.

After dinner I returned to my compartment where I listened to music and looked through the latest copy of Vogue magazine. Then I went to sleep in my bunk, which was comfortable.

In the morning I went to the dining car for breakfast. The food was different from what I was used to in America. For breakfast instead of eggs and bacon I had what was called a "Continental Breakfast" that consisted of different rolls, croissants with jam and butter with some fruit on the side.

Instead of American coffee, I drank something called Espresso for the first time. I immediately loved the thick strong Espresso which was served in a tiny coffee cup in shots.

So far, the beauty and allure of Europe was like nothing I had ever seen, and the movies I had watched growing up had not done it justice. I had picked up a "teach yourself Italian" book that I was struggling with before leaving the States. So far language had not been a problem, because everyone I had met so far spoke fluent English or broken English that I could understand.

As I traveled on that train, I wondered why so many people from Europe left and moved to the United States. Why would anyone want to give up their citizenship from this beautiful place? I had not even reached my destination yet and I was starting to think that I never wanted to go back to the States.

CHAPTER 90

For the first time in my life, I truly felt free as I took a deep breath and relaxed. My old life already seemed like a distant memory of a dream, and now I had awakened into a new and better reality.

I spent five days traveling by train, and during that time period I became educated about different races and cultures. I met and had dinner with a full-blooded African couple which was extremely exciting to me, because African Americans were mixed with different races. I had only seen full-blooded Africans in National Geographic magazines.

Their skin tone was the most beautiful thing to me because it glowed. Impeccably dressed, they were tall, graceful and with slim body types that I wished I had inherited from my African genes. As well, their facial bone structure and eyes were a work of art to me. They both had left Africa and moved to France for school where they met and fell in love. Both had earned master's degrees in business, worked for investment firms in France, and were fluent in five languages.

I even met Germans from West Berlin who were fluent in English.

Everyone I met during that train ride seemed interesting and intelligent to me and I fell in love with the Europeans as a whole, including their unique looks. I was starting to think that I could never go back to the States, not after this experience.

When I arrived at the train station in downtown Vicenza, Italy, a small town in Northern Italy, 20 minutes away from Venice by train and not far from Verona. Vicenza was the home of the military base where Nick was stationed.

It was a little after four in the afternoon when I stepped off the train on to the platform of a small quaint train station. I collected my baggage, put it on a luggage cart and rolled it outside into the late afternoon sunlight. I stood outside the train station and just looked around at the colorful old buildings. Once again, I felt like I had stepped into another world as the feeling of having been there before washed over me again and again. It felt as if I had come home after being away for a long period of time, and I was falling in love all over again with my home.

I even wanted to take my shoes off and feel the dirt of the land between my toes once again. It was crazy because I had never been anywhere in Europe before, but I felt like I was finally home again.

I forced myself to snap out of it and focus on the task at hand, which was finding a hotel room for the night. I spotted a hotel across the street from the train station and figured it would be perfect for my immediate needs for the night, as well as being close enough for me to use the train station's luggage cart to get my luggage to the hotel without trying to carry it all by myself.

As I was beginning to cross the street, a train station porter approached me and asked if I needed help. I told him that I was going to the hotel across the street if he wanted to help me get my luggage over there. The porter happily helped me get my luggage into the hotel lobby. As I stood at the front desk, I could hear the hotel phone ringing, it looked like an antique from the 1950's. In fact, the whole hotel looked ancient and was furnished with 1950's furniture.

Again, I felt as though I had walked into an old movie and Ingrid Bergman would walk down the stairs any minute. I stood at the front desk and watched the desk clerk answer the phone. I heard him say "Pronto" instead of hello as I stood listening to him speak Italian on the phone.

After the desk clerk had finished on the phone, he looked at me and said something in Italian that I could not understand.

"Can you speak English?" I asked.

He smiled and said, "Ah, you Americano."

"Yes, I need a room for the night." I replied.

In broken English he told me the price for a single room in Italian and American currency. I told him that I would pay with American money, which turned out to be $20. He then told me that I needed to leave my passport with him at the front desk until I checked out. I gave him my passport, then signed my name into the hotel's registration book. As the clerk walked me to my room I asked if there were a telephone, I could use to call my boyfriend and my father on?

He said there was a phone in my room, and since I was unmarried, my boyfriend would not be allowed in my room.

At first, I thought he was joking, but I suddenly realized he was not. How old fashioned. Back home in Los Angeles no one cared if a man was in your hotel room, I thought to myself. Time truly stood still here. Both the hotel and the rules were from the 50s era. This kind of pissed me off because I wanted to spend my first night in Italy in Nick's arms, not in bed alone. I could hardly wait to call Nick to let him know that not only had I arrived, but we would both be sleeping alone that night.

After the clerk left my room, I looked around and noticed how small and clean it was. The bed was a metal twin bed made in the 50s that had a reading light attached to the headboard. There was a wooden nightstand by the bed with an old black phone and a Bible on it. And over in the corner there was a small dresser with a large wardrobe cabinet next to it. I had to share the bathroom, which was down the hall, with the other guests on my floor.

I sat down on the bed and picked up the phone to call my father collect. I knew he was worried about me, and I wanted to set his mind at ease and let him know that I had arrived in Italy safely. It took me a good 10 minutes to get the call through with the overseas operator, but finally I heard my father's voice.

I gave him the name of my hotel and the phone number. He was happy to know that I had arrived safely. I told him how beautiful Europe was and how much I loved it already. Before hanging up he made me promise to write home once a week.

Then I called Nick at the barracks. Once I heard his voice, I felt overwhelmed with excitement. I told him that I had arrived and was checked into a hotel downtown across from the train station. I gave him the name of the hotel, and he assured me that he would show up in 20 minutes.

Before hanging up I broke the bad news to him about the "no men in your room" rule. He was just as disappointed as I was.

Then he said, "At least we can be together, that's all I care about. I'm on my way."

I hung up the phone and rushed to the bathroom down the hall to shower and put on fresh clothes and make-up.

Back in my room I heard the telephone ringing. It was the desk clerk telling me I had a guest downstairs waiting for me. Man, he got here quick, I thought. I told the desk clerk I would be right down and hung up the phone. I quickly grabbed a pair of blue jeans, a Elton John T-shirt, and my short ankle Frye boots and put them on as fast as I could. I finished getting dressed, grabbed my purse and rushed downstairs like I was running from a fire.

And there he was waiting for me, wearing his Army fatigues looking handsome as hell. I rushed into his open arms, and we engaged in a long passionate kiss, neither one of us caring if the desk clerk was watching us.

We stood there for a moment in a long embrace holding one another, happy to be in each other's arms again. Nick took my hand and led me out of the hotel onto the street where we walked to the bus stop just across the street.

As we reached the bus stop, a very cool looking public bus called "The Autobus" pulled up. It looked like a trolley car to me. Instead of paying the bus driver when you got on the bus, you were trusted to put your money in a machine that printed out your bus ticket for you.

Nick told me that every now and then the bus police would get on and ask to see your ticket just to make sure that no one was riding for free.

"What happens if you get busted riding for free?"

"Then the Italian police will make you pay a fine." He said.

We found two empty seats and sat down. Nick put his arm around me and held me close to him. It was only a 10-minute bus ride from my hotel to the base where Nick was stationed. The bus let us off right in front of the base, and as we walked to the front gate of the base together, I saw a sign in front of the base that read "Welcome to Caserma Ederle."

I noticed military police with loaded weapons and bomb sniffing dogs at the front gate.

Nick walked me over to a small office just inside the front gate to sign me in as a guest, the two soldiers on duty in the office had loaded weapons as well. This is a crazy situation, I thought to myself as I looked around me taking in the whole scene.

I was told to leave my ID at the front gate, and in exchange, I was given a guest pass to put around my neck and told to always wear it while on the base.

Nick and I started walking and I asked him why there were soldiers and military police with loaded weapons and dogs at the front gate of the base.

He told me that a terrorist group called the "Red Brigade," had kidnapped a general named Dozier so the base was always on a 24-hour alert.

"We are part of something called NATO and there's a lot of terrorist activity in Europe. Everyone gets rotated to pull guard duty at the front gate, including me."

I knew nothing about terrorist groups. Back home in the United States the closest I had ever come to this was when Sandie and I went to see the "Palestinian" staring Vanessa Redgrave. I remember the movie theater in Beverly Hills had been bombed in protest of the film. So, although Europe was a cool beautiful place, you were also in constant danger of a terrorist attack which was not cool.

CHAPTER 91

I had never seen a military base before and so far, it was proving to be quite an eye-opener. It reminded me of a TV show called MASH, but this was the real thing, and it was a trip.

As we walked down the street together, I noticed other soldiers walking past us. Sometimes Nick would stop dead in his tracks to salute some of them as they walked past. I asked Nick why he was stopping to salute some of the soldiers.

He explained that they were officers, and whenever he saw an officer, he was required to stop and salute them. Almost everyone we passed on the street had on a uniform. The base was like its own little world of "GI Joe's."

I saw row after row of ugly green buildings that all looked the same which served as barracks for the different military companies. At least they could have painted the buildings nice different colors, I thought.

Nick took me on a short sightseeing tour of the base, which only took 20 minutes because it was so small. There was a small movie theater where American movies were played, and a pizzeria that made American style pizza and served beer. I looked at Nick and asked him why on Earth would someone want American pizza when they could eat the real thing outside the base gates?

"Some of these guys get homesick for America so everything on the base is mostly American." He replied.

He then showed me a supermarket called a Commissary where only American food was sold. Then he showed me an American department store called the PX which sold clothing and other items. There was also a section of the base that had barracks for the regular Army personnel that Nick referred to as "legs". There were barracks for the Army medics and military police as well. I asked him why he called regular Army guys "legs."

"They are called 'legs' because they do not jump out of airplanes. They serve as ground troops to back us up." He said jokingly.

Nick gave me the impression that he thought that he was somehow better than the soldiers that did not jump. It seemed to me like he had some sort of elitist attitude about the situation.

"Do you look down on them just because they don't jump out of airplanes? That is pretty messed up. Correct me if I'm wrong, but I thought they got shot at just like you."

"Sure, they do, but this patch I'm wearing means that I jump, and they don't. "He answered with a bit of an arrogant tone.

We approached the Airborne Company that he had been assigned to called "Charlie Company first of the 509th." After that sign you saw another that read, "Welcome to Airborne Country."

Now all the soldiers I saw were Airborne soldiers who wore bright red berets, tilted to one side of their heads.

We walked into the building of his barracks and when we reached the front desk, he signed me in on a guest roster then took me upstairs to show me his room which was on the second floor of the building. As we reached the top of the stairs, I heard a guy yell, "female in the building."

"Why did that guy yell female in the building?" I asked Nick.

"So, no one runs out of the bathroom naked in front of you," he answered.

As Nick led me further down the long hallway toward his room, I heard the same voice that yelled female in the building yell, "Hey Ortiz, I slept with your mother last night and she liked it and after I finished with her, I slept with your girlfriend Vicky, the one you keep sending all of your money to every month."

I looked around the hallway for the source of that voice and spotted a tall, light brown-haired guy with a muscular build and a bright pink sunburn on his face. He had bright blue eyes that just shined out at you with a mischievous gleam.

"What an asshole," I thought to myself. Then I looked at the poor Spanish guy he was saying all this too. The poor guy was standing in the doorway across the hall from the guy yelling out the insults.

He replied, "fuck you Jughead."

Nick saw the look of horror on my face and laughed.

"Don't worry. That is Pierson and Oliver joking around. Pierson just messes with him because Oliver was stupid enough to catch syphilis years ago and never went for treatment. Now it is too late for treatment; syphilis has traveled to his brain. The Army is giving him a medical discharge and he's just waiting for his paperwork to come through so he can be shipped to Walter Reed Army Hospital."

This was unheard of to me with today's medical advances. Really? The only person I had ever heard of this happening to was Caligula Cesar, the Roman Emperor. Back then there was no treatment for the disease. But this guy had no excuse; why did this fool never get treatment? I mean, who the hell catches syphilis and lets it go untreated?

Then I heard Oliver yell, "Hey Pierson, can I shine your boots?"

I could hardly believe what I was hearing; this guy was asking permission to shine Pierson's boots after all the insults he had just hurled at him. This guy really is brain-dead, I thought.

As we reached the door of Nick's room, I heard another voice yell, "Hey Vanderpool."

It seemed like there was a lot of yelling going on in these halls.

When we walked into his room, I saw four beds with matching wall lockers. There were three guys in the room going about their business.

Nick introduced me to a guy named Paulson who was lying on his bunk listening to an Air Supply album. He had his stereo set up on the side of his bunk, with a huge poster of Olivia Newton-John hanging above it.

He was a big boned, tall white guy who looked like he had been corn fed, breast-fed and raised on a farm. He chewed tobacco and had a big spit can proudly displayed on the floor between his bunk and his stereo system.

Nick then introduced me to his other two roommates. One was a black guy named Jim who had joined the Army on the buddy system with his cousin. The other was a Spanish guy by the name of Jose Sanchez, who took my hand and kissed it when Nick introduced us to one another.

He told me that everyone called him, "The Anaconda of Love."

I asked why people called him that?

He told me that many women came to him and loved him of their own free will, and that was why he was "The Anaconda of Love."

All righty then, I thought, this guy is really living in a dream world.

Just then the guy they called Pierson walked into the room followed by a guy everyone called the ant-man.

I asked Nick why everyone called him that and was told, "because he has a nose like an anteater although his real name is Jay Vanderpool," Nick said.

Pierson looked at Nick and told him that I was too good looking for him. Then the other guys started teasing him as well. Vanderpool had the nerve to ask me what I saw in an ugly dog like Nick.

"He's not ugly. I happen to love the way he looks." I replied.

Then to make matters worse, Pierson came up with the bright idea to welcome me into Charlie Company by picking me up and swinging me out of the barracks second-story window.

Pierson had my feet in his hands and Vanderpool had my arms as they laughed while swinging me out of the big open window in Nick's room. I screamed for my life as they were swinging me back-and-forth, and my life flashed before my eyes.

When they put me down and let go of me, Pierson told me to consider myself lucky that they had not dropped me out of the window like they did all the new "Cherries."

"It's a Charlie Company tradition to throw all the newbies out of the second-story window here at Charlie Company." Vanderpool proudly proclaimed.

"Then you're really Airborne." He said, as they all started laughing.

I looked at all of them like they were crazy and said, "I could care less about your company traditions. My life just flashed before my eyes you assholes."

By now, I was pissed off at Nick because he did not try to stop them and just went along with it.

They all got quiet for minute when they realized I was really pissed off. Then Nick broke the ice by suggesting that we all go to the pizzeria for some food and beer.

After sitting in the booth with Nick and his friends at the pizzeria for an hour I was bored and wishing that we could be alone for our first night together. I was tired of hearing the jukebox playing REO Speed wagon Styx and Journey songs. I did not complain to Nick because I felt he wanted to show me off to his friends. And when it came down to it, where could we really go to be alone?

We could not go back to my hotel room and his room was out of the question. It was a disappointing situation, but I told myself to just be happy that we were together again and getting married.

While we were eating pizza, Nick told me that one of his friends suggested that I check into a hotel called the "Hotel Elena" that all the Americans used across the street from the base.

"The rooms don't cost a lot, and no one cares if we are sleeping in the same room unmarried." He said.

I agreed with him, but what I really wanted was to go out and rent a small flat and live among the Italians. I figured I had spent all my life around Americans, now I wanted to experience living like an Italian.

After spending another boring hour at the pizzeria listening to Nick and his friends talk, we finally left, and Nick took me for a walk on the football field. We sat on the bleachers together and he held me in his arms as we looked up at the stars in the sky. Finally, a romantic moment as he kissed me under the stars and told me how happy he was that I was there with him.

Then he walked me to the bus stop in front of the base and put his arms around me as we waited for the bus to show up.

"I'll come to your hotel tomorrow after I'm released from duty to get you and your things. I'll get us a room at the Hotel Elena, and we can start waking up together again." He said.

When the bus arrived a few minutes later I realized that he was not going to take the short bus ride downtown with me. I tried not to get upset as he explained that he had to get up at four in the morning.

Once I was back in my hotel room, I put my pajamas on and went to bed. Before falling to sleep, I prayed to God to take care of me and Nick and to hurry and get us into our own apartment.

CHAPTER 92

When I awoke the following morning at 8, the sun was shining brightly, and it looked like it was going to be a warm beautiful day. I felt rested and excited, and I could hardly wait to walk around town as I hurried to put on a pair of jeans and a T-shirt.

In the bathroom, I washed my face, brushed my teeth, combed my hair and put on some make up. I grabbed my purse and headed downstairs to the lobby ready for coffee and breakfast.

As I passed the front desk, the clerk asked me if I wanted to pay for another night. I told him that my boyfriend would be coming to pick me up later that afternoon. The desk clerk then warned me that I had to be checked out of the hotel by 2 o'clock that afternoon. Otherwise, I would have to pay for another night.

I asked him if I could check out right then, but keep my luggage behind the counter until four or five that afternoon?

He agreed to let me do that, and I rushed back upstairs to get my things out of my room. A few minutes later I checked out of the hotel and walked out into the warm morning sunlight. I was happy as I looked around me at all the people walking up and down the streets.

I walked for few blocks and found a small restaurant where I sat eating a Panini and drinking a cup of Espresso. Everyone around me was speaking Italian, and even though I could not understand a single word, it sounded beautiful. I just sat there for a while listening to them speak, in hopes of learning the language.

After an hour, I decided to walk around town to get familiar with my new surroundings. As I walked around going in and out of the shops, I could not shake the feeling that I had gone back in time somehow and was home again. It was so strange to me because I had never been to Italy before, but inside of me it felt as if I had come home, and I felt an odd sense of inner peace. I felt so comfortable around the old buildings, and I could still see the bullet holes in them from wars fought long ago. It was like walking through a living history book.

I walked to the town Square where I purchased some bread and began to feed the pigeons, all the while thinking how I never wanted to leave Italy.

As men walked past me in the Square some of them would say to me, "Ciao que Bella." I looked it up in my little self-taught Italian handbook and found out it meant "hello beautiful" in English. This was new to me because no one in Los Angeles told me I was beautiful on the street, much less said hello in passing unless they knew you.

I liked the Italian way of treating women on the street a lot better than the American way. Here I was viewed as a beautiful woman while in Los Angeles I was just a small fish in a big pond.

I spent the entire day just walking around the little town of Vicenza looking at art, clothing and taking in the beauty of the Italian lifestyle. I was just totally amazed as I sat on top of Mount Barraco, after hiking up some very steep steps to visit the "il San Antuario Della Madonna" who was the city's patron saint. It had a two-sectioned archway that had been constructed to honor the Virgin Mary in 1746.

Then I saw something called "Piazzale Della Vitoria" that had a national monument dedicated in 1924 to honor Italy's fallen heroes from many battles fought against Australia during World War I. From a large oval balcony at "Piazzale Della Vitoria" I could see all of Vicenza below, along with the Pre-Alps and the Venetian Lagoon. It was like being in a lovely dream that I never want to wake up from, and I knew that I fit in here.

After Mount Barraco, I looked for a phone booth and called the Nicole Agency as instructed by Sandy. I let the receptionist know that I had arrived. I made an appointment for the following week to show up in Milan at the agency to meet in person. Milan was three hours away from Vicenza by train, which meant there would be times when I would be forced to stay there overnight for work.

I walked around for a few more hours just sightseeing, until it was time to return to the hotel to meet up with Nick. I had to get on the Autobus to get back to the hotel in time because I had walked so far away from it.

Ten minutes later Nick showed up with the guy conceited enough to call himself "The Anaconda of Love." He kind of reminded me of Ricardo Montalban from the "Fantasy Island" television show.

I asked Nick why he had brought his friend along? He explained that the guy had a car and had volunteered to give us a ride to the new hotel with my luggage. We retrieved my luggage from the desk clerk, and then loaded it into the back of the car.

When we arrived at the Hotel Elena, there was a cute Italian girl about my age, working behind the desk. She had curly dark blonde hair that reached her shoulders, and olive skin with blue eyes. She had a tall, skinny shapely frame and wore a trendy looking pair of blue jeans that I immediately wanted. She introduced herself as Mary Angela and welcomed us to the hotel in a thick Italian accent. I got the feeling that I could be friends with this girl, she looked like she could be fun to hang with.

After we checked in and were given a room key, Mary Angela showed us the little restaurant they had attached to the hotel in case we wanted food. The little restaurant was a cute area with tables as well as a counter with barstools in front of it where you could watch your food being cooked.

Then she took us upstairs to the second floor and showed us our room. The room itself was a picture right out of World I, primitive looking but clean. Everything, including the walls looked like nothing had changed since the Great War. The floor was hard and cold without carpet. The bed was a full sized antique cast-iron bed that looked like one of those old hospital beds I had seen countless times in old war movies on TV.

As in the last hotel, there was a reading light attached to the head-board. And instead of a closet there was a huge wooden wardrobe cabinet to hang your clothes in.

I asked Mary Angela where the bathroom was?

She took us down the hallway while explaining that we had to share the bathroom with the other guests on our floor. Just like the other hotel I thought to myself. The bathroom had two toilets, a normal one that looked like it was from the 1950s, and the other one was just a cemented hole in the floor, with cement footprints on the sides so you would know where to place your feet. I had never seen anything like it before in my life.

The shower looked like it was at least 50 years old like everything else in the hotel. As Mary Angela walked us back to our room I thought, it may not be the fanciest hotel in the world, but at least Nick and I are together. Besides, this is just temporary until we find our own place to live.

As soon as Mary Angela left and we were alone, Nick shut the door and was all over me. He pushed me down on the bed and said, "We're finally alone."

He began undressing me while kissing me. Ten minutes later he was finished and snoring next to me.

As I lay next to him, I realized that nothing had changed in the sex department. I lay next to him wishing that he would at least hold me, but he had some problem about not being able to sleep unless he was sleeping with his back to you on his side. Sometimes he reminded me of Woody Allen in a movie called "Annie Hall." The main character in the movie played by Woody Allen always had some weird reason about why he could not do something.

I wondered if it would kill him to hold me before he went to sleep, maybe make me the priority for a change. After asking him in the past if he could maybe make things last a little longer when we made love, I understood this would be the better or worse part of my wedding vows because there was no improvement.

Long ago I convinced myself that sex did not matter if you really loved someone. That there were a lot of men out there paralyzed from the neck down in wheelchairs, and a lot of them were married. I was not the only woman on Earth who loved a man enough to give up a normal sex life.

I turned over in bed facing his back and put my arms around him as he snored.

The next morning was Saturday. I got up before Nick and made my way downstairs to the little restaurant. I got us some rolls, butter and jam with Espresso shots for breakfast. Nick had the weekend off and was due to leave for Germany on Monday for a few weeks to play Army war games. I woke him up and we had our rolls and espresso together in bed.

That is when I told him about my plans to go to Milan while he was gone to sign up with the modeling agency.

"Then I plan to look around town for a small apartment to live in." I explained.

That is when he told me that he had to put in paperwork with the Army housing department, and how they would find us a place to live after we got married.

"You mean I can't just go out and rent a place to live?" I asked.

"We have to wait for our paperwork to be approved first but don't worry, we'll get married and have a decent place to live." He said.

"Okay, but I'm ready to get settled into my own place as soon as possible." I said.

I went down the hall to take a shower and get dressed since I wanted to walk around some more and see Italy. But Nick wanted to stay in bed and sleep as much as he could before going to Germany, where he said he would be forced to stay up for days at a time without sleep. I had mercy on him and went by myself while he slept.

When I ended up downtown at the Olympic theater, I was impressed by the architecture of the 15th century building and thrilled to be standing on the oldest surviving stage still in existence. I thought about all the plays that had been enjoyed in the place, and I thought of Plato and Socrates.

I felt honored to be standing in such a beautiful landmark of history, even if I was seeing it alone.

The next day I wanted to go sightseeing again with Nick this time, but he insisted on going to the barracks to shine his boots and pack his gear for his trip to Germany.

So, we spent Sunday in the barracks where I watched him pack while he and his friends drank beer and listened to loud music. I was learning fast that life was one big party for these guys, and I did not like the idea of being the only female in an all-male barracks. I could not help but notice how some of the guys looked at me as I walked into that company.

It was as if they were undressing me with their eyes, and it made me feel uncomfortable.

One guy even yelled to Nick, "You're not going to keep that shit for long" referring to me. I waited for Nick to tell the guy to go screw himself, but he said nothing and acted as if he had not heard a thing which was ridiculous. And by the end of the day, I thought I was going to die from a serious case of boredom.

The next morning Nick got up at five, dressed and kissed me good-bye calling me his kitten. Unable to go back to sleep I got up and went to the bathroom down the hall to shower and get ready for my day. I was still disgusted every time I saw the old shower and always wore flip-flops while in the shower out of fear of catching something because of the other people using it.

I practiced thinking positively like my father had taught me to do, but it was hard sharing a shower with other people, especially when they were strangers.

CHAPTER 93

A bright beautiful future was ahead of me, and I had to concentrate and focus on that. I felt lucky as hell to have the chance to live in Italy, and I was going to take full advantage of it. After all, how many 19-year-old girls got the chance to live and get married in Italy?

After I showered and dressed, I went downstairs to the little restaurant and ordered a cup of Espresso and a sweet roll. Mary Angela was on duty, and as I ate at the counter we began to talk.

She told me that her parents had owned the hotel for years, and now that she was 20, she was managing the place. She told me that she had a 16-year-old sister named Belinda who had been blind from birth and was a classical concert pianist despite her disability.

"I wish my sister had not been born blind, that way she could work here, and I could concentrate on my Diego," she said.

"Who is Diego?" I asked.

She then held out her hand and showed me her diamond engagement ring, saying Diego was a pig farmer she had fallen in love with.

"We're getting married, Diego and I have been going together for five years and I'm now planning our wedding." She said smiling.

"Strange coincidence, I'm getting married too. That's why I am here in Italy." I said smiling.

We bonded immediately over our pending marriages.

I sat there for a few hours talking to her and told her about my life in Los Angeles and what it was like growing up there. She volunteered to be my first friend in Italy, and we even shook hands on it.

The rest of my day was spent walking around the town sightseeing.

I awoke at 4 the following morning and got dressed so I could be at the train station downtown to catch the 6 a.m. train to Milan.

Once on the train I took a window seat so I could see the countryside during the three-hour train ride. I wished I had a camera so I could take pictures, so my father could see how beautiful it was here.

My train arrived at 9:15 at the station in downtown Milan. My appointment with the Nicole agency was at 10 am. so I got a taxi and gave the driver the address. I had no idea where I was going and was surprised to see that the agency was only 5 minutes away from the train station. I could have walked from the train station instead of paying for a cab.

The buildings in Milan looked old and well preserved. There were many businesspeople walking up and down the street and they all looked so classy and professional in their clothes. I was learning fast that Italians had excellent taste in clothing.

After I paid the driver, I stood outside the building for a minute adjusting my blouse and hair before walking in. Then I took a deep breath and walked into the building, where I was greeted by a receptionist. I told her my name and that I had a 10 o'clock appointment with Miranda.

I was taken into a large office where an attractive, tall blonde woman in her mid-30's stood up from her desk and greeted me with a smile. She introduced herself as Miranda and shook my hand. She looked at me and my photos and seemed to like what she saw.

"It says here that you are black, but you don't look full black. What races are you mixed with?" She asked.

I told her that my father was black, and my mother was a Creole from New Orleans, LA.

"I like your photos and I think you have a most unusual look that I can market here." She said.

She explained to me that they were a new agency, and how she had been looking for a few exotic looking girls. I was excited to know that I was in a place where there was a market for girls who looked like me.

Miranda told me that I would never be booked for runway jobs. "You're too short, but you can do print and commercial work."

I was so excited as I sat there looking at all the photos of models and magazine ads hanging on the walls in the office. I figured this was the chance of a lifetime for me, so when Miranda produced contracts for me to sign, I signed.

Miranda did not agree with me living three hours away by train.

"I would much prefer that you live here in Milan," she told me. "A few of the models have an apartment not far from here and I could arrange for you to stay there,"

I explained my situation with Nick and about my upcoming marriage. She reluctantly agreed to give me a couple days' notice by phone for my bookings.

After the meeting I walked around for a while sightseeing and bought a sandwich and a cup of coffee. I liked Milan where the younger people all looked so carefree and elegant as they zoomed passed me on their Mopeds. Once again, I found myself wishing I had a camera to take photos of it all. I was so in love with this place and the magical feeling that resonated from it. I was continually wishing that I had been born an Italian instead of an American. After walking around in a daze of happiness for a few hours, I made my way back to the train station for the three-hour train ride back to Vicenza.

By the time I reached Vicenza I was tired and ready to go to bed. I caught the bus back to the hotel, had something to eat and collapsed into bed where I slept like a baby.

CHAPTER 94

Over the following week Mary Angela invited me to her family home for dinner and took me to one of her sister's classical concerts. Louisa was one of the most phenomenal piano players I had ever heard. Although blind, she was literally a genius.

Afterwards, Mary Angela's father dropped her and Louisa off at their home first, then proceeded to drive me back to the hotel. As I thanked him and told him good night, he kissed me on both cheeks which was the Italian custom. But then to my shock and dismay he tried to tongue kiss me. Horrified I got out of the car as fast as I could. I did not know what else to do. Once I was back in my hotel room, I locked the door, and just stood there for a moment with my back against it.

I thought to myself what a perverted dog Mary Angela's father was, just thinking about what he had just tried to do made my stomach turn. Not only was this man married with children, but I was his daughter's friend and a guest at his hotel.

As the next few days went past, I felt uncomfortable every time I saw Mary Angela's father at the hotel. I was tempted to tell her what he had tried to do with me, but I had no idea how she would react to that type of information.

Besides, I figured the old fart would probably just deny it all anyway. Mary Angela was in the process of planning her wedding to Diego, and I did not want to trouble her. Especially after she had invited me to her wedding and had asked my advice on some of the preparations.

Reluctantly, I figured it was best to just keep my mouth shut, not wanting to put a strain on our new relationship. I was also excited because this was going to be my first time attending a real Italian wedding. I wondered if it would be like the wedding in "The Godfather" movie when Connie the daughter of Vito Corleone married Carlo. I could hardly wait to find out.

One afternoon, on Mary Angela's day off from the hotel, we drove downtown in her blue mini car to find clothes for her honeymoon in Rome. The clothes and shoes were so beautiful that I tried on everything I could get my hands on.

It was fun trying on things that I could not afford just to see what I looked like in them. Then we got a table at a café in the town square where we sat outside drinking dry red wine made from a local vineyard.

We dined on the best pasta and sauce that I had ever tasted, as Mary Angela told me about her plans to eventually quit working at the hotel to be a full-time housewife to Diego.

At sunset, I found myself wishing Nick had been there with me because the sunset was amazing and romantic. I realized I was lightheaded from the wine and was forced to drink two cups of Espresso before leaving the table to go back to the hotel.

I did not want to admit it to myself, but I was having a great time without Nick although I was relieved when the day came for him to return from Germany, and I was once again in his arms. I had enjoyed my little sightseeing tours while he had been away, but I had also been lonely without him there by my side.

As I showered and put on perfume and makeup, I thought about our bright future before us and how much I was looking forward to being his wife.

I chose a pretty cotton floral dress to wear with a pair of flat sandals. I had 30 minutes before Nick was due to arrive back at the base. Before he left for Germany, he had arranged for one of his friends who had stayed behind to sign me onto the base and get me a guest pass so I could greet him when he got off the bus from the airport.

Once I arrived at the front gate at the appointed time, I saw that the friend was Pierson: the same creep who was teasing that poor soldier who was dying from syphilis. He signed me onto the base, and we walked down to Charlie Company together where Nick would be getting off a bus.

I took my place in the area where all the families were waiting for the troops to come in. I looked around at some of the wives who were waiting with me, hoping that someone would introduce themselves to me or strike up a conversation. But unfortunately, no one even noticed I was there. A lot of them looked 18 and straight out of high school, and I was surprised to see that most of them had children already.

Not that there was anything wrong with that, but I was not ready for a child yet and I knew it. I was still a child myself and trying to figure out who the hell I was in the world, and what I was supposed to be doing in it. I wanted to have myself and my life in perfect order before attempting to teach another human being how to live in the world. In my mind having a baby was some serious stuff and a huge responsibility.

Just then a whole line of buses pulled up and interrupted my train of thought. I stood there in my pretty dress excited, looking for Nick as the soldiers started getting off the buses. After A few minutes I finally saw Nick step off the bus looking around for me. His face was painted with Army camouflage makeup. I rushed over to him and ran into his arms anxious to kiss him once again.

The first thing I noticed was the nasty smell that was coming from his body. He smelled as if he had not taken a shower since leaving for Germany, but I bypassed all of that, and kissed him anyway, knowing that he probably had not brushed his teeth either.

After our brief reunion he told me that he had to stay in his barracks for a few hours to clean and turn his equipment in, then wait to be dismissed. He told me to go back to the hotel and wait for him there. He asked Pierson to walk me back to the front gate and sign me off the base.

As we walked toward the front gate together, I noticed a group of soldiers across the street whistling at me and doing cat calls. It made me feel uncomfortable and embarrassed all at the same time.

I was not used to men treating me that way and did not know how to react. I did not think I was the type of girl that men whistled at on the street since I did not see myself as some raving beauty.

Pierson, to my surprise, suddenly yelled out, "Whistle at her one more time and I swear I will cross the street and open a can of whoop ass on you!"

The guys across the street quickly shut up and kept walking.

I looked at Pierson surprised that he had bothered to defend my honor since he did not even know me. I thanked him and told him that he did not have to defend me.

"No problem, those punks should've known better than to treat a woman that way especially since they're wearing a uniform." He said.

Once we were at the front gate, I thanked him for everything then shook his hand. As I walked away, I turned around and said, "I guess you're not the big butt hole that I thought you were."

He smiled at me and then turned around and walked away.

When I got back to my hotel room, I decided to kill time waiting for Nick by reading the latest Cosmopolitan Magazine issue and listening to music. After what seemed like hours, he finally showed up all clean and fresh.

We walked to an Italian pizzeria up the street from the hotel where we sat down and enjoyed an authentic Italian pizza together. While eating, he told me about his trip to Germany and how he hated going to the field there. Afterwards we went back to our hotel room and made love for 10 minutes.

Then Nick being the creature of habit that he was, rolled over and went to sleep with his back facing me. I put my arms around him and listened while he snored. A tear ran down my cheek as I wished that he were holding me instead, and because I was fully aware of the fact that I was about to marry a man who did not satisfy my need for true intimacy in a relationship.

I wondered if I was somehow emotionally crippled for craving that intimacy with another person. What if his way was normal and mine was not?

The next morning, I woke up and was excited because Nick had the day off, and we could spend it together. I suggested that we go to the Olympic theater and drink Espresso afterwards in the town square. But he said he had to hang out in the barracks and do his laundry, and he wanted me to go with him.

"How long is it going to take for the military to finish processing your paperwork again?" I asked.

He told me it would be a few more months. I was pissed off but kept my anger to myself since there was nothing, I could do about it except wait for the paperwork to finish being processed.

We walked to his barracks from the hotel, and as we entered the building an uneasy feeling washed over me again about spending time in an all-male barracks. All those guys running around made me uncomfortable since I was raised to believe that only girls with a reputation spent time in an all-male barracks.

It just seemed to me like I had no business in there at all, but Nick saw nothing wrong with it. I wondered if I was being too old-fashioned. I also wondered what Gloria Steinem would say on the subject.

After three boring hours in the barracks hanging out with Vanderpool, Pierson and a guy named Jeri Granger, they all decided that we were going downtown to get something to eat.

I had hoped to spend the night alone with Nick, not watching him eat and drink beer downtown with his friends. I noticed that Nick drank a lot when he was with his friends, and I did not like it. The last thing I needed was a husband with a drinking problem.

My common sense told me to move to Milan and concentrate on modeling where I could share an apartment with the other models from the agency without the Government being involved.

Nick was lucky that I loved him because I was doing my best to be patient and happy with these circumstances, when, I was very unimpressed.

CHAPTER 95

Another month flew by, and we were still waiting to get married. And to make matters worse, I had missed out on a few modeling auditions when the agent tried to reach me by calling Nick's barracks. Miranda left a message that I got four days later. By the time I had called her back I lacked the proper travel time to get there.

That resulted in a warning from my agent that if this continued to happen, she would be forced to drop me. I thanked God that she was willing to give me another chance, because anyone else would have dropped me.

The following week Nicole called and was impressed when I called her back a few hours later, which I felt really saved my butt. She told me that I had been chosen along with another girl from the agency to do print work for a beauty book some Italian guy had written.

She instructed me to get on a train early the following morning so I could be at the agency by 9 am.

The client would pick us up there to take us to the train station to catch a train to Pisa. The photo shoot would be at the very top of the Leaning Tower Of Pisa. All travel expenses would be paid, including meals, and I would be paid $250 an hour for a day's work. I was excited and thrilled; my first modeling job in Europe, where someone thought I was beautiful enough to be in their book.

I felt elated and optimistic as I ran back to the hotel to tell Nick the good news. When I entered the room, he was sleeping before pulling 24-hour guard duty the following day. The timing for the job was perfect because Nick and I would be working on the same day. Now I would not be stuck in the room alone while he pulled guard duty.

Excited, I woke Nick up to give him the good news. He said that he was happy for me but was annoyed because I had awakened him from his sleep. He complained about not wanting to pull guard duty the following day, then went back to sleep.

I thought to myself, why did you join the Army to begin with dude if you did not enjoy every aspect of this life? I sat on the edge of the bed looking at him while he slept; he had to know that 24-hour guard duty was part of his job in the military. Now he had an attitude about it and complained on occasion about the physical discomfort in private.

In front of his friends, he put on a brave face and acted as if his military duties were no big deal at all. I decided to go downstairs to share my news with Mary Angela and get a cup of Espresso.

Five hours later when Nick finally opened his eyes, I suggested that we go downstairs for some dinner. Nick wanted to eat his dinner in our room where he could hide himself from the world. He complained that he was homesick and as a result of that he was depressed.

I did not have a medical degree, but I thought his excessive drinking was leading to his depression. I suddenly remembered the first day I ever saw him, and God telling me that Nick was going to some dark places in life and how He did not want me exposed to all of that. I had to remind myself that I had made the decision on that day to try and protect Nick from going in that direction.

So, I gave in and got us some sandwiches and a few cokes, and we ate in our room. As we ate, I looked at the depressed look on his face and tried to cheer him up by telling him that I was thrilled to be away from home and living in Italy.

"Don't you realize what an adventure this is? We're living in Italy; how could you possibly be homesick." I asked.

"I miss my family and friends." He replied with a sad look.

"There are so many new things to see and explore here it looks as though you've made some new friends here, and we can make good memories if you would stop with the depression routine."

"It's normal for me to miss my family." He replied.

Then he got up from the chair he was sitting in and got back into bed.

I used to think that Nick was lucky to have had two parents who loved him and paid for everything he needed. Now I realized that it had handicapped him because here out in the world without that safety-net, he had no idea how to swim on his own.

For the first time in my life, I was grateful to my parents for teaching me how to survive in the world without them, and for giving me the backbone to do it with.

Strangely, I was also grateful to my stepfather Maxwell Rogers who taught me how to look fear in the face by pulling a gun on me every day for a year. I had developed a tough skin by living through Maxwell shooting at me every day and I had never realized it until that very moment.

My tough childhood had made me into a fearless adult. Now I was going to have to teach Nick how to be fearless and battle this depression and homesick routine. I had a vision about how I wanted our life together to unfold, and it sure did not include depression and alcoholism.

I went to sleep that night, I prayed to God and asked Him to hurry and get me and Nick married and into our own apartment as quickly as possible. And to give Nick the backbone he needed to stop being so homesick and depressed.

CHAPTER 96

The next morning, I left for the train station at 5 and caught the early train to Milan. When I arrived at the agency the client, a small dark-haired Italian man named Luigi, was already there along with the other model. I figured they both must have been quite early because I was punctual.

The other model was a tall handsome dark-haired Italian girl. I envied her height because she could do runway shows. She was warm and friendly as she introduced herself as Elizabeth and said that she looked forward to working with me.

Luigi then ushered us both out to a waiting cab that would take us all to the train station, where we would begin our three-hour journey to Pisa on the train. When we arrived at the train station in Pisa, we then took another cab to the Leaning Tower of Pisa where Luigi had a photographer and lighting crew waiting for us.

When we got to the top of the tower Elizabeth, and I were approached by a wardrobe woman who gave us nude-colored bodysuits to put on. Then a makeup man appeared to do our makeup, while a woman wet our hair with water from a spray bottle. She put some type of glossy hair gel in our hair to give us that wet combed back look.

I was ecstatic; not only was I modeling in Italy, but I had two different people working on me at the same time to make me look perfect. As a child I never saw this coming, not even in my wildest dreams. I looked up at the sky for a second and thanked God for the experience.

After the photographer had us placed in the spot, he wanted us in for the actual photo shoot, we were instructed to pose together standing up against a wall.

After an hour and a half posing in front of the camera, my body begin to ache because a few of the poses were in weird positions, and I was required to hold that pose for a period of time.

Following the photo shoot Luigi took everyone out to dinner at a small deli that had flies buzzing around all over the place. I saw one land on the deli meat that was being displayed behind the counter and decided to pass on the food. I thought how flies sat in shit and laid eggs, as I saw the fly eating its fill on the meat.

It was a relief to be back on the train to Vicenza. Hopefully, Nick would be in a better mood since I saw him last, instead of the state of depression I left him in. I walked into our hotel room at four the following morning to find him sleeping after his 24-hour guard duty. I put my things down and just stood there at the foot of the bed looking at him sleep for few minutes.

I had been gone over night and traveled to get back to him and wondered if this was a sample of what the next three years would be like. Would Nick go home to Los Angeles and go to college and make something of himself? Was my love strong enough for me to save him? I lay down in the bed next to him trying not to wake him as I put my arms around him.

As I drifted off to sleep my last thought was,

"I won't let Nick live a life of depression and alcoholism. Instead, I will teach him how to live a life of happiness and joy."

Another month went by, and I was still doing my best to be patient while waiting to get married. At this point the Army wanted me and Nick to go through premarital counseling with the post chaplain. According to Nick, it was a requirement that the military insisted upon.

CHAPTER 97

I also met two American girls that month that I liked and got along well with. One of them was Drew Hall, who had checked into the hotel with her husband Stewart Hall, a medic in the military. We met over coffee one morning downstairs. Drew had just come over from the States, and only had to stay at the hotel for a few nights. She and her husband were both from New York City, born and raised complete with the accent and attitude. They had been high school sweethearts, just like Nick and me.

She and her husband had their housing approved and set up before they even showed up in Italy. After talking to her over coffee, I realized that Nick should have married me in the states and then sent for me after he had secured our housing.

How could he have been so stupid? He had gone about this all wrong, and now I was stuck waiting for permission to get married in a foreign country.

A few days later Drew moved into her new apartment not far from the hotel and invited us over for dinner so I could see their new place. It was a cute little flat above a pizzeria that had a living room, one bedroom, a kitchen and a bathroom. It was within walking distance to the base on a hidden side street. It was just the type of place I wanted for us.

That night at dinner I met Kathy Davis, a long,-haired blonde, blue-eyed, six-foot-tall Amazon woman. I thought she was a guy at first glance.

Kathy was living in Italy as a pro basketball player. She was the only American on an all-girls Italian basketball team. She was originally from Albuquerque, NM. The basketball team set her up with a cute little fully furnished flat downtown near the Square. She had an expense account, a contract to play ball and a free, dark blue mini car that she could barely fit into because she was so tall. The team also supplied her with a language instructor to teach her how to speak and write fluent Italian in which she was now adept.

She spent a lot of her free time drinking in a local Airborne bar downtown called "Johnny's," where she met Stewart and Drew and drank them under the table the night before.

Kathy told us that she was friends with a lot of the soldiers from the base, "without sleeping with them all of course," she said.

I was thinking she probably did not have to fight off too many sexual advances, because the guys probably thought she would get them in a head lock or something in the sack. She told us that Airborne guys treated her as if she were one of the family. I liked her the moment she laughed at my nickname for Stewart.

I had started calling him "Little Ricky," because he reminded me of Little Ricky from the "I Love Lucy" TV show." Kathy saw the humor in it and almost fell out of her chair when I said it. Kathy told Drew and I stories about her wild hash smoking and drinking parties.

Her outlook on life was "I'm 22 years old living in Italy, making a fat paycheck and playing basketball, I'm going to party my ass off." This was the code she lived by. The three of us became pretty much inseparable after that night.

Drew and I were determined to stay as far away from the base and that lifestyle as we could. We were going to live like Italians with Kathy as our guide, because she had already been there for a year. Neither one of us wanted to have kids until later in life. We all agreed that marriage was okay, but we were still babies ourselves. Our bond was formed as we realized that none of us were yet prepared to give life to another human being.

When the day came to attend Mary Angela's wedding, I took Drew and Kathy with me. To us it was an adventure to see an authentic Italian wedding in the countryside.

Nick stayed behind in our room and slept; he had no interest in watching Mary Angela get married.

Kathy showed up in a three-piece pantsuit that reminded me of the one John Travolta wore in the "Saturday Night Fever" movie, while Drew and I wore cute little summer dresses with heels.

The wedding ceremony was held on the outskirts of town where people had their farms and vineyards. The church was on an old dirt road in an ancient looking building probably hundreds of years old. It was the most beautiful Catholic Church that I had ever seen with antique art murals of angels on the ceiling, and handsome statues of the Mother Mary and Jesus throughout the church.

Both the ceremony and Mary Angela's wedding dress was beautiful, and I found myself wishing it were my wedding. The reception was filled with joy, good food, liquor and dancing. We really had a fabulous time, and I was happy for my friend as she drove away with her husband Diego, the pig farmer, to their Roman honeymoon.

Time went by and Nick and I started going to Kathy's parties and cookouts. I was surprised to find out that she knew Pierson and Vanderpool who also attended her parties.

Kathy also asked me if I wanted to go on trips with her when she played basketball. She said that she wanted the company of an American with her.

So, whenever I did not have to be in Milan for a modeling interview or job, I would spend my free time traveling with Kathy to various little towns in Italy.

She was truly the star player on the team; the other players were good, but Kathy had that height advantage. The best part, besides watching my friend win game after game, was that the basketball team paid for all my travel expenses while I traveled with them.

Kathy had somehow convinced them that I was her personal companion, and that she needed another American by her side for help and support. Since these people were desperate to keep their star player happy and hitting winning baskets on the court, I got to see a lot of Italy for free.

Each town we went to the food was unique and once we stayed in Rome for a game and went to dinner afterwards. The restaurant was across the street from the Colosseum and was quite upscale and fancy. When I opened the menu, I saw that everything on the menu was in Italian. Not wanting to embarrass myself in front of the team's owner, I just pointed at something on the menu and told the waiter that was what I wanted.

How bad could it be I thought to myself? But when our food arrived and the waiter put the plate down in front of me, I saw how bad it really could be. There was a cooked pigeon on my plate, and the eyes were still intact staring right at me.

I looked up at the waiter and said,

"Dude I can't eat this; it's a dead bird and it's staring at me."

Kathy quickly took over speaking in Italian and told the waiter to take it back and to bring me some pasta with red sauce. That was the last time I would ever order anything in a foreign country without knowing what it was first!

The next day before leaving Rome, Kathy and I walked across the street from the hotel to a park where Kathy thought she could get away with smoking some hash before getting on the team travel bus to go home.

While hiding behind a tree smoking hash, we watched two older look-ing Italian gentlemen very well-dressed, with bodyguards walking behind them strolling along the pathway.

There was a black Mercedes-Benz slowly following alongside them. They stood out from everyone else at the park and they both looked serious as a heart attack, like you did not want to get on their bad side.

"They both look cool, calm and cold blooded." I said to Kathy.

"That's because they're probably Italian Mafia." she replied.

I was in disbelief and my jaw dropped as I watched Italian Mafia mem-bers meeting in a Roman park, just casually walking through this public park having an outdoor meeting, complete with bodyguards and a security car.

"Whew! Wait until I tell Daddy." "I'm speechless he's probably making him an offer he can't refuse." I said to Kathy and we both laughed.

"Get it?" I said, taking my finger and pointing it at her as if it were a gun.

"I get it." She said, "Why do you think I'm laughing so hard?"

I could have sat there all afternoon just observing those two men, but Kathy told me it was time to get back to the hotel before someone came looking for us.

On the drive back to Vicenza I sat there in my seat looking out of the bus window at the picturesque countryside and wondered what those two Mafia men had been talking about in that park. Maybe they had been plotting a hit on someone or negotiating some big drug deal.

Whatever the reason was, I found seeing real Italian Mafia men inter-esting, and a check mark on my "Tour of Italy" list.

CHAPTER 98

As the weeks flew past Kathy, Drew and I ran wild in the streets of Italy together. We would go on little adventures together in Kathy's mini car. We would listen to Kathy's Lynyrd Skynyrd cassette, and sing *"Free bird"* and *"Sweet Home Alabama"* at the top of our lungs while going at least 90 miles an hour on the Audubon.

In Italy there was no speed limit on the highway, and it reminded me of a race car track with no limits because everyone went so fast. I figured that most of the car crashes ended in death because of the high speeds. Not only was Kathy fluent in Italian, but she also knew where all those little out-of-the-way trattorias and quaint places were.

She taught me how to drink shots of an Italian liquor called "Grappa" along with one called "Sambuca" which Kathy sometimes mixed with Tequila. I loved the way she would throw a shot down her throat then slam her shot glass down on the table with a gleam in her eyes.

I was never able to handle any more than a shot or two myself, and I was convinced at this point in my life that my body did not like alcohol. But I was trying to live like an Italian in every possible way. The liquor, along with the wine, was a way of life for the Italian people.

It was normal in Italy to take a shot or two after a good meal, and then you had your Espresso. Even the children were raised drinking watered-down table wine at meals. And as far as I could see the result was 90-year-old men and women riding around on bikes and working in the grape vineyards healthy as a 20-year-old.

Whenever we went to the Airborne bar, Johnny's Trattoria in downtown Vicenza, we always ordered the cheeseburgers because they made the best American hamburgers in town. Kathy would take her backgammon board to Johnny's just to mess with some soldier's head by taking his money.

She would get a table, set her board up and ask a few Airborne guys if they felt like getting their asses kicked by a woman. Some of these Airborne guys had big egos and would easily take the bait. It would usually start with a $10 bet and would end with the soldiers losing $30-$40 dollars. Their egos would not allow them to accept the fact that a female was taking their money in front of their buddies by rolling doubles so often that they rarely got a turn to roll the dice. Then they would bet even more money, trying to win their money back.

It was not long before Drew and I got in on the action. I had always been good at backgammon, so why not earn a little money at it? I had never bet on anything in my life, so I was excited to whip some butt. As I played, I was amazed at how often I rolled doubles and won money. I figured that Kathy just had the lucky board and dice. Until one night she confessed to Drew and me that the dice she used were a fixed set. She had two sets of dice with her board, and she made the person she was playing with play with the unfixed set. Her set had doubles on all sides except one. We all fell out laughing because we could not believe that we had gotten away with it for so long.

No one ever thought to check the dice, they were too busy dealing with the fact that a female had just told them that she was going to kick their ass in backgammon.

One evening Nick came back to the hotel overly excited after working all day. He was happy as he told me that the Army had finally given us permission to get married.

"Our paperwork has finally come through and been approved, but first we have to go to the American Consulate in Milan to get married under Italian law." He said.

"Why do we have to do that?" I asked him.

"Because we're Americans getting married in a foreign country." He replied.

"Then we have to get married a second time on the base by the post chaplain under American law."

"You mean we have to get married twice? Do you realize how romantic that is?" I asked.

He kissed and hugged me and told me how happy he was that we were finally getting married and moving out of the hotel.

"I'm going to miss Mary Angela." I told him.

"Well, the two of you can still be friends after we move into our own place." He said.

"I know, but I've gotten used to having espresso with her every morning and I will miss that." I replied.

CHAPTER 99

Excited, I thought about how I was finally going to be able to wear the beautiful white satin fishtail vintage dress I had purchased in an antique store in Los Angeles to get married in.

"What are we going to do about wedding rings?" I asked him.

"I don't think we can afford them." He said.

"Well, the least you can do is buy us two plain wedding bands," I told him.

"They don't have to be expensive. We can buy nice ones later when we can afford them." I quickly added.

"We have to have rings when we get married Nick; we can't just get married and not have rings. The rings are supposed to be a symbol of our love and commitment to one another." I said.

"Well, if it's that important to you then you can look around downtown for something affordable." He said.

Damn, I thought to myself I cannot believe that this guy did not go out on his own and buy me a ring before he even asked me to marry him in the first place. It was bad enough that my family would not be at my wedding, but there was no way I was getting married without a ring.

He never even got down on one knee to propose to me, I thought to myself. I looked at him and said, "I can't believe you expect me to go ring shopping by myself for my own temporary wedding ring."

"I would go with you but I'm busy working for the Army, remember? I can't just take off from work and go searching through stores for two rings I can afford." He said.

"Fine, I will find us some affordable rings while you're working." I said in a disappointed tone.

My patience with Nick was being sorely tried concerning many things and I told myself that guys did not mature as fast as females did. Besides, if I really loved him, I would wait patiently for him to catch up with me. But truthfully, at this point his attachment to his family and being homesick for them was very infantile to me.

Especially when he spent the day in bed depressed over them. I wanted to tell him that he had lived around his family his whole childhood, wasn't that enough? I wanted to ask him did not you ever imagine as a child growing up having a life of your own. Didn't you ever want to go on an adventure? Did you ever imagine your wedding day and putting a ring on your wife's finger?

In my opinion what he needed to do was cut that freaking umbilical cord and leave childhood behind. We were young adults, and it was time to embrace that. I was excited because I was young and had my whole life ahead of me. I had big plans for my future and felt that anything was possible.

But every time I tried to impart this knowledge upon him, he would tell me that I did not understand what he was going through. I figured since I grew up in survival mode taking care of myself and my siblings, that I had one up on him when it came to making it in the world without my family. I was hopeful that through my example, he would learn how to make it in life without his parents bailing him out of everything. Like his father, I was hoping Nick's time in the Army would make a solid responsible man out of him.

Nick and I spent the following weeks doing everything we had to do to get married, including counseling with the post chaplain. We had a meeting with his company commander, whom I disliked at first glance. I just could not believe that the Army had so much bureaucracy when it came to getting married.

Eventually, I found and purchased two cheap silver coated wedding bands for $10 each at a small shop downtown in the Square. I felt we needed our savings to get and keep a roof over our heads.

Then we went to Milan with Kathy, Drew, Pierson and Vanderpool. They were our witnesses for the first wedding in blue jeans at the American Consulate. I was shocked when I walked into the building and saw all the guards and security measures you had to pass to enter that building.

Pierson said they had experienced terrorist threats and bombings in the building, so now they were on full alert all the time.

I felt sorry for the people living in Europe because they had to live this way, always being threatened with a terrorist attack.

Pierson was irritated because he had a pocketknife on him and had to go outside to hide it in some bushes, due to the full body searches conducted at the American Consulate.

After waiting in a short line and filling out the paperwork, we finally got married by an Italian dude in a black suit. Then we all went out to dinner before taking the train back to Vicenza.

I tried to make a little celebration out of the trip by having dinner, after all Nick and I were now married under Italian law. I wanted my first wedding to be as perfect as I could make it with little money to spend. I wanted this to be a beautiful memory that I could cherish forever. It did not matter to me that we were both broke as church mice, what mattered to me was we loved one another enough to get married in the first place.

The following week Kathy and Drew gave me a small bachelorette party the night before I was due to get married for the second time under American law on the base. They surprised me by coming by my hotel room and dragging me out to the local trattoria.

Pierson, Vanderpool and Granger came by and took Nick off to the barracks for a party they had planned with the guys there.

We dined on pizza, and I had a few tequila shots. Kathy double dared me to swallow the worm at the bottom of the bottle. By then I was so totally drunk from the first shot, that I did have enough courage to swallow that worm.

Everyone at the bar cheered me and clapped when I swallowed the worm successfully. Then some Italian guy got up from his seat and started serenading me in Italian. I could not understand most of what he was singing about, but it sure sounded nice.

After he had finished his little song, he asked me if I wanted to dance. "We have Frank Sinatra on the jukebox." He said in broken English.

I told him no and thanked him, "I'm getting married in the morning." I said.

He then took my hand in his and kissed it, and then he bowed to show respect and returned to his table. It suddenly dawned on me that a childhood fantasy had just come true. When I was a small child, I used to wish that someone would serenade me like Romeo had done for Juliet in my story book. Now it had truly happened to me, in a small trattoria in Northern Italy.

CHAPTER 100

The following morning, I awoke feeling so excited because my wedding ceremony was at noon. I got out of bed grateful that Nick had spent the night in the barracks. I did not want him to see me before I walked down the aisle in case it was bad luck.

I walked over to the window and looked out for a minute, the sun was shining brightly, and it was a bright sparkling May morning in Vicenza, Italy. Nick and I were finally going to be man and wife, and I was incredibly happy about it.

I took my beautiful satin wedding dress out of the wardrobe and laid it across the bed. As I looked down at my used satin wedding dress, I felt a little let down because it was second-hand, but told myself that was okay, that it did not matter if my dress was used or new.

Getting married today was all that mattered as I told myself that if I followed Marie and Phillip's example of marriage, then mine would be successful too. I believed that with all my heart and hoped that when Nick saw me coming down the aisle in my dress that he would think to himself how beautiful I looked, like a vision in white satin.

I could hardly wait for him to look into my eyes as he said his vows to me. I was so in love with him, and I was going to make sure that we were both the best that we could possibly be in life.

Kathy and Drew interrupted my thoughts by knocking on my door. They were there to pick me up to go to Kathy's apartment to get ready for the wedding. Drew was going to be my bridesmaid. Kathy had been my first choice, but she had refused. Wearing a dress was just too much for her, and being a bridesmaid was just something she was unwilling to do. She told me that she had not worn a dress since she was six years old.

The wedding was in three hours, so I hurried and slipped into a pair of blue jeans and my "Beat Dick" election T-shirt. I put on my Frye cowboy boots and reached for my wedding dress and shoes along with a tote bag that held my shampoo, blow dryer and make-up bag. I rushed out the door with my girlfriends and into Kathy's waiting mini car.

When we arrived at Kathy's apartment, we had only been there five minutes before the two of them were getting high on hash. Then Tiffany opened a bottle of Sambuca and proceeded to do shots. She asked me if I wanted a shot as well.

"I really have no interest in getting drunk on my wedding morning or any other morning. Damn, Drew, how the hell can you drink first thing in the morning?" I demanded. Then I asked Kathy if she had any coffee.

She said she would make some for all of us as we both watched Drew down yet another shot of Sambuca.

"Drew, please stop drinking if you are going to be my bridesmaid. The last thing this wedding needs, is a drunken bridesmaid falling out while walking down the aisle." I scolded.

She put the cap back on the bottle and walked away from it. Relieved, I went into the bathroom to shower and get ready for the ceremony.

After I had finished taking a shower, I got myself a cup of coffee and walked out into the small living room where Kathy and Drew were waiting for me. Drew was wearing a plain long white cotton maxi dress to match my white satin wedding dress. And Kathy had on a man's cream-colored three-piece bellbottom suit, with a plain white dress shirt.

With her shoulder length blonde hair feathered back, she looked like a handsome high school boy on his way to the prom. We all got into Kathy's little car and headed for the chapel on the base.

As Drew signed us both on to the base as her guests, I realized that this would be the last time I would have to go through being signed in on the base. In a few days I would be issued my dependent military identification card. Then I could come and go as I pleased.

When we reached the little chapel, I could see Pierson and Vanderpool standing in front of the chapel smoking cigarettes and talking. Vanderpool was wearing his dress greens while Pierson was wearing a dark blue three-piece suit with a white shirt and a pair of white high-top tennis shoes. The poor boy stood out like a sore thumb; it almost hurt my eyes to look at him.

I approached him and asked if he had any idea how ridiculous he looked wearing a suit with high top tennis shoes? "Why aren't you wearing dress greens like everybody else?"

He laughed and told me, "I hate dress greens. So, I wore this suit my parents bought me so I could wear it on a Mormon mission. I deeply upset them by not going on the mission and joining the Army instead, so the suit and the tennis shoes are my form of rebellion against man-made churches and religion."

"What's a Mormon?" I asked him.

"It's a religion. Haven't you ever heard of the Mormon Church before?" He asked.

"No." I said.

"Well, I don't like organized religion, so I'm wearing tennis shoes to church," he said.

With that remark, I figured he was simply crazy and out of his mind and I turned to walk away. Before I could walk away, he asked me the strangest question.

Pierson looked me in the eye and asked in a low voice, "Why are you marrying Nick?"

Insulted, I quickly replied "Because I'm madly in love with him and have been since I was 13 years old' you asshole."

He then leaned over and whispered in my ear, "You're making the biggest mistake of your life, and if you're smart, you'll pack your bags, move to Milan to model or go back home to Los Angeles."

I felt a chill go up my spine as he pulled away from my ear.

"And why do you say that; do you know something about Nick that I don't know?" I asked.

"I just don't think he can take care of you," He replied.

"Well, you're wrong" I said pissed off. "And who the hell asked you for your advice anyway."

On that note, I turned around to walk into the chapel.

Just then Drew walked past me and stumbled while walking up the church steps. I looked up at the sky and told God, this is going to be the wedding from hell; I can just feel it.

I pray that you make sure Drew does not embarrass me during my wedding. I found myself wishing I had just asked Mary Angela to be my bridesmaid instead of Drew.

As I entered the church all I could do was hope for the best and trust in God that the wedding would go off without any problems. There were about 20 of Nick's friends sitting in the pews all dressed in their dress greens (except for Pierson) waiting for the ceremony to begin.

I saw Nick standing at the altar with a guy named Kevin Ford who was his best man. For the first time that morning I was nervous and sad at the same time: because my family and friends back home were not there with me, and I wished my father were walking me down the aisle.

My wedding day fantasy was that this would be a joyous occasion filled with food, family and friends. Now, here I was on an Army base with a drunken bridesmaid, no wedding cake and a cheap ring that I had to purchase myself.

Calm down I told myself as the Chaplain's wife began playing the wedding march on the most messed up, out of tune sounding church organ I had heard in my life.

Drew began walking down the aisle, and I began to walk behind her. Then, suddenly Drew just fainted and fell to the floor. I was shocked and mortified. I stopped walking and bent down to help her as her husband ran to her side, along with a few other people.

Everyone in the church was gathering around her, as I heard Stewart scream "Someone call an ambulance!"

I suspected that all the liquor and hash that she had put in her body that morning was to blame for her condition. After the base ambulance showed up to take her to the hospital, we continued the ceremony without her.

As I began to walk down the aisle again, I wanted to cry because my wedding was so messed up. And to make matters worse when I joined Nick at the altar, I noticed that his hands were shaking, and he looked nervous as hell.

However, as I said my vows to him for the second time, I meant every single word that came out of my mouth, because to me Nick was the most beautiful man on Earth whom I loved with all my heart and soul.

After the ceremony, we went to the pizzeria on the base with Pierson and his sidekick Vanderpool. Kathy and a few of Nick's other friends came along as well.

While sitting waiting for our pizza at the table, the guys started ordering beers. I was trying not to feel let down over my joke of a wedding, and no wedding reception, when Vanderpool shouted out,

"Watch this everybody."

We all watched as he poured salt and pepper, Jalapenos along with some bread chunks, into his large beer mug. Then he started drinking the whole thing without stopping. When all the beer was gone, he had enough nerve to chew the chunks of bread and jalapenos at the bottom of the glass. Then he slammed the beer mug down on the tabletop and let out a loud burp.

We all sat there looking at him astounded, disgusted and speechless.

There was a moment of complete silence, and a crazed look in Vanderpool's eyes when the vomit came gushing out of his mouth and onto my wedding dress, hair and face.

I felt like Sissy Spacek in the movie "Carrie" when the bucket of blood was thrown on her during the prom scene. There was vomit dripping down my face and eyelashes.

I could see a few of the guys trying not to laugh, while Nick just sat there telling Vanderpool what an asshole he was. I wanted to yell out at him to get up and defend my honor, but I held my tongue.

Pierson was the one who came to my defense as he got up out of his seat and pulled Vanderpool out of his chair. He knocked him to the floor and yelled, "What the hell is wrong with you?"

Then he rushed over to the counter and asked for a towel and the bathroom key for me.

Tears of horror ran down my cheeks as I walked into the ladies' room to wash off the vomit. My dress was ruined, and I was going to have to wash my face with public bathroom soap. I was completely grossed out as I looked in the mirror and saw the bread chunks mixed with vomit in my hair.

Kathy came in and asked me if I was all, right?

I cried out, "I'm pretty damn far from all right at this point. Vanderpool is the most messed up disgusting person I have ever met in my life. And I expected more out of Nick when it came to defending me. Instead, he just sat there and watched while Pierson physically removed Vanderpool from his chair. To make matters worse, now Nick is out there getting drunk.

I do not want my husband to be in that condition on my wedding night. I wanted him to carry me over some sort of threshold and make love to me." I cried.

As I washed my face and dunked my head into the sink, Kathy helped me get the vomit out of my hair. When we were finished, I asked her to drive me back to the hotel so I could shower and change my clothes.

"I don't think I can spend another minute wearing a wedding dress covered in that asshole's vomit." I told her.

"Sure, screw these guys. Let's get the hell out of here." Kathy said.

When we walked out of the bathroom Vanderpool was gone and everyone was asking if I was all right. Nick invited everyone back to our hotel to finish the celebration there. I was so mad at Nick that I thanked Pierson for helping me without even acknowledging Nick's presence and left with Kathy.

Nick could walk back to the hotel for all I cared.

I got back to the hotel room and thought how upsetting it all was, Including having to throw my wedding dress away. I went down the hall to the bathroom and took a shower in hopes of washing the horror of the day away. Then I dressed in the bathroom slipping into a pair of blue jeans and a Elton John tee-shirt.

When I got back to the room Nick was there changing his clothes high on beer, knowing I was angry as hell, so he kept quiet.

CHAPTER 101

We walked downstairs in silence to the people waiting there for us in the little restaurant. I sat down at the table next to Pierson who had purchased a bottle of Grappa on the way over. He sat a shot glass in front of me and told me I looked like I needed a drink.

As I downed the shot, I tried to forget I was covered in vomit on my wedding day.

Mary Angela had attended my wedding, but had skipped the pizzeria, and was horrified about the whole situation when I told her about Vanderpool showering me with vomit instead of rice. She came over to the table and sat down asking me how I was. She was so horrified that she started speaking in Italian.

I asked her to repeat what she had just said in English. She told us that men in Italy had been killed for less, and that Vanderpool was fortunate that he had not done this at an Italian wedding because he would not have made it out alive.

I laughed for the first time that day, knowing that every word she spoke was true.

An hour had not passed before Nick was in the bathroom throwing up from all beer he drank. He ended up in our room where he collapsed on the bed with his clothes on.

I was extremely disappointed to say the least and decided to stay downstairs with our little wedding party and tried to enjoy myself.

After a few games of backgammon on Kathy's board, we all said good night and I went up to bed. As I drifted off to sleep my last thought was, this will go down in history as the worst wedding known to man.

Three weeks after we were married our name came up on the military housing list. I was so happy and relieved to leave the hotel for my own apartment.

As I hugged Mary Angela goodbye I promised to keep in touch. She was sad that I was leaving the hotel because now we would not be having coffee together every morning. I promised her that I would come by the hotel to visit as often as possible and told her she was always welcome to come by my new place.

Although I had wanted to rent one of the older antique looking apartments in the downtown area, like Kathy and Drew had, Nick did not like them; they looked too primitive, and he wanted something more modern. We ended up getting a two-bedroom apartment that had just been built that was fully furnished with new modern Italian furniture. It was located 20 minutes away from the base by car, in a small village called Longarie.

The area was covered in vineyards as far as the eye could see, complete with ancient ruins. The beautiful countryside had lots of old villas with land attached to them. It was satisfying to see that people still lived this way. The land was most likely passed down from generation to generation.

There were old restaurants and bars where elderly men sat at tables with friends they grew up with in the village. They would play cards and drink Grappa shots chased with espresso shots. There were very few Americans living out there, and I harbored the hope that I would finally have Nick to myself.

CHAPTER 102

The village had no supermarkets instead there was a little country store run by a local family which sold Italian goods, pasta and other food items. There was a vegetable stand, a small butcher shop run by a nice man named Giovanni. There was even a little pizzeria and bar run by an elderly Italian woman whom everyone called "Ma."

This innocent looking elderly woman turned out to be a little gangster. She started out by asking if I could get her a bottle of Jack Daniels and a pack of Marlboro red cigarettes from the base with my ration card. The American Marlboro cigarettes had different tobacco in them, and the Jack Daniels was extremely hard for them to get. This was against the law and the military called it "black marketing."

You could get into some serious trouble for this. Military members and their families were given ration cards to buy liquor and tobacco on the base. The minute you were given that ration card, you were cautioned not to buy things for the Italians with it.

I evaded Ma's request by telling her that my husband used our rations for his own smoking and drinking habits which was true.

The locals who lived in the little village had been born and raised there, as well as their parents and grandparents. These families went back generations, inheriting the land and working it. I felt like I was living in another time or a history book because their customs had never changed as people clung to the old ways.

As my first few months went by living in the village, I got to know everyone at the shops, and they became my friends. As I walked down the dirt roads like a peasant girl wearing my sandals and sleeveless cotton mini dresses, I knew I was living a dream that even I had not dared to dream. It was a miracle from God that I was experiencing this lifestyle and living among these beautiful people. I truly wished I had been born in Italy and never had to leave.

Nick and I purchased a used moped from another soldier who was going back to the states. This way he had transportation to and from work without catching a bus. Transportation was a must because the bus only ran out there four times a day.

After a few months of being together in our apartment Nick started getting depressed and homesick again. He started spending all his off-duty time sleeping instead of exploring and enjoying our surroundings with me. It was hard to understand how anyone could be depressed living in Europe.

I tried to keep him out of the barracks where he drank too much. This worked for a while, but once the depression set in the barracks and the liquor started coming home with him. Suddenly, every weekend, the guys were hanging out at our apartment.

Pierson, Vanderpool and few other guys would show up with steaks and liquor expecting to use our deck and barbecue pit to enjoy them on. They all missed America so much that they hung out together drinking, eating and listening to American music. Pierson was not a big drinker like the other guys and did not need to drink every day to have a good time.

And he most certainly was not homesick for America or his family. Pierson just wanted to have a good time traveling and dating a variety of women at the same time. We both agreed that the more exploring we did in Europe the better. Usually, Pierson would play backgammon with me or help me cook while telling me stories about his little sister Jane using her bare hands to steal food off his plate back home. Or how he would take his three little brothers hiking and trick them into eating deer shit by telling them it was milk duds he had dropped on the ground. His stories were amusing, and I could relate to his sick sense of humor because I used to do stuff to my little sister Helen, like drinking the juice from her bottle while my mother was not looking.

Sometimes Pierson and I would sit back on the sofa like two gossips and make fun of the drunken fools before us. One night, Pierson and I watched a guy jump off my balcony thinking he could fly for real, while listening to Lynyrd Skynyrd singing *free bird.*

I now realized that Pierson was not such a bad guy, and he became like a brother to me as time went by. The thing that amazed me about him was he had women stashed all over Europe, yet he was not a flashy guy; in fact, he was quite normal looking and shy.

Every now and then Pierson would ask my help to get him out of an unwanted relationship. He once talked me into calling some Italian girl on the phone for him to inform her that he had jumped out of an airplane and died. I told her that his parachute did not open.

The poor girl screamed out crying over the telephone as I tried to reassure her by telling her, "At least he loved you enough to leave a note saying you were to be called if something ever happened to him."

When she inquired about his funeral services, I told her that his body was already on its way back to the States.

CHAPTER 103

At this point Nick was starting to get mean when he drank. And he started embarrassing me in front of other people by telling me to shut up or calling me a stupid bitch. To avoid an argument and further embarrassment, I would go for a walk outside so no one could see me cry. I would always come back to overhear Pierson telling Nick that he should treat his wife better. Sometimes it would help, and Nick would listen to him. I was grateful to Pierson for sticking up for me because I was trying hard to concentrate on my modeling and making some money. Nick made it hard for me to focus on anything but an argument with him.

In addition, I was having a hard time dealing with being a model. The past two jobs I had been offered were for underwear print ads. It felt inappropriate for me personally to be seen in my underwear before the world. I did not feel comfortable with that at all. I had already come to the realization that I was not thrilled with modeling, in fact I kind of hated it. It made me feel like I was a disposable piece of meat. If you did not concentrate on being beautiful and skinny, then you were done for in the modeling business.

I felt that I had a lot more to offer the world other than the I way I looked as well as not getting paranoid about gaining weight or messing up my looks for fear that I would not be able to make money. What disturbed me the most was that the models in the magazines were not a true representation of your average woman on the street.

To me, women came in all shapes, sizes, heights and skin tones. Your average every day woman was not six feet tall and bone thin. I was not morally proud of helping to spread that false belief system.

So, when Pierson invited me and Nick to go on a ski trip with him and Vanderpool to Innsbruck, Austria for New Year's weekend, it was a welcome distraction. I was excited because I had never skied on snow. The only real snow I had ever been exposed to was when Daddy took the family for a drive up to Big Bear, in the mountains outside Los Angeles, to play in the snow when I was a kid. I water skied quite well and hoped that would help me to snow ski.

Pierson and Vanderpool spent the entire Christmas holiday with us, along with Kathy, Drew and Stewart. We were all Americans away from home during the holidays, so we clung to one another as if we were family.

When Pierson saw I had no Christmas tree, he hatched a plan to borrow one that looked like a Christmas tree from the front of my apartment building.

On Christmas Eve after it had turned dark outside, Pierson and I went outside and dug up the tree from in front of my apartment building. We carried it inside with the roots exposed and the dirt still attached to it. This way the tree could be put back the following morning without anyone knowing what we had done, and the tree could continue to live.

Pierson took a rope and tied it to the top of the tree, he put a nail in my ceiling to tie the rope to and had the tree standing in no time. I was impressed by his resourcefulness as he took tin foil from my kitchen to make fake Christmas bulbs to hang on the tree.

Nick and Vanderpool were drunk and laughing at us. Pierson and I looked at one another unamused. Everyone else thought the idea was a stroke of genius.

Kathy, Drew and I went into the kitchen to start Christmas dinner. Pierson followed insisting on helping us, claiming he was a master turkey stuffer.

After we had finished cooking and had eaten everything in sight, Kathy and I did the dishes while Pierson and Stewart took out the garbage.

When they came back into the apartment Stewart announced that it was Christmas present opening time. Everyone produced their Christmas presents except Nick, who did not think to buy me a Christmas present, or anyone else for that matter.

I gave Nick the new down jacket I had purchased for him, asking him to try it on. I was trying not to let anyone see how let down I was. I received gifts from Pierson, Kathy and Drew, but nothing from my own husband. I excused myself saying I had to use the bathroom, but I was really having a hard time holding back the tears that wanted to explode down my face.

I sat on the toilet and cried silently while telling myself that maybe Nick thought I was not worth a gift, maybe Austria was my Christmas present. But still, he could have spent two dollars for a Christmas card. Wasn't I worth a two-dollar Christmas card? I told myself to pull it together and go back out there and act excited about the trip.

After drying my eyes, I went back out to the living room and told Pierson how excited I was about the trip.

Trying to make small talk, I said. "You and Vanderpool have built up quite the reputation for adventure. Is it true that the two of you were chased in Monaco by palace guards and nearly beaten by them?"

"Yeah, that happened," Pierson admitted.

"A group of us decided to go to the Grand Prix in Monaco and we tried to watch the races for free by sitting on a hillside, but it turned out the hillside belonged to the Royal Family. When we saw the guards, we all ran, and everyone got away except PFC. Brown who was badly beaten and hospitalized." He elaborated.

"Well, I'm hoping to have a good time on this trip with you guys without any drama," I said.

"I won't have time to get into trouble since the twins from Switzerland may be meeting us at the hotel." He said.

"What you really mean is they're coming to keep you company at night," Vanderpool said.

"What twins," I asked.

Vanderpool explained, "last time we were in Switzerland Pierson here met twins at a nightclub. They were attracted to him and took us home with them for a week. They made me sleep in the guest bedroom while Pierson here shared a bed with the two of them. The bizarre thing was, they lived with their parents and the parents did not care that Pierson was sleeping with both of their daughters at the same time! They acted as if the whole situation was normal."

Surprised, I looked at Pierson and said jokingly, "Dude no offense but you're not a rock star in the looks department. How on Earth are you getting these girls to do all this?"

"I don't know; they just hit on me for some strange reason," he replied.

"It's true, the girls just approached him for some unknown reason," Vanderpool said.

As I searched Pierson's face trying to see the magic for myself, the only thing I saw that was appealing about him were his eyes. His eyes were blue, but they looked like opals that turned gray then blue again. This was the only thing that was special about his appearance to me.

CHAPTER 104

The next morning at the crack of dawn, Pierson and I had a cup of coffee then returned the stolen Christmas tree to its place in front of my apartment building. We wanted to put it back before anyone could get up and complain that it was missing.

Then on Friday morning the four of us boarded the train in downtown Vicenza headed for Innsbruck, Austria. We were going to the same ski resort where the Winter Olympics had been held a few years back. This was something I could tell my children about one day, if I ever had any.

We shared our train compartment with a few Italian guys who had a Bro Box with them playing Jimi Hendrix and Pink Floyd music. We drank red wine and partied our butts off on the train, but you could always find a good party on the train in Europe.

After what seemed like a lifetime we finally arrived in Innsbruck. We were all ready to eat a full course meal in a restaurant and to check into our hotel. We checked into the hotel and had dinner at a restaurant down the street, then walked around the town sightseeing.

Innsbruck was scenic and reminded me of a lovely Christmas Card photo of Santa Claus town' in the North Pole with all the snow and decorations.

When we returned to the hotel, the twins from Switzerland had called and left a message for Pierson at the front desk saying they were unable to come because one of them was forced to work at the last minute. So, we all went to a nearby nightclub where I danced until my feet hurt and everyone yelled happy New Year at midnight. At the hotel, the night manager was nice enough to serve us hot wine in the dining room, on the house, in honor of the New Year.

I had never heard of anyone drinking hot wine before, and it did not sound too good to me, so I turned it down. Nick, who had been drinking steadily all night, had the nerve to accept the glass of hot wine. Oh my God,

I thought to myself, the last thing Nick needs is more liquor in his system. I suggested that he drink a cup of hot coffee instead.

Drunk, Nick suggested that I shut the fuck up. I was pissed off and embarrassed all at the same time. Everyone got quiet when he said that to me, and Pierson tried to lighten the mood and break the ice by suggesting that we all go up to our rooms to get some sleep.

"We need to get up early to hit the slopes." He said.

The minute we all got off the elevator on the second floor, Nick threw up on the carpet in the hallway. Then his legs gave out from underneath him as he collapsed to the floor.

Vanderpool said, "Let's get Nick to his room and just walk away from the vomit and act like we know nothing about it; the hotel might charge us for the cleaning bill."

Then things got even stranger, as two Italian men ran past us in the hallway butt naked singing some song in Italian.

I looked at Pierson and asked, "Did you see that? two naked men just ran past us singing."

"Yeah, I did. What a way to start out the New Year." He said smiling as we watched the two men disappear into a room down the hall.

Pierson and Vanderpool helped me get Nick into our room and into the bed. He was completely passed out.

The following morning, we all got up and had breakfast together before going skiing for the day. Everyone acted as if nothing had happened the night before, and Nick had no memory of throwing up in the hallway or passing out. But I remembered and worried about his drinking.

When we reached the ski resort, I was filled with optimism about learning to snow ski. After renting a pair of skis, I started out on the beginner slope.

No matter how hard I tried to stay up on those skis, I kept falling on my butt. To make matters worse, Nick and Vanderpool thought it was funny every time I fell. I thought Nick had a lot of nerve laughing at me because if the Army had not taught him how to ski, he would also be falling on his butt.

Pierson kept helping me up and teaching me, but the minute my feet were wet I was finished with the whole business of snow skiing. I told them to go skiing without me. I was left on my own while they skied on the advanced slope.

After I turned my skis in, I went to the resort restaurant which had a magnificent view of the whole area from large glass windows in the dining room. I sat down annoyed that my jeans and feet were wet, I hated that. I ordered a large cup of hot cocoa and just sat there for a few hours observing the people around me and watching people ski down the mountain from the window.

I felt lucky as I sat there because I was a poor girl from Los Angeles, and here I was drinking hot cocoa at the same ski resort where the Winter Olympics had been held.

If someone had told me when I was a child that I would be here, living in Europe I would not have believed them. I looked out at the sky and told God that I felt special and thanked him for helping me get here.

After the guys had finished skiing, they found me waiting in the restaurant and we all went back to the hotel to have dinner, then pack so we could leave in the morning. During dinner, Nick got drunk once again; apparently, he really thought that it was cool to get smashed every time he drank. I was not impressed and found it stupid and unattractive.

We caught our train on time the following morning and I tried to keep myself preoccupied by reading a Jackie Collins novel on the train ride back to Italy. I felt the need to escape into someone else's reality for a while.

When we arrived in Italy, I was relieved to be back in the warmer climate, and our apartment which happened to be liquor free now. I planned to do my best to make sure that it stayed that way. I was going to tell people to stop bringing liquor to my apartment for my husband to drink.

CHAPTER 105

A week after we returned, I started having nightmares that involved Nick leaving me and ending our marriage. They were frightening dreams that I did not remember in full detail once I awakened. The one thing that I did remember was the fact that Nick had only married me because he was homesick and then he ended our marriage.

I would wake up next to Nick looking at him as he slept not wanting to believe what I had just dreamed. I told myself that I was delusional and that the dreams meant nothing. Also, I told myself that God would not be so cruel as to allow that to happen to me because I had prayed to God every day for years to marry Nick.

Over the years, I had rearranged my life to accommodate his.

Then I thought about his sexual problems and the drinking, and how I had overlooked all that and just loved him for who he was and married him despite those problems, hoping for a brighter future. Now he was going to leave me. I should be the one leaving.

As he snored, I asked myself why I was so in love with this guy? He was truly a scared confused little boy inside and out, who did not know his ass from a hole in the ground. I was always wishing that he were more than he was, while he was still hanging on to his parent's coattails every time life got hard.

Then I thought, "you're just as stupid as he is because you're still with him."

Yet the thought of being without him still petrified me. So, I tried to ignore the dreams without saying anything to Nick about them and concentrated on trying to be a better wife.

Along with praying for my marriage every day, I really did not know what else to do. I had given up hope on the little boy on the moon, whom I had dreamt about when I was a little girl. I figured he did not exist, and it was just a stupid dream, a fantasy that was never going to come true. The only thing I knew for sure was, Nick was not the little boy on the moon that I had planned my future with.

As each month went by Nick was getting meaner and more distant as he enjoyed his drinking. Even worse, when he was not drinking or working, he was depressed and sleeping for hours on end. I realized that it did not matter if I kept liquor out of the apartment, he would just go to the barracks and drink there. I would try to suggest romantic things that we could do together that did not cost money and did not involve drinking, but he always refused.

After six months of hanging in there with him I finally lost my temper one night after we had dinner with Pierson and Vanderpool downtown one Saturday night. Our Moped was in the shop getting new spark plugs, so we were at the bus stop waiting for the last bus back to our apartment. It was late, and Nick was drunk as usual. I was cold despite the sweater I was wearing. I told Nick I was cold and asked him to put his arms around me to help keep me warm. He told me that he was too busy trying to keep himself warm. I was so hurt that I called him an asshole as the tears rolled down my cheeks.

He reacted by telling me to stop crying because it irritated him when I cried. As I continued crying, he started yelling at me, "You're nothing but a fucking bitch and I can't love you the way you want to be loved. No matter how hard you try to make our marriage work it won't!"

I screamed back, "all I want is a normal loving marriage where we work together as a team. I have given up everything for you: my family, my friends everything! And if I lived in Milan, I would be working a lot more, but I chose you over that.

It was then that he spit in my face. I was in total shock and disbelief as I wiped the spit off my face with my sleeve. It felt as if a knife had gone through my heart. The bus pulled up and we both boarded it sitting a few rows away from one another.

I kept asking myself on that bus ride home what was so wrong with me that my own husband could not love me back. Why the hell did I marry this guy in the first place? Where was God in all of this? Why wasn't God helping me to have a healthy happy marriage? I felt helpless and afraid as I prayed silently for some divine intervention.

When we got back to the apartment we went to bed, I lay there next to him still talking to God silently. I wondered if God had forgotten that I even existed. Was it because I had stopped talking to God every day and visualizing my future being happy, the moment I hooked up with Nick? I began to realize that Nick had become my entire life and my God. I realized that I had put him above all else in my life, including my flute playing.

I had given up going to church because Nick thought it was bullshit. But worst of all I had given up being me. I should have gone to college and taken a totally different path in life right out of the starting gate. It also occurred to me that if I had put as much energy into making money as I had in being in love with Nick, I would be a rich woman already. Despite being conscious of the fact that I was being stupid with Nick did not stop me from being in love with him.

"Please God," I begged, "Show me how to stop loving him because my heart is feeling a lot of anger that I have no outlet for."

I also asked that if it was his will for us to remain married, then to make our marriage a happy one. Because we were fighting and making up just like my parents did.

CHAPTER 106

We went home for a month each summer on leave where everyone pat-ted Nick on the back for being a big bad paratrooper. He would spend most of his time home on leave drinking with his friends from high school.

It was then that I realized Nick was not drinking because he lived in Italy, as the property of Uncle Sam. He had been drinking with the boys in high school, long before I had even started dating him. He was drinking because he had been doing it so long, that now he could not stop, and I did not know what to do about it because he would not listen to me. Since I could not control his actions, I gave up.

Therefore, I did my best to enjoy myself by soaking in as much of Europe as I could. I enjoyed every moment that I spent in a museum, or classical concert, modeling and traveling with the basketball team. I enjoyed seeing Gypsy children for the first time in my life, begging for money outside the base or the train station. None of this stuff was important to Nick, but it was to me.

Appreciation of beauty was in all of it for me. I also did not want to be one of those people who looked back on their life wishing that they had appreciated various life experiences while they were happening.

Now I would be able to look back on my life in my old age and honestly say that I had experienced living in Europe, and that I did it to the fullest; and how I felt so at home there that I never wanted to leave.

Nick, on the other hand, was thrilled once he was within three months of ending his tour of duty in Italy.

I had just received a booking for a modeling job, a print ad for an Italian magazine. When I showed up for the shoot, it took everything I had in me to smile and pretend that I was happy and carefree for the camera. I found myself thinking once again that I should have just lived in Milan and concentrated on modeling, but I had put my marriage first, and now I felt like a fool for doing so.

Nick and I continued to fight and argue about everything. For instance, now he wanted to spend money we did not have for round-trip airline tickets to Los Angeles. He wanted to take his one month leave in Los Angeles before he was due to check into his new duty station.

To me it made more sense to go straight to his new duty station and spend that free month getting set up there. That way the Army would be flying us for free, and we would not be out of pocket for airfare. If Nick went home to LA, we would have to pay for the airfare there, and to his next duty station.

But Nick was acting like a spoiled brat, saying he wanted to party with his friends back home. I kept telling him that we could not afford to fly to Los Angeles, and we needed to save every dime we had to set up a home for ourselves in the States. Plus, I still had a paycheck coming from the modeling job I had just finished, and I wanted to stay in Italy for an extra two weeks to collect my money. It was just financially wiser to skip going to Los Angeles.

Nick would not listen and purchased an airline ticket for himself anyway. He figured I could stay in Italy alone while he went to Los Angeles. Then I could fly to his new duty station alone and wait for him there, while he lived it up back home. I thought it was pretty messed up that my husband was willing to leave me in a foreign country alone while he went to Los Angeles.

A week before Nick left for the States, we cleared out our apartment and moved in with my friends Mary and Keith Cross. They were a married couple who were both Army medics on the base. They had a small three-bedroom apartment which was within walking distance to the base in case one of them got called in for an emergency.

I saw it as a blessing from God when they offered us the room. Since we were staying in someone else's home, instead of fighting with me Nick was nice. Knowing he was going home to Los Angeles soon, his mood was more upbeat, excited instead of depressed for a change.

We made love the night before he left for Los Angeles. Before Nick boarded the bus to the airport the following morning, he kissed me goodbye and told me that he loved me. We both agreed that I would call him every other day just so we could stay in close contact with one another. But as I watched the airport bus pull away with my husband on it, I had a bad feeling about the whole thing deep down in the pit of my stomach.

He was completely unpredictable when he was with his friends, and his lack of maturity scared the hell out of me. I was trying to be patient with him by waiting for him to grow up and start acting like a responsible adult.

I knew in my heart that he was going to get off that airplane in Los Angeles, where Glen Smith would be waiting for him, and the party would begin. The liquor and drugs would flow, and Nick would start telling Army Airborne stories. It was all so pointless and stupid to me as I listened to some of the shit that flowed from Nick's mouth.

When I returned to Keith and Mary's apartment, they both tried to cheer me up by making me dinner. Later that evening my hairbrush came up missing from my nightstand, and I asked Keith and Mary if they had seen it.

Mary told me that they had no idea where it was, and said, "It must be the ghost that lives here."

I laughed at her and said, "You must be joking."

They insisted that there was the ghost of a little boy living in their apartment.

"He's a prankster," Keith said.

Mary said that the little boy was always taking their stuff and leaving it in the other spare bedroom.

We all walked down the hall to the other spare room, and when Keith opened the door all I saw was a room filled with boxes. But on the window ledge was my missing hairbrush.

I looked at Keith and Mary and laughed out loud because I really thought they were playing a joke on me.

"You don't expect me to believe that the ghost of a little boy put my hairbrush in here on the window ledge, do you? One of you did this to cheer me up and pull my leg. I don't believe in ghosts." I told them.

Keith and Mary just looked at one another and smiled. "Have it your way, but I'm telling you that we never touched your hairbrush." Keith insisted.

Later that night while I was sleeping, I was awakened because I was unable to breathe. It felt as if someone were sitting on top of my face, literally covering my mouth and nose preventing me from breathing, but no one was there. Petrified, I tried to scream out for help, but no sound come out of my mouth. My vocal cords were frozen.

After what seemed like forever, I finally heard myself scream and I felt whatever it was pinning me down get off.

I ran to the bedroom door as fast as I could, as Keith and Mary rushed into the bedroom.

They both looked panicked as they asked me what was wrong, standing there in their pajamas. At this point tears were rolling down my cheeks, as I told them what had just happened to me.

I saw them exchange a look as Mary said it was the ghost, "You shouldn't have laughed at him and said he didn't exist. You probably pissed him off."

"I'm not sleeping in that room tonight." I replied.

"You can sleep on the sofa with the light on if that makes you feel better." Keith said.

I went into the living room to spend the rest of the night on the sofa, after what had just happened in the bedroom. Mary made the sofa up for me and turned on the television so I would feel more comfortable. After they both returned to bed, I lay there on the sofa nervous about every single sound I heard. Finally, while watching Italian television, I went to sleep.

CHAPTER 107

The next day I walked to the base to buy a few groceries at the post super-market. I was still trying to shake off the horror from the night before. I had never experienced a ghostly presence before, and I never wanted too again. Sure, I had seen my brother shortly after he had passed away. I had seen angels, but that was different because they were heavenly visitations. They did not try to prevent me from breathing.

I had enough common sense to know that any spirit that was still hanging around in this dimension was bad news.

I wondered if it was a disembodied spirit that did not cross over, or a demon pretending to be a little boy. I was happy I did not have to live in that apartment, and that my stay would be temporary because living with a ghost was not normal.

After purchasing my groceries, I began to walk back to the apartment just as it started to rain. By the time I got a block away from the front gate my paper grocery bag began to tear open at the bottom as the rain hit it. A few cans of vegetables fell out of the bottom of the bag and began to roll on the sidewalk, as people walked past.

I heard someone yell out, "Let me give you a ride with those groceries. Your bag is breaking."

That is when I saw Jimmy, my friend Connie's husband. She was a female medic I knew from my stay at the Hotel Elena. I welcomed the ride and picked my cans up off the sidewalk and got into the car.

The minute we drove off the base and stopped at the first red light, the car was suddenly surrounded by six Italian men dressed in civilian clothes. I recognized one of them as Palo, the Italian CID agent who worked with the military police on the base. We had eaten lunch together at the pizzeria on the base a few times when it was overcrowded with the lunch crowd, and you were forced to share a table with someone.

I remembered making fun of him for being CID one day while eating lunch because he looked like a simple grape farmer to me.

Terrified, I looked over at Jimmy who was eating chunks of hash still wrapped in tinfoil. I was shocked because I had no idea that he was even selling hash. It dawned on me quickly that I was in the middle of a drug bust.

Everything suddenly became unreal and dreamlike, as if in slow motion. Suddenly, Palo opened my car door and whispered in my ear to get out of the car and to walk away as fast as I could.

He did not have to tell me twice. I got out quickly and started to walk away while the agents were pulling Jimmy out of the driver's seat.

Then one of the Italian CID agents stepped in front of me and yelled "Bastia, Bastia, Bastia, Bastia" which meant "stop" in Italian.

I stopped in my tracks and stood there frozen, afraid this guy wanted to shoot me.

Palo approached us and told the agent that he knew for a fact that I had nothing to do with the situation.

"I know this girl," he said.

Despite Palo vouching for me and trying to get me out of the mess, I was still put in handcuffs and pushed into a police car.

Palo walked over to the car I was in and told me not to worry that he knew that I was not involved in this, and that he would do his best to get me released as soon as possible. For now, however, I had to go downtown to the police station with them.

As the agent started driving the car away from the scene of the bust with me in the back of it, I was scared out of my mind. I kept telling myself that everything would be all right, and that I was going to get out of this mess because I had done nothing wrong. I also told myself there was nothing to worry about, all I had to do was tell the truth. It was not against the law to accept a ride home in the rain with your groceries.

Instead of pulling up at the Italian police station, we pulled up in front of Jimmy's apartment building. I was taken out of the police car and taken inside the apartment with Jimmy.

I watched as the police forced this poor guy to show them where all his hash was hidden. His wife was freaking out, and his three children were crying for their father because he was in handcuffs.

Within minutes the CID agents emerged from his bedroom with four plates of hash. I figured poor Jimmy would be going to prison for a long time. It broke my heart to see the look of fear on the faces of his wife and kids as they cried and begged the agents not to take him away.

I heard one of the agents asking Connie if she had any knowledge of her husband's hash business. Smartly she replied, "no".

Jimmy backed her up by saying, "My wife had no knowledge of what I was involved in. I was just trying to make a little extra money to further my education once she got out of the military."

Not paying attention to Jimmy, one of the agents looked at me and asked, "Are you Jimmy's hash selling partner?"

I told the truth; "I have no knowledge of Jimmy selling hash, much less smoking it. I know this couple from the Hotel Elena where we were waiting for housing together. And I have seen them at the base swimming pool and some base barbecues after the football games, that is it." I paused, took a breath and continued. "He offered me a ride home with my groceries in the rain because my bag broke and he tried to help me. He was literally just trying to be nice and help me out with a ride. That is all I can tell you." I said. Thinking fast, I quickly added. "This is just a case of me being in the wrong place at the wrong time I guess."

"How do we know you are telling the truth?" One of the Agents asked skeptically.

I defensively replied. "Because I was walking home with my groceries, that's all. You have searched me and found nothing but the food and the change from the $20 dollar bill I used to buy it with. I'm telling you again, I'm not involved in anything illegal."

Despite my adamant denial, they put me back in the police car and this time Jimmy was sitting in the backseat next to me. He did not say a word, his face looked frozen, and I could tell he was in shock. As we were being driven downtown to the police station, I saw a tear roll down one of his cheeks. I felt sorry for him and his wife, most of all, I was heartbroken for the children. We both knew without speaking that he was in a shit load of trouble.

I figured that all the hash I watched him eat in his car was probably starting to affect him because his eyes looked as if all the life had been drained out of them. I thought to myself, they are going to lock this poor guy up for years in some primitive prison in Italy. From this day forward, his life as a normal American is going to be over for a long time.

Once we arrived at the police station Jimmy and I were taken into separate interrogation rooms. I was then handcuffed to a chair that sat facing a desk.

Hours later one of the agents that had picked us up sat down behind the desk holding a file in his hands. He opened the file and started naming off names of other Americans who were in the military. He wanted to know if I knew any of the people, and if I had any knowledge of their drug activities.

Once again, I told the truth; I knew a few of the people from the base swimming pool and other functions on the base, but I had no idea what they did in their private lives. Nor did I have knowledge of Jimmy selling hash until today.

I repeated. "My busted grocery bag and groceries are proof that I was telling the truth."

I thought about Nick for the first time since the whole thing had happened; he was going to be pissed off at me if I got arrested. I knew Keith and Mary were probably wondering why I never returned to the apartment.

The agent got up and left the room. He was gone for so long that I dozed off knowing I was not going to jail in Italy. I awoke to the sound of the door shutting as the agent re-entered the room, this time with Palo. He uncuffed me and told me that I was free to go, and how lucky I was that Jimmy had insisted that I had nothing to do with his hash business. I was incredibly happy that I had eaten lunch with Palo enough times for him to vouch for the fact that I was a military housewife and not a drug dealer. He then asked me where my husband was.

I explained that I was waiting for my last modeling paycheck, and that my husband had gone home on leave. He then informed me that without my husband in Italy to sponsor me that I would have to leave the country because I was now in the country illegally.

I assured him that I would be leaving for the States in a few weeks with no delays.

He asked where I was staying, and I told him with a military couple who had a place a few blocks from the base.

"You better stay out of trouble for the remaining few weeks you are here," he cautioned me. Palo assured him saying, "Don't worry she's a good girl." Then he looked at me and said, "I'll give you a ride to your friend's home."

Once we were alone in his car, Palo told me that Jimmy had tried to commit suicide.

"Oh my God, how?" I asked.

"He somehow managed to stab himself in a main arm artery with an ink pen," he replied.

"I really can't blame him; his life is pretty much over for years to come," I said.

"Did you see his wife and children? How dumbfounded and shocked they were? I think I would have been thinking about killing myself too. All I can say is you must have a heart of stone to be able to do your job."

"I have a heart. I stood up for you and got you out of this mess tonight, didn't I? Now, give me your friend's address so I can take you home and then go home to my wife and children," he said.

Palo dropped me off in front of Mary and Keith's apartment building. As I got out of the car, he leaned his head out of the car window and said, "You stay out of trouble. And I want you to know that I do have a heart and I do feel sorry for your friend, but he broke the law and I have a job to do."

I replied, "I am sorry, I did not mean to offend you. It was just heart-breaking to see the effect this had on his wife and kids. Thank you for helping me. I'm incredibly grateful for everything you did to get me out of that situation, and I promise to stay out of trouble."

When I walked into the apartment at 11:30 p.m., as I had expected, Keith and Mary were worried sick. All they knew was I left that morning to get groceries from the base commissary and never came back.

I told them what happened that day, they were both shocked. They also had no idea that Jimmy was selling hash; like me they viewed him as a family man who played with his kids in the pool on the base.

I thanked God that I had gotten out of the mess, because my life flashed before my eyes while I was sitting in that police station. I knew that nothing in this world was worth giving up your freedom for. I believed that God gave everyone freedom of choice, and prison took that away. I took my tired and worn-out butt to bed and slept with the door open and the light on in case the ghost wanted to mess with me again. Just the thought of some ghost watching me or being near me made my skin crawl. It was wrong on so many levels and I considered it an invasion of privacy. This was only supposed to happen in the movies, not in real life. The only thing I knew for certain was, I now slept with one eye open.

The following morning, I was extremely tired, because I kept waking up throughout the night with every sound I heard. I kept thinking it was the ghost trying to mess with me again.

I made myself a cup of espresso, got dressed and made my way to the telephone calling center on the base to call Nick. I missed him so much already and could hardly wait to hear his voice. I wondered how he would react once I told him about Jimmy and my little brush with the law the day before.

When I arrived at the telephone center on the base, I paid $20 dollars for a 10-minute telephone call. Then it took five minutes for the overseas operator to connect to me to the States. It was always such a pain in the butt to call the States from Italy. Finally, I was connected, and after a few rings my mother-in-law answered the phone. Thrilled to hear her voice, I asked her how she was.

In a strange, guarded voice she replied, "I'm fine. I suppose you want to speak to Nick," she said.

"Yeah, that would be great," I said.

I could hear her yelling for him to come to the phone. She returned to the phone a minute later saying that he must have slept next-door at Glenn Smith's house. "Hang on, I'll go next-door to get him."

I waited for a few more minutes, and then finally I heard him say "hello" over the phone.

"It's so good to hear your voice," I said. "How are things in LA?" I asked.

All I heard was silence on the other end of the phone. He finally replied, "I'm having a good time."

"What have you been doing?" I asked.

"Glen and some of the guys picked me up from the airport and we all went to a welcome home party my parents had for me," he said.

"That's nice. I wish I had been there to be a part of all that. So, what else have you been doing," I asked.

"Just going out to some clubs with Glen and the guys." He replied.

I noticed that he kept sniffing over the phone. "Do you have a cold? you keep sniffing," I said.

"No, I was drinking last night," he replied.

"Well, it sounds like you've been doing a little more than drinking, and you seem different," I said.

"Don't worry about it; I just did a little coke with Glen last night." He said.

"Why are you messing around with that nasty stuff? What's wrong with you?" I asked.

He instantly became defensive and yelled, "Calm the fuck down it's no big deal!"

I thought about our money and how he was supposed to be holding onto it so we could rent a place to live. I asked him if he still had our money to rent a place to live with. That is when he told me that he had spent some of it.

"Why would you do that? What's more important than having a roof over our heads?" I could hardly believe what I was hearing as he explained how he had to pay to get into a nightclub and for his drinks.

"Look, it wasn't my fault. Glen knew a few girls at the club, and he invited them over to our table for a few drinks and I had to help pay the tab." He said in his most convincing tone.

"You bought drinks for another woman?" I was in shock and total disbelief.

"I'm tired of worrying about money; it's my money and I can spend it any fucking way I want," He yelled.

"But don't you realize how messed up this is?" I asked.

He blew up and started yelling at me over the phone, saying he wished he had done more than that.

"And what the hell is that supposed to mean? Have you been sleeping with other people?" I asked.

"No, but I wish I had. Fuck this shit. I want a divorce!" He blurted out.

I could hear Glen in the background as the tears rolled down my cheeks saying, "Come on Nick it's time to go."

Nick said, "I have to go. People are waiting on me."

The last thing I said to him before he hung up the phone on me was, "please don't do this to me."

CHAPTER 108

A s he hung up the phone, I fought hard to hold back my tears as I rushed out of the call center. My goal at this point was to get back to Keith and Mary's apartment as quickly as I could. I just wanted to cry my eyes out in private. But as I walked, I was unable to control the tears running down my cheeks. I felt hurt, abandoned and rejected all at the same time. Worst of all I felt ugly, as if I were not beautiful enough for anybody to love. It felt like I would never measure up to be good enough for Nick as crazy as that sounds. I also realized that the horrible nightmares I had were finally coming to pass. It felt like my whole world was slipping through my fingers and there was nothing I could do to make it stop. I did my best to walk down the sidewalk as fast as I could, making sure to keep my eyes looking down towards the sidewalk. I did not want anyone to see the tears I kept wiping from my cheeks, I just wanted to be invisible.

As I walked past Nick's old company I bumped into Pierson.

"Hold on a minute where are you going so fast? You're just going to walk right past me and not say hi?" Pierson asked, in his best imitated hurt voice.

Feeling embarrassed, I looked at him and said "Hi, I'm in a rush right now."

"Wait a minute; you're crying." He said. "What is wrong?"

"I really don't want to talk about it right now, I just want to have a shot of Grappa and be left alone" I said.

"What did Nick do to you this time?" He asked.

I just let it out and said, "Well for starters, he went home without me, and then he spent our money in nightclubs buying drinks for other women. And he has been doing cocaine. I heard him sniffing over the phone. But the worst part is he dumped me over the phone! He told me he wants a divorce. And, oh yeah, I got picked up by the Italian CID with Jimmy the other day he is suspected of drug dealing. I just want to get out of here before people see me crying in public," I said.

"Look, I just got back from Germany, and I get off in a few hours. Let me buy you a pizza downtown later." He said.

"Why?" I asked.

"Because I'm your friend and I want to make sure you're all right. Okay?" Pierson insisted.

"Yeah, I guess. Do you know where Mary and Keith Cross live? I asked.

"Sure, in that apartment building on the side street across from the base." He said.

"Well, I'm staying with them, and you can pick me up there when you get off." I replied.

"Okay, see you then and between now and then try to stop crying. Any guy that leaves his wife in another country, then dumps her over the phone isn't worth a tear." Pierson said.

"Thanks for the support," I said and walked away.

On my way back to the apartment I stopped and bought myself a bottle of Grappa.

When I arrived at the apartment, I let myself in and brushed past Keith and Mary who were sitting in the living room shining their boots. I headed straight for the kitchen for a shot glass. I had never been a big drinker but now I suddenly felt like a character in an old movie who had received bad news and needed to throw something hard back just to snap out of the shock.

I opened the bottle as fast as I could and grabbed a shot glass from the cabinet. I took a shot and welcomed the burn that ran down my throat. Mary walked into the kitchen and asked me what was wrong.

I turned around with tears in my eyes and said, "Nick just told me over the phone he wants a divorce and that he wants to sleep with other women. The fucker had the nerve to marry me twice," I cried. "I didn't even get the chance to tell him about getting picked up by the Italian CID with Jimmy before he hung up on me!"

Mary reached over and hugged me as I cried out loud, "Why, God why?"

"I'm sorry I have to say this to you honey but I think God is doing you a favor. For as long as I have known the two of you, I always felt that Nick should have treated you better. I used to get pissed off when he would tell you to shut up every time you tried to speak up in a conversation." She said.

"I was offended for women everywhere when he told you not to talk, because you would draw attention to yourself. Like that was wrong or something, like you did not have anything worthwhile to say. I know that it hurts now, but you're better off without him," Mary insisted.

I muttered, "He's also out there in LA blowing cocaine up his nose with our money."

"Shit, he's really gone off the deep end, hasn't he?" Mary said.

"I swear, Mary it was like talking to a stranger off the street, and they're nicer. Then, after telling me he wanted a divorce, he even hung up on me. I have had nightmares about this for months. I thought if I prayed to God every day to save my marriage, that he would. But I guess God cannot force someone to love you back." I said crying harder now.

I took another shot of Grappa and slammed the glass down in the sink and shouted, "screw it! If he wants out of our marriage, there is nothing I can do but accept that it is over. I should have known that he was just using me to keep his homesick butt company while he was in Europe. I cannot believe that I was dumb enough to trust him with my heart.

Weeping, I looked at Mary and said, "I feel like a security blanket that has been used and thrown out. I could've gone to college instead of wasting the best years of my life on him."

"Maybe you should go lie down for a while and try to relax." Mary suggested.

"You're right; it would probably do me good to just close my eyes and clear my head. Oh, I ran into Pierson on the way back here and he is going to come by later so we can grab a pizza. He probably felt sorry for me when he saw me crying, and I felt like a fool because he warned me not to marry Nick. He actually stood outside the church and told me not to marry Nick."

Mary laughed, "You should've taken his advice."

"You and Keith are welcome to come along with us," I invited.

"Thanks, but I have a big inspection tomorrow that I have to get ready for. Listen, honey, I do not know why Nick is such an asshole, but I believe things happen for a reason. I think you are going to be better off without him in your life. Right now, just go lie down and try to relax and we'll talk some more later."

I went to my room and lay there crying until I finally cried myself to sleep. I was awakened hours later by Mary telling me that Pierson was waiting for me in the living room.

Feeling like shit on a stick, I got up and went into the bathroom to wash my face. I felt no need to put on any make-up because I did not care how I looked at that point. I grabbed my antique leather bomber jacket, put my Frye boots back on, straightened out my wrinkled blue jeans I had been sleeping in, and walked into the living room where I heard Mary giving Pierson the details of Nick dumping me.

Pierson and I walked downtown to Johnny's Bar and Trattoria. I walked in there looking like I had been crying all day. Right then, I did not care if my eyes were bloodshot and puffy, all I knew was my heart was broken and I was in pain.

Soon, I would be a divorced woman and I just wanted to drink the pain and disappointment away.

Pierson got us a table near the jukebox and the pool table. We ordered our pizzas and talked about the horrible details of Nick dumping me over the phone, and my brush with the Italian CID agents.

He said he was not shocked about Nick's behavior because of the way he acted when I was not around.

"I told you not to marry him," Pierson said.

"And I thought you were an asshole for telling me the truth on my wedding day, but you were right. How did you know that Nick and I would not be riding into the sunset together?" I asked.

"Because I have run into Nick's type before," he said.

"What type is that?" I asked.

"You know, the type of guy that follows the crowd just to be part of a group because he has low self-esteem. The type who makes sexual comments about other women along with the other guys when you are not around. I did not want to say that to you on your wedding day, because it was not my place. Nick is one of the most confused individuals I ever met. That is how I knew he would not be able to take care of you, because he cannot even take care of himself; plus, he is selfish and should have always put you first.

I would never leave my girlfriend or wife alone in a foreign country and I would not have gone home on leave when I could not afford to. When you are married you cannot just run off and do that type of shit," he said.

"That's exactly what I was trying to get him to understand, but he refused to listen to reason." I agreed.

Then suddenly it dawned on me: maybe Nick had this whole thing planned. Maybe this was no random act.

I looked at Pierson and said, "I strongly suspect that Nick actually preplanned this. How fucked up is that? How could someone that I grew up with treat me this way after marrying me twice? I would not treat a dog the way he is treating me. You should have heard his voice on the phone. It sounded so cold blooded."

"Listen, Nick is an asshole who was too stupid to see what he had in you. I think he is crazy for dumping you. A lot of guys in our company think you are the finest thing they have ever seen. Everyone wondered how he was even able to get a girl like you to fall in love with him." Pierson added trying to make me feel better.

"Well, the funny thing is I don't think I'm all that good looking," I replied.

"You've got to be kidding me! You attract attention everywhere you go because you are so pretty. Hell, I have had to stand up for you a few times in the barracks, and when guys cat call you on the street. A few guys in the barracks tried to insinuate that they could be with you if they wanted to." He reminded me. "Nick was constantly teased that he was too ugly for you. That is one of many reasons I would never trust him to cover my ass in a wartime situation. If you do not have the balls to defend your wife's honor in the barracks, then how can you cover my ass when bullets fly?"

"I never knew that anyone on that base gave me a second thought. You are just trying to make me feel better by spinning these lies," I said.

"No, I'm telling you the truth. Every time you walked into that company there were always a few guys talking about you in the shower that night," He insisted.

"Well, that doesn't excuse the fact that I married a creep who wants to divorce me," I said. "It really doesn't matter much if other guys think I'm attractive; the only thing that matters to me is that my husband doesn't."

"Look, all I'm trying to do is get you to see that you were too good for him in the first place, and Nick is just a stupid fool and that's just the plain truth." He said.

Just then the waitress appeared at our table with our order. Pierson looked at me with a grin on his face and said, "now eat and try to cheer up. Afterwards we can put some coins in the jukebox and shoot some pool. Just try to relax and enjoy yourself. Believe me, Nick isn't worth your tears," he said. "It may not seem like it now, but you're going to have a brighter future without him." He predicted.

I knew he was telling me the truth because Mary and my family said the same things about Nick.

We ate and drank shots, then I kicked his butt in pool and darts, while the jukebox played songs by Journey, and Styx. I suspected that he was just letting me beat him to cheer me up.

We stayed there until they closed at 3 a.m. then we started walking back to Mary and Keith's apartment. There were no buses running and not a taxicab or person in sight. The streets of Vicenza looked deserted, quiet and very still as we walked. I was drunk and feeling no pain.

Nick and his bullshit seemed a million miles away. I felt happy and free as the cool night air hit my face and I felt free enough to walk out into the middle of the street and start yelling, "FUCK YOU, NICK AND YOU CAN HAVE YOUR CHEAP ASS FAKE RING BACK!"

With that, I took off my wedding ring and threw it as far as I could. Pierson just stood there watching me laughing and clapping his hands.

"Finally, you're standing up to him. I'm proud of you." He said.

"I'm kind of proud of me too," I replied.

CHAPTER 109

Once we arrived at Keith and Mary's, I asked if he wanted to come in and have some coffee, so he would not have to walk on the base drunk.

"Maybe that's a good idea. I am just getting out of trouble for making a joke about Nancy Reagan. The LT overheard me, and I got written up for denigrating the Commander and Chiefs wife."

I laughed, "What was the joke?" I asked.

"You don't want to know," He replied.

"That bad," I said as I opened the front door.

Once inside, we went into the kitchen where I made coffee.

"I want to listen to my Andy Williams cassette while I drink my coffee," I told him to follow me to my room so we would not wake Keith and Mary.

We quietly went to my room where I shut the door and turned on my cassette player low. The Andy Williams *Greatest Hits* cassette was still in the player from two days prior.

As we sat on the edge of my bed drinking coffee, Pierson said,

"I can't believe you like Andy Williams," as we listened to him belt out his version of "The Days of Wine and Roses."

"I was a music major in school and played the flute in marching band and orchestra, so it's not really all that unbelievable. Besides, I like a little bit of everything and that includes easy listening to Andy Williams."

"Well, I'll let you in on a little secret: I actually like a few of his songs, but "Moon River" is my favorite. I play it on my harmonica all the time." He confided.

"I didn't know you played the harmonica. Are you any good?" I asked.

"No, not really. I can only play a few songs that I've figured out on my own and "Moon River" is one of them." He said.

"How on Earth did you get into Andy Williams?" I asked.

"I grew up watching the Andy Williams Show once a week with my parents in the living room." He said.

Just then Andy Williams started singing "Moon River." We both sat there singing together for a moment. Then I looked over at him and said, "would you mind dancing with me to this?"

He looked at me and smiled as we both stood up and he took my hand. We begin to slow dance for moment in total silence, and I realized just how tall he really was for the first time. I looked up at him and saw in his eyes that he wanted to kiss me.

I said, "you want to kiss me, don't you?"

He shyly answered, "yes."

"Well, now that I'm single again I'm giving you permission to kiss me." I told him.

Then he kissed me to my surprise it felt right and natural. I did not know why but it just did. He pulled away and looked into my eyes for a moment, then he kissed me again. This time it was longer and more heartfelt, as we both began to take our clothes off at the same time with our mouths still embraced in a kiss.

Pierson was a lot taller than me, and his body was larger and more muscular than Nick's. I had never noticed that he had such a perfect body before, and I was pleasantly surprised. Who knew that such a perfect work of art was underneath his horrible clothing? No wonder he had all those women chasing him.

Before now, Pierson had just been my friend; the guy who took out my trash whenever he came over for dinner, and occasionally helped me cook dinner, just because he loved cooking. I never viewed him as attractive; he was just my friend who defended me.

As he began to make love to me it felt like my body was being made love to for the first time. Just the way I had always imagined it would be with my husband. Pierson made love to me for five hours straight, as if I were the most precious, beautiful woman known to man. I thought my body had died and gone to heaven.

Afterwards we lay there in bed, bodies wrapped together as one, watching a light rain hit the bedroom window outside. As he lay there running his fingers through my hair, we looked into each other's eyes, and I noticed that his eyes changed color while I was looking at them.

"Your eyes just changed colors," I said.

He replied, "That happens from time to time; they just can't seem to decide what color they want to be I guess."

Then he took me by total surprise saying, "I love you, Maya."

And without giving it a second thought I replied, "I love you too Pierson."

"I think we're a little past you calling me by my last name," He suggested.

"You're right, from now on we're on a first name basis Jake."

As I lay there feeling totally at peace in his arms, he asked me if I wanted to take a trip to Venice and Amsterdam with him.

"I want to take you to Venice, so I can buy you dinner at my favorite restaurant."

"I can't afford to go to Venice," I told him.

"That is why I said I would take you to Venice, meaning I would pay for the whole trip. In two days, I start two weeks leave." He announced. "I was going to travel around with Vanderpool, but I would much rather go with you. And don't worry about the money because I have plenty saved up."

"Well, all this sounds pretty tempting." I replied.

"All you have to do is say yes." He said with a pleading look in his eyes and a smile on his face.

"Okay, yes I'll go with you," I told him.

He hugged me and said "Great, then it is all settled all I have to do is break the news to Vanderpool that he will not be going with me. We can start in Venice and then go to Amsterdam, or we can go where our sense of adventure takes us."

Like an excited child, I lay there in his arms, and it felt good to be wrapped in his arms. I felt secure and safe from the outside world because, I knew that Jake would never hurt me or let anyone else harm a hair on my head. It was the way I had always wanted it to be when I was with Nick, but it never was and now it never would be.

CHAPTER 110

Over the next few days Jake Pierson and I spent every free moment together when he was off duty. We would spend the nights together making love and talking about our childhoods, and our most intimate thoughts and secrets as we played with each other's hands. I felt as if I had finally found what I had been waiting for since childhood.

I now understood the relationship that twins shared, that feeling of being so totally connected to another human being that you knew what they were thinking before they said it. Never had I felt this close to another human being, and it felt like a whole new world had opened for me. It felt like we were one person as we lay there at night looking into each other's eyes, knowing what the other was thinking without speaking words.

Soon I began to realize that one door had closed and another one had opened. The one that had just opened was filled with love, light and unspeakable joy.

We discovered that not only did we have a lot in common, but we both viewed life the same way. It was freaky how opposite we were yet the same.

I told him about my childhood friend De-De who used to take me flying in my dreams so I could plan my future with the little boy on the moon, who was supposed to be my husband when I grew up. I told Jake that at first, I thought Nick was the little boy because I loved him so much. As time went on, however, I realized he was not. After I told Jake all this, he got a strange look on his face.

"What's wrong," I asked.

"I used to have dreams like yours when I was four or five. I would dream I was on the moon sitting on a cloud playing Pat-a-Cake and other games with a little girl who had two dark long pig tails. She had tan skin and looked like she had come from an island, and I knew that she lived in a big city near the ocean.

She was my secret best friend from my dreams when I was a kid. I haven't thought about that in years and as I got older, I thought the dreams were just that, dreams."

"Did you have freckles on your face when you were a kid?" I asked.

"Yeah, I did." He confirmed.

"And was your hair short and parted on the side?" I continued.

"Yes, it was," he replied.

"So, this means those dreams were real, and we're not crazy," I said.

I told him that I remembered seeing the angels coming and going up and down a set of twin ladders side by side. "They were coming and going up and down those ladders from heaven to Earth like a work force. I saw this each time I traveled out of my body to see you and I knew that they were on missions to help people on Earth. That means that we are not down here by ourselves without help. I saw another dimensional level, next to ours it had nasty freaky looking stuff in it. And when I asked De-De about it, she told me bad souls were there with demons and cast-off negative emotions like fear, greed and hate that had taken physical form. Along with souls that had refused the light and God does not live there. I never want to encounter anything like that because it feeds on the light that we embody."

Then I told him about how I remembered being in time and space, flying up among the stars. And how in the middle of all that it looked like we were floating on a white cloud on the moon when we were playing together.

"Do you remember any of that?" I asked him.

"The only things I remember is flying around the "Moon" and wanting to take rocks home with me. I remember playing games with you and feeling like you were my best friend who lived by the ocean. I also remember someone telling me that I would have to be patient once I found you because you would be in love with someone else." He said.

"I wonder why we didn't recognize one another when we first met," I asked him.

"I guess we look different than we did when we were kids, and you were too focused on Nick to see anyone else." He said.

"You're right; I was too focused on Nick." I agreed.

Then we both said at the same time "I guess that's why we didn't recognize one another." We both laughed because not only were we thinking the same thing, but we said it out loud at the same time.

"And to think, I wasted all this time believing Nick was my future," I said.

"Well, I'm ready to make up for lost time." He said.

Then he kissed me like I had never been kissed before and I knew in that moment that I was not crazy, the little boy on the moon was real. So that meant those angels and all the things I saw as a child were real.

After two days of total bliss together I felt like I was in some sort of magical dream state as we boarded the train to Venice together. We each had our clothes in back packs, my cassette player in hand and happy hearts.

When we arrived at a quaint little hotel overlooking the water in Venice, I knew I had been swept off my feet. We checked into our room which had a perfect view of the water. Then he took me to his favorite little restaurant where we dined on the best pasta and steak-sized pork chops I had ever tasted.

After dinner, Jake took me on a gondolier through the water canals of Venice as the sun set. In my wildest dreams, I never thought that a man could be this romantic and nice. That night we took a shower together, then slow danced naked in our room overlooking the water to Gordon Lightfoot singing "If You Could Read My Mind Love."

This man even liked Gordon Lightfoot. This was a dream that I never wanted to wake up from. After making love to me and talking all night into the early morning hours, we finally fell asleep, our bodies intertwined as one.

I woke up to butter croissants and coffee in bed, and he served it to me on a tray with fresh flowers. The flowers were so fresh that they still had the root and some dirt attached to them. "What a special way to wake up and start the day, but where did you get these flowers?" I asked smiling. "The roots and dirt are still hanging from the bottom of them, kind of like that Christmas tree we ripped off and put back."

A boyish mischievous grin appeared on his face as he confessed to stealing them from a flower box hanging from some Italian's window across the street from the hotel.

"Why didn't you just buy some?" I asked.

"Because I wanted you to have them with your breakfast when you woke up, and I didn't see an open flower shop on the street," he replied. "And I didn't think I had time to go hunt for one before you woke up, so I did what I had to do."

I thought to myself, "Is this guy for real? Do guys like this really exist?" A girl reads about this type of thing, but it never really happens to anyone except in the movies. But this was real life, and this was happening to me. The fact that the flowers still had the roots and dirt still attached was just so damn romantic.

After I had eaten, showered and dressed, Jake and I saw everything that Venice had to offer before leaving for Amsterdam the following morning.

Our last night in Venice, Jake took me to yet another beautiful outdoor restaurant by the water where we dined on seafood with a vintage bottle of wine. After dinner we slow danced to ballads played by an old Italian accordion player. I felt like Cinderella at the ball, the prince found me, and the slipper fit. I had waited for so long to be loved this way by Nick, and now here was Jake doing everything right without even being asked. He even pulled out chairs and opened doors for me.

On our way to Amsterdam, he told me that he had something that he wanted to talk to me about before I went back to the States.

"What is it?" I asked.

"Just a few ideas I've had running through my head. Nothing to be freaked out about; we can talk about it later. I just want to make sure that I don't lose you after finding you." He said.

"Okay. After Venice, God only knows what you have in store for me next." I said enthusiastically.

I then pulled out a paperback copy of Erica Jong's "Fear of Flying" to read, as Jake read Stephen King's book "The Stand," one of my personal favorites. He leaned his back against the window, then told me to lean back against his chest so we could read together. We listened to Elton John's "Friends" together as we read. We both listened to the music as if we had done that many times before together.

CHAPTER 111

When we finally arrived in Amsterdam, Jake got us a taxi in front of the train station and gave the driver the name of the hotel he wanted us to stay in. Fifteen minutes later we pulled up in front of a really nice hotel, again overlooking the water.

In our room, we took a quick shower together, where Jake insisted on washing my hair and back for me. I had never had a man wash my hair for me or my back, and I knew that I wanted this to happen every day for the rest of my life. I could hear a little voice in my head telling me, "This is the way love is supposed to be and feel."

After our shower, Jake took me downstairs to the restaurant and left me there to order food for the both of us. He left saying that he would be back in 15 minutes.

"Where are you going?" I asked.

"It's a surprise. Just order me some food and I'll be right back."

"Okay," I said reluctantly. By the time the food had arrived at our table Jake was back.

"Where did you go that quickly and what were you doing?" I asked him smiling.

"It's a surprise. You will find out soon enough, now eat. We have to go soon."

After we had finished our food, he paid the bill then took me outside the hotel and got us a taxi. He instructed the driver to take us to some stadium I had never heard of in the city.

"Why are we going to a stadium?" I asked.

"Don't worry; it's a surprise." He said.

Right before we reached the stadium, he put his hands over my eyes. When he removed them, I saw that this man was taking me to see the Rolling Stones, Tattoo You tour concert in Amsterdam.

"Oh my God, I love The Rolling Stones," I said hugging him. I kept saying, oh my God repeatedly while he laughed at me.

He paid the driver, as we got out of the taxi, he took my hand and said, "I figured this would give you a thrill."

"I'm more than thrilled; I'm blown away!" I cried in joy.

We waited in line for a while to get in, but we were in our seats just in time to see Mick Jagger and the boys start the show. Mick Jagger, whom I had nicknamed "Lips" years ago because his lips were so luscious, danced around the stage as he sang doing his best funky moves. Keith Richards and the boys played like they were in a class of their own. In my opinion, no other band had their sound. Jake and I danced and sang for hours, as if we did not have a care in the world.

After the concert we went back to the hotel and made love. As we lay there in each other's arms, he asked me if I was happy with him.

"Well, who wouldn't be," I replied. "Now I know why all those girls fell for you. I always wondered what those girls saw in you and now I know," I said smiling.

"But I didn't treat them the way I treat you," he said. "Don't get me wrong, I was nice and respectful to everyone I dated but I never gave them this."

"Gave them what?" I asked.

Then he reached over and took a small box out of the pocket of his blue jeans which were on the floor at the side of the bed.

"Look, I want you to wear this," as he handed me a jewelry box. My heart skipped a beat as I opened it and saw the most unusual opal ring I had ever seen. It seemed to change colors every time you looked at it, just like his eyes. The colors of the ring were hued in white, blue, pink and green.

He put the ring on my finger and said, "Listen, I'm not trying to rush you but now that you're getting divorced, I'm asking you to wear this promise ring I bought for you." After a slight pause he swallowed hard and continued, "This ring is my promise to you that I will always love, cherish, and treat you well. I will always do my best to treat you with nothing but love and respect. This means that I never want to be with anyone else but you, and when you're divorced and ready to start your life over again, I want to marry you," he said.

Struggling to breathe, because I was so shocked that this was even happening to me, it was hard to believe that this was even my reality.

"Please say something?" he said looking worried.

I struggled to find my voice to get some words out.

"So, this is what you were up to earlier today and how did you know I like opals?" I asked.

"I remembered hearing you say once that you hated diamonds but loved opals."

Jake continued, "The moment I laid eyes on you I thought you were the most beautiful woman I had ever seen. Now I want you to understand that I never secretly lusted after you. I truly never thought about us being together before now, and I respected your choice to be with Nick."

"I even went to your wedding and watched as you played house with him. Now that he has walked away, I want my chance with you. I know you need time to get things straight in your head, but I wanted you to know how I felt before you leave for the States, and I never saw you again."

A tear rolled down my cheek as I looked at him and then the ring again. Someone was giving me a ring and telling me that they never wanted to be with anyone else but me.

And he really meant it. The little boy on the moon was a real person.

CHAPTER 112

"I love you too and I'm willing to be your girlfriend, but I have to get divorced before I can even think about getting married again, I'm not a Mormon ya know." I said laughing.

"Very funny Maya, don't worry, I have all the time in the world to wait for you, if I know that you're going to be mine in the end." He said.

Tears of joy ran down my cheeks as I looked at the ring on my finger and back at him again. I was speechless for a moment still finding it unreal that someone was giving me a ring without me asking him.

He said he had a few months left in Italy. Then a year to serve in the United States.

"I want you to wait for me in Los Angeles until I get out of the Army. I'm even willing to move there when I get out, if that's what it takes to be with you."

"Don't worry I'll be waiting for you," I said as I lay back down into his arms. And I thought to myself how safe and happy I felt with him. Jake even had what I called "The body nook." The body nook is that perfect spot on your man, where you can lay your head and feel like your heart was finally at home. It had never felt this way with Nick and then I realized it was because he was never really in love with me to begin with.

Our relationship had been based on me putting in all the effort, and even that approach failed. But with Jake everything was easy and natural and there was no effort involved at all. And to think, I never even saw him as attractive, or even noticed how great he truly was.

That is when I realized that I may have been dumped by Nick, but at the same time a new door had been opened for me and my biggest dream was finally coming true.

As I lay there that night, I knew that God had my back. He must have had an angel hit this man with a love arrow because Jake Pierson was a miracle and a gift to me, and I knew that this gift was from above.

We ran around Amsterdam for the next few days like two demented romantic fools on a honeymoon. We concentrated on enjoying the time we had left together. We talked about our childhoods and how we grew up, Jake told me that he had been raised in a Mormon family in Utah. Then he explained why he never believed in the religion.

"It's a bunch of bull crap that I will never believe in. My parents forced me to go to church until I was 18. Then they expected me to go on a mission for a few years before going to college.

"That's when I accepted a basketball scholarship from Snow College for a year, got bored and then the Army and went Airborne cause it sounded exciting."

"What do Mormons believe?" I asked.

"They believe that a guy named Joseph Smith had a revelation from God and was given some plates written by God. Then God told him to start a church. The guy had like 40 wives and a bunch of kids." He said.

"You're kidding me."

"Not kidding. He said. "Back then Mormons had more than one wife until the church outlawed it."

"Do they believe in the Bible?" I asked.

"Yes, but they also follow the "Book of Mormon". Anyway, I never drank the Kool-Aid." He said with a smirk.

"So that's how you ended up in the Army. You were running away from the church," I reasoned.

"What was it like growing up in Utah?" I asked.

"I'm from a place called Dugway high up in the mountains in the middle of nowhere, on a restricted military base that looks like a little oasis in the middle of the desert. That is why I loved growing up there; I had my own desert to explore every day with no people around. It was just me and the wild horses that early Spanish settlers left more than 200 years ago, and all the other animals that lived out there."

"So why were your parents living there?" I asked.

"My father had been in the Army, and when he got out, he took a Civilian Government job working for the base telephone company. My mother works as the base librarian. I have three sisters, three brothers and I am the oldest of the boys," he explained.

"I'm the oldest kid in my family, but growing up in the middle of nowhere sounds boring, what did you do for fun out there? Go cow tipping?" I joked.

"No, I built a fort in the desert and kept all my secret stuff out there, like my Playboy Magazine collection. I camped out all the time with my Sears and Roebuck .22 caliber rifle that my dad gave me for Christmas one year. I also loved sitting out there drawing pictures of all the animals I saw. He said.

"I caught rattlesnakes and cooked them on Dad's grill in the backyard, and I had a pet hawk. My sister Lilly and I collected as many animals as we could, then we would open our own zoo during the summer in our backyard. We used to charge the neighborhood kids twenty-five cents admission to get in." He recalled smiling.

"The zoo thing sounds fine but eating and playing with rattlesnakes is awfully weird to me. I cannot believe you ate snake meat. That is just plain nasty. I said wrinkling up my nose, as if smelling the cooking snake.

"What was your high school like?" I asked.

"It was pretty small. My graduating class had a total of 17 students in it. I played basketball on my high school team, and dated a cheerleader named Serena who wanted to marry me. She actually had a wedding dress picked out." He said.

"Are you serious?" I asked.

"I'm telling you the truth! She really wanted to marry me." He said laughing.

"Did you ever tell this poor girl that you were going to marry her?" I asked.

"No, it was all her idea, she figured that since we had been together for two years and sleeping together that marriage was the next step. When I joined the Army and left home, she cried. She used to write me a lot when I first joined, but eventually she met someone else and got married and moved to Tennessee."

"So how come you didn't want to marry her? I asked.

"Because she wasn't you and I've been waiting for you. When I was a kid, I thought of you as my little island girl. Now I realize that after all these years subconsciously I was waiting for the girl who lived by the sea." He said. "My mom used to dream about you from time to time. She would tell me that she had dreamed that I had brought a tan skinned girl home and announced that I was going to marry her. The first time I made love to you I knew that you were the girl I had been waiting for; that's why I bought you the ring so fast." He said.

I knew he was right because I felt the same way about him. Our first night together I knew he was the one for me. Now we knew everything about one another, including all the people the other had slept with. Jake's list was extremely long.

CHAPTER 113

We cherished every moment we had together as we went and listened to live music at small bars; we read together in a cool bookstore that he had discovered on his last trip. And we looked at antiques together, we even checked out the hookers in the red-light district. I felt like heaven was here on Earth and I was a spoiled child just enjoying it all.

Sadly, we both had to head back to Italy and the little twin bed at Keith and Mary's. We wished we were rich enough to just take off and go live by the sea on the French Rivera.

Unfortunately, I was planning on returning to the States in a few days and I had to go to Nick's old company to get my modeling job paycheck from the mail room. I was dreading walking back into his old company without him being there.

The day after Jake and I returned from our trip, I got up enough nerve to go get my check from the company mail room. I turned around to leave to book a flight to Los Angeles, when the Company Commander walked in as I was walking out and said, "I need to have a word with you in my office please."

Suddenly, feeling nervous I said, "sure no problem."

I followed him into his office, he shut the door and told me to have a seat and pointed to the chair facing his desk.

I sat down as he said, "Word has reached my ears that your husband has gone back to the States without you. I have been trying to locate you. May I ask where you have been staying since you cleared out of your apartment?"

"I've been staying with a married couple I know who live near the base. I have been waiting for this modeling paycheck to come in the mail which I have here in my hand. And it's true sir, he did go back to the States without me. He wanted to go home on leave before going to his next duty station, and there wasn't enough money for me to go with him." I explained.

"So, he just left you here?" He said shaking his head in disappointment.

"Yes sir," I replied.

"Well, you're now in the country illegally without your husband here to sponsor you. Your husband is halfway through his leave, so I want you to go over to the travel office when you leave here." He handed me some paperwork and said, "Take these orders with you, and they will give you the airline ticket that your husband never picked up for you. You will be taken to the airport tomorrow on one of our busses. Once you arrive in Fort Bragg, NC, you are to check into the guest house on the base. You are to wait there for your husband until he shows up, and I am going to notify his new Company Commander of his actions here. If he were still here under my command, I would slam his ass to the wall for this."

I told the Company Commander that I had my own money to fly home to Los Angeles. "See my check," I said as I held it up to show him.

I don't need the Army to buy me an airline ticket, I just want to go home to Los Angeles," I told him.

He looked at me and said, "You will take the ticket and go to North Carolina. Once you get there you are free to go to Los Angeles, or wherever you want. You do not have a choice in the matter. You should not be here at all. You are in this country illegally without your husband to sponsor you" he said.

Amazing! I could not believe the Army was telling me what to do and I had not even joined. I did my best to contain my anger and remain calm before he restricted me to the base guest house as well while I was still in Italy.

I smiled at him, thanked him for his time, and got out of there as fast as I could. I begrudgingly headed to the travel office where I spent a few hours being issued an airline ticket and reservations for the guest house at Fort Bragg once I arrived there.

This really sucked, now I had to leave at 9 the following morning.

When I rushed back to Keith and Mary's where Jake was waiting for me, I had to give him the bad news, and I wanted to spend as much quality time with him as I could before I left. The whole thing just sucked as I realized I would not be able to tell my other friends goodbye.

In the apartment Mary and Keith were sitting on the sofa listening to *John Denver's Greatest Hits*. I gave them my bad news first, then proceeded to the kitchen where I found Jake busy marinating two large steaks for us to put in the broiler for dinner. He looked at me with a smile, but that smile faded once he saw the unhappy look on my face. He immediately stopped what he was doing and asked. "What's wrong?"

I showed him my airline ticket and told him everything the Company Commander said to me.

"So, we only have tonight then," he said pulling me into his arms.

I looked up at him with tears in my eyes and said, "Now that we have found one another I'm not ready to leave you yet. I thought we would have a few more days together."

He held me close and said, "Don't worry baby we will be together, because when I get out of the Army, I'm coming to LA for you. You just do what you need to do legally to get yourself free from that joke of a marriage you've gotten yourself into."

"Don't worry, Nick has probably gone to his parents to begin the process already." I said.

"Good, the sooner the better. I am going to write you every night and call you at least once a week until we are together again. And when things get rough, I want you to look at that ring on your finger and remember how much I love you." He said.

"Okay," I said holding onto him never wanting to let go.

He took my face into his hand looked into my eyes and said, "Now let me see that beautiful smile of yours. Let's just cook a nice dinner together, enjoy a bottle of wine and our last night together."

"You really have a way of helping me see the brighter side of things," I told him.

After we had finished cooking, we used two of Mary's TV dinner trays to set up a small dinner in my little bedroom. Jake lit a thin white candle and put in a Elton John cassette while we ate.

When the song "We All Fall In Love Sometimes" began to play we slow danced to it as he sang the words softly in my ear. It was Hard to believe coming from the background he did, that Jake even knew who Elton John was, much less the words to the song.

"I'm surprised that you like Elton John," I said.

"I don't know why. I also like James Brown, BB King, Buddy Guy and Howlin' Wolf. Just because I was raised a white Mormon, does not mean that I do not know good music when I hear it." He said.

"So how did you get exposed to the blues living in the middle of nowhere in Utah?" I asked.

"Well, we had this little thing called a radio that had blues and soul music on the radio stations, plus, I was friendly with some of the black soldiers who were stationed on the base where I lived. When I get out of the Army, I will take you home to meet my family, and you will see for yourself that Utah is not that far removed from any other place in America. It's not filled with polygamists wearing pioneer clothing. We have a variety of music and people living there, especially in Salt Lake City." He informed me.

"You're taking me to meet your family?" I asked.

"I plan on it. I put a promise ring on your finger and once you are divorced, I plan on replacing that with a wedding ring when you are ready. So why wouldn't I take you to meet my family?" He asked.

"It's all just happening so fast. It is like Nick just walked out of my life and you just moved right in. I need some time to deal with all this." I said.

"We can take our time and go slowly. I do not want you to ever feel pressured to be with me. Are you having second thoughts about us being together?" He asked.

"No, that's not it; I want to be with you, but I must get divorced before I can meet your family. The time we have already spent together has been the happiest time of my life, but I definitely need to get free from Nick." I told him.

"I understand," he said.

That night we lay in each other's arms unable to sleep, afraid of missing even a single moment of being together.

We got up in the morning and thanked Keith and Mary for allowing us to shack up together in their apartment. Jake then walked me to the base to get on the bus that would take me to the airport. After we hugged goodbye, I got on the bus, and a tear ran down my cheek as the bus pulled away and I could no longer see Jake.

CHAPTER 114

I arrived at the airport, got on the plane and thought about how I was going to deal with Nick once I saw him again. I could hardly wait to give him a piece of my mind. Now that I saw a better future for myself, part of me did not even want to see him after the way he had treated me. Despite my anger, part of me still loved him probably because we had known one other since we were kids. I remembered reading somewhere that once you absolutely loved someone that love never really went away. That did not mean we were suited for each other because we were not a good match.

I knew that his former Company Commander had contacted the new one and that Nick was in trouble for leaving me in Italy alone. I figured I had better do as I was told, and check into the guest house until Nick showed up. Then we would come to a mutual understanding about ending this messed up marriage. I would let him know that I was in love with Jake and show him the ring that Jake had put on my finger. The ring that he had not seen fit to buy me himself. I would proudly proclaim to him that someone else wanted to marry me. I was fully aware that this was my ego talking because I had been dumped.

I figured Nick would not give a damn because he certainly was not in love with me.

I sat in my seat smiling because the little boy on the moon was real, and I knew that God had my back, God was real, and everything I remembered from my childhood dreams was real. Since the little boy on the moon was real, then De-De and the angels I saw going up and down that ladder was real. Unbelievable and all true.

The minute my plane landed on US soil, I put my headphones on and turned on my cassette player to Linda Ronstadt singing *"Living in the USA,"* which seemed fitting for the occasion.

As I walked through the airport it felt strange to be back in the United States again after being gone for so long. Everyone had a southern accent here and it felt different from being in Los Angeles. In the airport, I saw elderly people in wheelchairs or walking with canes instead of riding around on bicycles healthy and vital like the Italians. I also remembered that a lot of Americans were not as nice and accommodating as the people were in Italy.

No one was going to be calling me beautiful as I walked down the street here.

I got my luggage and hailed a cab, giving the driver the address to the guesthouse on the base. While looking out the cab window during the drive to the base, it did not take me long to realize that I was truly in the south. I saw a lot of trailer parks for the first time in my life. They looked like little boxes with people living in them.

I saw a lot of large, wide open spaces with small homes on them that looked like they had been built long ago and one good storm could blow them over. No doubt there was probably a lot of history that went along with those little beat up houses, and the land they stood on. Some of the bigger, nicer homes we passed looked like the plantations I had seen in the "Roots" miniseries in high school.

Once we approached the front gate of the base, I saw a big sign that said: "Welcome to Fort Bragg," in big bold letters. As we drove through the front gate and onto the base, we passed the barracks of all the different Airborne companies.

I saw the soldiers walking in and out of the buildings wearing camouflage uniforms and red berets tilted to the side of their heads. It reminded me of how being on a military installation was like entering an entirely different world. The taxi pulled up in front of the guesthouse, I paid the driver and gave him a tip. Despite that, I asked him to carry my luggage into the front office of the guest house. He did not leave his driver's seat; just popped the trunk open and sat there. In Italy, the driver would have automatically opened my door and carried my luggage inside. I was already feeling homesick.

I checked in at the front desk, got the keys to my room, and using a luggage cart, had to get my things to my room by myself.

CHAPTER 115

That is when I felt the first wave of nausea. I got my door opened and rushed to the bathroom where I reached the toilet just in time to throw up everything I had eaten on the plane. I was starting to feel sick, clammy, lightheaded and weak. Oh my God, I thought, either I ate some bad food on the plane, or I caught some sort of virus from someone on the plane. Shit, I thought, as I lay down on the bed in hopes that the room would stop spinning. I felt like I was going to die; all I could do was lay there until I finally fell asleep.

When I awoke hours later, it was night, and my room was dark. I reached over to the nightstand on the side of the bed and turned the lamp on. I looked at my watch and saw that it was only a little after 8 p.m. I realized I had been sleeping for hours. As I sat up in the bed and put my feet on the carpeted floor, my legs felt weak. It was as if I had no energy or strength in them at all.

Maybe if I eat something, I will feel better, I thought. I saw the Yellow Pages sitting next to the telephone and looked for a place that delivered food. I realized that my options were extremely limited, it was pizza or a greasy hamburger. I choose the pizza and a ginger ale. As I sat back down on the bed, I found myself wishing that Jake were there to feed me soup or something healthy. I missed him already and thought about something my mother said to me when I was a kid. "The only thing a weak man can do for me is to introduce me to a strong friend." This certainly applied to me in my present situation. I was too young at the time to understand what she meant when she said it, but I sure as hell did now.

I heard the pizza delivery guy knock on the door, got up from the bed and grabbed my wallet out of my purse. I opened the door, paid the guy and gave him a tip, took my pizza and ginger ale back to bed, and got in. After one bite, I came to the conclusion that American pizza tasted like cardboard; the red sauce sucked. Italian brick oven pizza had truly spoiled me. I wondered how do you go back to this after eating the real thing in Italy for so long?

Halfway through my first piece, the nausea started again. I quickly ran to the bathroom just in time to vomit until I was dry heaving. I sat on the floor, my head resting on the toilet seat; bewildered by what was happening. What the hell did I have? In the morning I would find the doctor at the base hospital and find out what was going on if I did not feel better. I hardly ever got sick unless I had bad menstrual cramps, but whatever this was, it prevented me from keeping food down. With that decision, I felt another wave of nausea, dry heaved in the toilet again then went back to bed for the night.

When I awoke the following morning, I still did not feel well. I dressed and called a base taxi to take me to the Army Hospital Emergency Room. After waiting almost an hour, finally I was examined by a doctor who took a blood sample. He returned to the room and told me that I was pregnant.

"You're just having a little bit of morning sickness which is quite normal," he said.

Shocked and horrified at the same time I told him that it was impossible because I was on birth control pills and was still having a period.

The Doctor informed me, "It's common for some women to still continue having a period for a few months after becoming pregnant. You are about three months along and since you are new to the base here is a list of OB/GYN doctors. You need to call one of them and make an appointment as soon as possible."

He handed me the list of doctors and wished me luck.

As I watched him leave the room, I thought, "What the hell am I going to do now? My husband has dumped me, I am getting a divorce and now I am three months pregnant."

There had been a time when I had wondered what my children with Nick would be like and even wished for it to happen one day. How would Jake react to the fact that another man's baby was part of the package now? Would he still want to marry me? All these thoughts rushed through my mind within seconds. I hurried and got dressed, then caught a taxi back to the guesthouse.

CHAPTER 116

Once I was back in the room I sat on the bed and cried. I cried because I was 22 years old and having a baby with an asshole like Nick. I cried because raising a child without its natural father around everyday had not been in my life plan. I cried because I had been dumb enough to marry Nick in the first place. I cried because now I felt ashamed to tell my entire family that I was pregnant and getting divorced, after they all warned me to stay away from Nick. I thought about getting an abortion but that was not an option for me, because I remembered being in my mother's womb, after my body had formed.

It was a small memory, but a memory just the same and it was real to me. I believed in a woman's right to get an abortion, but I personally felt that it was too late for me. I could already sense the baby was a boy. I felt like I had already let the kid down because I was getting divorced before it even came into the world.

I had promised myself when I was younger that I would never have a baby without the father; I would have tons of money and a nice home before I ever gave birth to anyone. Now here I was, in a guest house on a military base with no job or home of my own for the baby to live in. I looked at Jake's ring on my finger and thought, I guess I am about to find out just how much Jake loves me.

I called him in Italy to tell him the news. He was excited to hear my voice over the phone and started telling me how much he missed me already.

"Well, you may not feel that way when you hear my news." I said.

"What happened?" he asked in a serious voice.

"There's no easy way to say this so I'll just say it, I just found out that I'm three months pregnant with Nick's baby. I have been sick and throwing up ever since I got off the plane. I went to the emergency room today because it did not stop. I thought I had food poisoning from the airplane food, but the doctor told me I am pregnant. And I have already made up my mind to keep it, so I won't be mad if you want your ring back. I wouldn't blame you for walking away," I informed him.

"I'm not walking away. When I told you that I loved you I meant it. So, we start out together with a kid. We can deal with this together. Besides, I like kids." He said.

"I can't believe you still want me?" I replied.

"Everything is going to be all right." He said reassuringly.

"Yeah, but I still don't want to rush into getting married again. I think we should live together first. I am not going to rush into marriage just because I am having a baby. I want us to start from the beginning with our relationship and take it slow with each other. I just need to take a breath between marriages." I told him.

"In other words, you just don't want to make another mistake." He said.

"No, it's not like that," I said. "You could never be a mistake; you're the best thing that ever walked into my life. I am just making sure that our relationship is a healthy one and that it starts out on solid ground."

"The only thing I know for sure is I do love you, and I do remember you from when we were kids. He said.

"When you come to Los Angeles, we can start out fresh and go from there." I said.

I started to feel sick again and told Jake that I had to hang up so I could go throw up.

We quickly said our goodbyes, and I ran to the bathroom and threw up. When I finished, I crawled back into bed, placed my hands on my stomach and wondered if my son would look like Nick or me. I was hoping he would look like me instead of his father. That way it would not be such a constant reminder that I had been dumb enough to marry him in the first place.

I had considered calling Nick at his mother's house to give him the news, but what if he hung up on me again? I figured it would be better to tell him in person; then I was going home to Los Angeles. I was thinking that I would have to stay with my father and stepmother in the beginning until I found a job and got my own place.

Getting my life together before the baby was born was a priority.

CHAPTER 117

I spent a week in that room alone with morning sickness, until one afternoon I was taking a nap and was awakened by the telephone ringing on my nightstand. I reached over and answered it and was surprised when I heard Nick's voice on the other end of the line. He sounded normal this time, like nothing had happened the last time we spoke. He told me that he had just arrived at the base that morning and had just come out of a meeting with his new Company Commander.

"I'll be at the guest house in an hour." He said.

After I hung up the phone, I thought about how he had treated me, and how badly he had hurt me. I was relieved that I would be going home soon and putting this whole mess behind me. Only problem was I would be forced to see him for the next 18 years, because of visitation rights with the baby.

My anger towards him was so strong that I could physically feel rage run through my body, I never wanted to see him again at this point. I told myself to be calm and not start a fight. Just get away from him as soon as you can I cautioned myself.

When he knocked on the door an hour later, I was sitting in a chair praying that the morning sickness would leave. I got up and opened the door for him.

He saw that I was not well, and asked, "What's wrong with you? It looks like you're sick."

I walked back to the chair and sat down and said, "Yes, I'm sick because I'm pregnant with your child. I have morning sickness and it feels like I'm going to die."

The look on his face was priceless. He looked like someone had knocked the wind out of him. He put his duffel bag down and sat on the edge of the bed, speechless. He managed to mumble, "I thought you were on the pill."

"I was but I got pregnant anyway. It happened because the pill is not 100% fool-proof. Trust me, the last thing I want right now is to be having a baby with you at my age, and in our current situation." I said flatly, pausing for effect, before continuing. "I had no idea until I arrived here and got sick and when it wouldn't go away, I went to the emergency room, the rest is history."

He walked over to the chair I was sitting in and put his arm around me and said, "It's going to be okay. We can get an abortion."

My anger rising, I replied. "I'm three months along. It is already a person. I can't just throw the baby away," My anger toward him exploded as I continued. "You're the biggest asshole I've ever met in my entire life. You lured me all the way to Italy to marry you and even had the nerve to marry me twice! You did not even have enough respect for me to buy me a wedding ring on your own, I had to buy my own piece of shit ring. And what is worse you have spit in my face." I paused to gather my thought and continued. "Then you decided to leave me in a foreign country alone. You got fucked up on Coke and slept with who knows what from some night club. You spent our money on a trip you never should have taken. You're the worst husband in the world and I'm still trying to wrap my head around the fact that I actually fell in love and married a weak little asshole like you!" Then as hard as I tried not to cry, I did anyway.

Nick looked remorseful and kept telling me that everything was going to be all right, and how sorry he was for the way he had acted. How if he had to do it all over again, he would have done things differently. I looked at him and saw guilt written all over his face. This was foreign to me, because he had never felt guilty about anything he ever did or said to me in the past.

He continued to say how sorry he was that he went home and spent our money on partying. "I don't know what got into me," he confessed.

"Look, you told me on the phone that you wanted a divorce and that you wanted to get laid in Los Angeles. You made it perfectly clear that we were finished before you hung up on me." I reminded him.

"Well, I've changed my mind. I really don't want a divorce and I didn't sleep with anyone else in Los Angeles." He replied.

Boldly I informed him, "Guess what? I slept with someone else. I believed you and took you at your word when you dumped me over the phone, so I threw my wedding ring away that night and slept with someone else."

Suddenly a look of anger and jealousy washed over his face as he said, "You sure didn't waste any time. Who the fuck did you sleep with?"

"After you dumped me, I ran into Pierson who saw me crying over you and invited me to Johnny's for dinner. We had a couple of shots and we slept together. I initiated it so, don't blame him. He also took me to Amsterdam and Venice, where I spent the happiest few weeks of my life." I replied.

"Don't tell me anymore!" He raged. "Spare me the fucking details! You slept with my friend?" He fumed.

"Yeah, I did. You said that you were unable to love me the way I wanted to be loved, then you dumped me. What the hell else did you expect me to do, kill myself?" I asked, angrily.

"Well, you sure didn't waste any time finding someone else, did you?" He repeated. "Were the two of you screwing around behind my back the whole time we were in Italy?"

"No, we were never even attracted to one another, he was always just my friend. I never found him attractive or saw him alone until you said you wanted a divorce over the phone." I answered. I figured you had told your parents to start the divorce process already. I was so heartbroken I just figured screw it, so I got drunk and slept with him," I said.

CHAPTER 118

Nick looked at me with total disbelief on his face.

"Don't look so shocked. You told me our marriage was over, so to be honest I didn't think you cared about me, and I don't regret what I did," I said.

"Okay look, I guess I am partly to blame for what happened. I did not know what I was saying. I had been up all night with Glen when you called." He said in a calmer tone.

"You mean you were on Coke and alcohol all night," I said.

Deflecting Nick responded. "Whatever, the point is, I never should've treated you that way and I'm sorry for that. But now we have a baby on the way, and we're going to have to figure out what to do about it."

"I am not getting an abortion. I plan on keeping my baby with or without you and I want to go home and start my life all over again without you." I informed him.

"I don't want you to leave. We should get a place to live and stay married," Nick insisted.

I wanted to say, "But I'm in love with Jake and I don't want to get a place to live with you." But the words did not come out of my mouth, I remembered how it was for me when my parents got divorced, and what my siblings and I went through with Maxwell and his gun. Would my son resent me for getting divorced?

Suddenly I felt like throwing up again and ran to the bathroom just in time to throw up in the toilet yet again. When I finished, I looked up from the toilet bowl to see Nick standing in the doorway of the bathroom watching me. It looked as if all the color was drained from his face. I could see that the reality of our situation really hit him after watching me throw up.

In a guilty voice he asked, "how come your stomach isn't big?"

"I don't know," I answered while reaching for my toothbrush.

"Do you need anything?" He finally asked.

Feeling exhausted, I said "Yes, some ginger ale from the machine outside would be nice," and started brushing my teeth as I went back to the chair, I was sitting in.

When Nick returned with the ginger ale, he told me that he had run into a couple of guys from Italy while signing into his new company, "They're going to pick me up in a little while to go have a couple of beers."

"Fine," I said. I welcomed the time alone to think about what I was going to do now that he wanted to stay married. After he left with his two friends, I turned on the television set for a distraction and got back into bed. My mind kept going back to Jake and how right it felt to be with him. I wanted to kick myself for marrying Nick. Maybe if I had waited in Los Angeles, I would have met Jake somehow and married him instead.

I considered buying myself a plane or bus ticket back home to Los Angeles with my modeling check. But I was ashamed to face my family because of my marital problems and the fact that they were all right about Nick. I felt conflicted, I did not know what to do. What I did know for sure was that I loved Jake and he was the little boy on the moon.

I fell asleep with the television on, and when I awoke the following morning Nick was off duty because it was the weekend. He walked down to the Officer's Club and brought back eggs and bacon.

While we ate, I told Nick that I had decided to go back to Los Angeles to stay with my dad for a while.

"I want you to stay here. I'm going to find us a place to rent, and you can get free medical care here on the base." He said.

"I don't want to stay married just because I'm having a baby." I replied.

"Look, I'm willing to forgive you for sleeping with Pierson because of the circumstances. But if you ever see him again, I am going to kick his ass," Nick said, putting a piece of bacon in his mouth.

"Why didn't you feel this way before I was pregnant? I think you're just jealous because someone else wants to be with me, or you just don't want to stay here alone," I said. "You know Nick, my emotions and my life are not a toy that you can just play with and then throw away when you're finished. I continued. You broke my heart, and treated me like I was dirt on the bottom of your shoe while we were in Italy and now you just expect me to trust you again?" I said with disgust.

"Well, I'm willing to act like none of this ever happened and start over. Besides, how are you going to take care of yourself in this condition? And you will have a hard time finding a job like this." Nick argued.

Unfortunately, he was right. I would probably have a hard time finding a job while I was pregnant. I had to stop being selfish and think about what was best for the baby.

As much as I hated it, it was time to do the right thing. As screwed up as it was, I had married the wrong person and now I was trapped in a bad marriage because of my unborn son. If I had known a few months earlier, I would not be in this situation, but it was too late to get an abortion.

CHAPTER 119

Two days later after Nick left for work on the base, I wrote Jake and told him that I loved him, but I had to stay married to Nick for the baby's sake.

"Because of my mistake, we have missed our chance to be together. I should have listened to you that day outside the church when you told me not to marry Nick. Now it is too late, and I have to put the baby first," I wrote with tears running down my cheeks.

I ended it by writing, "I will always love you." Then I took the precious ring he had given me, wrapped it in toilet paper, then placed it in the envelope with the letter. As I mailed that letter, I felt in my heart and soul that I was passing up my one true chance to be happily married. There was no one to blame but myself for marrying the wrong man after everyone told me to walk away. I just did not have the heart to deny my son the right to wake up with his father every morning. I had created this problem and now I had to live with it.

A week later Nick got a car loan and purchased a used pale blue Pinto complete with an oil leak, for a little over $1,000. Then he rented a two-bedroom trailer that he found on the base housing list. When we pulled up in front of the place, I saw a sign that read, "Woody's Trailer Park."

I thought to myself, "Oh my God, what a dump! I never dreamed that I would be living in a trailer, ever." It also occurred to me that it was at least a 25-minute car ride from the base hospital. What if there was a problem with the baby?

"Are you serious about living here." I calmly asked Nick, "You really expect me to live here? This trailer is in the middle of nowhere out in the woods. There aren't even sidewalks."

Irritated by my lack of enthusiasm, he said. "it's just temporary and it's all that we can afford right now."

I got out of the car, looked around me, and counted 12 different trailers on the wooded property. One of them had a big sign in front of it that read, "Nona Sue's Beauty Parlor." The only non-wooded area was the two-lane road that ran in front of the property.

Nick got out of the car and took the keys to our trailer out of his pocket, and unlocked the door so I could walk in. Then he unloaded our few belongings from the car.

When I walked into the trailer, the first thing I noticed was the nasty looking furniture. The sofa was a checkered multicolored mess and looked as if it needed a good cleaning years ago. The small kitchen, which could be seen from the living room and front door, had a small portable ice box, and a compact stovetop and oven. Continuing my self-guided tour, I walked down the short narrow hallway and saw a small bedroom that needed a deep cleaning, and a tiny bedroom next to it in the same condition. The bare mattresses had stains on them from years of use by other people.

I went back into the kitchen just in time to see a cockroach stroll across the counter. I slapped my hand down on the counter hoping it would run away, but it just stood there as if nothing had happened. I took off my shoe and killed it. I looked upward and said, "God, I hate roaches." Turning to Nick I asked. "Nick, did you know that this place had roaches?"

"We can buy some spray or roach traps." He replied.

Then I heard a voice with a southern accent yelling at the front door, "Anybody home?"

"That's the landlord," Nick said.

I looked toward the front door as a heavyset, old white man with long, gray unkempt hair came walking into the trailer. He had a long gray beard that reminded me of the guys who played in the rock group ZZ Top. He was wearing a pair of dirty dark blue jean overalls and a pair of old work boots that looked like mud or shit was all over them, I could not tell which.

Whatever it was it smelled.

He extended his hand to me and said, "Hi, I'm Woody" in a thick southern accent. As he smiled at me, I noticed that a lot his teeth were missing and the two in the front, had strange looking brown stains on them. Probably had something to do with the chewing tobacco he had stashed in the corner of his mouth.

"I just came by to welcome you folks into the trailer park." Woody said with an odd Jacko-lantern like smile. "Normally my wife Nona Sue would be with me to welcome you, but unfortunately she's fixing someone's hair in the trailer over yonder. If you ever need your hair attended to, well you only have to walk a few feet out your front door over to Nona Sue's Beauty Parlor and she'll do you up right mighty fine she will."

"We have everything you need here. I have propane for sale if you want to heat your trailer, and if you need to purchase some fresh meat, I have fresh pork and chicken for sale. I have a little farm area back there in the woods where I raise pigs and chickens to slaughter." He said proudly.

He chuckled and said to Nick. "I also make a good brew of moonshine. I make it myself from an old family recipe and sell it." He looked around at our meager belongings and added. "If you happen to need a TV, I have a 19" color one for sale for $15."

Does this guy ever shut up, I thought?

"Looks like you are a jack of all trades. Now, if you will excuse me, I must use the lady's room. It was nice meeting you," I said walking toward the bathroom. Once I was in there, I locked the door and sat down on the toilet with the lid still down. I cried with my hands over my mouth so no one could hear me.

Surrounded by grimy fake wood paneling and plastic tiling, I cried out in prayer to God. "This place is depressing and reminds me of some of the dumps my mother had us living in when I was a kid. You know I promised myself that I would never live in a place like this when I grew up. And here I am, pregnant and about to live in a run-down trailer park in the middle of nowhere. Please help me to get out of this" I pleaded.

Then I saw another cockroach stroll past me, walking up the wall like it had more right to be there then I did. I took off my shoe and killed it. "This is going to be trailer park hell with these roaches." I silently screamed. I looked upwards and said in a small voice, "help me, God help me."

I tried to tell myself that this was just temporary until the baby was born then I could go home and get a job.

Then I thought of Jake, He was everything I had ever dreamed of and then some. I missed him and knew he would never have rented this place for me to live in. He was too much of a gentleman for that, but now some other girl was going to benefit from my loss. I knew I was doing the right thing; this way my child would not grow up with stepparents like I did. So, if I had to give up my own happy ending for my child's sake, I would. I was just going to have to roll with the punches until the baby was born.

CHAPTER 120

After a few weeks of living in the trailer I thought I would lose my mind. I spent at least an hour each day spraying "Raid" on the cockroaches, whom I discovered can live in your refrigerator.

Nick only came home on the weekends because he claimed he could not afford the gasoline for the roundtrip to the base every day. So, I was alone during the week, and when he was home, he drank beer and watched the cheap television set that he had purchased from the landlord.

I still had not seen an OB/GYN and Nick kept putting off driving me in for an appointment. I was getting nervous about it because I was starting to show. Nick even told me one day that I did not look as good as I did before, which made me feel ugly.

On the weekends he would drive me to a supermarket called The Piggly Wiggly that had a big pig on the front of the building as the store logo. I would take $75.00 to buy a week's worth of groceries for myself. Nick was eating most of his meals in the mess hall since he was practically living in the barracks.

I ate a lot of canned soup on the budget I had to work with and hoped that it would be enough for the baby to grow on.

Being out there alone at night in the trailer was creepy. At night I could hear animal noises coming from the woods and it scared the shit out of me. I loved watching Mutual of Omaha's Wild Kingdom on television while I was growing up, but I never dreamed that I would live close enough to hear the animals while in bed at night.

Crying and feeling sorry for myself occupied much of my time and I awoke every day feeling helpless because I was stuck in the middle of nowhere with no transportation and no Jake in my life. I soaked in a hot tub and held my stomach having conversations with my unborn son. Somehow, I knew the baby was a boy. I told him my hopes and dreams for our future and how much I loved him already. I told him that after he was born, I would make sure that we both never lived in a squalid trailer again.

Then, just as my father taught me, I would visualize on the TV screen in my mind us living in a nice place. I had to remember to think positively everyday if I was going to make it through this hell. I told myself that if I could make it through being shot at every day by my stepfather when I was a kid in the seventh grade, then I could make it through this nightmare.

At this point, I was six months pregnant but still skinny. I was a little pregnant person with a small baby bump.

Nick and I argued constantly. He would drink beer then pick a fight with me. One day, to make matters worse, I found a letter from his mother in his coat pocket. That is when I found out that he still had not told his parents or anyone else for that matter that I was having his baby. They believed that he was living alone on the base and getting divorced. I wanted to call and tell his parents the truth, but he would not let me. It was crazy. I was fed up with his lies and drunkenness.

My father knew I was pregnant which meant my whole family knew as well. I purposely did not tell my father about my marital problems or my living conditions. It was too difficult to tell my him that my husband had turned into some sort of monster whom I no longer recognized.

CHAPTER 121

As time went by, I begin to realize that Nick had hidden me away in a trailer park in the woods as if I was some sort of shameful secret. He would just show up on the weekends, drink beer in front of the TV set and blame me for everything that was wrong in his life. One night he told me that if he did not have a wife and a baby on the way that he would have plenty of money to do with as he pleased. Once again, he told me that I was not good looking anymore.

Sitting on the sofa crying, I thought: "God, how am I supposed to look?"

Then I heard Nick screaming at the top of his lungs, "Will you just shut the fuck up with that crying?"

Unfortunately, I could not stop crying and felt like a wounded animal trapped in a cage. Then out of nowhere I felt my head explode with pain as Nick hit me in the face with his fist. I could feel myself falling off the dirty sofa onto the floor.

Then suddenly he was on top of me with his hands around my neck, choking me while lifting me up off the floor.

He was screaming, "Are you ready to shut up crying now?" Just as quickly, he let go of me and said, "Your eye is bleeding."

He took me into the bathroom and sat me down on the toilet seat, started running bath water while I sat there crying silently to myself and praying for God to help me, because I could not open my right eye. It was almost swollen shut and all I could see with was the left one as blood ran down my face. I wanted to get away from him but felt too dizzy to walk by myself and my legs felt weak, and I wanted to go to sleep.

Nick had the water running as he began to undress me, saying he was sorry and had not meant to hurt me. He put me in the tub of hot water and began to wash the blood off my face with a washcloth as I continued to cry.

Then I heard someone banging on the trailer door. I heard Nick say. "Shit someone must've heard us fighting. Be quiet and stop crying." He demanded. He helped me out of the tub and grabbed my robe from the hook on the back of the bathroom door and put it on me.

"I'm going to put you in the bedroom closet in case it's the police, that way I can tell them I was watching television and the sound must've been too loud." He said.

After hiding me in the bedroom closet and shutting the door, I was in total disbelief that I was even in this dilemma.

I heard Nick talking to someone and he sounded really pissed off.

Then I heard Jake's voice demanding. "Where is she?"

I could not believe he was here! What was he doing here? I never expected to see him again. He sounded extremely angry as I heard him ask again, "Where is she? I heard her crying from outside as I passed the bathroom window. I know she's here."

Then I heard Nick say, "It's none of your fucking business. Get the fuck out of here. You got a lot of nerve coming here after fucking my wife."

Then Jake said, "You mean the wife you treated like shit and dumped over the telephone? And I did not fuck her, I made love to her. As far as I am concerned, she was single the minute you said you were divorcing her and then cut out on her." Now, I am telling you to your face man, you are a piece of shit. I plan on marrying her and I do not care if you got her pregnant, I still want her." Jake paused, in my mind I could see him look around in disbelief, then he continued. "I can't believe you have her living in this backwoods trailer. Now, do I have to kick your ass to get past you to get to her? It's your choice man."

Then I heard Jake walking down the hallway as he called my name. I was too ashamed and shocked to answer.

Just then Nick said, "She's in here," and opened the closet door.

I suddenly felt Jake's arms around me as I sat on the closet floor with my head between my legs, hiding my face from him. As he lifted my face up with his hands, I saw him bite down on his bottom lip with anger as he saw what Nick had done to me. He told Nick that he had a good mind to kill him, but he would not be worth the time on death row.

Nick just stood there looking nervous, drunk and remorseful.

"It's taking every ounce of my self-control not to beat the shit out of you right now. What the fuck is wrong with you man? Who the fuck treats a woman this way?" Jake shouted at him.

Then Jake picked me up and told Nick "We have to get her to the hospital now."

Nick whined, "If I take her to the hospital then they will start asking questions about what happened to her."

Then to my surprise, Jake said "We can tell the doctor that she fell, hit her head and we found her this way. I'll back you up if you get your car keys, otherwise, I'm walking to the phone booth and calling a taxi to take her to an emergency room."

Nick answered reluctantly, "I'll go start the car."

Jake then carried me over to the bed where he hurried and put a sweatshirt over my head and a pair of sweatpants on me. While telling me repeatedly, you are going to be all right.

I felt a sharp cramp in my abdomen area and doubled over in pain clenching my stomach with my hands.

Jake muttered "I'm going to get his ass for this."

Then he kissed my swollen eye and said, "don't worry baby I got you now."

He carried me outside to the car where Nick waited for us.

CHAPTER 122

When we reached the hospital emergency room on the base, Nick carried me in. The next thing I knew I was on a stretcher being wheeled into an examination room with Nick by my side. I heard a nurse tell Nick to follow her to the front desk to fill out some paperwork.

Everything blurred as I fought to stay awake. I heard the doctor ask Jake what happened to me.

Jake told him, "Her husband did this to her then put her in a closet to hide her. I found her in the closet in this condition. I had to trick him into bringing her to the ER.

The doctor looked at me and asked, "Did your husband do this to you?"

"Yes," I answered.

The doctor looked at Jake and told him that he was calling the military police, and then he left the room. Jake took my hand and said quietly. "Everything's going to be all right; he's not going to get away with this."

Nick walked into the room and said to Jake, "I can take things from here; you can leave now." Just then the doctor walked back in with the nurse and told Nick and Jake to go take a seat in the waiting room. Shortly after that, I could overhear Nick being arrested in the hallway of the hospital. The last thing I remembered before I finally allowed myself to relax enough to go to sleep was the doctor putting the wet ultrasound gel on my stomach.

When I awoke Jake was sitting next to my bed reading a book. I could feel a big bandage on my eye where Nick had hit me. Next, I felt my stomach to see if my baby was still there. Just then the doctor walked into the room and told me that he was keeping me in the hospital overnight for observation, because I had a minor concussion and a blackeye. Then he told me to get some rest, as he left the room.

I looked at Jake and asked, "what on Earth are you even doing here?"

"I'm stationed here now," Jake replied. "I got your 'dear John' letter and my ring back in the mail before I left Italy. I tore the letter up and decided to look for you after I got here. Then he asked. Do you know why I came looking for you?"

"No" I replied.

"Because you cannot stay married to that drunk, depressed fool. He will be the death of you. Besides that, I know that you love me, so I knew I had to try to talk some sense into you. I really had a bad feeling about your being with him. I was just wondering what part of 'I'm in love with you' do you not understand? I gave you a ring and told you that I wanted to marry you. Then you find out your pregnant by this fool and dump me," he said.

"Honestly, I thought I was doing the right thing for the baby," I explained.

"Hopefully by now you know that you cannot trust or depend on Nick, but you can trust and depend on me. I don't care if you are pregnant, I still want to marry you and I will love that baby like it's my own," He promised.

"How on Earth did you find me?" I asked.

"Once I arrived at my new company I asked around and found out what company Nick had been assigned to and then it was easy. I talked to some guys in his company and found out that Nick was living in the barracks as a single man. That asshole has everyone in his company believing that he is single and getting divorced. To hear the guys in his company tell it, he acts like he is single too.

Nick went on to say. "Meanwhile he has you stashed away in a backwoods trailer park with his baby on the way. I want to fuck him up just thinking about it. I knew that asshole was up to something, so I went looking for him and found out that he was signed out to the address of the trailer. I took a taxi out there to confront him and talk some sense into you. I could hear you crying as I walked up to the trailer, with Nick screaming at you to shut up. And here we are," he concluded.

"Wow, now I understand why Nick wouldn't let me call anyone in his family to tell them about the baby.

Also, why he wouldn't take me to an OB/GYN. He had a whole plan in motion. A couple of times he hinted at abortion when I first told him about the baby. But I told him I was too far along for an abortion." I said.

"Well, it looks to me like he was trying to make you lose the baby, but who knows what goes through the mind of an idiot. I'm not going to try to figure out the thought process of a weak-minded fool like him," Jake said.

"All I know is we're supposed to be together, so forget this fool and walk away now," he said. "I know without a doubt that you're the girl that I dreamed about as a kid. I passed the time away with other women waiting and looking for you. I know it sounds crazy, but I think Nick was just the delivery man that brought you to me. I want you to know that I am for real and mean everything that I am saying to you. He took my hand and continued. "I'm willing to fight for you and our future together if I have to. I promise I will love you and the baby; all you have to do is walk away to a new life with me." He said.

"I want to be with you too," I admitted. "But you have to give me some time to get my head together, everything is just happening so fast. I am still trying to wrap my head around the fact that you are even here right now. And I do agree with you about Nick. He cannot be trusted. I cannot believe he is as cold blooded to me as he is. He just left me out there in that trailer alone for days at a time without a phone or a car," I said.

"You have to go back to Los Angeles and wait for me to get out of the Army and stay away from him. I figure now is the perfect time to get you out of here while he is locked up in jail. One of the nurses gave me the phone number to a Rape Crisis Center. "It's a good idea if you called the number," he advised.

"I'm so grateful for you and everything you've done for me. I feel like you've saved both my life and my baby's life."

"I want you and the baby to be safe. Divorce this fool and wait for me to get out of the Army." He repeated.

"I'm too embarrassed to tell my family that they were right about Nick, so no one even knows how horrible it's been. Add to that, I am also ashamed because now I am going to be an unwed mother. I promised myself when I was a kid that I would never have a baby without the natural father's support." I confided.

"Hey, it's not your fault that Nick decided to be a wife beating asshole, and you have nothing to be ashamed about; you didn't do anything wrong," He assured me. "I'm going to make sure that you get back home safely. When you get there, you hold your head up high. You are not going to be an unwed mother, because I am going to marry you. Once the divorce is over, you and I can get married whenever you are ready."

After some time in silence Nick announced. "I've been here for a week, and I don't have to start duty for three more weeks. In other words, I can drive you home. Normally, I would have gone home to see my family, but something told me to come here and find you instead. Now get some rest and I will pick you up tomorrow and get you out of here," Jake said smiling.

CHAPTER 123

As soon as I was released from the hospital the following day, Jake took me to the Rape Crisis Center on the base. There the counselor called my Aunt Marie and Uncle Phillip and explained my situation. Uncle Phillip wired me $1,000 that afternoon and instructed me to use the money to get home. I was happy I had my modeling money stashed away. Aunt Marie told me over the phone that I could stay with them once I was back home in LA.

After we left the Rape Crisis Center, Jake and I took a taxi to the trailer so I could get the spare car key while Nick was still locked up. We then went back to the hospital parking lot to get the Pinto where Nick had been forced to leave it after getting arrested.

Since I had no driver's license, Jake did the driving. We went back to the trailer so I could get my clothes and pack them into the Pinto. Jake took me to a lovely off base hotel and paid for the room. He ordered a steak dinner from room service. Then gave me a bath and changed my eye dressing.

After the food arrived and we were eating, Jake asked me if I had any map reading experience.

"No, in fact, I really don't have a lot of car driving experience either." I told him.

"Didn't you take driver's education in high school like everybody else?" Jake asked.

"Yeah, and I passed, but never got to drive around on a regular basis. Sometimes my father would let me drive his Cadillac to school, with him in the car of course. Occasionally, I would drive Nick's brother-in-law's old Volkswagen, but I never got a driver's license because the bus system works so well in Los Angeles."

"Don't worry, I'll drive for both of us. So, here is the plan: in the morning I am going to swing by my bank and get some traveling money, go to the barracks and pack a few things, sign out and let Uncle Sam know where I'm headed."

"Don't forget I have to pick up the money my Uncle Phillip wired," I said.

"You need to save that money. I can pay the expenses for you to get home." He said. Then to my surprise he touched my stomach with his hand and told my baby, "I'll get you home kid, safe and sound."

Again, I thought to myself, "I cannot believe this is happening to me. Jake's got to be the sweetest man on Earth." That night he held me and told me that everything was going to be all right as he ran his fingers through my hair saying, it reminded him of angel hair.

As I lay next to him in bed that night, he told me to relax as he placed his hand on my heart so he could heal it. I watched him close his eyes and concentrate on me. I could feel heat coming from his hands and going into me, then suddenly I felt safe, secure and surrounded by love.

I fell asleep with him holding me with his hand on my stomach, our bodies locked together as one.

The following morning Jake and I took off in the Pinto with the oil leak, and 300 miles down the road I was impressed as I watched Jake slide underneath the car at a gas station to plug up the oil leak that had gotten worse, with bubblegum to my amazement, it worked.

We continued down the road happily with the radio blasting loud rock music, singing together as if none of the bad stuff had ever happened. I felt so happy and was having such a good time with him despite my condition and circumstances.

Being with Jake was like having a little bit of heaven on Earth because he always acted as if he were my guardian angel. He always bought me good food to eat, and we always slept in decent hotels. Also, I loved the way he tucked me into bed each night, never trying to make love to me not only because I was pregnant but confused as well. He just held me and respected the fact that I needed my space and time to heal. This man made me feel safer than I had ever felt with Nick or any of my family members.

Somehow, he also managed to turn our little trip into an adventure. Along the way he kept telling me not to feel ashamed when I got home, but to go knowing that I was about to start a better life without Nick.

When we finally reached Los Angeles, it was 7 p.m. It never ceased to amaze me how beautiful the city lights looked at night. I was happy that Jake thought they were beautiful too. We were both relieved and tired when we arrived at my aunt and uncle's home in Los Feliz. Marie and Phillip were happy to see me, and relieved and thankful that Jake got me home safely. But I could tell that they wondered what my relationship was with Jake.

CHAPTER 124

My aunt and uncle had started their own mortgage company and had done well enough to purchase an elegant three-story Spanish style old Hollywood home complete with a nice sized swimming pool. They lived across from Griffith Park in a gated community in Los Feliz. I loved the view of the sunset strip, which you could see from every window of the house.

That night over dinner, my Aunt Marie had prepared for us, I could tell that she was quite disappointed when I told her that Jake and I were romantically involved.

After giving us separate rooms to sleep in, she asked me privately if I was having marriage trouble because of some sort of illicit affair I had had with Jake.

"I know what this looks like, but I never had an affair with Jake," I told her. Then I explained how Nick had dumped me in Italy, and the horror of the trailer, but the fact that Jake and Nick had been friends only made matters worse in her mind.

"You're not even legally divorced yet," She protested.

I told her that I would probably be dead if Jake had not saved me, and how I thought that he was the person God meant for me to be with. Then I made the mistake of telling her the truth about us meeting in our dreams as children. As well as the angel that I called De-De that took me flying to meet with him in my dreams so we could plan our future together.

My aunt looked at me like I had lost my mind and told me I was very confused and needed professional help. She also told me that I was wrong for wanting to be with Jake.

She also told me that she was happy to be driving him to the airport the following day, so he could fly right out of my life. All she could see was the fact that I was still legally married and about to have my husband's baby.

It made my heart sad to know that my Aunt Marie could not see what a Godsend Jake really was for me.

The next morning, I called Sally Hudson since I needed the support of a good friend at this point. Plus, I wanted to introduce her to Jake before he flew back to his duty station. Jake and I drove over to her house in the Pinto, which, surprisingly was still holding up considering we were using bubblegum to plug up that oil leak.

Sally was happy to see me, and it was like I had never left. We just picked up where we left off at before I moved to Italy. After introducing Jake, I told her everything that happened between me and Nick.

She was disappointed that I was pregnant, and it did not matter that I was married. The whole baby thing freaked her out. Her only reaction to the break-up news was: "I told you to dump that fool in high school. And frankly I am glad it is over for your sake. In my opinion, he had no redeeming qualities at all; he was bad in bed, broke and boring."

She then invited me to move in with her rent free.

"You can sleep on the sofa," she said. "This way you can save money for your own place." Sally suggested that I sign with a temporary employment agency for receptionist work, "Then you can sit on your ass and answer phones while you're pregnant."

It sounded like a good idea since it would save me from having to deal with family gossip over my failed marriage, and I would not have to rely on anyone in my family. "Great idea." I replied.

"It will be like old times," Sally said. "My sister Mary is staying here too."

Surprised at this news, I said. "When I left for Italy Mary had her own apartment and was doing well. Why is she living with you?" I asked.

"She had a mental breakdown and disappeared for six months. Mom found her living on the streets in Hollywood like a homeless person. She's been diagnosed with schizophrenia but now that she's on medication she's doing fine," Sally explained.

"Where is she now?" I asked.

"Working two jobs so she's really not around much except at night to sleep." Sally answered.

I got up from the sofa and said, "I'm going to walk down to the corner liquor store for some orange juice."

Jake got up to go with me, but I told him I would be right back. But when I returned, he was waiting for me outside on the sidewalk. "What are you doing outside," I asked him slightly confused.

Jake looked uncomfortable as he told me that Sally had taken off all her clothes in front of him and told him that he was a cute white boy. I was impressed that Jake was man enough to step outside and wait for me after being put in that situation. This was a true sign of loyalty on his part in my opinion.

However, I knew Sally, and this was normal behavior for her. I had to explain to poor Jake that Sally saw no shame in the human body and walked around her apartment naked all the time. "Her mother and sister do the same; in fact, I've seen her mother naked on countless occasions, just walking around her Hollywood home."

"That's some crazy shit! I do not care how normal she thinks it is, I think she needs to keep her damn clothes on in front of me. And if you were walking around the house naked in front of other people, I would have a big problem with that." Jake said. "Besides, I got the impression that she was trying to hit on me and that's why I went outside to wait for you."

Suddenly pissed off, "I said what the hell is wrong with her?"

"In my opinion, your friend is really not your friend," Jake observed.

I started walking back to Sally's apartment with Jake following behind me saying, "I really don't want to go back in there." Once inside, we found that she was taking a shower with the bathroom door wide open as usual.

"We'll just sit down until she gets out of the shower so I can have a little talk with her," I told Jake.

I drank my orange juice and went into the kitchen to throw the empty bottle away. As I reentered the living room, Sally was just walking out of the bathroom butt naked with a towel wrapped around her head.

I asked, "what's up with hitting on my boyfriend?"

By now, Jake was looking in the opposite direction on purpose so he would not have to see her naked again.

"I called him a cute white boy and you don't have to get all upset over it and trip out. All I meant was, he was an improvement from the last guy you were involved with."

Then Sally asked Jake, "aren't you a little old to be afraid of seeing a naked woman?"

Jake replied, "where I come from women don't walk around naked and tell you you're cute unless they want to have sex with you, and frankly, I would feel more comfortable if you put something on because I don't want to see you naked."

"Okay enough," I said. I looked at Sally, still irritated with her and said, "I'll call you later." Then we left.

A few hours later, Aunt Marie and I drove Jake to LAX Airport to catch his flight back to the base. It was a tear-filled goodbye as he asked me to promise him that I would wait for him to get out of the Army.

"I'll call you as soon as I get back to the base," he said as he gave me a final hug goodbye.

After seeing Jake off at the airport, my aunt and I drove back to her house where I got my things and moved in with Sally. I was too ashamed to be around my family because of the sad sorry situation I was in. All of them had told me that Nick was bad news, and they had all been right. I was not going to let them know all the horrible details of what he had done to me, and how he had torn my heart into pieces. It was bad enough that I had a healing black eye.

Part of me just wanted to disappear from the planet and be nonexistent. That is how badly my heart hurt. My father was jumping for joy about the divorce because he hated Nick with what my mother used to call "a purple passion."

CHAPTER 125

Two days after I moved in with Debbie, I got a phone call from Nick which was a surprise. "How did you know where I was?" I asked him.

"I called your father's house, and he gave me your number." He went on to tell me in detail how pissed off he was at me for getting him arrested.

The nerve of this guy I thought to myself; he is acting like I am to blame.

"How did you get out of jail?" I asked him.

"My First Sergeant got me out." He said.

"So, I guess you're just going to get away with beating up a pregnant woman. I left town because you're too dangerous for me to be around." I told him.

"Well fuck you!" he screamed into the phone. "Where the hell is my car and keys?" he demanded.

"I have the keys right here in my purse, and the car is parked right outside the apartment building here with me safe and sound," I replied.

"I can't believe you drove my car all the way to Los Angeles with no driver's license," he said angrily.

"Well believe it because I did take the car, and I'm keeping it for the baby." I said.

"Fuck you and the baby!" he yelled into the telephone "You can go apply for welfare like every other black bitch in America. Or better yet just give the thing up for adoption, or let the welfare office buy you a car, but I want mine back."

All I could manage to get out of my mouth was "Wow! I can't believe you just said that."

I felt like someone had taken my breath away and stabbed me in the heart all at the same time when that comment came out of his mouth. That is when I realized for the first time that I had been married to a racist asshole and that was a bitter shocking pill to swallow.

Fighting to hold back my tears I said, "you're scum Nick and I hope you burn in hell." Then I slammed down the phone and broke down crying. There was no way I was going to give him the satisfaction of knowing that I had even cried over him. Especially after he had just called me a black bitch and told me to go on welfare and insinuated that all black women in America were on welfare.

I just could not take any more crap from this idiot. I had to be strong for myself and my baby. How can anyone treat another human being this way? What kind of a person spent all their free time drinking and treating their wife this way? Nick did not care that I was pregnant with his kid and alone on the streets of Los Angeles. At that moment I realized that this was genuine Nick and had been the whole time; it made my skin crawl that I ever let him touch me.

CHAPTER 126

The following day I got myself a doctor with Nick's military medical insurance. I was still covered because I was still legally married to him. I purposely chose the best hospital in the area, Cedars-Sinai Medical Center near Beverly Hills.

After my last conversation with Nick, I wanted to saddle him with a high co-pay bill from the hospital.

As I sat in the lobby waiting for my name to be called, I noticed all the perfect glowing mothers-to be sitting with their husbands looking serene and happy. I quickly noticed that I was the only woman in that waiting room without a man by her side. It made me feel bad for myself, and my baby.

These women were having babies with men who loved them, and the baby they had made together. They would not be in the delivery room alone giving birth, like I would be. Their child would wake up every morning to eat breakfast with both of its parents. My kid was going to be shipped off to a daycare center and spend maybe three hours a night with a single parent after work.

I wondered if these people in the waiting room knew just how lucky they were, or if they took it all for granted. I felt sorry for my baby, and it was not even born yet. As it was, I thanked God for my savings to feed myself on and keep gas in Nick's ugly Pinto.

I felt pressured because I knew my little boy was depending on me, and I only had a few months to make a home for him. Not only would I have to find an apartment quickly, but I needed rent money each month. I knew that I would have to go straight to work after the birth and leave my newborn infant with a total stranger while paying them.

Of course, I knew that Jake wanted to marry me and raise my son as his own, as he continued to assure me. He called every other night offering to send me money to live on. I loved him, but I did not want to start my relationship with him based on financial support and a baby. My trust level for any human at this point was pretty much zero. I had learned from Nick that depending on a man for your happiness and financial well-being was a mistake that I had made once and did not plan to make again.

I needed time to get divorced, and to deal with everything that had happened because I was filled with hatred for Nick for doing this to me. He taught me that even the people who claim to love you the most could rip your heart out and leave you floundering. I hated myself because I had been stupid and lovesick enough to marry him, now I was starting to think that I never wanted to get married again. The whole situation was a huge mindblower to me, and I knew that I would never view the world or fully trust many people again. I had to be independent and rely on only myself and God if I was going to make it successfully with this baby.

My innocence was now gone forever, along with that feeling of natural joy and happiness that one feels waking up in the morning. For the first time in my life, I was depressed. After everything I had been through so far, I had remained strong through it all because I had no choice.

I never would have guessed that Nick would be the one to hurt me the most. It all seemed so unfair because he just got to walk away after throwing me and the baby away like we were yesterday's garbage. I went into full survival mode and knew it was sink or swim now.

After being told by the doctor that everything was going well with the pregnancy, I took Sally's advice and signed with a temporary employment agency for work. Four days later I was working downtown as an assistant for wardrobe accessories on a photo shoot. The shoot was for a new up-and-coming clothing company called LA gear. They had a young fresh hip look to their garments and shoes.

As I watched the models pose for the photographer, I could not help thinking that could have been me. I had not fully taken advantage of my opportunity to model while living in Italy; instead, I had been stupid enough to think Nick was more important than having a career. If I could go back in time, I would have moved to Milan and concentrated on modeling even if I did hate it.

As I watched the models pose for the photographer, I told myself that after the baby was born my body would go back to its normal size. My life was not going to end just because I had a baby. I thanked God that I was a small woman and was able to hide my pregnancy under a pair of blue jean overalls. None of these people had any clue that I was expecting a baby.

After working on the LA Gear shoot for a week, I was lucky enough to get a temporary job at a big law firm downtown. Once again, I kept quiet about my pregnancy, and was still able to hide my growing belly by wearing loose fitting dresses.

CHAPTER 127

Each time I went to a prenatal appointment and saw the other mothers to be, it made me feel depressed and unsure of my ability to give my unborn son the life that I felt he deserved. For one thing, I knew I had to be out of Sally's apartment before the baby was born. Not only was Sally against me keeping the baby and bringing it home to her apartment, but her sister Mary also often awakened me in the middle of the night by making tea for an invisible man named Daryl.

I lay there on the sofa and fearfully watched her talk and drink tea in the nude with someone who was not even there. It scared the hell out of me because I had never been around anyone who was schizophrenic before. I watched her talk to the air as if a real person were there. Was she talking to a spirit? I could feel male energy but no one was there...that I could see. It was really freaking me out and I wanted it to stay away from me and my baby. At one point it was so disturbing that I just lay there silently, pretending to be asleep.

As my due date grew closer, I still had not secured a full-time job so I could rent a place for myself and the baby to live. I had decided when Nick told me to go apply for welfare like every other black bitch in America that I was not going to depend on a man again. After Nick, all the trust had been sucked out of me. I felt like I was losing my mind because the feeling of sadness would not leave my heart.

Suddenly, all I wanted to do was die and disappear from the planet. I thought that maybe Nick was right when he told me to give the baby up for adoption. Maybe I was being selfish and unrealistic that I could take care of this baby on my own. I always thought I would at least be a homeowner before I had a child.

I was starting to think that my son would probably be better off with someone who had their life in order with plenty of money to buy clothes and food for him. The one thing I knew for sure was I did not want my son to suffer because of me and my stupidity in trusting Nick. Now I did not trust people, even if they claimed to love me like Jake did.

Finally, I decided to drive over to Nick's parent's home to talk to them about the baby and the divorce. I was hoping that they would help me somehow get a safe place to take the baby to after he was born. Maybe his parents would care enough about their own grandchild to help me to keep him.

The following day I drove over to their house and knocked on the door. His mother Dorothy opened it and was shocked to see me standing there. As I began to speak to her, she acted as if I were the bad guy in the drama. I asked her why she was treating me so coldly?

She looked at my stomach and replied, "Because you're pregnant with another man's child."

I just stood there for a second in total shock and disbelief at first, not knowing what she was talking about. I could not believe that Nick had told his parents that his own baby was not his. Who does that? He lied to his own mother and father, plus dragged my name through the mud for his own selfish reasons. I tried to tell her that it was not true, but she refused to hear anything I had to say. I asked her if I could speak with my father-in-law. She told me that he never wanted to speak to me again after the way I treated his son.

"If you had any shred of decency at all you would take that poor unborn baby you're carrying and put it up for adoption, because I'm sure whoever knocked you up isn't around to take responsibility for it, otherwise you wouldn't be on my doorstep." She scolded me.

I was still reeling from the fact that my husband had lied to his parents, and God only knows who else about me and his baby. He had made up a whole story that was untrue about me just to justify to his family that he was entitled to divorce me while I was pregnant. I could totally see what he was doing but just could not believe it. Not only was Nick throwing his wife and son away so he could drink, take drugs and party with his friends in nightclubs, but he was also a lying, selfish, racist asshole. I kept trying to tell Dorothy that Nick was not telling her the truth, but she refused to believe me.

At that moment, in my mind's eye, I saw this movie running in my head of my mother-in-law having a relationship with a black man who was married to a white woman. Their daughters were best friends, and my father-in-law was on friendly terms with the man. Neither one of their spouses suspected that they were attracted to one another. I could see the whole situation just the way God saw it when it happened years before. That is when I snapped and lost my temper with her.

I told her that I had been faithful to her son, "It's you who's been unfaithful in your marriage with a black guy. Maybe that's why Nick is so fucked up in the head today and called me a black bitch." My anger grew white hot, and my words came out like daggers, "He walked in on you and this guy kissing, when he was a little boy. Then you took him out to a movie to keep his mouth shut. What kind of mother screws around with the father of her daughter's friend?" Still wanting to hurt her I continued. "You were even friends with his wife while you were screwing him. You're a disgrace to women everywhere and you are pointing a finger at me…Really?"

I stopped for a moment and looked into her shocked eyes. I had no idea how I knew about her affair with a black man, but I just did. Suddenly, it was as if I was looking right into my mother-in-law's past reading her life story through God's eyes. I could also feel her inner confusion because she was afraid that Nick had told me and perhaps others. All those thoughts I sensed going through her brain in a matter of seconds.

Still fuming I continued: "I guess Nick learned how to tell lies from the best because you've been lying to your husband for years. And whether you like it or not, this is your grandson I am carrying and about to give birth to. Make no mistake; one day God will hold you accountable for the way you have treated me. Everyone dies eventually and is accountable for everything they did or didn't do." The shocked look on her face was priceless. " Don't worry, I won't bother you again," I said, and walked away with as much dignity as I could while hot tears ran down my cheeks.

I figured it was okay to cry, just if Dorothy did not see me doing it. At this point, I was almost desperate enough to call Jake and accept his offer of financial help, because my greatest fear was how I was going to rent an apartment without a job. I stopped myself because I did not want to be put into another situation where I was depending on a man. Besides, Jake deserved better than being used for his money. I still wanted to be with him because

I loved him not because he would be a solution to a problem. By now I was positive that I did not want to get married again at this point in my life.

Maybe everyone was right; my son will be better off without me. The last thing I wanted to do was give him up, but I kept questioning whether I loved my baby enough to do what was best for him in the long run.

As the days came and went, I began to panic even more because I had no place to take my son after he was born and no full-time job. I went to an OB/GYN appointment and told my doctor I had no place to take my baby after the birth. He asked whether I had ever considered adoption. I thought why do people keep suggesting adoption to me. Is this some sort of sign from God that I am supposed to investigate adoption?

I told my doctor that the baby's father wanted me to give the baby up because we were getting a divorce.

"As it happens, I know a lawyer who handles adoptions," he said. "I'm going to give you his name and number when you leave just in case you decide to give him a call. He has an office right off Wilshire Boulevard in Beverly Hills,"

"I would like to keep my son," I said.

"I'm not telling you to give your baby up for adoption, I just wanted you to know that there were other options besides living on the streets with an infant." The doctor told me.

"I'm not living on the streets. I'm staying with my friend and sleeping on her sofa." I informed him.

"Well, can you continue to stay there after the baby is born?" He asked.

"No, my friend hates babies and refuses to let me bring him there." I replied.

What about your family?" He asked.

"They're not real thrilled with me right now because I married my husband after they warned me not to. I don't want to go to them for help, so I'm pretty much on my own," I explained.

"I'll send you home with the phone number, just in case things don't work out the way you want them to." He said, handing me a business card.

I returned to Sally's with a newspaper, I was determined to rent a place even if it was a one-room dump. My baby and I were going to make it; I could not give up yet. I found six different low-rent, beat up apartments that I felt I could afford, but I was turned down for all of them because my income was not solid enough. Turns out that working through a temporary agency turned out to be an obstacle in being approved for an apartment.

CHAPTER 128

Two days later I drove out to Venice Beach after work, feeling depressed and defeated. I sat on the sand watching the ocean while begging God to help me find my own apartment in time.

Now, for the first time I began seriously considering adoption. Not to relieve myself of responsibility for my son, but to make certain he had the best chance in life possible, and to make sure that he did not suffer because of my mistakes.

I sat out there on the beach that day thinking about how I really had nothing to offer this baby but years at a daycare center, and financial struggle while I worked my way through college. I refused to use Jake to get me out of this since my heart was not allowing me to truly trust anyone yet. Remembering my childhood, I recalled how I could not trust my mother who did not protect us from Maxwell and that gun. Sadly, I thought, "if you could not trust your mother, who the hell could you trust?"

By the time I returned to Sally's it was almost midnight, I sat down on the sofa and watched Mary talk to the invisible man in the kitchen again. I could still feel someone there with her, and it was really freaking me out. I was positive now that an actual spirit was in the room. Then it hit me like a ton of bricks that this Daryl was not a dead man, but a demonic disembodied spirit disguising itself as a man named Daryl. Instinctively I knew that it had come from that place that I saw as a kid while flying with De-De to play with Jake on the moon.

Daryl was from the place that people referred to as hell, the dimension with all the cast-off negative emotions and feelings from souls on Earth. It was a dumping ground of spiritual shit, I thought about seeing the demons and negative disembodied spirits there as well, hungry to attach themselves to any source of light that they could feed upon. Or any human body that it could enter in order to live again through that person.

I remembered De-De telling me that you had to have an opening through some negative emotion, or belief system, or you had to invite it in to open the door for that to enter your life. Somehow Mary had not only been attacked by this thing, but it had attached itself to her pretending to be her friend in a romantic way.

I realized that this thing was romancing her, and she believed he was some sort of invisible boyfriend. Chills ran down my spine because this scared the hell out of me. "What if this thing came after me and my baby?" I thought, or was I just going insane with Mary?

That was my breaking point; the moment I decided to call the adoption attorney the following morning. I had to admit to myself that I did not have my life together and had nothing to give my son but love. How could I ever explain to him that his own father wanted nothing to do with him? I needed to make sure that he was loved and cared for properly.

The next morning, I called the phone number on the business card the doctor had given me and was given an appointment for 4 that afternoon.

As I drove to Beverly Hills for the appointment, I kept telling myself that I was doing the right thing for my son.

When I arrived, I noticed how plush and fancy the office was. I approached the reception desk and gave the receptionist my name.

"I have an appointment with Mr. Rothstein." I told her.

She handed me some papers to fill out and offered me some juice to drink. I requested orange juice, then sat down on the sofa to fill out the forms.

Twenty minutes later I gave the receptionist the completed forms.

"I'll let Mr. Rothstein know you're ready." She said smiling.

I sat back down on the sofa, and a few minutes later a short elderly man approached me and introduced himself as Frank Rothstein. He led me down a hallway with exquisite artwork covering the walls, to a big office with a panoramic view of the city.

Mr. Rothstein offered me a seat on an elegant dark brown antique leather sofa. He sat down behind his desk and looked through the forms I had just filled out. He then asked me to explain to him why I wanted to give my baby up for adoption.

I explained my circumstances to him in detail, including my pending divorce and that the baby's father wanted nothing to do with the child.

"In fact, he and his mother told me to give my baby up for adoption," I said. Then I took a wallet sized photo of Nick out of my purse and showed it to Mr. Rothstein. "This is a photo of my soon to be ex-husband he told his mother that the baby wasn't his; that's how messed up this is. I had planned to raise the baby on my own, but I am sleeping on my friend's sofa with no place to take the baby after it is born. It's important to me that my baby has a better childhood than I did. I want him to have choices in life, not live in a broken home, and be raised in a daycare center."

Mr. Rothstein then told me that I could chose the adoptive parents myself and interview the couples he represented. "We have done extensive background checks on our clients to make sure that we are placing the baby in a loving healthy permanent home." He said.

"I want them to be church going people, because I want my son to be raised going to church. I want them to be homeowners who can send him to college when the time comes. If I give my son up, I want him to have a better life than I ever could have given him." I told him.

"I have a very impressive client list. I represent some doctors, lawyers and even a judge, along with a broad range of other professionals who were unable to have children of their own." Mr. Rothstein informed me.

"Well, professionals with money can be just as freaky and crazy behind closed doors as a poor person can be. So, their money and job will not be my deciding factor." I told him.

"When you leave, I'm going to send you home with client profiles to review. We require that our clients provide photos of their homes, so you can get an idea of what type of home your baby will be raised in. In addition, I want you to fully understand before you leave my office that no one here will ever pressure you to give your baby up. That decision is going to be yours and yours alone to make." He said.

I went back to Sally's apartment and looked through the files. All the couples were either upper middle class or wealthy. One couple that stood out from the rest were named James and Hannah Lieberman.

They were a young Jewish couple who owned an apartment building in Culver City and a home in Santa Monica near the beach, my favorite place on Earth. The Lieberman's were both doctors who met and fell in love in medical school. According to their file they loved music and the arts, as well as hiking and other outdoor activities.

I even liked their head shots and family photos and noticed there were a lot of children in their family. That appealed to me. Cousins, aunts and uncles for my son to grow up with was a priority. They looked like nice down-to-Earth people whom I wanted to meet and to see how I felt about them in person.

CHAPTER 129

The next day I went to work and called the attorney on my lunch break and made an appointment to meet the Lieberman's.

Two days later I met with them in Mr. Rothstein's office and knew immediately that they were genuinely nice people. I sat down with them, and we talked and got to know each other. Hannah was unable to carry a baby to full-term and had tried to fix the problem with surgery more than once, which proved to be unsuccessful. They told me that they concluded that God meant for them to adopt.

I explained that I did not really want to give my baby up for adoption, but I felt I had no choice. And I needed to know that they would explain that to my son; that I had no place to take him once he was born. "Please let him know that I did not throw him away like yesterday's trash. That I had taken the time to find loving parents for him. I want my son to know that his natural mother really loved and wanted him."

They both agreed to do this for me including showing him photos of me when the time came to tell him the truth.

Before leaving the office, I consented to spend time with them to get to know them better, before making my final decision. As I left that office, I thought that if I had to give my baby up, I wanted him to be raised by people like James and Hannah.

We started out by having dinner together at their home by the beach in Santa Monica that weekend. I was happy to accept the invitation because this way I could see what environment my son would be living in and get an authentic feel for their lifestyle.

I drove up to a large three-story Spanish style home, with a long winding beautiful driveway that had a large fountain with flowing water near the front door. It was surrounded by a large well-kept lawn landscaped to perfection. The place looked like a mansion to me. I parked my beat-up Pinto, which looked totally out of place in their driveway, walked to the front door and rang the bell. They opened the door together, gave me a hug and invited me into their home. James and Hannah began to show me around their home which had high ceilings with wood beams. The floors were a mixture of Spanish tile and wood. They even had their own library with built-in floor to ceiling bookshelves that had a large wooden ladder on wheels to reach the books on the upper shelves.

Their home also had a magnificent panoramic view of the ocean from almost every window in the house. Then they showed me the bedroom they had prepared for a baby. It was so adorable that I thought I had walked into a real-life fairytale nursery. The wallpaper had nursery rhymes written all over it, with a darling white crib in front of a huge window overlooking the ocean. There was also an antique baby cradle just the perfect size for a newborn infant.

In addition, the room had its own bathroom, two changing tables and a few large antique dressers that looked like they were from the turn-of-the-century. I loved the way the walls were lined with built-in shelves filled with children's books and toys. The room also had plush wall-to-wall carpeting that any baby would be safe crawling on.

Their impressive home even had a swimming pool and a hot tub in their back yard.

After the grand tour, we sat down to a lobster dinner with salad and grilled corn. Everything tasted so delicious that I thought I had died and gone to heaven. I thought to myself, "my son could live this way every day." Then I thought about the pain I knew I would feel when I gave him up; however, knowing he would be living this type of life would make it more bearable. My child would have everything he required and more.

CHAPTER 130

I returned to Sally's apartment that night totally impressed by this couple and what they could offer my son, but I was still heartbroken because I loved him already and did not want to give him up. He was a real person to me after feeling him kick and grow inside me for so many months.

It would require courage and digging deeply within myself to do the right thing and give him up. I sat on Sally's sofa and took a long look around me knowing that I could not give birth to my son, then bring him back to her apartment. I began to cry because I wished with all my heart that I could keep my child. My hatred toward Nick exploded for putting me in this position to begin with.

My apartment, my bank job and my life, all given up for him: a man thinking I was a black bitch in the back of his mind. I felt stupid for believing that Nick would love me forever, no matter what. Now, I was unable to trust Jake's love for me. Deep down, I knew he loved me, and wanted to step up for me and my baby, but what if he changed his mind after a year or two of being together, like Nick did? Then my son would be crying because his stepfather had walked out the door like his natural father had. I just could not take that chance again. This was a little boy's life I was dealing with and his emotional well-being, and I was responsible for him. I kept telling myself that I was doing the right thing. After all, Hannah and James were stable, happy and in love with one another. They were financially stable with tons of money so my son would want for nothing.

It took me about two weeks to finally call Mr. Rothstein back and tell him that I had decided to let Hannah and James adopt my son. From that day forward, the Lieberman's made sure I had excellent care. I was not asking them for money; that would be selling my baby. Hannah and James, however, insisted on going to my doctor's appointments with me and buying the best prenatal vitamins on the market for me to take. They also bought me groceries to ensure I was eating properly.

One afternoon after telling them about Mary and the invisible man she was talking to, they showed up at Sally's place with a newspaper saying that they were taking me out to lunch and then apartment hunting. They explained to me that since I was trusting them to raise my son, that the least they could do was make sure I was all right after the birth. They wanted to pre-pay my first six month's rent and wanted me to accept some cash to live on until I found permanent work instead of working through a temporary agency.

"We just want to help you out and make sure you're all right after everything you've been through with your husband." They said. By the end of the day, they had rented me an apartment in the Wilshire area not too far from downtown Los Angeles. Ironically, it was also not far from Nick's parent's house.

Three days later I moved in. Hannah and James had furnished my little apartment and stocked the cupboards and refrigerator with food, telling me that they did not want me to be stressed out about anything while I was pregnant. I was so grateful, I just stood there taking it all in with tears of relief running down my cheeks. These people were trying to leave me with a solid foundation so I could start my life all over again and I was truly touched and grateful.

No more Mary and Daryl, no more fear of sleeping in the same room with the disembodied spirit that was trying to live with this poor girl. No more Sally looking at me and saying, "I can't believe you are knocked up."

After I moved in and got settled, I found myself sitting alone in my new apartment holding my stomach while talking to my unborn son. I was sure he could hear me. I wanted him to know just how much I loved him, and how important it was to me that he have a happy family life and a successful future. I explained to him that I was giving him up for his own well-being.

CHAPTER 131

I decided I would sit down and write my son a long letter, explaining why I felt I had no choice but to give him up. I explained my whole situation to him and put the letter in an envelope along with photos of Nick and me. I wanted him to see what his natural parents looked like so he would not have to wonder if he looked like us. I also wrote down the names of my family members in case he wanted to find them one day. In my heart I was hoping that he would look for me and want to meet me one day. Maybe he would even love me for being strong enough to give him a better life with decent parents.

When I called Jake to give him my new phone number, and tell him about my new apartment, I also told him about my decision to let Hannah and James adopt my baby. Jake became upset and advised against it.

"You will regret this for the rest of your life; besides, I'm willing to raise that little boy as my own," he said. "I may not be a rich man, but I can support the two of you right now if only you would let me. I offered you money to rent a place to live, and I offered to mail you money every month to live on. I can support the two of you." He protested. "Why won't you just let me marry you and we can raise that boy as our own?" He pleaded.

"Because I can't marry you while I'm still married to someone else," I told him. "I can't put my life in someone else's hands. I would be making the same mistake as I did with Nick. Only fools make the same mistake twice," I said.

"But I'm not Nick," he insisted.

"Can't you see I need time to get over the fact that I was married to that fool in the first place, then dumped. I am trying to forgive myself for being dumb enough to believe him in the first place. I need to fix myself." I said. "It's not possible to marry you yet; the only thing I can offer you right now is being your girlfriend. I love you enough not to hurt you. If we end up together, I want it to be under the right conditions not because my baby needed a father. When you get out of the Army, we can be together, but we must take it slow," I told him.

As I hung up, I knew that the main reason I would not marry him was that I no longer trusted anyone. Between Nick and my mother, they had sucked the trust right out of me. I figured if your mother and husband could betray you then anything was possible here on Earth. I also realized that I no longer trusted the institution of marriage itself. I once believed that marriage was about loving one another forever. To me it meant that the person you married was your partner through life, and the two of you wanted to be together every day until you died.

It looked to me like I was living in a world where people no longer valued marriage or true love. People did not stay together through thick and thin. How could I trust anyone to show me that type of love? I now believed that only God himself could love me that way.

CHAPTER 132

A week later Saturday at 4:30 p.m. I went into labor. I was sitting on the sofa watching television when I felt the first sharp pain in my stomach. It felt like a lightning bolt going through me. At first, I paid no attention to it, but then it happened again and again, each time the pain was more intense.

Oh my God, I thought, is this the beginning of labor? I reached for the telephone which was sitting on the coffee table in front of me. My first thought was to call Hannah and James, but then I thought, I want to be alone with my son for just a little while longer. Instead, I called a taxi. I was not going to take a chance on driving myself to the hospital just in case the pain got worse. The last thing I needed was to be on the roadside unable to drive.

When the taxi driver showed up and saw that I was pregnant, and that I needed to get to the hospital as fast as I could he came to my rescue. He did his best to make sure that I was comfortable in the backseat and got me to Cedars-Sinai Hospital as fast as he could. He was from India and spoke with a thick accent, and I could tell he was nervous about getting me to the hospital in time.

When we arrived at the hospital emergency room entrance, he even got out of the cab and walked me into the emergency room. He had no idea what he had just done for me: this kind stranger made me feel like my nervous husband had driven me to the hospital because he did everything a real husband would have done. He gave me that one moment of feeling like a normal expectant mom, before someone else took my son home as their own.

As I entered the emergency room and was wheeled up to labor and delivery, everything became a blur. The labor pains were so strong at this point I thought I was going to die. I found myself wishing that Nick were there to hold my hand, and then I quickly snapped back to reality and told myself do not even allow yourself to mentally go there. He has probably got his penis in someone else or is celebrating the fact that he is free from his black wife and mixed-race baby.

I watched as a nurse hooked me up to an Ultra-sound machine. Then I felt wet from the waist down, and heard the nurse tell the doctor that my water had just broken. The pain was becoming unbearable at this point, so I was hooked up to an IV with pain killer in it.

After the painkiller had taken affect, I gave the nurse Hannah and James' phone number and asked her to call them. My doctor already knew that I was giving my son up for adoption, all the arrangements had been made for circumcision and for James to cut the umbilical cord.

I made it completely clear to them that I wanted to hold my son and to tell him goodbye alone, without anyone in my hospital room. It was going to be our little moment together. It would be my only memory of him to hold in my mind, possibly until the day I died. I could only cling to the hope that one day he would read my letter with an understanding heart and come looking for me. I was sad because I would not have the joy of my son sleeping with me in my room after his birth like the other mothers on the ward. My baby would be taken to the hospital nursery before Hannah and James took him home. Following the birth, I would be going home alone, without my little bundle of joy.

With an aching heart, it all seemed so unreal, like I had left my body and sat down to watch a sad movie starring myself.

Eventually, Hannah and James showed up happy and excited. They asked me if I was in much pain? I told them that I was so drugged at that point I did not feel anything. "Everything just seems so unreal," I told them.

"It's a side effect from the epidural they gave you; just try to relax." James advised.

I did as he suggested and drifted off to sleep, until suddenly the nurse was waking me up telling me it was time to push. I still could not feel anything because my body was numb, but the machine they had me hooked up to was showing the contractions in real time.

Not long after that my son was born, and I could hear him crying. It was a delightful sound, one that I never wanted to forget. I looked at him from across the room, as the nurse cleaned him up. I saw his little beautiful face surrounded by dark hair like mine and he had taken my dark brown eyes, but his skin tone was fair like Nick's. He was so cute and healthy, thank God. The baby was taken from the room, and I was taken to the recovery room where I fell into a deep sleep.

CHAPTER 133

When I awoke the following morning, I was allowed to spend time with my son for the first and last time. The nurse brought him into my room and placed him in my arms. It felt like I was holding the cutest little thing in the world. He was wide awake as we looked into each other's eyes. He was perfect. I could tell already that he had Nick's slim nose and mouth. And he had a gorgeous head of hair.

I told him how much I loved him and wished I could keep him. "I'm giving you up for your own good and I hope you don't hate me one day for doing this," I said crying. "And I hope and pray that one day you will come looking for me. I left you a letter explaining everything so that you know just how much I really wanted you." The rest of my time with him was spent cuddling and hugging and kissing him all over his little face and hands; I even kissed his little feet.

When Hannah and James entered the room, I could not help crying as I handed the baby over to them, knowing that he was no longer mine. They were both overly excited as they left the room with him. I laid back down on the hospital bed and cried myself to sleep.

When I awoke a few hours later I tried to collect my thoughts and pull myself together. I did not feel like me anymore, it felt like a part of me was missing because the baby was no longer with me. I told myself that this was a normal reaction; that my son was better off now and I would get over the feeling of not being with him.

An orderly walked into the room and set a lunch tray in front of me, but I had no appetite. Then the doctor came in and checked me over and gave me a clean bill of health, along with a prescription for some pills that would dry up my breast milk.

"If you don't take these pills," he warned "you could get a nasty infection and feel a lot of pain. I'll be releasing you to go home in a few hours." Then he left telling me goodbye for the last time.

I was just about to get out of bed to take a shower and get dressed to go home when my father burst into my hospital room! I was shocked to see him as he frantically yelled, "Where is my grandson?" A nurse ran in right behind him as he continued to ask me where his grandson was. My mind was racing a mile a minute, how did Daddy even know where I was and that the baby had been born? What was he doing here? Besides, I thought he was mad at me, and we were not speaking. I had purposely stayed away from the family and their disapproving looks and gossip. He was starting to make a scene as the nurse told him to calm down.

My father looked at me and said, "I had a dream last night that you gave birth to my grandson and gave him up for adoption to some white people. "So, I got up and called Sally who said you moved out and refused to give me your new address. I called every hospital in the city until I found you." He looked desperate as he stood there asking where the baby was.

I was still freaked out that he knew that the baby had been born and that I had given him up. I had no choice but to tell my him that it was true, I had given the baby up for adoption.

Daddy shouted, "You're out of your mind!" He looked so pissed off that I thought he might kill someone. I had not seen him this upset since Dennis died. "Well, I'm not going to let you, do it? Why would you do something like this?" He demanded.

"Nick and his mother put the idea in my head, and when I asked Nick for help to keep the baby, he told me to go apply for welfare like every other black bitch in America. "I was trying to do the right thing, Daddy, I swear, I just didn't know what else to do," I sobbed.

"Why didn't you just come to me for help? You could have stayed with me." He said.

"You were mad at me," I replied.

"You still should've come to me for help because that baby is my flesh and blood. You need to get dressed so we can go get my grandson back, whoever you gave him up to is about to give him back. If you do not want to raise him, then I will." He insisted.

By now, I was thinking, this must be a sign from God himself. It had to be God that gave Daddy that dream. This meant that I was supposed to have my son and raise him. I went into the bathroom and got dressed with a full heart. Just the thought of being with my son forever made me feel whole and complete. I no longer felt like one of my arms was missing, and the empty feeling in my stomach was now gone because soon we would be together.

Then I remembered: the apartment, food and money Hannah and James had given me, as well as how nice they had been to me, but most of all I felt bad because I really did not want to hurt them, and this would break their hearts.

CHAPTER 134

I explained to my father about the apartment, and everything Hannah and James had done for me.

"Don't worry about all that, you can just give it all back and move in with me and I will help you get an apartment when the time comes," He promised.

"I'm not going on welfare, even if I have to work two jobs I refuse to be on welfare," I said.

"Don't worry about all that either, you just concentrate on getting my grandson back," he said.

When we arrived at my new apartment, my father was even more pissed off than he had been at the hospital. Now he was saying that Hannah and James basically paid me off to get my baby.

I kept telling him that it was not true, "I was not asking them for money they just insisted on helping me."

"Well, you can just give it all back. I want you to call the lawyer that got you into this mess and tell him that you've changed your mind and you're not giving the baby up for adoption." He insisted.

I took the lawyer's business card out of my wallet and called Mr. Rothstein.

After I had broken the bad news to him, my father grabbed the phone out of my hand and told Mr. Rothstein that he needed to prepare Hannah and James for the harsh reality that we were picking the baby up in the morning.

My father reached over and put his arm around me after I hung up the phone and said, "you're my daughter and I love you and my grandson, and I will make sure that nothing happens to you or him." I was so touched by his words that I hugged him for standing by me and acting like a real father. He had just prevented me from making the biggest mistake of my life and I was grateful.

At nine the following morning Daddy showed up at my apartment in his Cadillac to take me to the lawyer's office. Mr. Rothstein knew we were coming and so did Hannah and James. When we arrived at the office Mr. Rothstein did not look to thrilled because he already knew why we were there. He explained to my father that the adoption had not gone through yet, and that I was legally entitled to take my son back.

He told us that he had already spoken to Hannah and James and given them the bad news. "They're both heartbroken, but you can go to their home and pick your son up. They have requested that it be done that way."

As Daddy and I drove to Santa Monica, I could not help feeling sad for Hannah and James because I liked them both so much. I did also feel sorry for them because they could not have children of their own. The last thing I wanted to do was hurt either of them, but it could not be helped. I just couldn't live without my son, and I knew now that it was God's will for me to raise my son. Otherwise, He would not have given my father the dream and send him to stop me.

When we arrived at the house, Daddy looked at me and said. "This is a mansion by the ocean. These people must be wealthy, but no amount of money in the world could ever compare with my grandson growing up with his real family. I know that you will be a good mother to him because I raised you right."

"Certainly, I'll do my best," I said. "I'm going to ring the doorbell alone, and I have to talk to them without you interrupting our conversation so please stay by the car." I said.

When I rang the doorbell, James opened the door with Hannah standing next to him. Hannah was holding the baby in her arms and had tears rolling down her cheeks. Just looking at her face broke my heart and I felt guilty for being the cause of it. I explained to them why I had changed my mind. After they heard about my father's dream and how he hunted me down, they understood better and agreed that it was God.

It was then that Hannah handed me my son. Then I told them, "I'm ready to move out of the apartment and give back everything you gave me, since I'll be moving in with my father."

"No, we don't want anything back," James said. "We were never trying to buy your baby; we just helped a young girl get back on her feet. We wanted to help you so please keep everything. Besides, you are going to need every bit of help you can get now that you are keeping Jack. That is what we named him. I don't know if you want to keep that name, but he just looked so wise and serene, and the name seemed appropriate."

I looked at my son and thought to myself, the name does fit him well. And he does look calm. I looked at them and said, "I think you're right; Jack is the right name for him."

Then James produced a suitcase and told me they had packed some baby clothes for Jack to take with him. Hannah said, "We have a few other things we want you to take with you that Jack will need."

That is when James asked, "Is that your father standing by the car?"

"Yeah, that's my Daddy." I replied.

James waved and motioned for him to come up to the door.

When Daddy approached us, James and Hannah introduced themselves.

Daddy looked at his grandson for the first time, and kissed him on the forehead, and said to James, "Sorry for all of this, but my daughter was confused when she did this, but God sent me to stop her."

"We believe you. Can you help me get this baby stuff into the trunk of your car?" James asked.

Daddy and James went inside and came back with everything a new-born could ever need, including baby bottles with the warmer, a bassinet with folding legs, diapers and so much more. By the time they were finished loading up my father's car, not only was the trunk full but the backseat as well. They even gave me a car seat for Jack. Hannah and James really wanted to make sure that my baby and I got off to a good start, even if they were hurting inside themselves.

I realized then that what they had done was a selfless act of kindness and I would be grateful to them forever. I thanked them and told them that I knew they would have a baby of their own one day soon.

"After everything you've done for me, God has to give you two a baby to raise." I told them sincerely.

We hugged goodbye, then I turned around and walked back to my father's car with my baby in my arms and my father by my side. Daddy had already strapped Jack's car seat into the backseat of his car, next to an endless supply of Pampers. As we drove back to my apartment, I kept looking at my Jack in the backseat, now wide-awake and looking right back at me. He had not cried once; I could tell immediately that he was not a fussy crying baby. He just looked alert and peaceful.

"It's time to celebrate," Daddy said. "I'm going to drop you off at your apartment and then I'm going to the supermarket to get some ready-made barbecue pork ribs and some potato salad." He said.

I had never seen Daddy so happy. He was just beaming with pride and joy. Every time he stopped for a red light he would reach into the backseat and squeeze Jack's little hand and say to him, "I'm your grandpa little fella, I'm your grandpa." It was as if the baby had turned my father into melting ice on the sidewalk on a hot California day. I was beyond happy; I was overjoyed every time I looked into the back seat. I thought my heart was going to burst with love for Jack. I just loved him without limit from the very beginning. He was going to be my little partner in life.

CHAPTER 135

I began to imagine his first day at school, and his first girlfriend and how I would watch cartoons with him while he had his cereal in the morning. Jack and I were going to have fun together. I was looking forward to watching him grow and become a good decent man.

When we arrived at my apartment, I put the key in the lock and opened the front door while Daddy held Jack. I noticed that my door was already unlocked, I looked at my father and said you forgot to lock the door when we left earlier.

That's when I walked in and saw all my aunts and grandparents. They were all in my living room yelling surprise. I could not believe it!

They were giving me and Jack a welcome home party. They had laid out food, presents and decorations. But Daddy still wanted ribs, so he left and went to buy them. Everyone gathered around me congratulating me for having a baby. My grandmother took Jack from my father the minute she saw the baby and all my aunts were waiting for their turn to hold him. Jack was wide awake, quiet and cute. By the time I got my baby back, he had four different shades of lipstick on his little cheeks.

My Aunt Gina immediately began calling him Jackie. They all said he looked like an angel and my grandparents were thrilled to have their first great-grandson.

After Daddy returned with the ribs, and everyone had eaten, grandmother showed me how to make a baby bottle of formula since I was not breast feeding, as well as how to hold him while feeding him, how to burp him, change his diaper and give him a bath in the kitchen sink while everyone watched fascinated.

Then I put Jack in the bassinet that Daddy and grandfather had set up in the corner of my bedroom. Jack immediately went to sleep with no problem; he just closed his eyes and slept.

"You've got a good quiet baby and believe me after raising 13 children I can spot the quiet ones right off," Grandfather said. Then went back into the living room where my Aunt Janie was waiting to cut the cake, and for me to open the gifts they had brought for the baby.

After eating German chocolate cake, baked by my grandmother, I sat on the sofa to open the gifts. Each one had a card attached with money inside. By the time I had opened all the cards I had a little over $300 in cash and checks. "You should save that money since you never know when you're going to need extra money with a baby around," grandmother counseled me.

"I will, I promise." I said, kissing her on the cheek.

After everyone had gone home and day turned into night, I put on my pajamas and got into bed. Then I decided that I wanted my baby to sleep with me, it was our first night together and I wanted to hold him while I slept. I managed to pick him up without waking him. I put him in the middle of the bed and placed pillows on the side of him to protect him from falling off the bed. Then I held him as close as I could to my chest.

I lay there thinking that God truly blessed me, somebody had my back up there in heaven. Then I remembered a Bible verse that said, "God works in mysterious ways." That is true I thought. I gave my son up for adoption and God sent my father a dream about it. Then He somehow gets the adoptive parents not only to give the baby back peacefully, but to supply us with a fresh start financially. And I could hardly believe how generous my family had been and the fact that they threw a party to welcome my son into the family. I lay in bed and thanked the God that I knew was there but could not see. Just a few months ago, I had no hope but now everything seemed to be turning around. I felt hope in my heart for the first time in a long time.

I was confident that I could build a successful life for my son and myself, and that made me smile. I fell asleep feeling complete because I had my son in my arms.

CHAPTER 136

When I awoke the following morning, I looked at the clock on my nightstand and saw that it was six o'clock. My first thought was of Jack. I looked at him wondering why he had not cried during the night like other babies did for a bottle or a diaper change. I wondered if something was wrong with him that I did not know about. What if he was deaf or blind? "You are crazy," I told myself, the doctor would have told you if something was wrong with him. He is probably just a quiet baby.

Jack was just lying there with his eyes wide open. I carefully picked him up to support his little head. I kissed his little cheek and hugged him good morning. Then I checked his diaper and saw that it needed to be changed.

After I changed his diaper, I took him into the kitchen with me to prepare his bottle, then fed and burped him. I bathed him in the little baby tub Hannah and James had given me. Then I dressed him, thinking we could go for a walk, but he fell asleep before I could get him into the stroller. I laughed to myself, all this kid does so far is shit, piss, eat and sleep. I could hardly wait until he could walk, talk and play. So far taking care of the baby was not difficult, and I was excited to put him in the stroller for his first walk once he woke up.

A pleasant surprise was that I could still fit into all the clothes I had before my pregnancy. Although my stomach still poked out a little, the clothes fit. I just looked up and said, "Thanks God."

CHAPTER 137

I called Jake and told him that I had decided to keep the baby. I told him about my father's dream and everything that had happened.

"I'm glad you came to your senses. It was the right thing to do. Send me a photo of you and baby Jack together so I can keep it in my wallet." Jake still tried to get me to accept money from him every month until he got out of the Army. It was tempting, but I just could not allow myself to start depending on him. I had learned a hard lesson with Nick and was not going to make that mistake again. I had to be independent because the only thing I figured I could depend on for sure in life was myself and God. Now that I had a little boy to think about, I was not going to drag my son through relationship drama.

"Hopefully, I will be divorced by the time you get out of the Army. You can look for a job and stay with me. We can start our relationship with a clean slate when I'm single." I told him.

"You are single as far as I'm concerned. You were single the minute Nick dumped you over the phone and told you he wanted a divorce." Jake said.

That night my father came over straight after work. He made dinner for me, and we ate it together. Then he spent a few hours playing with his grandson, until Jack fell asleep. From that night forward, my father came to my apartment every night after work. My stepmother did not seem to mind that he was not coming straight home after work. I figured she understood that he was trying to make sure we were all right; besides Daddy loved little babies. He would come over, make dinner for us, play with the baby then watch television until he was ready to go home to my stepbrother.

The minute my so-called girlfriends found out I had kept my baby, they all dumped me. Sally even called Jack "It." she told me that I was messing up my life by keeping him. I wanted to smack her face, instead I told her to get out of my apartment.

Jake and my father stuck by me. Jake called me every other day from a phone booth with a roll of quarters in hand to feed the machine with. Daddy was around so much that he even went grocery shopping with me. He would drive me to distraction in the store by telling me to buy ninety-nine cent hotdogs instead of the higher quality hot dogs which cost three times more money. There was no way I was eating anything but quality hot dogs. Daddy was so cheap that he could squeeze a buffalo off a nickel. He constantly nagged me in the car about overspending on food, that he insisted I could have gotten cheaper. I kept reminding him that one of the great things about being an adult was you could choose what food you put in your own icebox.

CHAPTER 138

By the time Jack was six months old I was working full-time with benefits as a mailroom clerk at a law firm on Wilshire Blvd not far from my apartment. I contacted Social Services to get a list of licensed childcare providers for infants. I wanted someone who had been through a background check. After my experience with Nick, I now believed that people were capable of anything. Since Jack was unable to tell me if someone treated him badly while in their care, a thorough background check was critical to me.

I left Jack with my grandmother while I interviewed the daycare providers on my two-page list. I really would have preferred to have my grandmother take care of him while I worked, but Daddy said that she was getting older and had raised enough children.

"She wants to work at your grandfather's furniture store now," Daddy said.

I found a Hispanic woman named Martina in Hollywood. She had an in-home daycare center, licensed by the state of California and had glowing references. I chose her because she was an older woman who had children of her own. Martina had eight infants in her care, and all the parents I talked with told me they were happy with her services. She charged a little more than the others, but I figured it would be worth it to ensure Jack's safety while I worked.

I was proud of myself since I now had enough money to support the two of us by myself. I told God that He was the coolest thing ever. As usual I talked to Him like He was sitting in the room with me. I figured that if He had the ability to create me and make breath come out of my nostrils, then He could hear me.

I thought about all the great things that had happened in my life that year: I now had a savings account with four thousand dollars in it thanks to my family, Hannah and James; plus, my rent was paid up six months in advance, so I was able to stay home with my son after his birth for a little while. Add to that Jake Pierson was in love with me, the little boy on the moon was real.

Again, I thanked God because all this was a miracle. It felt like some unseen force loved me enough to look out for me. Sometimes I could feel the presence of something loving and wonderful, but it was always a fleeting moment.

The only negative situation in my life at this point was the Pinto breaking down two days before my first day of work at the law firm. Daddy had it towed to his car mechanic where we were told the car needed a new engine. We were also told that the car was not worth fixing, so I sold it for parts.

I bought a monthly bus pass and made a schedule for myself: get up at five in the morning to feed the baby, then wash and dress him; pack his diaper bag with all the things he would need throughout the day; feed myself, shower and get dressed in business attire.

After walking a few blocks with Jack in a baby stroller to the bus stop, I had to take two buses into Hollywood to get to the daycare center. Then I had to take the bus all the way back downtown to where my job was. In total, I was spending two hours a day on the bus just commuting. But that was okay because Jack and I were making it together.

Each morning to keep my spirits up, I once again started listening to the theme from "The Mary Tyler Moore Show." I would take my little cassette player and headphones with me for the bus rides. The lyrics inspired me by declaring," *You're Going to Make it After All.*" I could relate to the song because I was a city girl trying to make it on her own.

As soon as Jack was old enough to talk, I planned on going to college at night somehow. I figured my father would have no trouble watching Jack at night for me. In fact, I was counting on his help because I had decided to study law. I found law and politics enjoyable, and I had a natural interest in world events.

But most of all I wanted justice for the poor, weak and innocent people of the world. I wanted to somehow one day help influence laws to be made that allowed fairness and freedom for everyone. I wanted to make sure there were laws in place, to ensure that my son and every other kid in America continued to go to good public schools and get college scholarships.

Every day I saw politicians on TV trying to chip away at these opportunities, and I believed that everyone should be able to live the American Dream, not just a few. I used my free time to plan a future for myself and my son. It was my meditation time, and my time to talk to God about stuff. I would visualize myself being the woman I intended to be, on the little movie screen I had in my mind.

That is when I would ask God to heal my heart from the disappointments that life had shown me so far. I truly did not want to be one of those people who became physically ill from having a hard heart. I was trying hard not to hate Nick or think about him. Easier said than done since my heart still felt ripped to pieces and the thought of him made me sick emotionally.

Jake, on the other hand, was calling me on the phone every other night enthusiastically lovesick for me. Every time he called, he made me put the telephone receiver to Jack's ear so that his voice would become familiar to him.

One night while talking with Jake on the barracks payphone our conversation was suddenly interrupted by shouting in the stairwell where the payphone was located. I could not quite tell what was being shouted but it sounded very urgent. A moment later I heard Jake say, "Holy shit!" I got to go now; I will call you when I can! I love y…" And the call went dead.

"Are you going to be all right?" I asked no one.

As I hung up the phone that night, I thought. Maybe Jake was being sent to the Middle East, and I became very worried and afraid for him. But the next morning when I turned on the news while I was feeding Jack, I heard the news reporter announcing that Jakes unit had just invaded the Island of Grenada. They were on a mission to capture the Island's Airport and rescue American medical students. I watched as they showed grainy lowlight camera footage of tiny paratroopers jumping onto the airfield behind enemy lines.

I could see small smudgy puffs of black smoke appear around the airplanes the jumpers were falling from. Strange bright arcs of light sprayed up from the ground towards the descending troops. It looked to me like people were shooting at them before their parachutes hit the ground. I could not even imagine jumping out of an airplane, and having people shoot at me while I was still in the air. I would probably shit my pants, I thought to myself. I could not believe what I was seeing, and I was afraid for Jake. "Oh my God, please let Jake be alright, please keep him safe," I said out loud. "Send those angels that you sent to protect me when I was a kid, to protect him," I beseeched God.

CHAPTER 139

I was frightened for Jake and freaked out, as I waited day after day for any word from him. Weeks's passed before I heard from him again. One day I came home from work, opened my mailbox and found a letter written on a green leaf in a Ziplock baggie. The man was crazy; while in Grenada he wrote me a letter on a leaf, and it got to me through the mail. "Who does that?" I thought. He wrote that he had taken a pair of my underwear the last time we were together and kept them in his rucksack for good luck when he jumped onto the island of Grenada. I had no idea that he even had a pair of my underwear.

Jake said wonderful things to me in that letter written on the leaf. He wrote that in his eyes I was already his wife, and that a marriage license was just a paper formality. "I just know that you're going to marry me one day," he wrote. "I plan to fly to Los Angeles the minute the Army sets me free and sweep you off your feet."

The leaf letter was the most romantic thing that anyone had ever done for me. And the part of my heart that was still able to trust someone loved him for it. On the bottom of the letter he wrote, "I'm alive and well baby." Then the words, "wait for me, love Jake. P.S. Didn't have any paper so I used this leaf."

He had written my address at the very top of the leaf and there was no stamp. I was amazed and impressed that the leaf letter had arrived intact. Thank you, God, for keeping Jake safe, alive and for the letter on the leaf. I then walked over to Jack and picked him up out of his baby carrier and hugged him saying, "Jake is okay."

My father was still showing up at my apartment every night after work, to check on me and play with his grandson. We were still going to the supermarket together and arguing over my choice to buy quality hot dogs instead of the slim price brand. I continued to stand my ground.

I slowly came to the realization that I might be suffering from mild depression. I could still function, but my inner joy was gone. It felt like all my happy cells had just packed up and left my brain. Through self-reflection, I began to examine why I felt so sad. Looking at myself in the bathroom mirror, I could see the effects of trauma in my eyes. Nick was now out of the Army and living with his parents. They were helping him file for divorce which was stressful for me.

I also saw in my eyes that falling in love with the wrong guy had caused a lot of emotional damage. I saw where giving myself away to another person had been bad for my mental health, because Maya Johnson had been lost along the way. To be with Nick, I had stopped being myself. Now I wanted to be me again. The problem was the girl I was before Nick was gone forever and she was not coming back. The empty shell feeling was strong, and I had to change that.

I reminded myself that after everything I had experienced in life so far, I had remained optimistic about my future. Hadn't I waited to grow up so that I could control my own life? Surely, I told myself, I could still be happy, and that Nick was just a bad experience that I needed to move on from. I also told myself, that many of my dreams could still come true.

Thinking this way, positively helped me feel better.

Since Nick had returned home, he made no effort to contact me or see the baby and I was grateful for that. Then one day I was served with divorce papers at my father's house. Shortly after that, Nick shocked me by showing up at my apartment in the middle of the night high on cocaine and liquor, demanding to see his son. After telling me to give the baby up for adoption, and telling everyone that the baby was not his, the asshole had the nerve to knock on my door at three in the morning.

The first time I made the mistake of letting him in. He drunkenly looked around my apartment and said, "Where did you get all this stuff from?"

"Don't worry about that, you filed for divorce so it's none of your business," I replied.

He stumbled into the bedroom where he saw Jack sleeping in his crib. Nick walked over and examine him. "He's a good-looking kid," Nick said.

"Well, if I had given him up for adoption like you and your mother wanted me to then you would have no idea what he looked like, now would you?" I chided him. "And the thing that really bothers me is you told your family he was not yours, when you know that he is. He even has some of your facial features."

Nick picked Jack up as he continued to sleep, then just stood there looking at him. Then he put the baby back in his bassinet. Before I knew it, he had his drunken hands on me. He pressed his body up against mine and pushed my back against my bedroom wall, as he tried to kiss me. His breath and body smelled like alcohol was coming out of his pores. Being the germophobic freak that I was, my body immediately recoiled from his touch. I certainly did not want his tongue or saliva in my mouth; his breath was foul.

I pulled away from him as he dropped his pants and revealed himself to me. I looked at him in shock as he stood there with his pants and underwear down around his ankles. He looked pathetic showing me what he had to offer, which was nothing to be proud of or to brag about. Then I became even more disgusted as I noticed the sore on his penis, with dried up white stuff all over it. I wondered for a moment, is this his way of telling me that he had VD?

I realized that he had engaged in sexual intercourse with someone else before he showed up at my door. My stomach turned, as I looked at the true nature of the guy I had grown up with, loved and married. He just had sex with someone else and had not even bothered to clean himself up afterwards. Now he was looking at me like I was sloppy seconds. Disgusting!

I pushed him away from me and said. "We're not having sex Nick. I am not going to allow you to put that diseased looking thing near me. Don't you realize that you have someone else's dried up fluids on your penis? With a sore as a companion? Who the hell do you think I am? Oh wait." I said. "You must think that black chicks just put up with this type of shit while we're collecting that welfare check. Get out of my apartment; go home Nick.

Better yet, go back to the woman you just left before you came here because she can have you. And do not come here again looking for a late-night booty call, because I am not going to open the door. I don't have time for this crap I have to get up for work in the morning."

Drunk, stoned and bewildered Nick looked at me, and all I saw in his eyes was a confused, sad pathetic little boy. He pulled up his pants and I walked into the living room to open the front door for him. As he approached the door, I was relieved that he was leaving and that I did not have to call the police to get him out. He walked out the door and I shut it, making sure that all three locks engaged.

I leaned my back against the door as a tear ran down my cheek. I had been married to him, and now he was just a total stranger who made my skin crawl. It made my heart sad that he was even the father of my child. I wanted to just run away and forget that Nick was ever in my life.

The following month I was awaken in the middle of the night again. But this time it was a loud sound in my living room. At first, I just lay there in bed frozen in fear, then I heard someone moving around in my living room. I silently thanked God that my bedroom door was shut, as I quietly slipped out of bed and picked my sleeping baby up. As I sought refuge in my closet, I prayed that Jack did not wake up and cry. I sat down on the floor in the back of the closet behind some clothes.

I felt around in the dark and picked up a high heeled shoe to use as a weapon just in case I needed it. I was scared out of my mind as I sat hurdled on the closet floor. Holding my baby in one arm, and a shoe in the other, I heard my bedroom door open and thought my heart was going to beat out of my chest. The closet door opened and without thinking, I pushed past the man standing there and ran for my life with my baby in my arms.

I ran out of my apartment screaming, "someone's in my apartment." I ran to the managers apartment and banged on the door screaming. A few other guys opened their doors to see what all the commotion was about. I was telling the manager my apartment had been broken into when we all saw the guy running across the courtyard. My manager and two male tenants went after him and tackled him down to the ground. I heard the managers wife yell, "I just called the police." I saw the guy struggling to get away, but he could not because he had three guys restraining him at the same time.

He was a tall skinny guy in blue jeans and a black ski mask pulled over his face. My landlord pulled it off his face, and I was surprised to see that it was the guy who lived across the street. He was high on something and had a sort of super-strength. Another guy from the building had to help the three that were already restraining him, to keep him down until the police showed up.

Turned out the guy was a crack addict, who had gotten into my apartment through an open window in the living room. He was looking for money to buy more crack. The police cuffed him and took him away. I realized then that the days were gone when you could sleep with an open window in Los Angeles. Now you had to worry if your neighbors were dangerous. The next day I bought a fan and kept my windows shut at night.

CHAPTER 140

A few weeks later I had to work through my lunch break because we were so busy at the firm. My boss was nice enough to let me off an hour early. I decided to pick Jack up early and take him to the park. I took the bus to Hollywood and showed up unannounced at the daycare center. Upon arrival I was horrified to find out that my baby had been left with the sitter's 13-year-old daughter. There was no adult there to watch my child. This was unacceptable on so many levels. "Where is your mother?" I asked the girl.

"She left to run some errands." The girl told me.

"Your mother left you here to care for all these infants by yourself?" I asked in an alarmed voice.

"I always watch the babies for her when I come home from school." She said.

I rushed to the nursery to get my son, and found Jack lying in a crib by a window with the sun beating down on his little face. Then I noticed that his bottle was in the sun and the formula looked like it was spoiled, and his diaper needed to be changed.

Is this what I was paying hundreds of dollars a month for, my son lying neglected in his own shit? I wanted to kill that woman; if she had walked in the facility that moment, I would have gone to jail that day.

I looked at her daughter and said, "tell your mother that she's fired. And tell her that I'm going to report her to the state for child neglect." I picked up Jack's diaper bag and changed his diaper before carrying him out of the front door for the last time.

As I sat on the bus riding home, I wondered how many times my child had been left crying in the crib. Or how many times he had needed to be picked up or attended to, and no one had been there for him. All I could do was hug my baby and tell him how sorry I was for leaving him there in the first place. I felt guilty as hell and stupid at the same time, as though I had let my son down. I had done everything I could to check this woman out. Most likely the other parents were as clueless about this woman as I had been. We had all depended on the State of California's background check. First thing Monday morning I was going to call the State and report her and put an end to her so-called daycare services. I was relieved that it was Friday, and I would have time to talk to my grandmother about babysitting for me on Monday until I found someone else.

When I told Daddy that night, he was tempted to drive over there and tell the woman off. I told him that she was not worth getting arrested over.

I called my grandmother the following morning and explained my situation to her, she was just as angry as I was. She agreed to help me out until I found somewhere else to leave Jack while I worked. This time I was determined to find an actual daycare business in a building instead of someone's home. It took me a few weeks of interviewing places after work, but I finally found one in the Wilshire area where I lived. It was called Bright Horizons Day Care Center. They took infants until preschool. It was professional looking, clean and had a playground. They promised to start preparing my son for preschool as soon as he could walk and talk.

CHAPTER 141

Things were on the upswing again and I started getting regular letters from Jake in Grenada. The fighting had stopped, and the medical students had been rescued. Despite that, for some reason Jake was still there. He wrote me beautiful love letters about marrying me one day, and how he could not wait for us to be a family.

He wrote about taking Jack fishing and hunting once he was old enough. What impressed me most about his letters was he was willing to raise my son as his own and was excited about it. I was grateful that another human being loved me that intensely to accept my child as his own. Despite Jake's commitment I still felt that getting married could be a threat to my independence.

When the court date was set for my divorce hearing I was grateful. I had done nothing to defend myself, so my father hired a well-known lawyer, for my hearing. Daddy liked him because he used to date my Aunt Marie when they were in high school and considered him a friend. I really did not care who handled my divorce, so my father arranged everything, including making certain that Nick paid my attorney fees. And when it was time to show up in court, Daddy went with me.

Nick showed up with his mother and had the nerve to lie to the judge in a court of law that Jack was not his son. He just lied in court as if it were nothing, as if he never creeped over to my apartment in the middle of the night to see his son. In fact, he denied even doing that or seeing the baby. I was so hurt and angry that I wanted to kill him.

When I was on the witness stand, I told the judge the truth: that Nick was my son's father, and how he and his mother had suggested that I put my baby up for adoption. I told the judge everything Nick had put me through, and how he told me to go get on welfare like every other black bitch in America.

I told him about the abuse I suffered at his hands, and how he tried to hide the pregnancy from his family while we were still living together as man and wife.

When I finished the judge looked at Nick like the piece of shit that he was and said,

"I'm ordering a paternity test. You will pay child support if the results show that you are that child's father."

After court ended, Daddy and I were walking back to his car when we spotted Nick getting into a brand-new Ford. I approached the car and asked Nick where he got the new car from. I noticed that he had changes of clothes in the backseat, which told me he was already regularly sleeping with someone else.

"My father bought me the car." He replied.

It pissed me off that Nick had it so easy. I felt like the universe was rewarding him for being an asshole. Dump your wife and kid, get a new car, job and a girlfriend.

I looked at him and said. "You're going to regret the way you've treated me one day, as well as denying the fact that Jack is your son."

"Well, I may be stuck paying child support for him, but I'm not going to let that kid ruin my life." He sneered.

I spit on one of the new shoes he was wearing and said. "You're really scummy you know that? I hope you have a nice time trying to live with yourself." My stomach turned as I left with all the dignity I could muster and walked toward my father's car, got in and left before I did something I would later regret.

CHAPTER 142

A week later Jake called me one night after work and said, "I'm back from Grenada." I was so happy to hear his voice that I wanted to scream out in a fit of joy. He had made it back safely, except his voice sounded differently.

When I asked him if he were okay, he responded by telling me what I wanted to hear.

"I'm really okay. I'm not trying to downplay anything," He responded.

When I asked about Grenada, he refused to talk about it. He told me that he was not allowed to talk about it; that the government made him sign papers saying that he would not talk about it.

After that, I told him everything that had happened in court, and how the judge had ordered a paternity test.

"I so regret the fact that Nick is the father of my child. I am already having visions of Nick treating Jack like a piece of crap for the rest of his life. Now I am going to be connected to that creep until Jack's 18, when I would rather never see him again. And my son is going to grow up knowing that his father doesn't love or want him."

Then I suddenly had a thought, just do not show up for the paternity test. That way the judge would rule that Nick was not the father because I failed to show up. And if Nick did not pursue it, which he would not, the divorce would be granted without a child being involved. But if he did pursue it then I would be forced to take the test.

Nick did not want anything to do with his half black son, so this would suit him well.

I could hear Jake on the other end of the phone saying, "I'm going to be out of the Army in a few months. I intend to stick by the two of you and I promise everything is going to work out.

When I hung up the phone, I revisited my idea, would it be worth it to have a judge and the world think I had lied the whole time? Yeah, it would just to protect my son from rejection. I wanted Jack to grow up with a role model. A father who was going to tuck him in at night and read him a bedtime story. And if I took it real slow with Jake, it might just work out. He was already acting like he was Jack's father and he had not even met the boy yet.

I heard a voice from within my heart saying, "You love Jake, and you know that you can trust him. He wants to take your son fishing and hunting, plus spend the rest of his life with you. You can always trust him with your heart, and he will always love you and have your back. This is your only opportunity for true love, and it will never come across your path again."

I made the decision not show up for the paternity test. Nick reacted just the way I thought he would, he never complained about my not showing up. After that, he went his way, and I went mine.

CHAPTER 143

A few months later Jake was on my doorstep with a cute little smile on his face. He picked me up as he took me into his arms and kissed me, then he just held me for a long time as time seemed to stand still.

He brought his suitcase and a large green duffel bag into my apartment, as I shut the front door. "Where is Jack?" he asked excitedly. I took him into the bedroom where Jack was taking a nap in his crib. Jake leaned down and kissed him on the forehead. He looked at me and said. "He's even better looking in person."

"He's really quiet and sleeps a lot and he's easy to take care of," I said.

"I guess you got lucky then, because when my little sister Jane was born, she cried a lot." He said.

That night for the first time we had dinner together as a family, and while I was washing the dinner dishes Jake was on the living room floor trying to teach Jack how to roll a ball across the carpeted floor. Then he changed his diaper and helped me bathe him before putting his pajamas on. Jake fed him his nighttime bottle and told him some bedtime story he had made up about a little boy growing up in a magical animal kingdom.

My heart was truly touched by watching Jake with Jack, and I recognized what a gift from God he really was. I felt like this finally was the beginning of having my own family, and it felt good.

I awoke the following morning to the smell of bacon and fresh coffee coming from the kitchen. I got up and put on my robe while walking into the kitchen where Jake was cooking breakfast for us while feeding Jack oatmeal in a highchair. I just stood there for a moment amazed by this man.

He kissed me on the cheek, as I walked over to him, he said, "Jack and I are making you breakfast."

"I could've done this," I replied.

"You looked like an angel while you were sleeping, and I wanted to let you sleep." He said.

I poured myself a cup of hot coffee and put some cream in it. I noticed that he had changed Jack's diaper and the two of them were already dressed. Jake placed a plate of eggs and bacon in front of me and sat down at the table. While we were eating, he told me that he had gotten up at 5 a.m. and Jack was wide awake in his crib just playing with a stuffed animal.

"I bathed him in the kitchen sink, then dressed him, and I can tell that he's really smart," Jake said. "Jack and I are going to the park after breakfast. I want to show him some stuff."

"What stuff," I asked.

"Stuff like the trees in the park and the birds you know; teach him to respect nature. Kids like collecting frogs and lizards to bring home." He explained.

"I never looked at it that way." I replied. "Okay, the park it is," I said smiling at Jack.

After breakfast I got dressed, and the three of us caught the bus down to La Brea Tar Pits Park. The first thing Jake did when we got there was catch a frog for Jack to see up close. Then he took him to the trees so Jack could touch the leaves.

After introducing Jack to nature, Jake then insisted on buying tickets for the tar pits museum, claiming that he and Jack wanted to see some fossil exhibits. Surprise—Jake was the one who really wanted to see the exhibits. Afterwards he bought us some sandwiches for lunch which we sat down on the lawn to eat, while I fed Jack some Gerber baby food. I was hooked on the Gerber plum dessert and always bought an extra jar for myself. Jake thought I was insane until he tasted it. I had to make him give me the jar back, he liked it so much.

"Maybe you should buy an extra jar for me next time you go to the store." He said laughing.

"When we get home, I'll give you some of the Arrow Root Baby Cookies they taste just like shortbread cookies." I offered.

Jake burst out laughing.

"What's so funny?" I asked.

He pointed and said, "That woman over there is looking at us like we're crazy because we're eating baby food with the baby."

I saw the woman who looked at us like we were taking food from the baby's mouth. "I buy an extra jar for myself," I yelled over to her. Still laughing, Jake took a photo of her with this camera, capturing the shocked look on her face.

"We should get going" I said and began to gather up our stuff. We caught the bus back to the apartment where I put a sleeping Jack into his crib.

Jake walked down to the grocery store, claiming he was going to make me a pot of his mother's homemade chicken noodle soup. When he returned, I sat in the kitchen and watched him put a whole chicken into a pot to boil in water with fresh onions, carrots and celery. Then he took fresh eggs and flour to make homemade noodles.

A few hours later the apartment began to smell like chicken soup heaven. "Damn dude, who are you? The 'Galloping Gourmet?'" I asked him smiling. Next, he was busy baking French bread and squeezing lemons for lemonade. I was starting to feel very well taken care of and spoiled.

My father came over and I introduced him to Jake. Daddy was impressed by the smell of the soup and wanted some. Jake wasted no time telling my father of his intentions towards me and Jack and how he was looking forward to raising Jack as his own son. I could tell that my father was impressed that someone loved me enough to step up and be a full-time father to his grandson. As Jake and my father talked, Daddy tasted the soup and said that it was the best he ever had.

Obviously, I was relieved that my father and Jake got on well together, and I could tell that Daddy approved of him. That night I went to bed happy and fell asleep in Jake's arms only to be awakened in the middle of the night by my doorbell ringing.

Jake said, "I'll go see who it is, you stay here." He put his jeans on and walked into the living room to answer the door. I heard the doorbell ring again, got up and put on my robe and walked out into the living room and stood behind Jake as he looked through the door peephole. "It's Nick and he looks pretty wasted." Jake said.

Nick rang the doorbell again and yelled out. "Open the door."

Jake asked. "Does he do this sort of thing often?"

"No, just once months ago. I think he gets drunk and high on cocaine and thinks he can bang on my door in the middle of the night. Last time he wanted to see his son without his parents or anyone finding out and then he tried to have sex with me." I told him. "He just dropped his pants and thought I was going to sleep with him. His private parts had a bump and were still dirty from the last person he had been with. I told you about that over the phone, remember?"

"Please spare me the memory. I'm about to make him leave you alone for good." He said. Jake opened the front door as I stood behind him. The shocked look on Nick's face when Jake opened the door was priceless.

"What the fuck are you doing here?" Nick said.

Jake replied, "I live here now, and you don't. I highly suggest that you move on and leave my girlfriend alone. You are divorced, with no children remember? You do not have to pay child support, and you have got your freedom. Now go away and don't come back."

"I want to see my kid," Nick insisted.

"Look man, you told the judge that the baby was not yours, then signed divorce papers saying there were no children from the marriage. Now, unless you are willing to pay child support and be a good father to that defenseless little boy in there, I strongly advise you to leave us alone." Jake warned him. "The sad thing is you know that he's your son and you know you had a good wife. Jake continued, "That's why you're showing up here in the middle of the night drunk trying to see them. Part of me feels sorry for you man because you lack a backbone, but you got to go, and I am telling you not to come back. It is over between you and Maya; I'm going to marry her. The minute you filed for divorce you lost the right to invade her apartment in the middle of the night. Now that we have had this little talk, I am going to shut the door and we're going back to bed. If you come here again, I'll call the police." Jake slammed the door in his face, and we went back to bed.

I did not know it at that moment, but that would be the last time that I would see Nick for many, many years.

CHAPTER 144

When I awoke the following morning, Jake already had breakfast going again. I walked into the kitchen in my pajamas, and Jake told me to sit down and relax while he handed me a cup of hot coffee. Then he placed a plate of scrambled eggs, bacon with toast in front of me. He had fed Jack, dressed him and already placed him in his highchair again. He also had the employment section open in the Sunday Los Angeles Times. I was impressed that he was already looking for a job just days after showing up here.

I took a sip of my coffee and said, "all this cooking and helping with Jack is making me feel spoiled."

"It's the least I can do," he said. I figure you have been taking care of Jack by yourself for all these months. You probably never got the chance to sleep in or have someone take care of you. So, I thought I would give you a break."

"I'm just curious: who taught you to treat women this way?"

"My parents. This is the way my father treats my mother. I've never even heard my parents argue." He said.

"You're lucky. I grew up watching my parents fight and argue and a lot of the time the police would show up. I swore to myself that when I grew up and got married, I would never allow that to happen to me or my children. And look what has happened already: I got divorced just like they did. History repeated itself except Nick and I were fighting while the baby was still in my womb." I said.

"But it's not your fault. I was there from the beginning till the end. You were serious and Nick was playing house. Basically, you just married the wrong guy the first time around," Jake said with a big grin on his face. "Now I'm here to correct that mistake."

I smiled shyly and said, "You're crazy; you know that don't you?"

"Crazy for you." He said and reached over and kissed me on the mouth.

Over the next few months, I went to work five days a week and Jack went to daycare, while Jake went on countless job interviews. For some reason unknown to us, no one wanted to hire him. We wondered if it was because of his voice. It had changed since going to Grenada I had gotten used to the sound of his voice and had hardly noticed it now.

Instead of looking at him as the capable individual that he was, he was being discriminated against because of his voice and we both knew it. Nobody seemed to care that he had served in the Army. One guy had nerve enough to ask him if he had a drinking or drug problem because of his voice. It was pretty messed up that you could go into combat for your country, suffer a disability because of it and be unemployable. The dog pound even refused to hire him to pick up dog shit. It was shocking, and I felt bad for him because, he was living off his savings at this point.

I, on the other hand, seemed to fit in with the Los Angeles work force. I never had any problems finding a job because I was a city girl and had grown up in LA. But Jake was from Utah and grew up on a remote military installation. The closest thing to a city for him was Salt Lake City, which was a two-hour drive by car. The jobs he had growing up were easy to get because the community was smaller. People knew him and his family.

Los Angeles, however, was a whole different arena.

One night I was awakened by Jake muttering, and thrashing in his sleep.

"What the hell is this about?" I thought before waking him up. I reached over and gently shook him awake. When he opened his eyes, he looked like a startled deer looking into the headlights of a car. He had sweat dripping down his forehead and the side of his face.

"I'm going to get a washcloth for your face," I said going into the bathroom. When I returned, he was just lying there looking up at the ceiling with a blank look on his face. "You were talking in your sleep. Are you okay? What were you dreaming about? What's up with that?"

Jake just lay there looking up at the ceiling for a moment, then he said, "my roommate decided to blow his brains out in our apartment."

"What apartment?" I asked.

"When we got back from Grenada, my friend Jules Henley, asked me if I wanted to share this apartment he had off-base. We had fought together in Grenada and hung out in our free time. Anyway, I never told you about the apartment because I only spent two nights there then I moved back into the barracks.

"The second day we were there I went out to buy us some hamburgers from a fast-food place. While I was gone, Jules decided to kill himself with his own gun in the living room. I walked in with our food and his brains were scattered all over the walls and the carpet. After I called the police, and they had finished doing their investigation, I moved right back into the barracks. I ended up having to clean up the mess to clear out the apartment. As I scrubbed his brain tissue off the wall then repainted it, I became angry because not only did I have to see him go out that way, but I had to clean up parts of his brain tissue as well. No one had a clue or suspected that he was suicidal. He explained.

Taking a deep breath, he continued. "We were in the same fire team so we both saw and did some messed up shit together on that Island. We fought side-by-side. You know it changes you inside when you end someone's life at first you justify it as just part of a soldier's Job. But eventually a guy, meaning me has some down time to really think about it and he might realize that he was the one that volunteered to be put in a situation where he might have to kill someone. What does that say about that person?

He paused for a moment I could tell he was struggling to explain what he was trying to tell me in a way I would understand. You know something? I concluded that killing those soldiers didn't really bother me much. Is that bad? He asked.

He quickly continued as if he was afraid of what answer I might give. "What messes with me the collateral damage I witnessed, you know small dead children, Hungry orphan children whose parents died in a collapsed house, mistakenly targeted by Uncle Sam."

He was silent for some time, then shaking his head he continued. "It also bothers me That one of the guys in our platoon lost his arm. Poor guy was just out of jump school. I feel partially responsible because I was the patrol leader when it happened. The idiot thought he was going to pick up a grenade that a Cuban soldier tossed in the middle of our patrol. I guess he thought he had enough time to toss it back in the direction it came from. Stupid cherry, he's lucky as hell he aint dead" he said bitterly. "That is one of the first things they teach us not to do in basic training. They taught us to yell "GRENADE" and immediately fall to your belly as low as you can get, facing the grenade in hopes that your helmet would take the brunt of the shrapnel." He paused and as an afterthought added. "So low an ant could piss on you," "they told us."

He stopped for a moment put his head down and covered his eyes like one does to shield them by the sun, and continued reluctantly, "Well it blew up. I could not hear anything but a loud ringing coming from the middle of my head. I looked around and saw him trying to leverage himself up with an arm that wasn't there. I could tell he was screaming but I could hear nothing. I rushed to him yelling for the team to set a perimeter around the wounded soldier. The medic beat me to him and began assessing the damage. It looked really bad."

He looked up at me and went on. "The guy kept asking me to get his missing arm. It took me a minute, but I found it a few feet away in the bushes. I came back to him and placed his arm on his chest. He held it with his good arm while the medic worked to stop the bleeding. Last I saw of him was when they loaded him and his arm on a medevac. We learned later he was alive and recovering in Walter Reed Army Medical Center."

"Why did he want his arm so badly?" I asked him.

"Sometimes they can reattach the limb if it's a clean cut. I think he mostly just wanted it back with him, attached or not. In his case reattachment was not an option because it looked like the upper half of his humerus was missing or shattered."

He paused, looking thoughtful. I could tell he wanted to end this conversation and get to the point. Then he continued. "Listen, I got way off track here so I will cut this long sad story short. The thing that I have fucked up dreams about the most is Henley killing himself like that and leaving me to deal with the mess and his devastated parents who insisted on viewing the scene. That's why I am mad at him. He did this to me, Jake said pointing to his throat. I started talking like this a couple of days after he killed himself, and I blame him.

"Maybe you should go talk to a counselor," I suggested.

"How? I signed a paper saying I would never talk about a military operation," he said.

"Well, you just told me some stuff," I said.

"I didn't tell you anything that hasn't been made public already on the news. Do not worry, I will be all right. It is just a stupid dream. Besides, the more I am with you and Jack the better I feel. He said sounding confident. "Let's just go back to sleep."

We lay there our bodies tightly press together holding on to one another like a lifeline. Both of us feeling safe because the other was there, and for a change I held him as he fell asleep with his head on my chest.

CHAPTER 145

After months of looking for a job, Jake decided to go back home to Utah. He sat me down one afternoon after job hunting all day and told me he thought it would be easier for him to find a job back home in Salt Lake City.

"I still have plenty of savings left for us, but I don't want to deplete them by fighting a losing job battle in Los Angeles. No one is going to give me a job here and I do not feel right here, there is too many people. I know if I went home, I would have no problem finding a job. We could have a fresh start in life and really leave the past behind us," he said.

"You're right," I agreed. "I'm ready to start my life over again with you and Jack. A lot of bad things have happened to me here in Los Angeles. Maybe a fresh start somewhere else would be good for us and I would never have to deal with Nick again or see him for that matter. There is nothing really holding me here except my family. So, let's do this."

We sat on the sofa brainstorming about how we could do this smoothly without problems. Within an hour we had come up with a plan that we both felt would be fool-proof. Jake was my best friend and our planning together reminded me of when we were little kids, and my friend De-De would come and take me flying in my dreams to see him. I thought about us planning our lives together with the angels, while we played pat-a-cake together as if we were twins.

That is how close I felt to him back then and I still felt that closeness. I could still remember the freckles on his face, his hair was cut short and parted to the side of his head and his cowlick, which he still had today. Now, we were all grown up and still planning.

Jake had been saving money since he was a kid working on his uncle's cattle ranch, so he had the financial means to rent us a two-bedroom apartment and buy a used car. After he found a job, he would buy me and Jack train tickets out of our savings fund. Jake figured it would take him a month or two to accomplish everything.

Three days later Jake flew home to Utah, stayed with his sister and within a week he had a job at a plastics company in Salt Lake City. Two weeks later he rented a two-bedroom apartment for us and moved into it after buying his sister Lilly's used mustang before she left for a Mormon mission in Europe.

He even had a phone installed in the apartment and called me immediately to complain about being lonely without Jack and me around. He wanted us to get on the train as soon as possible.

Although my father was not too thrilled about us moving out of state, he trusted Jake and had respect for him because he had stood by me when Nick had not. My father knew Jake was a solid guy.

After reminding him that my grandparents had done the same thing back in the day, my father gave us his blessing. Now all I had to do was believe my own words. I kept telling myself that my grandmother had left her family and her home to be with my grandfather. "If grandmother had not followed her heart, I never would have been born into the Johnson family." I told him.

The following day, I threw caution to the wind, gave two-week's notice at the law firm, and sold anything I could not fit into a suitcase.

On a Friday morning, Jack and I boarded the Amtrak train and left Los Angeles and the past behind us. I told myself that one day we would move back, but little did I know at the time that I would not be living most of my adult life in California.

I was excited about taking Jack on his first train ride. He was 11 months-old now and getting better looking every day. His dark hair was growing longer, and his face was becoming more chiseled looking and defined like his father's. He looked like a little curly haired Greek or Middle Eastern baby. Every time I looked at him, I could see bits and pieces of Nick. I figured that was a fact I would have to live with until the day I died.

After I boarded the train and it had taken off, I held Jack up to the window so he could see the countryside through the train window. Jack would see cows from the window and get excited. We were going to spend the night on the train and arrive in Salt Lake City at nine the following morning.

CHAPTER 146

At least four women approached me on the train asking to hold Jack telling me how handsome he was and how he would be a lady killer when he grew up. I felt quite proud that I had such a good-looking son who was my little partner, and I was looking forward to watching him grow up.

Despite my pride, I just wished the stab wound in my heart would heal and go away. Having Jack and Jake in my life really helped, but the wound Nick inflicted was still raw. I was ready for the wound to heal.

Depression was draining, I felt like I had to fight my way out of a box every morning and hide the sadness I felt deep inside. I really had to fight hard with myself to get up each morning and function like a normal human being.

Truthfully, the Nick debacle had changed me inside forever. I thought of it as emotional scar tissue. I told myself to remember my childhood; no matter what happened I would wake up happy. I had refused to allow anyone to steal my joy when I was a kid. I told myself now that for some reason unknown to me, I was blessed, God loved me enough to send Jake into my life and help me keep my son. I could not forget what a miracle it was that we had played together as children in our dreams, only to end up together as adults. I had no reason to feel sad deep inside I told myself; you do have every reason to be happy and you must make that conscious decision to be happy.

When the train arrived in Salt Lake City the following morning, Jake was there waiting for us. He had flowers in his hands for me with the roots and dirt still hanging from them, and a water gun for Jake. He gave me a big kiss and hug then put Jake on his shoulders as he exclaimed, "Come see our 'new' used car." He took us to the parking lot where he had a blue Mustang parked. I noticed that he already had a car seat set up for Jake in the backseat. He put Jake in it, then told us to wait in the car while he got our luggage.

I gave him my baggage claim tickets as he kissed me on the forehead saying, "I'll be right back."

After Jake had put our luggage in the trunk of the car, it was a 10-minute car ride before we pulled up in front of a three-story apartment building. I got out of the car and looked around me, the neighborhood looked nice and clean, and reminded me of the Wilshire area back home. There were beautiful Victorian homes everywhere I looked. I was impressed.

Jake took us inside and showed us the apartment. He had done well: there was a decent sized living room, a small kitchen and two bedrooms, with a large bathroom that had a shower and bathtub. The best part was that Jake already had the place completely furnished. He even had a new crib set up for Jack and stuffed animals along with a few toys in his room. He had gone out and purchased towels, bedding and dishes. I was absolutely blown away by how well he had set things up for us and all by himself. I could not have done better myself.

He said that the rent included a laundry room in the building basement. "And there's a big park down the street called Liberty Park that has a playground and swimming pool for small children. So anytime we want to take Jack to the park we only have to walk a few blocks. Plus, the University of Utah is within walking distance so we can go to college when we're ready."

After we had unpacked the clothes, I brought with me and put them away, Jake took us to lunch, then drove us around the city for a personal tour. He showed me the University of Utah, which was six blocks up the street from our apartment building. I appreciated all the big beautiful antique homes in our neighborhood that reminded me of a Norman Rockwell painting.

Jake told me that the early Mormons built most of the homes in the mid-1800s. The mayor's mansion was in our neighborhood and looked like a mini-version of the white House to me. But my favorite house was a place called Ellis Mansion, you were really looking at some history when you looked at that place. You could still see where they tied up their horses and buggy's long ago in front of the house, everything was original.

While showing me the downtown area, we passed a big building that looked like a 200-year-old castle.

"What's that big building?" I asked.

"It's the Mormon Temple," Jake said. "That is the church my family believes in, but you'll never see me in there. I decided it was all bullshit by the time I was old enough to think for myself."

"When was that?" I asked.

"I was around eight years old when I started sneaking out of church, but I hated it from the start, and I never swallowed the Kool-aide" he said.

"I loved going to church," I said. "I used to go to the church bookstore with my father after the service to buy books about the betterment of your soul. After that we would go to lectures three nights a week to hear positive thinking speakers, I thought it was fun," I said.

"How could that be fun for you?" he asked.

"Because I would go home and practice visualizing in my mind's eye what I wanted in my life. It is fun like being a painter with an empty canvas called your life. You can create things in the physical world with your imagination. If you apply faith and the light of God you can sometimes choose what you manifest into your physical reality. It is based on the concept that we create situations, moods and actions for our lives all day long, every day. We do this by the actions we take or the way we think or the words we speak, for example. Sometimes I think it is fate for a situation to happen, for a soul to learn a lesson. Like us being together is fate. But it must be the will of God, and you must ask in prayer. My personal relationship is with God, who made me, and he is my church," I said.

"Well, you're welcome to do all that just don't expect me to join any church," Jake replied. "Part of the reason why I joined the Army was to escape organized religion, and the mission my parents had me set up to go on. I really never want to sit through a church service again."

"I guess if someone forced me to go to church and I didn't believe in what the preacher was saying, I would have a hard time going too," I told him.

The Mormons have tons of rules and hoops you must jump through. They build expensive temples when they should be giving all the money to people in need. The church owns a lot of businesses, as well as the tithings they pocket from every church member's paycheck. Jake told me.

"All because they believe some dude named Joseph Smith received some plates and "The Book of Mormon" from God. When I was a kid, it gave me the impression that all churches were cults, and I think God is bigger and better than all of that. I believe in what made me and nothing else," he said.

"Don't worry Jake, I won't be joining the Mormon Church." I said smiling.

Jake showed me the Great Salt Lake, which the closest thing to a beach that Salt Lake City had to offer. "You can sail a boat on it, but no one really swims in it," Jake explained. On the way back to the apartment, Jake pointed to the Mountains on the eastern edge of the city and said, "We are 30 minutes away from four different ski resorts, and an hour away from Robert Redford's Sundance resort in Provo."

I had heard something about that on the news back home in Los Angeles. I replied.

Robert Redford had married a Mormon girl from Utah and bought a ton of land in the mountains in Utah. He built a ski resort and a film studio giving unknowns the chance to write, act and make quality films. He had even started an annual event called the "Sundance Film Festival." Giving Utah a little bit of Hollywood, according to Jake.

Just as he was making that statement, we passed a pasture of cows on the side of the freeway. I looked at him and said, "I hate to tell you this, but I think Utah reminds me more of Hemingway and Idaho then Hollywood. But it's a plus knowing I can take advantage of the University up the street from us and walk to school."

"I can see myself working and getting a degree here," I said to him.

"Good, all I want is to see you happy every day." Jake responded.

That night we had our first dinner together as a family in Utah. Afterwards we bathed Jack together. Jake told him a bedtime story and we tucked him in with a cute little Winnie the Pooh night light by the side of his bed.

We went into the living room, and I put in an Elton John cassette. Jake took my hand as "*Mona Lisa and Mad Hatters*" began to play and spoke. "May I have this dance?" As we slow danced and he held me tight, I felt safe and loved. My old life in Los Angeles seemed a thousand miles away as we danced. Later we went to bed, made love, and fell asleep in each other's arms.

The next morning, I got up before Jake and Jack and walked to the corner store for the Sunday paper, determined to find a job immediately. Over breakfast, Jake told me that he was going to take me and Jack to Dugway to meet his parents for the first time.

"I've already told them about the two of you, and our plans for the future. I have to warn you that they're not too thrilled about our having a baby out of wedlock," he said. "I told them that Jake was my natural born son since no one in my family has ever married outside of the church or had a baby outside of marriage." He said. "But then again they're not too happy about my decision to live my life outside the Mormon church either. Guess you could call me the black sheep of the family." He laughed.

He went on assuring me. Don't stress about it, I am going to live my life as I see fit with no regrets. I'm hoping that once they meet you and get to know what a wonderful person you are, that they will love you and Jack as much as I do."

"You lied to your family about Jack being your son?" I asked.

"Yeah, I did; if we're going to raise him together then we should start telling people that we have a kid." He informed me.

"Well, Nick's name is on the birth certificate as the father," I said.

"My parents are not going to ask for proof, don't worry I have everything covered," he assured me.

"I feel kind of nervous about meeting them now; what if they don't like me and Jack?" I asked him.

"That would be their problem. They live two hours away so it's not like we have to see them every day," he said.

I thought to myself, "At least he is not attached to his parent's hip like Nick; at least he has enough balls to stand up for what he believes in." I was certainly impressed by that and realized again what a stand-up guy Jake was.

"So, let me get this straight: nobody in your family has ever married outside the Mormon Church?"

"Nope," he replied while taking a sip of his coffee. "I'm the first one. My family has been Mormon for so long that I had a relative who knew Joseph Smith and fought in the Mormon Brigade. A few of my ancestors died building the temple downtown that I showed you yesterday. There is a Mormon Museum downtown that has furniture in it that one of my ancestors built for a guy named Brigham Young. My family has been with the church pretty much from its beginning."

"That's a trip. Well, at least you had the freedom to reject it; a real cult would prevent you from leaving," I said laughing.

CHAPTER 147

I continued to search for a job in the paper and circled a few to call the following morning. Jake then took me and Jack shopping for thick wool sweaters and socks. He insisted on buying us heavy down jackets along with mittens and neck scarfs. "You're going to be happy that I bought this stuff when the snow starts falling," he said.

He then took us to a shoe store and bought us both snow boots, saying he did not want my beautiful feet to get wet or cold. This was one of the sweetest things any guy had ever said to me. This man was an angel, and my best friend in the world. He even interviewed daycare centers before I arrived and had Jack all prepaid and set up in daycare three blocks away from the University. Jake had thought of everything and had carried it out with military precision.

One day Jake called his parents. I overheard him telling them that he was going to drive out the following Sunday to introduce them to me and Jack. After he hung up the phone, he sat down next to me and said. "They're expecting us at two o'clock next Sunday after church."

"Okay," I said smiling, "I'll be looking forward to it. I just hope they like me."

"Don't worry," he said. "I have a nice family."

I spent the following week looking for a job and going to the University to see what I had to do to enroll. Jake and I planned for me to go to college first, then he would start after I graduated. This way one of us would always be working full-time to keep the bills paid. After we both had degrees and jobs, we would buy a spacious lovely Victorian home, get a lot of pets and take wonderful vacations every year while growing old together. That was our life plan.

Three days later I was hired by a little family-owned Italian Restaurant called "That Italian Place." The best part was it was only five blocks away from our apartment.

The restaurant was owned and run by a couple named Harriet and James Smith, who were Mormon and had six children. It seemed that Harriet had them one right after the other because they were all so close in age. The family lived on a farm somewhere in Sandy, UT which was a suburb of Salt Lake City.

Even though they were devout Mormons, they lived like hippies without the drinking and pot smoking. Harriet and I were the only waitresses in the place, and we both doubled as dishwashers. Harriet and James were trying to save up enough money to do repairs on the building and could not afford to hire a dish washer. But they always had a good lunch and dinner crowd which meant the tips were good.

I was making anywhere from $100 to $150 dollars a day in tips. I had never waitressed before and I found it to be hard work because the restaurant was like a mad house, especially at lunch. There were a lot of office buildings on the street and the restaurant was always filled during lunch. In addition, there were also takeout orders to fill so the whole thing was a juggling act.

CHAPTER 148

The following Sunday, Jake, Jack and I got into the Mustang and started on our long drive to Jake's parent's house. We drove on the freeway until we got to a small town called Tooele. The town was so small that it looked like maybe 20,000 people tops lived there. But Jake said the population was closer to 43,000 people.

On the outskirts of town Jake took a short detour down a dirt road so he could take a photo of an old gas station he grew up seeing every time his family drove to Tooele or Salt Lake City to and from Dugway. He stopped the car in front of the place, which looked like it had been closed for years. Jake told me its hay day was back in the 1950s.

Being city minded, I immediately saw an antique goldmine. The old gas pumps and signs were from a lifestyle long ago when Roy Rogers and Mr. Ed were household names. It had an old store attached to it with an antique cash register caked with years of dust on it as well, and there were empty shelves that once held products.

On the side of the building was an old garage that once repaired cars and had a large deer set of antlers hanging in the front. Jake decided to remove the skull from the building to take home for a wall hanging. The old gas station stood alone out there, old and deserted for years. There was nothing in sight but the mountains and tumbleweeds.

The tumbleweeds were so large they reminded me of an old Twilight Zone episode where a bunch of tumbleweeds had come alive and had a few folks on the run for their lives. Jake took his photos, and I was relieved when we got back on the main road to Dugway, which was on the other side of a mountain we had not passed yet.

As we drove up the mountain on a narrow highway, I began to understand what environment Jake had grown up in. He had been surrounded by nature. Being in his environment was like watching "Wild Kingdom" on television. With a gleam of excitement in his eye, Jake pointed out deer and other animals that we saw along the narrow mountain pass.

Finally, the mountains opened into a vast deserted area that looked like an endless desert. The only thing out there was a small distant military installation called Dugway Proving Grounds. Jake looked at me and said, "I want to show you something before we go to my parent's house."

We drove into the desert for a good 20 minutes, when I suddenly started seeing horses. Jake looked at me and explained, "These are wild horses that the Spanish settlers left here over 200 years ago. I grew up with them and they are my friends. People call them ghost horses because they are so hard to find, but I know where their hangouts and watering holes are."

Jake turned off the ignition in the car and told me to get out. He took Jack out of his car seat and held him as we walked toward the horses. I swear those horses recognized him. They began to run toward us and gathered around us. It was the most awesome thing that I had ever seen so far in nature.

I immediately knew they were battle horses because they had so many cuts and scars from living outside in the elements and fighting. What amazed me was one of them even allowed Jake to pet him. It was a magical moment that I will never forget.

After spending a good 30 minutes with Jake taking photos of them, we left and began driving to Jake's parent's house. We drove up to the front gate of the military installation, where Jake and I had to show our ID and give the soldier on duty his parent's address and phone number to get on the base.

After they called his parents to verify the visit, we were given a pass to drive on post and sent on our way. I asked Jake why we had to get a pass to drive on the base.

He told me that Dugway was a highly restricted military base.

"You're joking," you really grew up here? I asked.

"Yep," he said.

"Well, it looks pretty boring out here to me. I observed.

I grew up here and I'm fine," he said.

"What on Earth did you do to pass the time?

"I'll show you," he said. "See that building over there?"

"Yeah," I replied.

"That is where my mom worked as a librarian, and I would go there to get books to read. Over there is the movie theater where I used to go to the movies with my friends, and right now we're passing by the bowling alley where I worked in high school."

He pointed across the street and showed me the PX and commissary. We turned a corner and he pointed to a plain brick building and pointed out Dugway High.

"That building was your high school? That is the smallest high school I have ever seen," I admitted.

"It's a small high school because it's only for the kids who live here on the base. There was 16 of us in my graduating class and maybe 200 kids in the entire combined Junior high, and High schools. I played basketball and dated a cheerleader and earned a college scholarship to play basketball for Snow College—all from that tiny high school. He informed me. I also had a dirt bike to ride around in the desert, it was a blast!" He exclaimed happily.

"Everyone was expecting me to go on a mission when I graduated, and that's when I joined the Army and went to Italy. I figured I could finish college when I got back." He said.

"I still remember the suit you wore at my messed-up wedding. Now I understand what you meant when you said your parents bought it for your mission."

He pulled up in front of a one story plain yellow house and parked the car. Before I could get out, a little girl with light brown hair came running off the front porch down the walkway yelling Jake's name, followed by three guys. I assumed they were Jake's three brothers. They were clean cut and innocent looking, like the Osmond Brothers or Bud from "Father Knows Best." They were teenagers, one of them had dreadful acne.

I wanted so much to reach out to him immediately and tell him about alcohol rubs and Clearasil, but I held back that impulse from fear of offending him. His siblings started introducing themselves to me as Jethro, Doug and Ray. "I'm Jane" the little girl said, already in the backseat taking Jack out of the car seat. His family members seemed warm and inviting and I started relaxing a little.

As we were walking up the walkway towards the front door, his parents came out of the front door and stood on the porch. His mother was a beautiful woman, and still had her figure after giving birth to seven children. She had bright blue eyes, and I wondered if they turned gray like Jake's. She had soft light brown hair which she wore pulled back from her face. His father had short cropped blonde hair, wore glasses, and was good looking. I saw why Jake looked the way he did, an equal combination of them both.

Jake introduced me to his parents as his fiancée and Jack as his son.

His mother extended her hand to me and said, "Hello, I'm Anita."

Then Jake's father shook my hand and said, "I'm Taggart."

"Dinner's almost ready, why don't you come into the kitchen and give me a hand," his mother said to me.

Jake's younger sister Jane said, "I'll take Jack into the living room and play with him."

I followed Anita into the kitchen, where she handed me some plates to set the table with.

Then she asked me if I belonged to a church.

I told her that I had grown up going to church like Jake had.

"Would you be willing to take Bible study with a few of our church missionaries?" she asked.

"I don't think Jake would be very happy with that; I don't think your son likes religion very much," I replied.

Then she said, "If you really love my son, you will give him up."

I was stunned because I really did not see that coming. She continued by saying that she and her husband did not believe in inter-racial marriages or marrying outside of the Mormon Church.

"I'm sure you're a nice girl, but we have to set an example for the other children in our household."

Wow! I thought is she serious?

She continued: "if you do this your life will be a hard one together."

CHAPTER 149

I t was then that Jake, walked into the kitchen holding Jack looking angry. "Let's go; we're leaving."

It occurred to me that his father had said something to him about not wanting him to marry me because of my race. I grabbed Jack's diaper bag and my purse, and before I knew it, we were driving back to Salt Lake City.

I had never seen Jake so mad and pissed off. I asked him what happened.

"My father took me outside alone and told me that he and my mom did not approve of us being together, because you're not white and you don't belong to the Mormon Church. Then he said that it was a sin against God to have a baby outside the institution of marriage." He told me.

"See why I hate religion? It divides people and they all think they are the one true religion. I think that God is bigger and smarter than that," Jake insisted. The race comment really threw me for a loop," he said. "My parents never raised me to be prejudiced, hell our neighbors are black. I grew up with them being friends with our black neighbors."

"Well, maybe they think it's okay to be friends with black people but not to marry them," I said.

"They never told me that while they were raising me," Jake replied.

"My father said that if I married you, I would be on my own; I would lose contact with the family." He said angrily.

"You can't be serious! it's 1983. I thought people were beyond this kind of thing now. I had no idea that your parents would feel this way."

It was sad to me, since growing up in Los Angeles, I saw mixed couples all the time.

"I apologize that you had to be subjected that," he said.

"So, what happens now?" I asked.

"We go on with our lives without them. We don't need anybody; we can make it on our own," he said. "When I turned 18 and left home, I quit depending on my parents to support me and make my decisions. My father taught me that real men stand up for what they believe in, and I believe in you and me." He assured me.

When we returned to our apartment, Jake acted as if nothing had happened. He just went on with his life. He helped me give Jack his bath and we made dinner together since we had missed it at his parent's house. Later We read Jack his bedtime story together and tucked him in as usual. Then went to bed and fell asleep holding one another.

Now I had even more respect for Jake. Nick would never have walked away from his family for me. I loved Jake even more for this: I was worth giving up his family for. Someone was actually going the extra mile for me.

The next morning, I wanted to show him how much I appreciated and loved him, so I made him breakfast and put the song *"You Make Me Feel Like a Natural Woman"* by Aretha Franklin on my cassette player and sang it to him. He always serenaded me by playing *"Moon River"* on his harmonica so why not serenade him too? I picked that song because of the lyrics, and I meant every word as I sang it to him. But most of all he deserved to have it sung to him.

His reaction was to say, "Listen to Maya" with a big smile on his face. He always said that to me whenever I said something worthwhile. I could tell that he was touched that I had recognized all his sacrifices for me and Jack.

CHAPTER 150

I enrolled in school at the University of Utah, and that, along with my job, made me feel comfortable in my new home. Things were going well for us: Jake was working at the plastics company, and we were both happy being the little family that we were. We talked about getting married, but when I found out that it would affect my scholarship money for school, we both decided that it would be cheaper for me to stay single.

In order to stay honest, I had to keep Jake as my boyfriend. It was okay with me because I was in no rush to get married again.

I loved Jake and wanted to spend the rest of my life with him, but I still needed time to catch my breath between marriages. I had learned the first time that a piece of paper was not going to keep you together anyway. Our plan was to save enough money after college to have a real wedding with my family attending, since we were estranged from his.

Winter came it got so cold in Salt Lake City that I thanked God for the heavy coats, socks and outerwear that Jack had purchased for us because it was colder than a bear's ass outside and I hated it. Especially when it snowed, and it snowed so much that at times it was up to my knees, even in the valley where we lived. I could only imagine how deep the snow was in the mountains. I would walk to school and work, all the while complaining to God that I was a California girl, a water baby. I was not used to cold-weather, and I longed for the sunshine and the ocean.

Jack on the other hand was walking, running around and talking. He was one and a half at this point and a handful. Jake was now dropping Jack off at daycare every day and picking him up after work. I would cook dinner for them before I left the house in the mornings if my schedule allowed that day, but usually Jake cooked with Jack as his assistant. I started calling him Mr. Mom because he even did laundry and house cleaning while holding down a full-time job himself. I loved the type of Father Jake was turning out to be, a man who played and watched cartoons with Jack every day.

They both loved the snow and would go to the park and spend hours sledding, building snowmen and having snowball fights. I would occasionally go and watch them from a park bench as they played without a care in the world, but most of the time I had to stay behind and study for a test or write a paper.

Every now and then Jack would have what I called, "a special moment" which was a temper tantrum. Jake and I did not believe in hitting kids, because of being spanked ourselves as children so instead we would put him in "timeout."

Jack would get angry because not only did we stop him from doing what he was not supposed to be doing, but he also had to sit in his room or a chair to give his actions some thought. The thing that really embarrassed me was his reaction when I refused to buy him more than one candy bar at the supermarket. When I told him that one piece of candy was enough, he would break into what I called the "back arch." His little body would go stiff as a board, then he would arch his back and scream as loud as he could in the store. People would look at me like I had done something to cause the outburst.

One day I found him in the bathroom putting my lipstick all over his face and the wall, he said he was playing GI Joe. When I took it away from him, he broke into the back arch and started screaming. I knew that he was only doing what he had seen Jake do at least a 100 hundred times. Jake would play Army with him and put military camouflage makeup on his face.

Jack came up with a solution and broke out his military camouflage make-up and made Jack's face up with it. He seemed to enjoy the camouflage make-up more than my lipstick. Then Jake gave him his own make-up so he would leave mine alone, on the condition that he not draw on the walls with it. He kept it on the shelf in Jack's closet with an Army cap he had given him from his basic training days. Because of Jake's support, I was able to put all my attention on school and work.

Jack called Jake dad, and had no idea that Jake was not his natural father. It felt good to know that my son had a father figure to depend on while I worked and studied.

CHAPTER 151

At this point, I was getting all my required courses out of the way at the AU as well as going to Salt Lake Community College three nights a week to get a paralegal license. I figured I could work as a paralegal while going to law school later. Every time I felt like I could not do it all, I remembered Nick telling me to go apply for welfare like every other black bitch in America, my energy and resolve would suddenly be renewed. I used his statement as fuel to keep going and overcome all obstacles.

On Jack's first real Halloween, Jake made him up as Colonel Kurtz from the movie "Apocalypse Now," and taught him how to repeat the words from the movie. "The horror, the horror."

He even took pictures of him in his costume so I could mail them to my father, who did not like the idea of us living so far away from him, but still liked Jake. When Christmas came Jake drove me home for the holidays to spend them with my family, to make my father happy.

Within two years of living in Salt Lake City I had managed to save up enough money to buy myself a used, dark blue four door Audi 5000s fully loaded with a sunroof. It was a beautiful car with a kicking stereo system. Little did I know at the time, but this would be the beginning of my love affair with cars. I felt a certain sense of pride when I remembered that Nick's father had bought the same car for his mom. Now I had one of my own and a man did not buy it for me. I thought to myself, God has a funny sense of humor.

One morning I was sitting at a table in the "Pie Pizzeria," the local college hang out across the street from the University. I would go there sometimes to study between classes and listen to great rock 'n' roll music. The pizza was made in an Italian brick oven and was the best in town. There was always a line outside the door to get in.

CHAPTER 152

O ne day, while sitting at the pie, drinking a cup of coffee and preparing for a math test I had that afternoon, I heard a familiar voice say, "Hi Maya." I looked up from my book and saw Jeri Granger and Greg Smith standing in front of my table. They both had served in the Army with Jake and Nick in Italy. It was a surprise to see them both and I stood up and hugged them.

"It's been a long time. What are you two doing here?"

Greg replied, "we both go to school here."

"And we're both from Salt Lake," Jeri said.

"I never knew you guys were from here, I'll share my table with you," I said.

We talked and I updated them on my life. They were both sorry to hear that my marriage to Nick did not work out but were shocked to hear that Jake and I were together raising Nick's son, since Jake and I had been strictly friends when we were hanging out in Italy.

Jeri said that he figured that Nick, and I would end up divorced. "I saw it coming because Nick was an asshole to you, and we all saw that."

Just then, an attractive brown-haired girl walked up to our table and said hi to Jeri. She had a cup of tea in her hand.

"This is Bobby Wright," Jeri said to me.

We said hello to one another. She looked like she played sports, her body was so fit and toned looking. She had a short pixie haircut and bright green eyes.

Jeri asked if she wanted to sit down then looked at me with a smile on his face and said, "Bobby here likes to hang around me and Greg so she can grill us about going Airborne."

I looked at her and said, "damn girl! Are you thinking of going Airborne?"

"I sure am. I have been thinking about joining the Army for a while. At first, I was going to join for the college fund money the Army offers, but after talking to a recruiter I have decided that jumping out of airplanes is right up my alley. I'm trying to get these two ex-paratroopers to help a girl out to get ready for basic training and jump school before I sign on the dotted line. Unfortunately, all Carey and Greg want to do is attempt to get laid, unsuccessfully, and go to frat parties," she lamented.

"I'm not surprised. They both had the same agenda when I knew them in Italy," I said.

I liked this Bobby girl right away. She was like the good-looking girl who blew you away because she could do anything a guy could do. I could tell that she was a strong, independent female which really impressed me. I knew immediately that I wanted to be her friend.

Greg interrupted my thoughts by saying, "go out with me Bobby and I'll work out with you in some very creative ways."

"Dream on pervert," she replied.

I looked at Bobby and said, "I think it's pretty cool that you want to go Airborne, but they don't allow women to do that, do they?"

"They do now. Uncle Sam has been allowing females to go to jump school," Jeri said to me.

"So why won't you help her train?" I asked Jeri and Greg.

"Yeah Jeri, why won't you help me train?" Bobby asked.

"Because I don't feel like running for miles with a heavy ass rucksack on my back again," he said. "I've been there and done my time. Now, I am ready to go to college, drink beer and get laid."

I looked at Greg and asked, "what's your excuse?"

"I just don't have the time with school and my work schedule," he replied.

I looked at Bobby and said, "my boyfriend was Airborne with these two jerks in Italy. I will ask him tonight if he can help you out and I promise he won't try to sleep with you."

"Could you?" she asked excitedly.

"Sure, give me your phone number." She quickly wrote her number down on a small piece of paper and gave it to me.

When I got home from working at the restaurant that night, both Jake and Jack were already in bed. But Jake was still awake waiting up for me. I told him about running into Jeri Granger and Greg Smith at the Pie earlier that day and told him about meeting Bobby.

I told him that Jeri and Greg wanted to see him, and that they had invited us down to some bar downtown called "Juniors" for a drink.

"I'm not interested in watching Jeri get shit faced at the bar," he said. "Haven't you noticed that neither one of us really drinks since you had Jack?".

"You're right." I agreed, "We have become non-drinkers. Let's invite them over for dinner one night, we can talk about old times."

"I'm ok with that, just as long as Jeri and Greg know I don't want them drunk and drinking in front of our kid. He's going to see enough of that in high school." He told me.

After putting my pajamas on I climbed into bed next to him and laid my head on his shoulders. I told him about Bobby wanting to go Airborne.

"She got me thinking," I said. "What if I joined the Army Reserve for the college fund money? That money could really help me avoid student loan debt, and I could get some good legal training working in a Judge Advocate General office one weekend a month. What do you think?"

"I think it's a good idea, but can you really deal with it? Basic training can be tough. The drill sergeants get nasty with the yelling in your face, and treating you like you are a piece of shit for eight weeks. It is all a mind game, along with a lot of physical exercise and weapons training. You get very little sleep, but I suppose you could make it through if you go in knowing what to expect. He said. "Be prepared for the physical workout of a lifetime. You need to be in good shape to make it through. Otherwise, the drill sergeant will mess with you and drop you for push-ups," he continued.

"Well, I've been thinking about it all day. I was thinking about getting the name of Bobby's recruiter and asking some questions."

"I told Bobby that I would ask you to give her some physical training tips for basic training and jump school," I said.

"Jump school? She's going Airborne?" Jake asked.

"She sure is, and I think it's pretty cool to see a female with a set of balls like that. I mean, it really takes guts to jump out of an airplane. What if your parachute doesn't open?"

"Well, I guess I could fill her in on a few things," he said.

I kissed him on the cheek and said, "thanks, I love you for this."

He kissed me back and said, "I love you too baby."

CHAPTER 153

The following morning, I called Bobby and told her that Jake was willing to help her out. We arranged to meet at the Pie Pizzeria for coffee after my drama class that morning. I was supposed to play a hooker that day in full costume. I grabbed a mini skirt and some high heels, stuffed them into my backpack with a halter top and I was good to go. My plan was to look as if I was hooked on hard drugs, by making fake needle marks on my arms with an eyeliner pencil.

That afternoon Bobby and I met up at the Pie as planned. Over coffee I told her that I was thinking of joining the Army Reserves for the college fund benefits. "You've inspired me; can you hook me up with your recruiter?"

"Sure, I can even go down there with you."

A week later Bobby and I were driving down State Street together in her convertible Jeep to see the recruiter. I liked her style; she had The Electric Light Orchestra blasting 10538 Overture loudly from the speakers as she drove.

She was a free spirit and wild at heart who, I learned, was also skilled at deer hunting and skiing. She even knew how to repair her own Jeep. I wanted to be self-sufficient like that. I looked at Bobby as an example from whom I could learn.

By the time we reached the recruiting station I decided that I now wanted a Jeep of my own. When we walked into the building, I could not help but notice recruiting posters all over the walls. My favorite one was a poster of an old white man in a striped Bicentennial suit and hat while pointing his finger at you saying, "Uncle Sam Wants You." Most of the ads were filled with promises of sending you to college without acquiring debt.

Bobby and I approached the receptionist and asked for Sergeant Sanchez. A few minutes later a 30-something Hispanic male approached us with his hand extended toward me for a hand-shake. He was dressed in uniform and seemed like a nice guy. He took me and Bobby to his desk and offered us seats sitting across from him.

Sergeant Sanchez looked at me and said, "so, Bobby here tells me that you're interested in joining the Army Reserves."

"I've been thinking about it," I said. "I'm a student at the University of Utah, and Salt Lake Community College three nights a week in the paralegal program. Right now, I am working part-time as a waitress, while raising my son.

There is a live-in boyfriend, but legally I am a single mother. My goal is to become a lawyer and I need money for school without getting into debt. When I met Bobby and she told me about her plans to go Airborne, it inspired me to check into joining the Reserves myself," I explained.

"Okay, I can certainly answer all your questions. For starters, we have a program through the University that will allow you to leave school for basic training and any other further training. You can pick up where you left off at when you return. First, you would have to pass a physical, then you would go to basic training for eight weeks. After basic training you would go to AIT school, which would be training for the job you enlisted for." He explained.

"I'm interested in working in the Judge Advocate General office," I said.

"I assume you would want your duty station to be here at Fort Douglas?" He asked me.

"Yes," I replied.

"Then It would depend on if they had a job opening at the JAG office here. I can check on that for you. How are you paying for school now?" Sergeant Sanchez said.

"I qualify for some educational programs for single mothers, and I have grants. And after failing Psych 101 twice the University tested me and found that I am completely thinking with one side of my brain." I disagreed with 80 percent of what the textbook said, so I had a hard time remembering the information when test time came.

I then told him. "That's when I was put into the Vocational Rehabilitation Program, so my books and classes at the University of Utah are paid for through that program. The test they gave me revealed that I would be good in the legal field. I'm already pulling straight A's in my paralegal classes without even trying." I told him.

Bobby and I spent almost two hours there getting information and asking questions. By the time we left, Bobby and I had decided to join on the buddy system. This would be for basic training only because there was no way I was going Airborne. She would go on to jump school, and I would go on to AIT school, to start from the bottom as a file clerk in an office at Fort Douglas. Then I could continue to go to different schools, and as time went on to move up the ladder. Plus, once I was ready for law school, my debt would be a lot lower because of the Army Educational Fund. Since I only had to miss a few quarters of college, it looked like a winning proposition to me.

I would have to sign up for a four-year commitment of working one weekend a month at Fort Douglas and two weeks every summer. Now, all I had to do was get up enough nerve to sign on the dotted line, but I was not ready to do that yet. Talking to Jake was critical first I had to see what he thought about the deal.

That night as we made dinner, I told Jake everything, then waited for a response to my plan. He thought for a moment and said, "It all sounds good, and that money would really help us stay out of debt once you get to the point of going to law school," he said agreeing.

Then Jake gave me this warning, "Just be ready to leave the outside world behind because the minute you get off that airplane and arrive at that reception station, you're in a different world. I can assure you that the first thing those drill sergeants are going to tell you is: "You no longer have the right to think for yourself, that they will be doing all your thinking for you." Then he stopped and smiled. "And I know you. You like to be in control at all the times."

"I can do it if you prepare me." I said.

"I'll give you some examples," he said showing me a raised index finger.

"One! If you do anything like moving without permission that could be viewed as thinking for yourself." He paused in thought.

Now holding up two fingers, Jake continued, "Two! You must ask permission to use the bathroom.

Then without a finger warning Jake said, "Three! The drill sergeant will make you drop and do push-ups or run in place, which is called getting hot."

Jake went on forgetting his count, "You will be yelled at pretty much every second of the day. You will get very little time to eat. You are only allowed 10 minutes to wolf down as much food as you can get into your mouth. Those drill sergeants go to school to learn how to break you down; to weed out the weak from the strong."

"Why do they do that? I don't see the point of breaking a person down to an empty shell or yelling in their face."

Jake countered me by saying. "But there is a point to it all, when you're in a combat situation the weak and undisciplined can get you killed. And even if you do not agree with what you are being told to do, you still must follow lawful orders."

Jake went on saying. "They train you to stay up for days at a time by giving you different types of guard duties to pull, where you're forced to stay up all night. Because if you are in a real combat situation when the bullets are flying, you cannot afford to sleep a lot. You must be able to stay awake and alert for days at a time. The drill sergeants will wake you up out of a dead sleep in the middle the night for surprise inspections and make you get into formation, while they tear the barracks apart, then come outside and punish everyone because the place is a mess. You will have to pull fire guard duty, which means staying up all night. And battalion CQ duty, which also means you are up all night."

"And" Jake said loudly, "You will be going on long road marches in combat boots with your M-16 machine gun at port arms, a heavy rucksack with all your equipment in it on your back. If you must use the bathroom and bullets are flying, you must piss in your pants or a bottle or dig a hole in the ground where you stand. You must be able to deal with killing someone and keep moving under fire. It takes real discipline and a strong mind to make it in a real combat situation. Otherwise, you can get the soldiers fighting with you as well as yourself killed. Therefore, a drill sergeant must push you to your limits. "The enemy is not your friend and doesn't give a damn if you are tired or have menstrual cramps, he will blow your brains out anyway."

"Just remember." Jake continued while tapping the side of his forehead. "It aint nothing but a mind-fuck, with some physical torture thrown in to keep folks from getting bored."

"Look," he said. "I hate to sound harsh, but it's the bare boned truth of it once the bullets start flying. So, there is a meaning to the madness and just remember that you are being trained to survive and do your job without getting yourself and others killed. If you go into basic training with an understanding of what the drill sergeants are trying to teach you and why, then it makes the mind games they play with you a lot easier to deal with," Jake said.

Jake continued. "I'll start taking you and your friend up to Red Butte Gardens hiking trail for some uphill running with some weight on your backs. You should start running in Liberty Park on your own every morning and evening and start drinking lots of water. You also should start doing push-ups and sit ups every day in the morning and at night before you go to bed,"

We both agreed that I would start my new routine in the morning.

CHAPTER 154

The following morning, I got up at 5 and started out by drinking two glasses of water, which was a great achievement for me because I had never been a big water drinker. I put on a pair of running sweats, shoes and a sweatshirt, and quickly looked in on a peacefully sleeping Jack. Then I got my little cassette player and put in my "Rocky" soundtrack cassette. The movie and the soundtrack had always inspired me.

I jogged the few blocks over to Liberty Park, stretched my legs out for a few minutes, then hit the track. I ran around the track once and walked around it once, then did it again doing a total of four miles that morning. Afterwards I speed walked home, where I did 100 sit ups and leg lifts.

When Jake got up, he showed me how to do push-ups properly. Unfortunately, I was only able to do 25 of those.

Jake told me that I lacked upper body strength, "You need to do push-ups constantly to build up your upper body strength," he instructed.

At breakfast I forced myself to drink even more water.

As promised, Jake took Bobby and me to Red Butte Gardens. He had Jack by his side who was excited about being at Red Butte because it was "animal world." to him. Jake had told him that the great outdoors was the world where all the animals from his bedtime stories lived. To me, it was a steep dirt hill that I had to run up with a backpack, that Jake put a few rocks in for weight.

Jake told us to run up the mountain, which was half a mile, while he and Jack walked up. Once he joined us at the top, he made us run back down, then made us do it again and again.

At one point he even made us carry tree branches at port arms as a substitute for the M-16 machine gun as we ran. Afterwards he dropped us down for push-ups. I noticed that Bobby had no problem doing 50 of them, but after 28 I was a dead woman lying face down in the dirt.

"At least you did three more than you did this morning. It's going to take a little time for you to build up your upper body muscles so don't give up," he encouraged me.

We all went to the village Inn restaurant and had a huge lunch afterwards.

A few days later I returned home from work one night to find that Jake purchased some used weights from a Mormon Church thrift store called The Deseret Industries.

"Look what I found for a $1.50," he said with a smile. He said that I was to use them twice a day to help me build my upper body strength.

I hugged him and said, "You're just a dream come true, you know that? I cannot think of a bad thing to say about you. I come home and you surprise me with hand-weights. You better watch out or you could end up with a spoiled brat on your hands."

He looked at me and said, "That's the goal: to spoil you. I will always support you in everything you do. You and Jack are my whole life now." He said hugging me. Then he showed me how to use the weights properly.

CHAPTER 155

That night we went to sleep only to be awakened by Jack climbing into bed with us. He was now almost three years old and sleeping in a twin bed instead of the crib that he had outgrown. He was now getting out of his bed and coming into my bedroom in the middle of the night to sleep. This would be the beginning of Jack wanting to sleep in our bed with us all the time. He would always say that there was a monster by his bed, or he had a bad dream that a monster took his cookie.

Sometimes we would wait for him to fall to sleep in our bed, then carry him to his own bedroom without waking him up. But we would usually take turns lying in his bed with him until he fell back to sleep. We could not understand where he was getting this monster thing from. The only thing he knew at this point was Sesame Street, characters such as Kermit the Frog and The Electric Company TV show, along with Mr. Rogers.

One Saturday morning before work, I was doing sit-ups in the living room while Jack was watching "Sesame Street. Suddenly, Jack was pointing at the TV saying "monster, monster." It was then that I realized that my son thought the Cookie Monster on Sesame Street was a real monster.

"Oh my God," I thought to myself. Jack has all those stuffed Sesame Street characters in his bedroom. A big Cookie Monster stuffed animal was sitting on the floor by his bed next to the nightstand. Now I understood why he was afraid. I did my best to explain that the Cookie Monster lived in TV land on Sesame Street.

"He's really your friend and he's friends with all the kids on Sesame Street. He would never hurt you," I told him. I went into his bedroom and got his stuffed Cookie Monster toy, then went back to the living room and put the animal in front of my face.

I started talking to him pretending to be the Cookie Monster. "Look at me: I'm the cookie monster, and I love cookies and little kids. Will you be my friend too?" I asked him. Jack started laughing and trying to pull the stuffed animal away from my face. The problem was solved.

CHAPTER 156

Over the next few months, I did nothing but study, work at the restaurant and work out. Bobby and I continued to train for basic training together and we were fast becoming close friends. I was getting really toned and now able to do 100 push-ups without stopping. I also had a muscle in my upper arm and was proud of myself.

We were now running Red Butte Garden without Jake. We were at a six-mile point for up-hill running with weight on our backs, and 12 miles for track running. I loved the running the best because I would get what Jake called a "runner's high."

I would run with my little cassette player blasting the "Rocky" soundtrack and I was in another world. My body would start to feel so light that I often felt like I was floating on air instead of running. I was starting to gain some nice muscle tone in my legs as well. I was on my way to having my body be in the best shape it had ever been in.

CHAPTER 157

When the day finally came for Bobby and me to sign the final papers and fly out to Fort Jackson, SC we were both confident about our ability to make it through basic training. We were both prepared for what was to come.

At 5:30 a.m. Jake and Jack drove me to Fort Douglas so I could report in at six. When we pulled up in front of the building, Bobby was already there with her parents kissing and hugging them goodbye. Family members were not allowed in the building; Uncle Sam wanted you to say your goodbyes outside the door.

My heart was sad because I was going to be away from Jake and Jack for almost four months, total with AIT school included. I kept telling myself: think about the free money for school and buying a house for your family to live in.

Jake and I said our goodbyes and kissed one another. I picked up my little boy, gave him a huge hug and kiss, and told him that I loved him. "I'll be back as soon as I can, and I will call you while I'm gone." I had tears rolling down my cheeks as I walked into the building backwards so I would not lose sight of them both as they got into the car to drive home.

Bobby and I stood there together watching our families drive away.

"Ready?" Bobby asked.

"Ready as I'm ever going to be," I replied.

The moment we walked into that building our freedom was gone. There was a sergeant posted by the front door with a list of names on a checklist. He asked me my name, I gave it to him and then he pointed to an adjoining room and told me to go have a seat.

I walked into the other room as I was told and took a seat in one of the folding metal chairs. A moment later Bobby joined me and took the seat next to me. Bobby looked at me and said in a low voice, "Are you nervous?"

"No, are you?" I replied.

"No," she said.

"Then I guess we're on our way to basic training," I said.

We were part of a small group of only 10 other people being shipped out that day. After we had finished in processing and taking the "Oath," we were given our airline tickets and taken outside to a waiting bus that drove us to the airport in Salt Lake City.

Once we arrived in South Carolina, there was an Army sergeant waiting for us to step off that plane. We were escorted to yet another waiting bus outside the airport.

Thanks to Jake's advice, Bobby and I knew to sleep on the airplane and the bus ride. The other 10 people we shipped out with stayed up running their mouths the whole trip there. Jake had warned us that sleep would be precious and to sleep whenever we had the opportunity instead of socializing.

We arrived at the reception station in late afternoon. A few of the guys in our group were laughing, wondering why no one had yelled in their faces yet.

I informed them that these soldiers were not drill sergeants.

"They are reception station military personnel used for in-processing. They are the calm before the storm; before you're transported to hell on Earth," I told them smiling.

"Once you see that 'Smokey the Bear' hat, you know you're in the presence of a drill sergeant," I explained.

We were instructed to leave our carry-on bags at the door. Then we were told to take a seat on some long wooden benches while we were processed into the military. We were told sternly by a sergeant who stood before us that, at this point, we were not allowed to speak unless spoken to.

"You're not to make any noise at all," he announced. "If you have any trouble staying up, then you can stand against that wall over there and quietly run in-place. If you need to use the latrine just raise your hand and one of us will excuse you to do that." He instructed.

We all sat there in silence for hours; the only thing we could hear was the clock ticking on the wall. At one point we were given pre-made sandwiches to eat and a choice of water or milk.

By now, more people who were beginning basic training were showing up from the airport. Before I knew it, there were at least 200 men and women from all over the country being processed into Fort Jackson, SC with Bobby and me.

Every few hours someone would call your name and you would follow them into another room for more in-processing. Then you would go back to your spot on the bench.

Later that evening we were told to line up and we all walked over to the mess hall for dinner which consisted of some sort of mystery meat with mashed potatoes, gravy and mixed vegetables. We were allowed to use the restroom and then we were marched back to the benches and boredom. As it got late into the night, some of the people in the room started nodding off while sitting up.

Whenever that happened a sergeant would walk over to the person with a long dark stick and bang it against the hard floor in front of the person to wake them up. Then they would be sent to run in-place next to the wall, which the sergeant called "getting hot."

Bobby and I glanced at one another both thinking, these people should have slept when they had the chance on the bus and the plane ride. They had spent all their time running their mouths and now they were paying the price.

By noon the next day, Uncle Sam was finished issuing us our uniforms, boots and an A-bag to hold all our Army issued uniforms. After lunch in the mess hall, we were all lined up outside the building in our new uniforms. We still had not been allowed to sleep.

We were taught how to speak to a drill sergeant, stand at "attention," "parade rest," and "at ease," all the basic commands and their meaning. We were taught how to march and how to run in-place. We were also told what would be expected from us during our stay at Fort Jackson.

A few hours later our actual drill sergeants showed up in their distinctive hats with clipboards in hand. Then the in-processing sergeants walked back into the reception station building and disappeared.

I was surprised and happy to see that two of the drill sergeants were not only female, but black. They both looked like they had invented the words "mean as hell." No doubt Martin Luther King Jr. was probably smiling down on them from heaven, while watching his dream become a reality. The rest of them were white males who looked like they had a chip on their shoulder. They all looked like they woke up angry every day.

We were told to stand at attention and that is when the mind game that Jake had warned Bobby and me about begin.

CHAPTER 158

The drill sergeants began sizing us up, yelling and cussing at us like vicious bulldogs looking for someone to devour. We were ordered to keep our eyes fixed straight ahead of us and not even blink. The verbal abuse ramped up, and they really started putting the fear of God into us.

We were now in another world. I silently prayed to God not to stick me with a female drill sergeant. I wanted to cross my fingers but was too afraid that one of the drill sergeants would notice and drop me for push-ups.

We were then told to start picking up the A-bags we had been issued with our uniforms, then load them into the waiting cattle cars that were parked in front of the reception station. We were told to do it as fast as we could and not stop until every single A-bag was loaded onto the cattle cars. As we were doing this, I heard one of the female drill sergeants yell at some girls, "All right you bitches move faster. You're not moving fast enough," She continued yelling "faster, faster."

Then they started picking on people at random, one girl started crying after being told how ugly she was. The drill sergeant showed her no mercy and got up in her face and said, "Do you want me to give you a real reason to cry little girl? Do you want your mommy little girl? Well, your fucking mother is not here. I am your fucking mother now! Now shut the fuck up before I make you my special project!"

After all the A-bags were loaded onto the cattle cars, we were told to get into formation and stand at attention again. One of the male drill sergeants stood in front of us and told us to start forming single file lines in front of the cattle cars, and to remain silent while doing so. Then we were given permission to board them. I assumed we were now being taken to our barracks and basic training station somewhere on Fort Jackson.

Bobby and I sat next to each other unshaken by the drill sergeants. Thanks to Jake preparing us for them, nothing they did or said shocked us.

This is it I thought; now the real horror begins. You are in the Army now!

While we were driving it was so quiet that all you could hear was the engine from the cattle car. We drove for about 20 minutes before stopping. The doors opened and the drill sergeants started yelling orders for us to unload the A-bags from the cattle cars.

After the bags were unloaded, we were ordered into a formation where we stood at ease for four hours while being assigned a drill sergeant and our barracks. There were two drill sergeants for each group which the Army called a platoon. I was relieved when Bobby and I were assigned to two male drill sergeants instead of the two females. I noticed the looks of fear on the faces of the privates who were assigned to the female drill sergeants.

Both women looked like permanent PMS in a uniform. I wondered if the two of them had graduated from drill sergeant school at the top of their class, with extra credit for intimidation.

We were then ordered to get "hot" and grab an A-bag while running to our assigned barracks, which were housed in a large building.

Once we were in our barracks, we were told to stand at attention facing our wall lockers with our A-bags placed on the floor by our feet. One girl, for some unknown reason, placed her A-bag in front of her. One of the male drill sergeants immediately went in for the kill yelling at her and asking her. "Are you stuck on stupid, deaf, dumb or all three?

The girl looked petrified. She was ordered to place her A-bag in the correct place by her side, then the drill sergeant put her down for 50 push-ups while yelling out a count. While she was doing the push-ups, he verbally attacked her intelligence. He did everything to make this girl feel lower than dust.

Finally, unable to do any more push-ups at count 33, she collapsed onto the cold hard floor face down crying for dear life. It kind of shocked me that a drill sergeant could get away with treating anyone that way, but I quickly remembered what Jake told me.

"The enemy doesn't care about your crying, or your feelings being hurt. He will do everything in his power to take you out."

So, I understood what the drill sergeants were trying to do. It had to be done to weed out the weak from the strong.

We were then ordered to unpack our uniforms and hang them up in the wall lockers. Then finally, we went to the mess hall to eat evening chow. It was now almost 7 p.m.

Then we were marched over to the mess hall and lined up outside the front door. We were then told to "get hot" or run in-place the whole time we were waiting our turn to eat in the mess hall. The mess hall could only hold so many people at a time and there were hundreds of us waiting in line.

I looked over at Bobby who was running in-place next to me and whispered to her without getting caught, "You all right?"

"Yeah," she said. "You all, right?"

"Yeah," I whispered back. Then we both continued to look straight ahead as we ran in-place.

Once we were in the mess hall, we were told that we had just 10 minutes to get our food and eat it. We were not allowed to talk as we ate our food. The drill sergeant said that the only reason for our mouths to be open was to put food in it.

After eating a meal of mashed potatoes, peas and a mystery-meat meatloaf, I figured I would probably lose weight during my stay at Fort Jackson because the food was so bad. We finished eating and were instructed to go back to our barracks to shower and sleep for the night. I silently thanked God because I was exhausted.

After the drill sergeant left our room, we were all finally able to speak freely among ourselves. I asked Bobby which bunk she wanted, "the bottom," she replied.

"Cool, because I want the top," I said.

"So, what do you think about basic training so far?" Bobby asked me.

"Well, it's going pretty much the way Jake said it would go. Thank God, we do not have it as hard as Jake did. Remember him telling us that his basic training was different because he had joined the infantry?" I observed.

"Yeah, he said they really dogged them out," she replied.

"Being here really isn't all that bad except I already miss Jake and Jack. I bet Jack is wondering when I'm coming home." I said.

"Just try not to think about home; focus on basic training," Bobby said.

"Yeah, you're right," I agreed.

Bobby and I talked for a few minutes, but we were focused on doing our best to make it. So, instead of socializing like the rest of the girls in our platoon, we both went into the bathroom and took our showers.

There was a row of open shower stalls against both sides of the wall with drains built into the floor. It looked like a gym locker room bathroom. I wore a pair of flip-flops into the shower so I would not pick up a bad case of athlete's foot. Just another tip from Jake. After our showers, Bobby and I were both smart enough to get into our bunks and sleep since the next day was going to be filled with nothing but physical activity and mind games.

When the other girls finished taking their showers a lot of them wasted a good 15 minutes talking about why they joined the military, or where they were from. By the time the drill sergeants came back into the room and yelled "lights out ladies," Bobby and I were already in our bunks for the night. I fell asleep quickly with no problem, but at 3:30 a.m. was awakened by the sound of the drill sergeants' batons hitting the metal on the bunk beds we were sleeping in, while yelling.

"Wake the fuck up little ladies, you have exactly 10 minutes to be outside in formation." He added, "you have permission to use the bathroom. Brush your teeth and wash your ugly faces. Wear your PT uniforms." He ordered.

I watched as one drill sergeant pulled the bed sheet right out from under a few girls who were too slow getting out of bed, forcing them to fall to the hard cold floor. Damn, I thought to myself, this is what happens when you do not get out of bed fast enough.

The room was in a state of total chaos, as girls ran around in their underwear trying to use the toilet and get dressed fast enough to get into formation on time. It reminded me of the way cockroaches scatter when you turn on a light. The only thing that caught me off guard about the situation was the fact that the male drill sergeants could see us in our underwear.

Jake never mentioned that part to me. I was glad that Bobby and I were prepared. We both slept in our Army issued T-shirts and PT shorts like Jake told us to do. We both used the toilet, put on our running shoes and were out the door.

That first morning Bobby and I timed it and made formation within six minutes. There were quite a few girls who were late to PT formation. They were put down for push-ups and I could feel some real fear coming off some of those girls as the drill sergeants yelled and cussed at them.

One of the girls who had been put down for push-ups could not continue doing them and collapsed crying with her face in the dirt. A drill sergeant yelled at her to get up, telling her that crying would not get her anywhere. As he yelled at her, I noticed the looks on some of the other girls faces. They were starting to realize that they were not only cut off from the outside world, but they were now in hell.

Of course, hell does not care if you cry or if your feelings are hurt. You could see that realization wash over their faces, and it was hitting some of them hard. Movies, photographs and books about the military could never compare to the actual experience itself.

Your recruiter can explain what basic training entails, but doing it is totally different.

Now, all the drill sergeants were standing in front of their platoons wearing their big hats, all of them looking meaner than a junk yard dog. I must admit, it was quite intimidating.

They yelled out, "Attention." As the company commander joined us.

Immediately everyone stood at attention. Eyes fixed straight ahead, trying not to move at all except to breathe. We were then marched out to a big grass filled area for our morning PT session as a drill sergeant yelled out, "left, left, left, right, left."

We did jumping-jacks, sit-ups and a bunch of other exercises; then marched over to a nearby track where we were told to run, as the drill sergeants monitored timers. I do not know how many miles we ran that morning, but Bobby and I had no problem keeping up.

Bobby and I ran past girls breaking down with leg and side cramps, a few of them were vomiting and crying. I felt sorry for them because it was clear to me that they were not in good shape, so this was a huge struggle for them. To make things worse, the drill sergeants were yelling and screaming insults at them lying there in the dirt trying to intimidate them into getting up.

I thought it was pretty messed up, but again I understood why they treated you this way. In a combat situation, you had to be able to run for your life and the lives of the people fighting next to you. You could not break down and say, "I have a cramp in my side." I remembered what Jake said: "when the bullets are flying you better keep running and shooting and forget about that cramp."

I was grateful that Jake made Bobby and I do the uphill runs at Red Butte Gardens.

CHAPTER 159

After we finished PT, we marched back to the barracks to shower and change into our uniforms. We were told we had 30 minutes to be back in formation standing at ease.

By now, it was 5:30 a.m. Bobby and I rushed upstairs to shower and get dressed as fast as we could. Once again, we were in formation early. I even brushed my teeth in the shower to save time.

From that day on, every waking minute day and night was spent training. We were put through classes where we learned how to take an M-16 apart and put it back together again. The M-16 was my favorite weapon out of everything they trained us on. I loved firing it, carrying it at port arms, taking it apart and putting it back together again.

I was so proud that my platoon of women out shot the guys during Basic Rifle Marksmanship, or "BRM" for short. We also learned how to throw hand grenades.

My other enjoyment was road marches because we got to sing songs like "In the Early Morning Rain with a Weapon in My Hand." I felt a camaraderie with the other soldiers as we all marched and sang together. I got a mental high off that togetherness and one force feeling.

The "bayonet" training was fun but staying up all night pulling Battalion CQ, and fire guard duty was not. We learned how to march at port arms, how to survive the gas chamber and many other things.

Not only did I feel empowered physically, but also mentally as though I could accomplish anything. I also knew now that I had it in me to defend my country and everyone who lived in it by killing the enemy then sleeping like a baby that night.

I was proud of myself, and my self-esteem was soaring through the roof. I thought about Nick and how he had complained about hating military training, and how physically uncomfortable it had been for him. Now, here I was going through basic training without a complaint, hell I liked it.

"You should see me now Nick, "I thought to myself.

I felt that every young person should go through this experience. The only time I was dropped for push-ups was when I failed the Compass Course Training. I had no natural skills for reading a compass. I ended up lost in the woods, twice.

But when it came time to graduate and go on to AIT school, I was presented with a major problem. I was looking at my pay stub one afternoon and noticed that my BAQ, which is money for your dependents, was missing. My drill sergeant gave me permission to go to the finance office to get the problem resolved.

That is when I found out that the Army had no idea that I had a child. My recruiter had enlisted me as a single female with no children. I was told that I was illegally enlisted in the Army; that I never should have been able to join.

The woman officially told me that the Army did not allow single mothers to enlist, and if I wanted to remain in the Army, I had to get married. I could hardly believe what I was hearing.

She asked whether my recruiter knew that I had a child. I told her yes, "And I even showed him a photo of my son that I carry in my wallet."

"Unfortunately, it looks as though your recruiter probably did this to meet an enlistment quota. He's about to be in a lot of trouble for this." The woman informed me.

When I returned to my barracks, someone had already called and informed my drill sergeants of my situation. Within a week I was processed out of the Army because of fraudulent enlistment.

CHAPTER 160

I was so angry and disappointed that this had happened to me, and I had gone through all this training for nothing. Now my educational fund, as well as my dreams of working for JAG, were flushed down the drain, all because of a dishonest Army recruiter. I literally wanted to kick that guy's ass.

The day my plane landed in Salt Lake City; I went looking for my recruiter. When I got to the recruitment office on State Street, I learned he was no longer there. My guess was he got into big trouble for this and ended up losing his job. Well good I thought, even if I was not able to cuss the creep out in person he is paying for his crime.

It was time to stop crying over spilled milk and find another job. Three days later that happened when I was hired as a hostess at a private membership-only restaurant and bar called Bourbon Street.

My job was to sit at a desk at the front entrance and check memberships as people came in. I had to dress nicely because most of the members were affluent people with high incomes, athletes, and local news anchors. I was learning that Salt Lake City had a small community of non-Mormon residents who liked to drink.

There were no regular liquor stores on every corner here, like in LA, and you could not go to a restaurant and have a glass of wine with dinner. Liquor was controlled by the State because the Mormon church wanted a liquor and drug free state. Bourbon Street was one of the few establishments at the time in Salt Lake City that served alcohol on the premises.

Things began falling back into place for me as I returned to school and began making enough money to meet my needs. I once again spent all my time studying, working and caring for Jack who was getting bigger and running around with tons of energy.

Jake suggested that we start looking for a house to rent with a back yard. He said that kids needed space to run and play in and he thought it was time to get Jack his first dog. I agreed and within a month Jake found the perfect little house in the Capital Hill area of Salt Lake City with a breath-taking view of the city from the front porch. The house had two bedrooms and one bathroom, a fireplace and a family room. The kitchen was big, and there was a large living room.

There were skylights in every room and big windows that let a lot of light in, but what I liked most about the house was the wooden sundeck and big yard out back. The house was built in the early 1950s and had been recently updated. I liked the neighborhood because it reminded me of the Benedict Canyon area in Los Angeles.

The one thing that worried me was winter season and driving in the snow because the neighborhood was on a steep hill over-looking the city. I would be driving downhill on icy roads and that scared the hell out of me.

Despite that concern, the rent was affordable, and the house was big and beautiful, so we took the place and moved in. Within a week Jake and Jack found a three-year-old yellow Labrador Retriever at the dog pound named "Sadie." She was sweet, laid back in temperament and was the perfect companion for Jack.

CHAPTER 161

A month after we moved in, my sister Stephanie called and said she was sick of Los Angeles and needed a change. She had broken up with her live-in girlfriend, was between jobs and her car had a dead engine. She asked if she could move in with us and give Salt Lake City a try.

I talked to Jake about it, and he thought it would be a good idea to have one of my family members around to keep me company. Two weeks later my sister flew out to live with us.

Stephanie was now a beautiful, 115-pound gay woman. She had sandy blonde hair with natural streaks running through it in a cute pixie cut that suited her well. She also had a very masculine demeanor.

It was cool having my sister around and we had a close easy-going relationship. We spent time listening to rock 'n' roll while getting tans on my deck and having sister-to-sister talks. It was like old times. It was a good thing for Jack to have his aunt around.

Stephanie nicknamed him "Baby Pringles" as in the Potato Chip, because Stephanie said Jack was cute enough to eat. She loved him intensely and spoiled him to death. I would put Jack to bed and awake in the morning to find him and Sadie sleeping with Stephanie. The dog would be on the floor and Jack would be wrapped up in Stephanie's arms. It was just such a happy time to see my son around a relative every day.

Until then it had just been us and no other family members. I had always called my relatives on the phone and kept in touch, but to live in the same state with one was a different thing. Now home did not seem so far away because of Stephanie.

Stephanie quickly found a job as a desk clerk at the Ramada Inn Hotel in downtown Salt Lake City. She started making a few friends and found the only gay nightclub in town over on the westside where she would go dance on weekends. Stephanie loved to dance and go to nightclubs. We shared that in common, except I could no longer go out like that because

I was someone's mother. Being a mom and going to school and being with Jake was my priority.

I loaned Stephanie my Audi whenever I could since Jake, and I had two cars.

One Sunday morning I took a break from studying so Stephanie and I could sunbathe on the deck in our bikinis and listen to loud Elton John music blasting from my stereo inside the house. Jack was playing catch-the-stick with Sadie on the lawn.

After a while in the sun, Stephanie and I both felt a shadow block out the light. I looked up I saw a tall, skinny white guy with wavy blonde hair in a pair of cut-off shorts and no shirt towering over us. For a moment I thought it was Tim Roth, an actor that I liked, because he looked so much like him.

"Hi, I'm Carson Baker, your neighbor," he said.

I sat up as he pointed to the house on the hill right above mine.

"Hi, my name is Maya, and this is my sister Stephanie and that's my son Jack over there with our dog Sadie." I replied.

"Wow," he said "You don't look like you gave birth to anything. In fact, you're both gorgeous."

"Well thanks. My boyfriend tells me that every day," I informed him.

Then Stephanie sat up and said, "And I'm a lesbian, but thanks for the compliment."

Not expecting that answer he looked a little shocked for a minute and replied, "Well, we can still be friends, I don't care if you're gay."

"Cool," Stephanie said. Then she laid back down on the deck chair to finish tanning her face.

"It's always nice to meet new people; Maybe if you're around later I can introduce you to my boyfriend Jake. I'm from Los Angeles and Jake is from Utah," I said.

"Really, what part of Utah?" he asked.

"He's from Dugway." I told him.

"That's way out there in no man's land. I'm from the Holiday area here in the valley," he said.

"Are you a Mormon?" I asked.

"I was raised one, but I don't belong to the church. We call people like me Jack Mormons," he said.

"Then I guess my boyfriend is a Jack Mormon too, so you'll probably get along with one another. I am putting some burgers on the grill later if you want to join us. Sunday is my only day off, so I try to make the most of it," I said.

"What do you do for a living," he asked.

"I'm the door girl at a private club called Bourbon Street downtown, and I go to the University of Utah and Salt Lake community college, so I have a pretty busy schedule," I said.

"I go to the University of Utah as well. Maybe we can carpool sometime," he said.

"What's your major," I asked.

"Electronic engineering," Carson answered.

"Wow, you must be a real brainiac," I said.

"What's your major," he asked.

"I'm going to become a lawyer and change the world." I said, and laughed, "Correction: I'm going to try and change the world."

"Sounds like a noble ambition." He said.

"Well, if you're up for a burger or if you want to put your own meat on the grill, you're welcome to come by later and meet Jake," I said.

"Cool, I'll catch you guys later then," he said.

After he walked away, I looked at my sister and said, "He seems like a nice enough guy."

"As far as guys go, he seems pretty cool. He looks like that actor guy Tim Roth." Stephanie observed.

"I was thinking the same thing, and I probably don't have to worry about him complaining about my loud rock music because he probably listens to it himself." I said.

When I looked over to check on Jack, he was butt naked; that boy had stripped off all his clothes and was lying on the lawn naked while the dog licked his face.

"Oh my God," I said as I got up to get him dressed again.

"You should just let him run around like that" Stephanie said, "He's not hurting anybody."

"We are living in Utah, not a California beach. You can't just let your kids play outside naked without somebody thinking something weird is going on," I told her. "Besides, I don't want him growing up thinking it's acceptable to run around naked in public."

Stephanie yelled to Jack, "I tried to win you some freedom baby Pringles, but your mother won't allow freedom to reign. I never thought while we were growing up that you would turn out to be an old-fashioned prude," she chided me.

"I'm not an old-fashioned prude; I just don't want one of my Mormon neighbors calling the child protective services on me because my son is running around naked in the backyard."

I ran over to Jack and collected his clothes off the lawn. As I approached him telling him not to do this again. I put his clothes back on him and said it is time for lunch.

"Follow me into the house and I will make you a peanut butter and jelly sandwich." I told him.

As we walked past my sister and into the house, Stephanie yelled out "Make me one too."

While we were eating, Stephanie asked Jack to tell her about his nursery school.

Jack replied, "I went to school and the girl pushed me. I told her to stop, but she pushed me again so I picked up the pencil can and hit her in the head with it and Miss Green made me go to time out."

"Don't forget to mention that the school told me that they were going to kick you out if you were violent again," I said.

"Well, I don't blame him. I would have hit the girl upside the head too," Stephanie said.

"But I don't want him to think it's okay to fight with people unless it's a life-or-death situation," I said.

"Next time just run and tell the teacher," I told Jack as he ate his sandwich. "Don't listen to your Aunt Stephanie."

That evening our new neighbor Carson came over with a six-pack of German beer and a steak to put on the grill. I introduced him to Jake, and they talked and drank beer for a while.

Carson explained to us that the house he was living in was owned by his father. In exchange for free rent, he had agreed to remodel the place so his father could sell it. Turned out his father owned a lot of other homes and apartment buildings in the area.

I got the impression that his father was rich in real estate and that Carson could be a trust fund kid. Any way you looked at it, Carson had no job, and his father was paying for his education.

Later that night in bed Jake and I were talking about Carson. We both thought he was lucky as hell to get a free ride like that. This guy had no worries about money, and no problem paying for his living expenses, plus he had a nice house to live in rent free.

"Some people are just born lucky," Jake said.

The following morning when Jake and I awoke to start our day, Jack was missing from his bed, and he was not with Stephanie. The three of us looked for him, calling his name and going from room to room. Then Jake noticed that the glass sliding door was open where the deck was in the back.

We went out into the backyard and saw no sign of Jack or the dog. Then I heard the dog bark, we all looked up towards Carson's house. There was Jack with Sadie sitting butt naked in the dirt right in the middle of Carson's Garden. He had a tomato in his hand eating it.

The three of us just stood there for a moment looking dazed and dumbfounded.

Jake walked up the small hill that separated the two homes and picked up Jack and his discarded pajamas.

When we got back into the house, I looked at Jack and asked, "What's going on Jack? I get up and you have let yourself out of the house to eat tomatoes from the neighbor's garden. What's up with that? Why do you feel the need to be naked in the grass and dirt?" I asked him.

Jack just stood there for a moment looking at me with tomato smeared all over his mouth and said, "I like tomatoes."

"I understand that you like tomatoes, but what I'm not understanding is why you're going outside and taking your clothes off?" I asked.

Jack said, "I don't like wearing clothes."

Stephanie said, "Maybe he's a reincarnated mystic or something. Obviously, he likes to get grounded by being naked in the dirt. Do you want Aunt Stephanie to buy you a crystal to lay in the dirt with baby Pringles?" She asked him.

"You're not buying my son a crystal; he might try to swallow it," I protested.

I looked at Jack and told him that when I got home that evening, we were going to have a little talk about why he could not run around naked.

"If we lived on a farm, it would be different," I said. "But people passing by in cars who see you out there like that will get the wrong impression. Or bad people could see you, and maybe they would try to hurt you.

I elaborated. "These people are called strangers. So, when I come home tonight, Dad and I will explain things to you, but for now I want you to promise me that you will keep your clothes on, okay?"

"Okay," he said.

"Now, come in here and take a quick bath and get ready for the day," I said to him. I could hear my sister and Jake snickering together as I walked into the bathroom with Jack and shut the door.

That night when Jake and I put Jack to bed for the night we talked to him about crazy people who like to hurt little kids. Also, why it was so unsafe to play outside naked as well as if anyone ever touched him in his private parts to run screaming, and to tell an adult as quickly as possible.

"If you need to be close to the Earth from now on just tell somebody, and we can put you in a pair of shorts with no shoes and no shirt, but your butt has to be covered when you're outside." Jake told him.

Jake and I kissed him on the forehead as he snuggled up with Sadie who slept with him every night. I looked at him for a moment with his Army glow stick in his hand that Jake had brought from the Army Surplus Store and given to him as a night light.

I thought about a song I used to hear on the radio when I was a kid, "oh yeah, they call me the streak because I like to show off my physique" the guy would sing. I hoped this was the end of my son's streaking days.

After I took a shower and got into bed, I read a chapter in my paralegal textbook for my class the following day.

A few days later Carson came by one night and knocked on my sliding glass door just after I had returned home after work at Bourbon Street. I had just taken my shoes off and sat down to rub my feet and eat a plate of Jake's fabulous gourmet tacos when Carson arrived.

I waved for him to come in and asked if he wanted a taco.

"Sure, if you have enough," he said.

I yelled to Jake in the kitchen, "Carson wants a taco."

Jake yelled back, "Carson can come in here and fix it himself. I have no idea what he wants on it."

Carson and I walked into the kitchen to get our tacos. He asked me if I had any classes at the University in the morning. "Yeah, bright and early at 9," I replied.

"Perfect, my economics class is at 9:20. Can I ride in with you in the morning? I have to replace the timing belt on my Honda this weekend, and the bus sucks." Carson explained.

"Sure, anytime you need a ride just holler."

"Cool" he replied, fixing himself a plate of food.

Carson and Jake started talking about fishing. I did not care too much for fishing since I did not like the fact that I had to touch a worm, kill it and then touch smelly fish after watching it die slowly on a hook. But it sure tasted great after it was cleaned and cooked.

From the sound of things, Carson enjoyed fishing and hiking just like Jake, and they were bonding over that. I listened to Jake telling Carson how he was preparing Jack to learn how to fish as well by buying him his own fishing pole and a little fishing kit with hooks and stuff in it.

Carson asked me where Stephanie was. I told him that she borrowed my car to go to the only gay nightclub in town.

"Oh yeah, she found that place on the Westside?" He asked.

"Yeah, I'm shocked they even have a gay nightclub here. I mean, the Mormon church has so much control over what happens here it's just kind of strange that they allowed the gay community to have their own club," I said. "Anyway, she met a girl at the club she's now dating so they go there a lot together. Sometimes Stephanie sleeps at her apartment then comes home at six in the morning to return my car before I have to go to work and school."

"Well, more power to her. Your sister is a cool chick and I like her," Carson said.

"Yeah, she's a pretty cool sister. Sorry I'm going to study now before I go to bed. I'll see you at my car in the morning." And wished him a good night.

"Okay, I appreciate the ride."

"I'll give you my schedule tomorrow and then you can compare it with yours and maybe we can carpool."

The following morning Carson was at my car on time.

I popped on my radio and "Erasure" was singing, their song "*A Little Respect*" we both sang to it while driving to school. I was surprised that Carson knew all the words,

"I'm a fan and have this on vinyl," He proudly proclaimed.

"You have to come by and see my collection and listen to a few records one day when you have some free time," He offered.

"Okay I'll do that." I said.

"What kind of music does Jake like?" Carson asked?

"Pretty much everything across-the-board, but his favorite is Pink Floyd," I said.

"I've got everything they made on vinyl. For sure, you guys should stop by sometime," Carson said.

Over the following months, Carson became a family member, it was like he was my brother from another mother. And little did I know then, but Carson would end up being my friend and my father's friend for life. We had a lot in common with one another like music, movies and we both loved to lay in the sun listening to everything from rock, jazz, blues, classical, punk rock, country, Elton John and this new underground stuff that Carson called Rap.

It was truly as though Carson was another brother from long ago and now, we were making up for lost time. No one had ever listened to music with me like that except my siblings when we were growing up.

Carson had such a genius IQ that most of the stuff he talked about had to do with electronics and physics which was way over my head. This guy spent time just playing with mathematical formulae for fun. I sometimes felt that having a conversation with him required a dictionary. His brain was a human computer system that probably used brain cells most people never did. Also, his mind was lit up with a constant energy flow of intellectual thought and wonder.

But the thing I liked most about hanging out with Carson were the metaphysical mental experiments that we did at his house. I had not done anything like this since before I moved out of my father's house. No positive thinking books, no lectures, nothing. So, with Carson, I felt like I was a teenager all over again at home with my dad throwing I Ching Pennies against the wall.

Carson also had gravity boots installed in his dining room ceiling. I would walk in the front door of his house and find him hanging from the ceiling facing a big window overlooking the city. He taught me how to hang upside down in the gravity boots while listening to music.

He and I made a list of what we wanted in life, and then visualized it happening. We would throw energy into the vision and believe that we had it already just like I used to do with my father.

Carson was the only other person I had ever met who admitted that they had a TV screen in their head. I told him that my TV screen had been turned off for years, because too many things I had seen on it had happened and they were not good experiences.

We kept records on a little chart about how many of our wants and desires came to pass and recorded how long it took to manifest it into our physical reality. For example, if you wanted a new car, you would see yourself in the car, then consciously put yourself in the car feeling the steering wheel in your hands and smelling that new car smell, knowing without a doubt that at that moment in time it was yours.

Both of us noticed that some things took a matter of days to manifest, while others, such as being financially wealthy, did not come to pass. But if I wanted to ace a test at school or find a certain shoe that I could not afford, then I was successful. I was learning that instead of money falling from the universe into my lap, I could manifest the actual physical things that I wanted to buy with the money.

One day I was driving down the street and thought: maybe I should stop by the Banana Republic store and look through the sale section. The 1960s-style purple suede go-go boots that I had wanted for months and had visualized were there. When I walked into the store, I found that the boots I wanted were on clearance sale in my size for $39.95 and they were the only pair left.

3 months prior, when I first saw them, they were $175 dollars. I looked upwards towards the sky and said, "thanks God," as I threw my new boots in the back of my Audi and drove off with a big smile.

My father flew out to visit for the weekend, and I introduced him to Carson. They got along so well that the two of them went to a night club. When I got up the following morning my father was passed out on my sofa in the living room in a three-piece disco suit.

I knocked on Carson's front door and asked him what had happened the night before with my father.

"He's passed out with his suit on," I said.

Carson started laughing and told me that my father had been the life of the party the night before. And how much he enjoyed being with him at the club.

"Your dad's a trip; he drank, smoked some pot and danced with some college girls we met. Your father had four girls hanging on his every word as he discussed the workings of the subconscious mind. Then, when the club closed, he went home with one of them, a 19-year-old. Your dad scored big," Carson said.

"Oh my God," I thought my father comes to visit me, and he has a one-night stand with a girl younger than his own daughter, and he is married. Why was I even shocked? This was classic behavior for my father. Jake and Carson thought the whole thing was funny, but I was unable to see any humor in it.

Carson had also become close to Jack and was like an uncle to him. He was always giving Jack magnets to play with as well as fruits and vegetables from his garden.

Carson's interactions with women were a great source of amusement for me, Stephanie and Jake. You could see the girls coming and going, Carson had what I called a stable of women. Somehow, he got them all to agree to a casual sexual relationship with no strings attached.

Carson also introduced me to his two best friends Clay and Mickey, who were both studying law at the University. We formed a study group and the four us spent a lot of time together. I now had a new group of friends, and they were all guys who looked at me as their sister.

One day, Carson's high school sweetheart, a girl named Jana, came back into town from New York City. Her mother had just died, and she had to clean out her mother's house in Salt Lake City and sell it.

She and Carson reconnected over the death, and before Jake and I knew it she had moved in with him.

Jana was attractive with blond hair and bright blue eyes. I found her to be warm, friendly and nice. It was refreshing to see "The Carson Man" hang up his condom collection for one woman. It took about a week for the two of them to come up for air after she moved In. And I was happy for him. Unfortunately, the move-in was short-lived. Some girl who worked for the airlines that Carson used to sleep with occasionally knocked on the door, and Jana answered it. Plus, there were phone calls from a few other girls wondering why Carson had not been calling them any longer.

Because of this, Carson said that a verbal fight ensued one afternoon while Carson was driving with Jana on the freeway.

"I kept telling her that I had quit seeing the other girls when I got back together with her, but she refused to listen to reason. She turned into a totally different person."

Carson continued, "Hell girl, I said, you just moved in. The girls I used to date are just finding out that I am no longer available, and that I am in a relationship with you. I was just getting used to the fact that I was sharing a closet with someone, and she acts like we are about to walk down the aisle or something."

He went on to say, "Then she started saying, that if I really loved her, we would be engaged; hell, we are living together, why couldn't she just be content with that? She wanted me to commit to getting engaged, can you believe that shit? He asked.

Not waiting for a response, he continued, "When I told her that I wasn't ready to do that yet, she became so infuriated that she grabbed a hammer that I had in the backseat of my car and hit me in the head with it while I was driving on the freeway at 60 miles an hour!"

My mouth fell open in shock, "damn dude, I didn't see that coming."

"Yeah, man I had to grab the hammer out of her hand before she could throw a second blow and kill my ass," he said. "Can you imagine going 60 miles an hour on the freeway while your girlfriend is attempting to bludgeon you to death with your own hammer?" He asked.

"That is crazy, she really didn't strike me as the type of person who would do something like that. She seemed so quiet and soft-spoken; I never would've expected that in a million years," I said.

"Well, obviously it's the quiet ones you need to watch out for." He added.

"Yeah, some women can be treacherous if they get pissed off. What will you do now?" I asked.

"I told her she had to move out immediately, and that I would pay for the first night in a hotel for her."

"Dude, you really kicked her out?" I asked.

"I'm not sleeping in the same house as a crazy female who wants to kill me; do you see stupid written on my forehead?"

"Well, I guess I can see where you're coming from; I would be afraid to go to sleep in the same bed with her too," I said.

After Jana moved out, Carson was through with serious relationships. He immediately went back to his old lifestyle of dating and sleeping with anyone who looked good to him. He was hitting the clubs with the boys again and talking about taking leave from school and moving to the Virgin Islands with Mickey to start a jewelry business.

CHAPTER 162

Stephanie was also talking about leaving. She was tired of the slow pace of Salt Lake City and wanted to move back to Los Angeles. My Aunt Carol's husband Victor had set her up with a painter's job working for MTA bus system.

I, on the other hand, was truly worried because I was starting to gain a little weight in my abdomen and had missed a couple of periods. My greatest fear was that I was pregnant. In fact, I was so fearful of being pregnant that I put off going to the doctor for a few days or getting a pregnancy test out of fear of what the results might be. Finally, I got up enough nerve to make an appointment at Planned Parenthood and went.

My greatest fear became reality when the doctor told me that I was about four months pregnant. Once again, my birth control pills had failed me. I wondered why I had been stupid enough to continue using them after getting pregnant with Jack while on them the first time.

Making matters worse was a recurring dream of a teenage girl who seemed to be my daughter. We never spoke in the dream; she would just stand there looking at me. She appeared to be a young adult already; not an infant, but completely grown up.

As I left Planned Parenthood, I knew that my baby was a girl, and those dreams had been God's way of telling me that she was on the way. I always knew I would have a son, but I never saw a second child coming. I also knew that it was no coincidence that both times I had become pregnant I had no idea I was pregnant until I was too far along to get an abortion.

Someone in the universe knew that I would have gotten one if I had known in the earlier stages of my pregnancies. I was into my fourth month and no baby bump. It was as if "someone upstairs" was trying to tell me that I was going to have these two kids no matter what I wanted.

As I drove home, I wondered how I was going to tell Jake that we were pregnant and wondered how this was going to affect our lives. How would I support another baby, work, go to school and study?

This was just the wrong time in my life to have another baby. After Jake and I paid our bills, bought groceries and clothed Jack, there was money for savings but that was it. I was worried about how I was going to add a baby into the mix because as it was, I barely had time to breathe.

That night after Jake and I put Jack to bed, I broke the news to him that I was four months pregnant. His reaction was better than mine; he was immediately happy and overjoyed.

I reminded him that we could not afford another kid since the medical bills alone would kill us financially.

"Don't worry about that," he said. "I can go back into the Army, then we won't have to pay any medical bills. To tell you the truth, I have been thinking about re-enlisting, but for the Rangers this time. I hate to admit it, but I actually miss being in the military."

He said that he had been a little jealous when I had joined.

"I never knew you felt this way," I said. "But if you rejoined, I would have to quit school and move."

"You can still go to school just in a different state," Jake said. "And you wouldn't have to work while you were in school. Are you alright with me talking to someone about getting back into the military? If this works out, are you with me?"

"Always," I said.

Then he said, "We would have to get married. The Army will not let me take you and Jack with me if we are not married and we would have to do it before I got back in. Plus, I don't want our baby to be born without us being married."

That is when he looked into my eyes and said, "Will you marry me?"

"Yes," I said without hesitation.

That night as we lay down to go to sleep, Jake held me as usual, but this time he held my stomach too.

The following morning, I drove Stephanie to the airport and told her I was pregnant. She was happy that she was going to be an aunt again and promised not to tell Daddy.

After her plane took off, I thought to myself how sad it was that everyone was leaving, and we would not be a little group anymore. Also, how fast things and circumstances in a person's life changed within the blink of an eye.

I had started out in life like a racehorse breaking free from its stall, with big dreams and high hopes for my future. Now at 28, I was living out my biggest dream as it came true. The little boy on the moon and I had found one another, and we were one force in life now. A life with Jake, Jack and our little girl made me a rich woman. Not a college degree or money, but to love someone and know that you are loved in return was priceless and hard to find in the world. That is why I agreed to walk away from everything I had built for myself in Salt Lake City.

CHAPTER 163

Two weeks later, Jake and I put Jack in the car and drove to Las Vegas to get married. At four years old Jack was Jake's best man in a small private ceremony in a little white chapel.

The guy at the chapel played *"We've Only Just Begun"* by The Carpenters while I walked down the aisle with flowers in my hands wearing tan Bermuda shorts and a white t-shirt and with tan sandals. Jake and Jack wore blue jeans and t-shirts.

A formal wedding ceremony did not seem important this time around. The only important thing was we absolutely loved one another with every inch of our hearts. It was all especially beautiful to me because this wedding was for real, and I knew it would be my last one.

That is why it did not matter that it was a cheesy shotgun wedding in Las Vegas.

Jake wanted to buy me an expensive wedding ring that we could not afford. I convinced him to settle on a less expensive Opal ring, that I preferred over a diamond.

After the ceremony, Jake took Jack and me out for a delicious steak and lobster dinner to celebrate.

"We're legally a real family now," Jake said to us happily.

Then we checked into an elegant hotel for the night where we got a good night's sleep before driving back to Salt Lake City the following morning.

Two days after we returned from Las Vegas, Jake joined the Army Rangers. He would leave in a month for six-weeks of training in a school called Ranger indoctrination Program, they just called it "RIP" for short and then "Ranger School for three months."

Then he would be stationed in a Ranger Battalion at Fort Benning, GA. I was not looking forward to living in Georgia, but I thanked God that he did not have to go through basic training again. I thought being in a

Ranger Battalion was way more dangerous than being Airborne. Also, I was a little afraid for him because these guys disappeared on dangerous secret missions. He was 28 years old and going through that type of training, but he had kept himself in shape, thank God.

Even so, he ramped up his workouts just to make sure he could handle Ranger training. Jake continued to work at Advanced Foam Plastics until the day before he left.

The morning that Jack and I drove Jake to the airport was a sad one since neither one of us wanted him to go. Jake kissed and hugged us goodbye and told us that he would be back before we knew it. I felt a tear rolled down my cheek as Jack and I watched his plane take off.

While Jake was gone, I quit my job and lived off our emergency savings, dropped out of school and Carson helped me pack. We were both leaving town, he was moving to the Virgin Islands to start a jewelry business. We both vowed to keep in touch and to be friends forever.

I also discovered a restaurant in downtown Salt Lake called "Shoney's." It had an all you could eat breakfast bar. I would sit there with Jack and Carson eating until my stomach hurt from being too full. I found this strange because I did not have a huge appetite when I was pregnant with Jack.

This time though I could not shove the food in my mouth fast enough. I figured it all must be going to the baby, because I was now six months along and only weighed 130 pounds. Since I was eating like a pig, I figured the everyday workout video for pregnant women I had purchased was working.

Jake called us whenever he could and wrote letters that included photos of himself in uniform. Jack was excited because in his mind he had a real GI Joe, like the cartoon, for a dad. He told everyone we saw, "My dad is a real GI Joe and a Rocket Man who jumps out of airplanes."

The day that Jake returned from Ranger training was a glorious day for us. We were now all together again as a family, and it felt good. I had everything packed up and ready to go to Georgia. Jack and Jake were excited and saw the whole thing as an adventure.

As for me, I was not thrilled about living in the South again. I was not impressed because of the trailer with Nick. Jake promised me that he would get us on the list for post housing, and that he would never allow me to live in a trailer again.

CHAPTER 164

We took off for Fort Benning on a sunny morning in our Renault Alliance, after I gorged myself at the Shoney's "all you can eat breakfast bar" for the last time. I was grateful that the Army had shipped all our belongings to Georgia for free.

Life had been an adventure up until now as I had survived a lot of bad times and overcome many serious obstacles. I did not allow any of my circumstances to hold me back from anything. I can honestly say that I never stopped or had the time to feel sorry for myself for long because I was too busy surviving to wallow in self-pity.

I believed in what made me and I lived on prayer in this crazy world, which I call the land of make believe.

Most of all I never gave up on my dreams or myself and I always knew that I deserved the best that life could give me, and now at age twenty-eight I knew that God was real because He and the Angels had kept their word to me.

I would marry "The Little Boy on The Moon" one day. He would knock on my door and take me away on an adventure through life with him, and he would love me like God himself.

Little did I know that morning we left Salt Lake City for Georgia that the real adventure was just beginning; we were about to experience and see things beyond even our young imagination's ability to understand and dream about.

Our drive to Fort Benning started out on a joyous note until we drove through St. Louis and our car began to break down on the freeway. Suddenly, there was a loud clicking noise coming from the front end. Then it felt as if the front end was going to collapse any minute. I was so nervous about the situation that I asked God to help us get off the freeway before the car broke down completely.

Horrifying visions went through my brain of our car coming to a dead stop on the freeway with cars going at top speed unable to stop in time before they hit our car. I sat in the passenger seat with my fingers crossed while praying, "Help us God and come through for me."

I was relieved once I saw an exit coming up and Jake was able to get us off the freeway safely. But the minute he pulled over to the side of the road our car broke down as the front end of the car just collapsed. I figured God had heard my cry for help, because if this had happened on the freeway the situation probably would have ended in a multi-car accident and physical injuries or death.

Jake made sure Jack and I were comfortable, and that Jack had toys to play with while he walked to a phone booth to call for a tow truck and find a dealership to have the car towed to. We were stranded in a place called Independence, MO near Fort Leavenworth.

At this point, I was an uncomfortable pregnant woman. All I wanted was a hot shower, some food and a bed.

The tow truck showed up and took us and our car to a dealership 15 minutes away where the mechanic told us that the universal joint had gone out on the car. The repair was going to cost hundreds of dollars, and it would take until late the following afternoon to complete.

Jake called a cab which took us to a nearby hotel where we got a room for the night. He also ordered Chinese food for us and had it delivered to our hotel room while I took a long hot shower. After the three of us had finished our General Tao's chicken and shrimp fried rice, Jake bathed Jack while I collapsed in the bed: pregnant and exhausted from the horror of the car breaking down and costing us a fortune to fix.

The following afternoon we picked up our car and decided to stay one more night, then get an early start in the morning.

I was grateful that the rest of the trip went well without incident as we sang along to my Elton John cassette collection, as well as Crosby, Stills, Nash and Young and the Beatles. We ate good food and enjoyed the rest of the drive. Jake was so excited that we were finally man and wife that he kept holding my hand while driving, and every now and then he would reach over and rub my stomach with one hand. I felt completely spoiled rotten.

When we arrived at Fort Benning, it was late afternoon and the three of us were exhausted from being on the road. We checked into the guesthouse on the base and ordered takeout pizza before going to sleep. The following morning, we had breakfast and went to the housing department on the base where we found a three-bedroom apartment with a swimming pool on the housing list just over the railroad tracks in Phoenix City, AL.

This was only a15-minute car ride from the base, so Jake would not have a long work commute. I was okay with it because I did not want to live near the base or in base housing. I wanted our home life to be separate from the military and for Jake to leave the Army business at the base when he came home.

I thought it would be nice to experience living in Alabama because my grandfather had been born and raised there. I was eager to see how much it had changed since his family had been run out of the state in the middle of the night in fear of their lives.

Unfortunately, I had no idea what truly awaited us in Phoenix City, AL and if I had, I never would have moved there. We called and made an appointment to see the apartment that afternoon. Jake dropped us off at the guest house for a nap while he went to his new company for a few hours.

When he returned, the three of us drove for 20 minutes to our appointment to see the apartment. The first thing I noticed when we pulled up in front of the apartment building was that it looked new and modern which was encouraging. We knocked on the manager's door, where Jake and I experienced being referred to as "salt and pepper" for the first time in our lives.

I whispered to Jake, "What does he mean by that comment?"

"It means that we are an inter-racial couple and it's an insult," He whispered back.

We should have a run right then and never looked back, but desperately wanting to be settled, we signed a month-to-month lease and rented the place. We moved in the following morning.

The first thing I noticed on television was instead of Oprah Winfrey being on to my shock and surprise the Ku Klux Klan had a TV show. Totally bold and out in the open about it. The men on the show were dressed in their Klan wardrobes for everyone to see as if it were normal.

Coming from Los Angeles this was just shocking to me that groups like this were still going strong. I remembered learning about this in history class and movies, but nothing can prepare you for the real thing.

The first tenant we met in the apartment building referred to us as "salt and pepper," as well.

Then a week later we found the words "Nigger Lover" written on our back door in mud. I also noticed that in passing none of the other tenants in the building really spoke to us, they just stared at us like we were a side-show event. And every time I took Jack outside to play, none of the other children played with my child except one little blond girl named Becky who claimed she played the mommy, Daddy and baby game in bed with her parents, whatever the hell that meant was a mystery to me. I had never experienced this type of crazy or real racism before in my life. I truly had been naïve enough to believe that racism had died in the world because I had been raised around kids who did not care what race I was.

One morning, Jake went out to the car to drive to work and found that someone had cut our front tires in the middle of the night. That was the straw that broke the camel's back for me, and I was pissed off to the point of no return.

These people were crazy. I thought that Martin Luther King Jr. had marched and died to end this type of behavior. But obviously Dr. King meant nothing to these people. Later that day I looked out of my kitchen window and saw three white men laying out by the pool with Budweiser beer cans in their hands, acting as if they did not have a care in the world.

I figured it was one or all of them who destroyed our tires and wrote those disgusting words on our back door in mud.

That is when my mind clicked over to crazy, pregnant and out of control. I got the bright idea to put on a bikini at six-months pregnant and take my son swimming while they were out there swimming and drinking Budweiser. I quickly took Jack upstairs and we changed into our swimsuits. Then, on our way out the door, I decided to take my cassette player with me so I could play James Brown singing *"Say It Loud-I'm black and I'm Proud"* at full volume.

Screw these fools, I thought to myself as I walked outside with Jack.

The look on their faces was priceless as they saw me headed for a deck chair in my bikini at six-months pregnant with Jack by my side. I spread out my towel on the chair and pushed the play button on my cassette player.

As James Brown started singing *"Say It Loud-I'm black and I'm Proud,"* one of the guys began to get up from his deck chair to confront me until my words stopped him dead in his tracks.

I looked him in the eye and said, "look, I'm about to swim in the same water that you swim in." Then I got up and dived into the pool.

When my head came up out of the water, I saw the guys packing up their beer cooler and towels. As they walked past me one of them spit in front of my deck chair just missing it, then he called me a dirty nigger as he walked away.

I yelled back, "I guess that makes you the racist that smells and looks like an asshole then."

He replied, "Go fuck yourself nigger" and walked away with his buddies.

Jack and I stayed out there enjoying the pool for a few hours and I kept James Brown going on continuous play the whole time I was out there. My whole attitude was: Yes, I am black, and I have a right to be here.

When Jake came home from work later that afternoon, I proudly told him what I had done earlier at the pool to fight back.

"Now maybe they'll leave us alone," I told him.

Jake told me that I was going to get myself killed and the next morning he was going to the housing office on the base and applying for base housing where no one cared what color our skin was. I told Jake that would be giving those racist bastards what they wanted, me gone from the building.

Jake said he did not care if they got what they wanted, "it's my job to protect you, Jack and the baby from harm and there's no telling what these crazy assholes will pull while I'm working. You know we can't stay here and send Jack to school in an environment like this," Jake said.

I realized he was right, and I really did not want my child living in an environment where he was considered less of a human being just because he was of mixed race. Within two-weeks Jake had us packed up and moved into a housing area on the base for our safety. The house we were given had two-bedrooms, a living room, bathroom and kitchen.

It also had a heavy cockroach problem, to the point where the base exterminator went to all the houses in our area to spray once a week. I had never seen cockroaches like this before; they had wings and flew in your house and adapted to living in the refrigerator and they were immune to the weekly exterminations.

Instead of dying from the poison, they would give birth to albino babies. It was unbelievable and I wanted out of there fast. Instead of stocking my refrigerator with food, I saved the money and bought our food daily.

Jake got us on the housing list for the newer nicer post housing. We had a three-month wait on that housing list. Until then I was doing my best to hang in there, at least I was living around people of different races now and not a building full of people who judged me by the color of my skin.

Unfortunately, we were forced to spend Christmas there with the flying cockroaches, but at least my son was able to play with the other children in the housing area. Within a week Jack was best friends with a little blonde-haired girl named Amanda who lived next-door with her mother, who was a medic in the military and a single parent. The two of them would spend hours in Jack's room playing with his toys.

Every morning at 7:30 sharp Amanda would show up at our front door so Jack could walk her to the bus stop on the corner to catch the base school bus to her kindergarten class. Jack was a year younger than Amanda and would not be attending kindergarten until the following September.

Joyfully, I watched my son play with his little friend and I thought it was cute that he walked her to the bus stop every morning and waited for the bus with her.

CHAPTER 165

Meanwhile, Stephanie had found our mother and was developing a relationship with her. Without asking me, she gave our mother my telephone number. The first time my mother called me, I was shocked to hear from her, and did not know how to react.

Part of me loved her because she was my mother, but the other part of me was afraid because you never knew when she was telling the truth and she was still married to Maxwell. She called to tell me that Stephanie had informed her of my pregnancy, and how happy she was for me and how excited she was to be a grandmother to my children.

At this point I was so pregnant that I could barely stand. My stomach was so big that it was becoming increasingly difficult to even get a good night's sleep, because I was unable to find a comfortable position to sleep in.

Plus, the baby was active, constantly kicking and moving around in my stomach. At times I could see her moving underneath my clothes. My doctor told me months prior that I had something called gestational diabetes and he ordered me to stay off my feet, get bed rest and not to have sex.

Staying off my feet was impossible because I had Jack to take care of, and I found it boring to just lay there in bed reading and watching TV.

Jake did his best to be home as often as he could, including coming home for lunch every day to check on me and Jack. But by the morning of New Year's Eve, I just could not take being pregnant anymore.

I was a week away from my due date and began to think of ways to give birth early without hurting myself or the baby. A few things ran across my mind, like going horseback riding or getting on a roller coaster. Then I remembered that the doctor told me not to have sex, and I wondered if that would do the trick.

That is when I lied to Jake for the first time in our relationship and told him that the doctor had called and said it was okay for me to have sex. I felt guilty about deceiving him, but I could not take it anymore. It felt like I was going to die from the lack of sleep alone.

After Jake and I had gotten in bed that night we made love for the first time in months, and after we finished, I got up to use the bathroom and water started spilling out of me onto the bathroom floor.

There was so much water spilling out of me that I could hear it hit the bare floor. Jake jumped out of bed in a panic and rushed to the bathroom.

He looked at me and said, "your water has broken, I bet the doctor never said it was okay to have sex."

I immediately apologized for tricking him and told him I just could not take being pregnant anymore, and how desperate I was for the baby to be born, "It's only a week early." I said to him.

Jake reached for his blue jeans and began to get dressed, shaking his head in disbelief, and told me to get dressed before the labor pains started. After he was dressed, he dressed Jack, then returned to our bedroom to get me. He rushed me to Martin Army Hospital on the base at top speed afraid that I would start having labor pains on the way there. He told me that he did not want me in pain.

By the time we arrived at the hospital I was still feeling no pain, but unfortunately, we found out that my labor and delivery doctor was out of town and would not be back for a week. So, I was stuck with whoever was on duty that night. Then to make the matter' worse, when I did meet the doctor who was going to deliver my baby, he informed me that they had a policy of not using pain killer for labor and delivery at Martin Army Hospital.

I told him that my regular doctor had promised me that he would give me an epidural. The doctor told me once again that I would not be receiving an epidural or any other pain killer.

Next thing I knew I was being wheeled down the hallway to a hospital room. I tried to get up out of the wheelchair once we arrived at my room, but the nurse pushed me back down which really pissed me off.

I now regretted having sex and making the baby come early, because now my regular doctor would not be there to keep his promise to me about that epidural. And with that thought, I felt my first labor pain and it was not pretty. It felt like someone was stabbing me from within.

I was then forced to take my clothes off and put on a hospital gown and get into the hospital bed. After that I was being hooked up to an ultrasound machine and attended to by a "mean ass I have a chip on my shoulder" Army nurse.

Her name tag said Sergeant Albright, but there was nothing bright about her. She reminded me of the cruel nurse from the movie "One Flew Over the Cuckoo's Nest" Nurse Ratched in the flesh.

I was stuck with her and no pain killer for what turned out to be 48 hours of labor and I thought I would die from the labor pains. Then I lost my mind and just wished I were dead so the pain would go away.

At one point I started throwing up from the pain and everything became a blur. I do not know how I gave birth to Lucy or how I even gathered up enough strength to push when I was told to.

All I know is the first time I saw my daughter she was so beautiful that she reminded of a princess, so I named her Lucy Sara Pierson. The Sara was for my grandmother. I could tell that Lucy had taken after Jake in her physical appearance.

She did not have much hair except for a few little blonde strands on top of her little head. I was madly in love with her from the moment I saw her and so was Jake.

Lucy cried from the beginning of her life and kept crying. I spent one night in the hospital and was released to go home to my relief. We had a beautiful beige wicker baby bassinet set up in our bedroom on my side of the bed so if Lucy cried in the middle of the night, I would be able to reach her quickly. I had elected not to breast-feed for the second time; there was something about it that just made me feel uncomfortable and I could not bring myself to do it. So, the doctor put Lucy on baby formula and gave me pills to dry up my milk. Once we had Lucy home and settled, she still cried pretty much 24 hours a day. I never imagined that a baby could cry so much. It did not matter what you did to try to soothe her, whether it was picking her up or just holding her and rocking her she just continued to cry.

Within a week I was suffering from sleep deprivation and the doctor ordered me to get bedrest and gave me a prescription for sleeping pills. He also supplied Jake with a note to give to his company commander so he could have a week off duty to stay home and take care of Lucy and Jack while I slept.

After a week of bed rest, I felt renewed and finally like my old self. Lucy may have cried a lot, but she was the cutest little baby girl I had ever seen. I could not help but kiss her little cheeks constantly and hug her and squeeze her all the time. Jake would rush home from work every day just to play with her, he was so happy to have a little girl.

At night he would bathe her himself and tuck her into bed in her little bassinet. Jack, on the other hand, was not thrilled to have a little sister. I think he was used to being the only child and did not like having to share our attention. I did my best to pay as much attention to Jack as I could so he would not feel as if he had to compete with his sister.

One afternoon I decided to put Lucy in her stroller and take Jack outside to the playground to play on the swings and slides. When we arrived, there were already a few other children out there playing. Jack quickly ran to the swings and got on one of them. I turned my attention to tending to the baby for a minute when I heard Jack cry out in pain. I looked over and there was a little boy standing in front of Jack's swing with a stick in his hand.

Every time Jack would swing forward this kid was hitting him in the nuts with the stick. I suddenly stopped what I was doing and ran over to the kid holding the stick and took it away from him. I ran to Jack who was crying at this point, to see if he was going to be all right. Still crying, I walked him over to the baby stroller.

I was so mad I took that kid by the arm and asked him where he lived so I could tell his mother what he was out there doing on the playground. I forced the kid to take me to his house. I knocked on the door and when his mother opened it, I told her what her son had done.

She did not seem to care much; her reaction was, "I don't know what you want me to do about it." Then she told her son to come into the house and she shut the door in my face. It was obvious that she and her son did not intend to apologize at all.

As I walked away with my children, I thought no wonder her kid is a violent little creep; she taught him well.

When Jake got home from work and I told him what happened that day on the playground, he told me that I should not have interfered because Jack had to learn to fight his own battles in life.

He said I would only be hurting him by fighting his battles for him. I did not quite see it that way; I saw it as another child with poor home training had a stick that could have punctured my son's testicles and damaged him for life.

A few weeks later a couple that lived next-door to us were being shipped off to a new duty station and did not want to take their pit bull mix with them. They asked us if we wanted to take the dog for Jack. Not wanting to see an animal go to the dog pound we agreed to take the dog whose name was Oscar.

In the beginning everything went smoothly until Oscar stole my ham off the kitchen counter in the kitchen. I had taken the ham out of the oven, went to the bathroom, and when I returned to the kitchen the ham and the pan were gone.

That is when I saw Oscar licking the pan in the corner of the living room floor. I knew then that the dog had to go. I called Jake into the living room and when he saw Oscar licking the pan that the ham had been in, he agreed with me that Oscar was more than we could handle at that point in our lives.

Jake looked at me and said, "This is probably why they didn't want to take the dog with them."

He quickly took Oscar back next-door and explained to the guy that we could not keep him. Jack, of course, was disappointed because the dog had been sleeping with him but taking a whole ham off the kitchen counter was just too much.

A few months later our name came up on the housing list for the new housing on the base. We went and looked at the place and the moment I walked in the door I was relieved because it was a lot bigger and newly built with no bug problem.

It had a nice big entry room by the front door, huge kitchen, spacious living room and dining room, on the first floor. On the second floor there were three bedrooms and a bathroom, plus a powder room downstairs next to a huge coat closet.

It also had a patio area with glass sliding doors and a big backyard. But the thing I liked the most were the hardwood floors. I was thrilled and excited, no more flying cockroaches, no more being cramped for space, and no more living in housing built in the 1950s.

CHAPTER 166

Lucy had just turned four months old and Jack six and ready to go into kindergarten that fall. There were a lot of kids to play with in our little cul-de-sac of 12 military homes which made me feel a little better after the racism we had experienced in Alabama.

We tried the dog thing again and adopted an Australian Shepherd from the dog pound for the kids to play with.

We were happy until we begin to have contact with our new next-door neighbors. We were now living next to a black couple who did not believe in inter-racial marriages. They were both in the military and had the wife's mother living with them and she proved herself to be just as racist as her daughter and son-in-law.

I remember wondering what the hell is wrong with people. It was 1986 and I thought racism was something we supposedly had moved on from a long time ago.

Occasionally, when I would step out my front door, I would hear someone from next-door calling me a white boy lover from their upstairs bathroom window.

At first, I just ignored them and acted as if I heard nothing.

This literally went on for months until one day our dog Fremont got loose and wandered into their backyard. The woman's mother knocked on my door and told me they had my dog tied up in their yard and that they were going to call the base dog pound and have my dog put to sleep.

At that point I just snapped because this situation was totally out of control. I held my anger in and asked the woman kindly to give me my dog back.

When she refused, I went into the house and got Jake's .22 caliber rifle that his father had given him for Christmas when he was a kid (which was now empty with no bullets in it and totally non-functional.)

I confronted her daughter with the gun, as she stood in her backyard with my dog. She had an ugly grin on her face. I told her that if she did not give me my dog back immediately, I would shoot her and take the dog anyway.

Believing that the shotgun worked, she immediately released Fremont who came running happily to me. Then she shouted out that she was going to call the Military Police on me for pulling a weapon on her. I told her to go right ahead and call them.

I went back into my house with my dog and put the rifle back in the closet. I figured once the MPs showed up and saw the busted gun, she had no case. I went into the living room, turned my television set on to the Oprah Winfrey Show, sat down on the sofa with my dog and acted as if nothing had happened at all.

About 15 minutes later I heard a knock at my front door, instinctively I knew it was the MPs. I opened the front door and acted surprised to see them standing there. I looked at the two officers as innocently as I could and asked, "Can I help you?"

One of them told me that they had received a telephone call from my next-door neighbor saying I had taken a gun outside and took a shot at her.

Doing my best to look shocked, I looked at the officer and said, "You've got to be kidding me. The only weapon we ever had is a busted Sears and Roebuck .22 that my husband's father gave him when he was a kid. I'm not even sure where it is or if we still have it."

"When was the last time you saw the .22?" the police officer asked.

"The last time I saw it was when we moved. I don't know if my husband threw it out or kept it. I answered."

"Well, if he kept it, where do you think it would be? The MP asked.

"Maybe the coat closet here." I replied.

The officer looked at me and said, "Well, can you see if you still, have it?"

"Sure, no problem." I told him. I walked over to the coat closet, opened the door rummaged around for a moment, and said, "There it is, back there on the floor."

I moved out of the closet to allow him to go in and pick up the rifle.

He examined it and said to his partner, "This thing is not even functional, and it definitely hasn't been fired. There isn't even a bullet in it and from the looks of things a bullet hasn't come through this thing in years."

They looked at each other and then looked at me and said, "Ma'am, we're sorry to disturb you and thank you for your time."

As I looked out the window by the front door, I saw them go next door ring the doorbell and tell my neighbor that they were taking her in for filing a false complaint. I knew I should have been ashamed of myself, but I could not help smiling a little with satisfaction that this woman was finally getting what I felt she deserved.

After weeks of yelling racist comments out her bathroom window every time she saw us, the final straw was my dog. I thought she was getting everything that she deserved because she never should have lied and said that I took a shot at her.

I walked into the kitchen happy and satisfied with myself and begin making spaghetti for dinner as if nothing had happened.

Not more than two weeks later Jake and I were coming back from the supermarket with the kids on a Saturday afternoon, when we noticed our prejudiced neighbors moving out. According to another neighbor, they had been kicked out of the housing area and had received an article 15, reduced rank and pay, because the woman had lied and said I shot at her.

I just looked at my neighbor and said, "I guess the MPs don't like it when you call in false claims." Then I turned around and went into my house to unpack my groceries. As an LA girl I was not used to prejudiced people. And it seemed that I was kind of surrounded by it from both blacks and whites.

This crap went both ways and was just so unbelievable to me, it was as if history had taught us nothing. What was wrong with people? I thought that being on a military installation would be better and reduce prejudice because all the soldiers fought together as one team. But that sadly proved not to be true.

Four doors down from us lived a woman named Charlene in charge of our little housing area. Her husband was a drill sergeant and looked the part. This woman was always bragging, in a super thick southern accent, about how she had been born and raised in Savannah, GA and how beautiful it was. I tried to befriend her, but she wanted no part of me.

She and her husband had three boys, two of them were around Jack's age, and one older from a previous marriage. Her two younger boys began playing with Jack and they were not nice little boys. They would do things like take his toys or his bike and refuse to give them back. Sometimes they would just gang up on him and hit him on the head and run after taking his candy from him.

As usual, Jake told me not to interfere. He kept insisting that Jack had to learn how to fight his own battles from the beginning if he was ever going to know how to fight for himself as an adult.

Jake sat Jack down and told him the next time anyone hit him or tried to take his candy, or anything else that belonged to him, to just ball up his fist and hit them in the face, "or better yet in the stomach area as hard as he could."

"You won't get into any trouble from me or mom for defending yourself." Jake got down on his knees and started showing Jack how to box and defend himself. He told Jack that he personally preferred hitting the person in the stomach area, that way as they balled over in pain, he could go behind them and kick them in the ass and get them on their way.

A week later I was in the house changing Lucy's diaper and Jack was outside playing when I heard my doorbell ring. I opened the front door to find Charlene standing there looking extremely pissed off. I immediately asked her what was wrong, but before I could even step outside, she started in on me with how horrible my son was and how my son had punched her son in the stomach and then kicked him in the butt which made him fall face down onto the cement ground.

I immediately thought about the fighting lessons that Jake had given Jack and I knew what was going on. My son had gotten tired of getting his butt kicked. I told her that her son had been picking on my son constantly to the point where his father had to teach him how to defend himself.

"I never knocked on your door screaming at you," I told her. "Just tell your kids to stop picking on my kid and there won't be any more fighting unless he has to defend himself again."

Then I walked out to the play area and took Jack by the hand and took him into the house thinking to myself that people were just plain crazy.

Once we were in the house, I sat Jack down on the sofa and I asked him if that kid was picking on him first. He told me that the little boy had purposely walked into him and tried to push him to the ground for no reason.

"So, I did what dad told me to do," Jack said.

"Don't worry," I told him "You're not in trouble."

Then I got up and turned on the television to cartoons hoping it would occupy his mind for a while.

In the kitchen, where Lucy was sitting in her highchair eating baby cookies, I began to cook dinner and tried to forget about the woman banging on my door.

As time went on, I assumed that Charlene was a racist, because she did not like me and had no reason to feel that way. She and I spent most of our time avoiding one another.

Eventually, I was able to make friends with another lady in our housing area named Sandy who was married to a military solider named Brian and had a two-year-old son.

She began inviting us over on the weekends for backyard barbecues with her husband and his friends. I really did not care much for her husband because he was one of those guys who bragged a lot. At one point we were sitting in their backyard eating barbecue ribs and potato salad when I overheard her husband Brian bragging to one of his friends how much money he was making off stolen military equipment.

Stuff like night vision goggles and other things that I knew cost a ton of money. He was asking his friend if he wanted in on the action.

It looked to me that he had a little thieving ring going on. He soon confirmed my suspicions by opening the storage shed in his backyard to show his friend some of the stolen equipment he had stashed in there.

Then the TV screen in my brain turned on and I saw a storage unit off base filled with expensive military equipment. I was just completely floored about the nerve of this guy since I knew he was an asshole and bragged a lot, but this really was a stomach-turning situation for me.

I knew for a fact the supply clerks in the military had to sign for all that equipment in their care. If anything came up missing, it came out of their paychecks. I had visions in my brain of some poor private who had kids, struggling to buy baby diapers, while the military took thousands of dollars out of his paychecks over time.

And this was the guy responsible for all the theft. Just the thought of some poor soldier suffering and paying for this idiot's crimes made my stomach turn. What kind of person stole from their own military?

It just made me sick to my stomach to even look at the guy after knowing what he was doing.

I went home that night unable to sleep, wrestling with my conscience. Part of me kept saying it is none of your business; the other part saw some kid going without food or baby diapers while Brian continued to steal and force innocent people to suffer over his actions. Not to mention stealing my tax dollars. In my mind the tax dollars of each American citizen were used to purchase that stolen military equipment. So, to me it was like I was just giving money away to him.

He had just purchased a new Camaro, and now I knew where the money had come from.

Jake and I talked about it the following morning. He had been playing ball with Jack when I overheard the conversation and saw the contents of that shed. I told Jake that I wanted to turn this guy in so he could not steal any more equipment.

Jake agreed that I should go down to the Criminal Investigation Division office to report him. After I drove Jake to his company and dropped him off, I headed to the CID office with my children.

I walked into the office, kids in tow, and told the receptionist that I wanted to report a crime. She told me to take a seat and that someone would be with me shortly. I sat down with the kids and waited 10 minutes before the agent came out to get me.

I sat by the edge of his desk and told him everything I knew and asked to remain anonymous since these people were my neighbors.

The agent assured me that no one would find out that I reported him.

I drove home feeling as if I had done the right thing and decided that I should stay clear of Sandy and Brian since they were criminals; besides who wanted to spend time with someone you just turned in for theft?

There was no way I was going to stand around holding casual conversation with them knowing that the CID was going to investigate them; that was a little too uncomfortable for me. Plus, what they were doing was so stomach turning, why would I want to spend time with them?

A few weeks later Jake and I, along with the rest of our housing area, were awakened at 3:30 am to hear people yelling outside, and a dog barking. We got out of bed and rushed to the window to see what all the fuss was about.

At the window, we saw Military Police and CID agents. We saw Brian standing in front of his house in handcuffs, as well as his wife standing there along with her mother and father who were visiting from out of town. Then we saw two MPs and a police dog coming out of their house with the handler.

We stood there at the window watching as Brian was put into one of the Military Police cars and driven away.

Jake and I looked at one another and I said, "Damn, they busted him in the middle of the night while his in-laws were visiting."

I kind of felt guilty about turning him in, but on the other hand I would have felt even more guilty just thinking about an innocent soldier's paychecks being robbed by paying for military equipment he did not steal.

"You did the right thing," Jake said as we stood there by the window watching the MPs go in and out of their house.

The next day part of me wanted to go over and ask his wife if everything was okay, but I already knew it was not. Also, I did not want to be an asshole and talk to her after turning her husband in. A week went by, and I assumed that her husband was locked up in jail because I did not see him coming and going.

One afternoon I decided to take my dog Fremont for a walk through the woods. Halfway through my walk I felt a rock hit my forehead, not knowing where it came from. I looked around and saw Sandy standing not too far away from me.

She looked enraged as she yelled, "I bet you're the one that turned my husband in, you fucking bitch."

I could feel blood dripping from my forehead on to my eyelashes as I lied and screamed back at her, "I don't know what you're talking about."

"Don't play dumb with me. I know that you overheard my husband talking about the military equipment because I was there, and I know that you saw what he had in the shed when he opened it up. No one else was there." She said angrily.

Sandy came toward me saying, "I'm going to kick your ass." The only thing that stopped her was my dog Fremont who saw her as a threat to me and began barking and growling like he was going to cut her a new asshole.

Not wanting to tackle my dog, she began walking away saying, "I'm going to get you if it's the last thing I do."

I hurried back home totally afraid for my life because Sandy looked and acted like she had lost her mind. I went to the bathroom to see what damage had been done to my forehead, took a washcloth and washed the blood off my face.

It was only a small cut and I put some antibiotic cream and a Band-Aid on it.

Then I went into the living room where Jake was watching cartoons with the kids. The minute he saw me he got up from the sofa concerned, asking what had happened to my forehead.

I told him and asked him where the car keys were because I was going down to the CID office to let them know that I had just been threatened, and that Sandy had figured out that I was the one who turned her husband in.

"How did she find out? You didn't tell anyone did you?" Jake asked me.

"No, I didn't tell anyone; you're the only person I discussed it with besides the CID agent. She told me that she figured it out on her own, because I was the only one there who overheard him talking and saw what was in the shed. She said that she was going to get me if it was the last thing, she did." I replied.

That is why I need the keys so I can drive to the CID office and tell someone that she threatened me.

"I'll come with you", he said.

"No, I want you to stay here with the kids, I can drive myself down there." I told him.

I drove down to the CID office and told the agent what happened and showed him the gash on my forehead. I also told him everything that Sandy had said to me.

He sent me home assuring me that everything was going to be all right saying that they might have to relocate me and my family until the court-martial trial.

"What do you mean relocate us?" I asked.

"We may have to place you and your family in the witness protection program and have your husband reassigned to a new duty station. In the meantime, I want you to try and stay indoors as much as possible. And if she approaches you again or knocks on your door, I want you to call the Military Police."

CHAPTER 167

Two weeks later Jake received orders saying that he was being relocated and stationed at Fort Lewis Washington in Washington state. Once again, we were packing all our stuff up into a U-Haul truck.

It turned out that the bust was a huge deal to the military because it involved more than one person and Cocaine. The CID agent told me that I would be flown back to Georgia to testify at the court-martial proceedings.

Jake decided that before leaving Georgia we should buy a new car and trade the old one in. He said that he had a feeling that our present car was on its last leg because of the high mileage and would probably break down on the way to Washington state.

After looking around a few auto lots, we settled on a used Pontiac 6000 LE, because with our trade-in and the money in our savings account we could pay cash for the car.

I do not know if the woman helping us with the paperwork was disturbed by the fact that we were a married inter-racial couple, or what her problem was, but she was extremely rude to us and her dislike for us showed.

The salesman had offered us an $800 discount on the car if we paid cash. This woman was trying to reduce our $800 discount to a $400 discount instead, and our salesman had left for lunch.

I could see the anger in Jake's eyes building and he looked frustrated as he just stared her down in deep concentration. Then suddenly, she flew out of her chair onto the floor as though someone had pushed her, but no one was there.

I looked at Jake, who no longer looked angry, and was smiling.

As I looked at his face, I knew that he had somehow pushed that woman out of her chair without even touching her. From the frightened look on her face, she did too.

Then Jake told her "Either you sell me that car for the amount agreed upon or I'm walking out of here without the car. I will give you a minute to think it over."

Fearful, the woman got up off the floor and sold us the car with our $800 discount.

As we got into our new car and strapped the kids into the back seat, I looked at Jake and asked, "What was it that you just did back there? I know that you pushed that woman out of the chair without touching her, I saw you."

"I just concentrated and pushed. I've been doing it since I was a kid with toys and marbles for fun, and if you ever tell anyone I will deny it." He added defensively.

That is when I thought about all the little unusual things I noticed about Jake, like occasionally catching him touching my head and my heart while I slept next to him. There was always heat coming from his hands which usually woke me up.

When caught red-handed he would say that he was healing me up.

He also had a way with animals, and they liked him for some reason. He would take Jack deep into the woods in Georgia and pick up rattlesnakes for him to examine without getting bitten. Any animal that Jake saw he loved, honored and respected, and they treated him the same.

However, pushing someone out of a chair without touching them was really something, and now, I wondered what other gifts he possessed.

The fact that we met as children playing pat-a-cake on the moon while two angels planned our future together, and the fact that I had a TV screen in my mind showing me at times the past, present and future, made it easier for me to accept the unusual things that Jake did from time to time.

CHAPTER 168

The following morning, we left Fort Benning with me driving the new car with the kids in the back and Jake driving the U-Haul truck with our dog. We drove for four days, and Jake ensured we slept in decent hotels and ate three healthy meals a day.

Once we arrived in Tacoma, WA, we drove to the base Fort Lewis and checked into the guest house.

The following morning, we started looking for a house to rent off the base. We found a place to look at just a short 20-minute car ride from the base on the freeway.

The minute we pulled up in front of the house I knew it was the place for us. It was a Victorian two-story home with three bedrooms and hardwood floors and an elegant staircase. I was totally in love with the place. We rented it and moved in the following day.

My early dream was coming true about living in a house with a beautiful wooden staircase and hardwood floors. This house even had a fireplace in the kitchen, as well as a nice sized fenced-in backyard for the kids to play in.

Since the rent was surprisingly cheap, I considered that a gift from God. We began to unpack and get settled in. We were getting the beds set up and the kids into their pajamas when suddenly we heard gunshots from outside as we all stood there in the living room, pajamas in hand. Then more shots sounded, they seemed to be getting closer and closer to our house when suddenly Jake pushed all of us down to the floor in the living room.

He covered us as a bullet shot through our living room window. It was unbelievable! I was lying face down on a hardwood floor with my husband lying over me because a bullet had just been shot through the window of my living room.

"Where the hell was I? South-Central Los Angeles?" I thought, it sure felt like it. Jake made us all lie there, until minutes later we heard police sirens coming. That is when he let us get up.

Jake told us to stay inside as he walked outside to see what the hell was going on. I looked out the window with my kids and saw Jake talking to one of the police officers.

The police were looking around our front lawn and walked up to the window and examined the bullet hole in the glass, then our wall. I heard one of the police officers telling Jake that we were lucky that no one was hurt.

I stepped outside just as a neighbor from across the street walked over to our front lawn to see what all the commotion was about. He introduced himself as Raymond and asked what happened.

After Jake told him what happened, he looked at him and said, "Just another day in the neighborhood. You know, those Rangers and gang members always clashing with one another and then the shooting starts."

I was surprised, "What do you mean Rangers and gang members?"

"Well, about five blocks over in that direction," he pointed west, "there are a group of Rangers from Fort Louis renting a house. It started when one of the gang members in the neighborhood stole one of the Rangers' bicycles and then he sees the guy riding around on it a few days later. Ever since then they have been at war with one another," Raymond said.

"Damn" I said, "we have gang members living in this neighborhood.? But it looks so calm and peaceful, and the homes are so attractive and old."

"Don't let that fool you. Welcome to the Hilltop neighborhood," Raymond said.

Raymond's comments really killed my enthusiasm for my new neighborhood. Here I thought we had it made because we were living within walking distance to the Puget Sound and the docks. We could walk the dog and go fishing and take our children crabbing.

We were all so excited and looking forward to living near the water. Now gang members had been added into the equation in this nice little neighborhood.

Jack was still excited about the experience. He said it reminded him of watching cops on television except that it was happening in real life. I looked at Lucy who was walking around as if nothing had happened and thought how resilient children are. I was still so shaken up over the whole thing my damn life flashed before my eyes.

About 15 minutes later the police left saying that they found the shell casings in our front lawn.

We got the beds set up, unpacked our bedding and went to bed.

CHAPTER 169

I spent the following week unpacking and putting everything in its place and decorating the kid's bedrooms. It made me happy to be living in an old house like my grandparents had when I was a kid. The old house on Bronson Street had been torn down with the rest of the houses in the neighborhood years ago.

But now I was living in an old house of my own with my husband, my children and a dog named Fremont and it felt like another one of my dreams had come true.

Raymond and his wife Shawn lived across the street with their three children: a girl around 13, and two boys who were in Jack's age group, seven and eight. Shawn and I became friendly because of the children. We would sit in her front yard watching the boys play, talking and becoming friendly.

Shawn started telling me how she really hated her husband and wanted to divorce him as soon as possible. She told me she had a boyfriend on the side, some guy named Earl she was in love with.

She was good looking with long brown hair that hung to the middle of her back. She was tall, had a sparkle in her brown eyes and a voluptuous figure. I looked at Shawn and wondered why a beautiful woman like her would get herself in this predicament.

Shawn pulled out a small photo of Earl from her back pocket saying, "I like to keep him close to my butt."

I looked at the photo and saw this scrawny looking dude who was maybe 5'8" at most and looked like he had spent one too many nights at the tavern. It was shocking to see how someone as beautiful as she was falling for someone like Earl.

It reminded me of beauty and the beast. At least Raymond was half-way tolerable to look at and responsible with a decent job. This guy not only looked like he was unemployed, but Shawn confirmed that he was unemployed and looking for work.

He looked like the hippie who would sleep on your sofa because he had no place else to go.

"Shawn," I said, "nobody wants to smooch when the lights are turned off and your belly's screaming for food."

She insisted that she was tired and fed up with Raymond, and in love with this Earl guy. Who was I to argue with her; I figured there was an ass for every seat.

One day Raymond came home from work and found her in bed with Earl and what really perplexed me about the whole situation was instead of Raymond kicking Shawn and Earl out, they both kicked him out! It was the strangest thing I had ever seen when it came to relationships and break-ups.

Raymond found a small trailer to rent not far from Shawn. I started driving Jack over to Raymond's trailer to spend the night with the boys whenever Raymond had visitation rights on the weekends.

With his newfound freedom, Raymond became quite a partier, so I decided to stop Jack from sleeping over there. Besides, Raymond was also smoking pot and doing God knows what else at the local nightclubs and taverns. I figured he was just trying to party and smoke the hurt away that Shawn had inflicted upon his heart.

Not long after that the owner of our house decided to put it up for sale and we had two months to move out. We were disappointed because we all really enjoyed living in that house and had only been there six months.

Jake and I quickly found a duplex to rent that had three bedrooms, one bathroom and a big backyard for the kids to play in that was not far from the docks.

But now we had to drive a short distance to the water rather than walk. The one good thing was that the rent was $125 cheaper per month. We moved in and Jack continued to be friends with Raymond and Shawn's little boys.

One day Raymond called and sounded scared when he asked me if I could come pick him up because his car battery was dead. Jack was at school and Jake was at work on the base, so it was just me and Lucy on our own.

I picked up Lucy, put on her coat and left to help Raymond. As I drove to his home, I had a feeling that something more than a dead car battery was bothering him because he sounded so frightened over the telephone. When I reached Raymond's house, I was grateful that Lucy had fallen asleep in her car seat.

I knocked on his door, expecting him to be ready to jump into my car and go. Instead, Raymond answered the door and motioned me into the living room.

"Lucy's asleep in the backseat of my car and I don't want to leave her unattended. I thought you were ready to go. What's going on?" I told him.

"This will only take a second," he assured me.

Sitting there in his living room was a young girl who looked about 19 or 20 whom he introduced as Susie, his new girlfriend. They had met at some club weeks ago and now they were in love. They had been inseparable ever since.

Then an older blonde woman came out of Raymond's bathroom and Raymond introduced her as Carly, Susie's mother. It looked like Susie had already moved in and she and her mother were in charge.

Both Susie and Raymond looked frightened, while her mother just looked irritated by my presence.

"Raymond, what's wrong?" I asked nervously.

"Susie and I see balls of energy floating through the air in the house. The other day we visited a friend who lived in an apartment building on the second floor, and as we were standing at his door, something we could not see tried to push Susie over the railing." Raymond explained. "Anyway, I figured since sometimes you know things, before they happen, maybe you could help us figure out what the hell is going on; and maybe tell me what those energy balls are," he said.

"Wow, I 'm not psychic, and just because I knew that you were getting a raise at work, does not mean that I have any knowledge about what is going on with you now. The most I could do for you is to go home and pray and ask God about this situation," I explained.

As the words "God" and "pray" came out of my mouth, I noticed that Susie's mother was nervously pacing around the room while giving me dirty looks. Then suddenly she just left the room. I wondered what she had against God and praying.

I looked at Raymond and said, "my child is in the car, so if you're ready, let's go."

Raymond got into the car, and I dropped him off at Shawn's house, then went home to feed Lucy her lunch.

After lunch we took a nap together. As I lay there watching her sleep next to me, I thought about Raymond and asked God to give him and Susie the answers they needed. I closed my eyes and got my brain to quiet down, and then it came to me: those balls of energy Raymond mentioned brought back memories of seeing my brother Dennis in that form.

Except in Raymond's case the whole thing felt dark as hell.

My gut told me they were seeing disembodied negative spirits. I felt that this was God's answer. I also got the feeling that this dynamic was nothing to be played with. I suddenly remembered back when I was a kid, and my angel friend De-De would come to take me flying after I had gone to bed.

I remembered seeing the other dimension next to ours which was filled with demons, lost souls, bad energy and every negative emotion and thought.

The light of God did not exist in that place, and that scared the hell out of me. Whatever was around Raymond was from this place and I did not want to be involved.

I finally fell into a peaceful sleep and when I awoke Lucy was still sleeping next to me. I lay there for a minute when it suddenly occurred to me that I needed to call Raymond and warn him. I thought about asking him if he had ever prayed, and if not, he needed to start now.

Something was not right with his new girlfriend and her mother; this dark crap was attached to them not Raymond.

After I got up from the bed, I placed pillows on each side of Lucy so she could not roll off the bed if she woke up. Then I called Raymond and told him that I had prayed and thought about his dilemma. I warned him that the stuff he was seeing floating in the air was not from God.

"I suspect they are evil spirits without a body, and they want to live in one. I do not understand what this is, and do not want to know. But whatever it is, it is demonic, and it is coming from your girlfriend and her mom. If I, were you, I would dump her." I warned him.

"I can't," he said.

"Why not?" I asked.

"Because she has already moved in," he replied.

"Well, if you can manage to think with your brain and not your penis, you will realize that this is some strange mess and you need to tell her to leave, then stay away from her." I informed him. "Like I said before, the only thing I can do for you is pray and you should pray too. I don't know if you have any religious beliefs or if you know who God and Jesus are, but you need to pray to God and Jesus to help you out of this mess."

"All right," Raymond said, "I'm going to break it off with her and tell her to leave."

"Wise decision," I said. Then I heard Lucy waking up in the bedroom and told Raymond that I had to go and hung up.

After deciding to get on with the rest of my life and not give Raymond's situation another thought. I went on with my day.

The next day I got another frantic phone call from Raymond telling me that his car would not start again and asked if I could come pick him up and drop him off at Shawn's again.

I told him I was busy and to call someone else.

Then he said, "Please, I'm scared." He said that he had broken up with Susie the night before, and now she had some guys there helping her load her stuff into their car.

"So, what's the problem?" I asked. "She's leaving."

"My car will not start; I feel uncomfortable, and Susie's pretty pissed. She cried when I broke up with her. I promise this is the last time I will bother you."

I do not want to do this, I thought to myself as I said: "Okay, I'll be there soon; be outside." Again, I put Lucy in her car seat and headed out to get Raymond.

When I arrived at his house the front door was wide open, and Raymond was waiting for me outside. I saw Susie's mother carry a laundry basket full of clothes outside and walk towards a parked car. I saw Susie standing next to the car with two rough looking white guys.

Raymond approached my driver side window and said, "I'll be right back. I left my keys on the kitchen counter."

"Hurry," I urged as I sat there looking at Susie standing at the far side of the trailer driveway. Suddenly she was at my driver's side window. It was impossible that within the blink of an eye she was there at my car window, but she was.

Within seconds, as her face contorted in front of me, a deep masculine voice came out of her mouth and said, "You bitch, I'll show you how much power I really have."

My body immediately froze. I could not move. I was so frightened that I could not even scream; I felt paralyzed. It was like Megan in the Exorcist movie, except this was real life. I forced myself to press my foot down on the gas pedal and took off at top speed.

I saw Raymond standing in front of his trailer with his hands up in the air through my rear-view mirror. I did not care. I was getting the hell out of there as fast as I could, and as far as I was concerned Raymond could call a cab.

Glancing into the backseat to check on Lucy, I saw that she was fast asleep and thanked God. I also thanked God that my child had not witnessed Susie's face changing into a demon face. All kinds of thoughts raced through my head, like what the hell just happened back there?

The minute I got home I locked my front door and called Jake at work to tell him what had just happened to me. Surprisingly, he believed me although I did not expect anybody to believe me. Especially since I did not believe it myself and I saw it. You only saw this in the movies and never really expected to see it in real life.

Raymond called to ask why I left him there and, I told him that Susie's face had changed in front of me like she was a demon from the Exorcist movie, and I was not going to wait around for her head to start spinning.

Then I told him to take a cab and tried to get on with my day and put that ordeal out of my mind. I was finished with this situation and Raymond.

CHAPTER 170

A couple nights later Jack showed up in our bedroom in the middle of the night claiming he had a nightmare about a little boy who had been hit on the head with a rock, kidnapped and tied up in a basement. Jack was pretty shaken up about the dream.

Jake and I told him to get into bed with us and tried to assure him that it was just a stupid dream and nothing to worry about.

But the following night Jack had the dream again and showed up in our bedroom once again in the middle of the night climbing into our bed telling us that the little boy needed help.

Jake and I continued to tell him that it was just a dream, was not real and to try to forget about it.

The next night I had the same dream. I dreamed that a little boy about five years old was playing in the front yard of a house. A white van pulled up in front of this house and some hippie dude with long black hair to his waist got out of the van with a big rock in his hand and hit the kid on the forehead with the rock knocking him out.

Then he picked the boy up and put him in the van and sped away.

That is when I saw this little boy still unconscious tied up in a wooden chair that I remembered using when I was in kindergarten. It was one of those wooden school chairs from the 1950s and '60s. The little boy was tied to the chair with a rope and his head was slumped over because he was unconscious.

I looked around and saw that he was in a basement made of brick instead of plaster.

I woke up not believing what I just dreamed. I knew instinctively that it was the same dream that Jack was having.

As I went about my day the following morning, I began to think to myself that it had to have been the power of suggestion into my subconscious mind from Jack telling me about his dream. And somehow my mind had grabbed the idea and I dreamed about it myself. There was no other explanation.

That night Jack showed up in our bedroom once again telling me that I had to hurry and get out of bed because we had to go into the living room and pray for the little boy.

Without giving it a second thought for some reason I got up out of bed and went into the kitchen with Jack. He told me that I had to get a pan from under the sink, put water in it and get one of his dad's white Army candles, set it in the water and light it. Then we could pray for the little boy and God would hear us.

I did what Jack said and removed the frying pan from the cupboard, put water in it and grabbed one of Jake's white Army candles and took everything into the living room. We set the pan on the floor in the middle of the living room, and I lit the candle. I sat there for a moment thinking to myself, "what do I do next?"

And then it came to me as I heard a voice from within say, "call on St. Peter," so I called on St. Peter out loud not knowing who he was.

Suddenly I looked up at the wall in front of me and watched it turn into a movie that was showing where this little boy was being kept. I could see the red brick in the basement and the little boy sitting in the wooden school chair tied up with a brown rope and his little head slumped over.

The next thing I saw was the room outside where the little boy was being kept. There was some sort of an altar in the middle of the room and there were a group of people around it maybe 13 or so, all naked having sex and snorting some white stuff up their noses. Every time they snorted the white stuff, their crown chakra would open and a black thing that looked like Casper the ghost entered in through that open hole on the top of their heads.

It would start out as a piece of darkness within their soul and then it would spread until the spirit had completely taken over. I somehow automatically knew that these black things were demons that wanted a body to live in.

Three other people: Susie, Raymond's girlfriend; her mother and that guy with the long dark hair whom I saw at the house the day Susie was moving out were also there.

I could not believe what I was seeing.

"Jack, are you seeing this? Are you seeing what I am seeing? Or have I gone crazy?"

"I see it too mom," he replied. Jack's facial expression was one of shock and wonder.

Neither one of us could believe what we were witnessing, it was like we were watching a movie on the living room wall. It seemed so unreal, yet you could feel the evil and the danger of what these people were playing with.

Jack and I continued to watch the movie before us. As I looked at Susie and her mother, I somehow knew that they were devil worshippers, and it made my stomach turn.

Next my attention focused on the white guy with the long dark hair. He walked away from the group and went to the room where the little boy was being kept. He opened the door to take him out of the room to put him on the altar to sacrifice him. That is when I saw a great force of light enter that room.

The minute this man encountered the light he moved backwards fast like a cockroach running up a wall.

He was screaming, "Ah! The burn, the burn."

And I realized as I watched the movie that calling on the Saint made the light of God burn him, because dark cannot co-exist with the light. Abruptly, the movie ended.

I could see my living room wall again, with black demon things stepping through it. It was as if they said where did that light come from that messed up our sacrifice and traced it back to me and Jack.

Suddenly I saw what looked like a bird man dressed in battle gear wearing what looked like a breastplate around his chest and groin area. He was on a white horse coming from a cloud in the sky and had a sword called justice and truth. I do not know how I knew the name of the sword, but I did.

Next, I saw a large Army of bird men behind him coming from the same cloud, they all wore the same armor and battle gear, and all carried a sword of justice and truth. They were all coming down from above in a perfect line each with big, beautiful wings coming out of their backs.

Their beauty took my breath away. They looked like cartoons to me, yet they were real. They flew into my living room and began fighting with the demons that were about to attack Jack and me.

Jack and I watched them fight and stab the demons with the sword of justice and truth which was filled with the light of God. The minute a sword went through a demon it would just disintegrate into nothing.

It was like "poof" you are not here anymore. It was the most bad-ass thing I had ever seen.

As I watched the Army of God in action, I knew without a doubt that these bad-ass warriors sat behind the throne of God. I also knew that these were the battle archangels that fought against the devil in heaven and won.

They were half-man, half-bird, that is why I called them birdmen, their beauty was breathtaking. And I knew I would never forget the exquisiteness of their wings and how they killed those demons without mercy while embodying angelic kindness and love for mankind at the same time.

After the Archangel Michael and his Army were finished killing all the demons, the living room wall was suddenly not there anymore, and we could see the street outside.

Jack and I saw two of the angels go outside our duplex.

One walked to one corner of our block and stood there, and the other walked to the opposite corner of our block and stood there. Then they both pulled out these weird looking trumpets that I had never seen before and began to blow them together in perfect musical unison.

Then suddenly the Army of God began to celebrate and as I watched them dance around in celebration, I realized that they celebrated after each battle they won.

It was one of the most beautiful things that I had seen in my life so far.

I looked at Jack and asked, "Are you seeing this?"

He said, "Yes, it's the angel's mom. It is the Archangel Michael and God's Army."

Then Jack said to me, "now the little boy's safe mom. Now I don't have to worry about him anymore."

I felt shocked, speechless and dumbfounded. I just could not believe what I had experienced with my son. How would I tell other people? Who would believe me? This was totally unbelievable. I tried to reason the experience out in my head. I thought maybe Jack and I had experienced some sort of shared delusion. I mean, there had to be an explanation for this.

Jack and I got up, went into the kitchen with the pan of water and candle, and put everything away. Then Jack got into bed with me, and Jake and we fell asleep.

CHAPTER 171

When I got up the next morning to make breakfast for the kids and drink my coffee, I still could not believe what had happened in the middle of the night.

I told Jake before he left for work that morning about the experience. He listened to me and Jack and when we finished said he believed us. I knew that when he left for work that morning, he was concerned about us.

I attempted to put the whole thing out of my mind and continue with my life. I mean, after all, even if it were real there was nothing that I could do about it. I did not even know who this little boy was or if he even existed.

Four days later on a Saturday around 1:30 p.m. Jake and I were sitting at the kitchen table with Jack and Lucy eating lunch when we heard a knock at the back door. I thought it was strange that someone would be knocking on my back door instead of the front door.

I got up from the table and opened the door, the first thing I saw was the little boy from my dream standing there at my threshold with a group of people. There was another little boy with him who looked close in age but older. There was a priest, a middle-aged woman and a sheriff in full uniform along with a lady who said she was a social worker from the Child Protection Agency.

At that point, Jake got up from the table and stood next to me. To my shock and surprise the little boy approached me and began hugging me and would not let go.

The sheriff explained that the little boy, now hugging my hips. Had insisted upon being brought here to my house.

Then the older woman said, "I'm his grandmother and he claims that you saved him."

The sheriff asked me if I knew anything about his kidnapping. I told him that I had nothing to do with his kidnapping.

"I had a dream about him, and I prayed for God's saint to save him, that's all I know. I am shocked that this kid is real." I said in wonder.

The sheriff said that the little boy had been playing in his grandmas' front yard with his brother here when, a white van drove up, and a man got out and hit him on the head with a rock, then put him in the van and took off with him.

It turns out that his mother had formerly been a member of a Satanic cult. But now she had broken away from the cult and was currently in rehab trying to kick a crank habit. "Grandma was watching her two boys while she was away getting herself together," The sheriff said.

He went on to tell me that a real Satanic cult will not allow you to leave once you have joined and become a member. So, when she decided to leave the cult, they wanted her younger son in return. He went on to say that they had a whole department that handled satanic crimes like this, and the people involved had been arrested.

The whole thing was unbelievable, yet here was this little boy hugging me for dear life not wanting to let go. He would look up at me periodically and try to speak, but his words were all jumbled.

I asked his grandmother what was wrong with his speech? The social worker from the Child Protective Service told me that little David had been traumatized by the experience that he had been through, and his speech had been temporarily affected. I thought back to my sister Stephanie and Dennis's shooting and understood.

Meanwhile, the little boy was still holding on to me for dear life like I was the only safe place in the world he could run to. The older boy looked at his grandmother and said, "Can we spend the night please, please, let us spend the night with the Army man!"

"What a strange request," I thought, "these people did not even know me."

Then it got stranger when, to my surprise, his grandmother said yes. Then she told Jake, "Thank you for the Ranger berets you gave them.

I asked the boy his name and he said his name was Kurt and he wanted to spend the night so he could look at Jake's Army gear.

It turned out that even though we did not know these two boys, they knew us. Kurt told me that they took the berets from our car.

Jake had been in the habit of coming home from work at the base and leaving his black Ranger beret on the passenger's seat in the car. We hardly ever locked our car, and Jake just though he had misplaced them.

We learned that these two little boys lived two blocks away from us with their mother and would ride their bicycles past our house in the afternoons. They had spotted Jake many times, had idolized him from afar and wanted to be a soldier like him. They had taken the berets and lied to their grandmother telling her that Jake had given them to the two of them.

The whole thing was strange. Who was I to be saying a prayer for some little boy I did not even know? Why would that prayer work to free him and how did he know that I was the one who prayed?

I asked little David that question. That is when he said, "I was asleep when I saw you praying for me. Then the bad man had to let me go.

Still shocked after the little boy's grandmother had left him and his brother in our care for the night, I offered them some lunch. After they ate, I sat on my back porch and watched them play with Jack in our backyard.

At dinner time the little boy hung out in the kitchen with me and watched me prepare dinner. After we ate, we watched some television and Jake showed the boys his Army uniforms and all his military equipment. Kurt was beside himself with joy when Jake let him put his feet inside Jake's jungle boots. Both boys idolized Jake like he was their own personal G.I. Joe.

At bedtime I put the two boys in Jack's room with him in sleeping bags. Jake gave them each a military glow light stick. And Jake told them all about jungle survival school and how he had to shoot a monkey out of a tree just to eat. The boys were in heaven as they listened with rapt wonder in their eyes.

The following morning, right after breakfast, their grandmother arrived to pick them up as she promised.

The boys hugged Jake goodbye and as little David hugged me, I heard him mumble "thank you."

I knew as I watched them drive away that I would never see those boys again because according to their grandmother they were moving, but I knew in my heart that they were now going to be okay.

CHAPTER 172

A week later I started noticing various items moving about my house. At first, I thought I was imagining things, but one morning I was in the kitchen making breakfast and I saw the coffee pot move by itself on the counter.

Then I started seeing strange people who looked as though they had no soul walk past my home. Just the feel of them made a shiver go down my spine and a few of them had wolf dogs that looked as if their souls were gone, as well.

I was beginning to get scared shitless when my children started waking up in the middle of the night claiming that a monster with red eyes was in their closet.

They started sleeping with us every night.

Everyone in the house was seeing paranormal activity except Jake. It seemed as if Jake was immune to what we were experiencing. The feeling in the house was something else was there besides us. And whatever the hell it was, it was not good.

The most valuable thing in our lives, which was our happiness and peace of mind, had turned into fear. I was ready to pack up everything and move home to Los Angeles just to get away from the unknown.

At this point Jake was drawing every night after work and cranking out some beautiful wildlife pencil drawings that looked like photographs. Our neighbor Phil was a distributor of posters, postcards and antique Indian artifacts. He saw Jake's artwork and fell in love with a large size drawing of a cougar.

Phil invited us to dinner with the kids to discuss buying the picture and the distribution rights for $800. We went to his house one evening with the kids for dinner to discuss the deal.

I told him about the paranormal experiences that I was having in my house and how I was thinking of moving with the children to Los Angeles to escape it.

Phil said that he knew someone who could help me. He called a woman on the phone who played something called a prayer flute.

As he handed me the telephone receiver, I thought to myself how crazy this was as I explained to her what was happening.

She told me that she would play her prayer flute over the phone. My first thought was, what in the hell is this woman talking about? However, the minute she started playing the flute I suddenly fell to my knees.

It was as if something had overtaken me, and I was zoning out of reality and rapidly leaving my body. I felt myself ascending upward like a bullet shooting out of a gun.

As I ascended upward my whole life on Earth, who I was, my husband and children, any connection to my life on Earth peeled away from me like an onion until I was just me in my rawest form, my original form which was spirit.

Within the blink of an eye, I was in time and space, literally floating but with no human body. It all seemed fine and natural as if I had always been this way and I was finally really me again. The acting role and storyline I had been playing on Earth was now nonexistent.

I was now constantly aware of everything around me, while all my natural senses were now coming back to me.

The different planets and the fact that each planet was a creation like Earth, birthed out as a seed that grew and evolved naturally, each in its own course of time, became a natural known fact to me.

As if I had always known this as fact to be true.

I could sense that each created planet had its own life form just like Earth. Even if that planet looked to be inhabitable from the surface to support one it still had a life form in some state of evolvement. Each life form was different but created by the same source as if I had known this forever yet had somehow temporarily forgotten that fact, but now remembered.

In my mind's eye the Red Planet was a young planet in its evolutionary stages and had fire on the surface, but underneath the layers on the surface there was a life form in a young almost infantile state. It was microscopic in its stage of growth, yet it was a form of life like an embryo forming in the womb.

Then I sensed another place, not far from Earth this place was old, even older than the Red Planet and I could feel all the souls that had lived on Earth there. I could literally feel the consciousness of more souls than I could count.

And I thought: I remember that place, my waterfall and black panther live there. I also knew that this place was where I remembered coming from. This was the place I knew truly as my home. The place that looked like the world of life and death but was better because everything was alive there and in a state of its highest perfection.

All the animals, plants and people lived in harmony as they communicated telepathically instead of using words. In this place all you had to do was think a thought like, I want to go swimming at the beach, and you were there. There was no death or sickness there or hatred or other negative thoughts, energy or emotions. As I remembered this, I realized that not only was this my true reality but being in the world of life and death was just a temporary situation like you are a soul going to sleep and acting out a play in your dreams. Death was just a necessary tool to help you wake up from that dream.

Next, I begin to feel a big strong presence driving me closer to it. And the closer I got to it the more loved and peaceful I felt and the more I felt like my true self. My soul had never felt this free and peaceful before on Earth. My heart was so full of joy words cannot describe it. Suddenly I realized that this was God, this was the source from which I had come. God was this infinite intelligence that was massive.

I was standing before the spirit of God completely naked; stripped down to my very soul as it drew me near. God was not a man or a woman, but God was ancient, timeless, and an infinite intelligence that is beyond comprehension to most humans on Earth.

I could see that every soul had knowledge of these facts, but the memory of all this was wiped away when they came through the birth canal to Earth. I realized that every planet, star, soul, everything was within God and had been created by this one source. It was like the song, "He's Got the Whole World in His Hands."

Everything and every soul is within God; not separate from God. This "I Am." Is no male or female, no shape or form, just "I Am." And I thought to myself, "people on Earth kill and hate one another over a false conception of what made them. What a waste of time."

I suddenly saw a beach with grains of sand upon it, too many to count. These grains of sand were souls, they were all the souls that "I Am" created.

The individual souls were separate from "I Am" but they were not, and they always came back to where they originated from. It was an "oh yeah, I remember that" moment.

Then I saw my house has many mansions. It started with a place called the throne room that looked like it was made of a type of stone that I had never seen on Earth before. The holy of holy's, I heard "I Am's" voice say.

I saw the throne, but no man sat upon it, the presence of "I Am" filled the seat of the throne and the entire room. I saw baby angels with wings flying around the throne, and even though they were small they were powerful.

Next, I saw a long hallway made of the same stone, and as I went down the hallway, I knew that I was in a huge house with many rooms and levels, too many for me to count. I entered a room that had a huge choir in it, they were all angels in robes with sounds and instruments of music built from within them. And the sound of music that came from them was unlike anything I have ever heard on Earth. It was as if each note was filled with the light of God, and nothing but love and joy came from that music.

Then suddenly I was back in the long hallway again, and I entered a room. In this room I saw souls that we call "Saints." These souls were numerous and each one was dressed in a white robe that tied with a rope around their waist. And on their feet each one was wearing a pair of black leather sandals. The sandals were real primitive looking, they had two leather straps going across the foot connecting to the bottom of the sandal. One was near the toe area and the other near the ankle.

Every soul in this room was crying in joy and anticipation of coming to Earth to shed their blood for Christ. Some of them had already done this, and some were waiting for the honor. Then I was back in the hallway again, and I saw a room filled with what I call "Master Souls." I call them this because these were the souls that had already mastered Earth and were only sent to Earth to make great change, history making change.

Souls like Martin Luther King Jr., Barack Obama, Gandhi, Muhammad were in this place as great teachers and leaders.

I found myself once again in the hallway, and I entered a room that held every word, every thought, every action and event, and every lifetime each soul had lived. I knew it was a hall of records. I then saw a stone surface which looked like a screen, I had never seen anything like it on Earth. I saw my face come on the screen, then I saw a rush of lifetimes with me wearing different faces, male and female, on that screen.

It finally stopped at a female who looked Egyptian. I realized it was me. I remembered being this person long ago. I remembered being one of 25 children in Egypt.

My father worshipped "The Sun King" and was a rich officer. We lived within the walled community surrounding the palace. Only the rich lived within these walls. The poor lived outside the wall and had their communities.

Next the face of a man appeared before me on the screen, and once again I recognized it as myself. I was a skinny, deckhand on a cargo ship that transported cargo like gold, silver and supplies for merchants.

We were far out at sea on a regular shipping route that lots of ships used regularly. I was happily working on the deck when our ship was attacked and robbed for its cargo, which was gold that day. I saw myself fighting with a sword then getting stabbed in the abdomen. As a sword went through me, I was pushed overboard into shark infested waters. The sharks were in a feeding frenzy already with the bodies that had gone in before me.

I went in the water feet first and was still alive when I felt them begin feeding on my body feet first. Then I was floating above our ship, watching the rest of the battle as everyone on board was killed. Afterwards, I watched the men that attacked us load all our cargo onto their ship and sail away after setting our ship on fire.

Suddenly, I was in time and space again. My soul was so flooded with joy that I begin to move my hands as if doing sign language, but in a dance. My spirit began to sway in a dance of worship before what made me.

All I wanted to do was dance before "I Am" in an expression of the inner joy I felt, and I never wanted to leave its presence again because I had everything I needed right here.

As I danced before "I Am" I had no fear. I had confidence that I was not only safe, but I truly felt and knew in that moment that I was its creation. I could ask this source from which I came anything, and it would hear me because I was an extension of it.

Then immediately I felt myself leaving that presence like being sucked back into a vacuum, and I did not want to go. I wanted to stay in the presence of "I Am" and never leave again. But I was falling back down into my body fast.

CHAPTER 173

The next thing I knew I was back in Phil's living room with my concerned husband and two children at my side. They thought that I had fainted with the telephone receiver on the floor next to me and the lady still on the other end.

I noticed I felt different inside and no longer afraid of the coffee pot moving inside my house. I felt like I could face anything without fear, but most of all I knew that "I Am" was real and that it was with me.

And I wondered why me? What was so special about me? Had this happened to other people?

I began to tell Jake, Phil and the lady on the phone what I had just experienced and the things I saw.

Jake looked at me not knowing how to respond to the story I had just told them.

To Phil it did not seem so extraordinary. He, along with the lady on the phone, told me that I had just been in the presence of God. Although I already knew this, it was nice to know that someone else knew it as well.

But why? I asked.

We sat down to dinner as planned and when we all returned home, I was still no longer afraid. Immediately after that event not only did, I feel differently, but I had a very vivid, strange dream that night.

I dreamed that I was looking at a lot of different roads in life going in different directions, but all intertwining. There were people coming and going on those roads, from every walk of life. I saw some were dishonest, while others were honest and kindhearted. The question was: which road did I want to follow?

Then the next thing I knew I was at an old brick well. Standing next to me was an old, black man with short, brown hair turning gray, wearing a minister's robe. I knew instinctively that he was a master minister from "I Am."

This man was immune to sin and temptation since he had already mastered it and had been sent here to save as many souls as possible.

The old man told me to look down into the water in the well and he looked down with me, and as we looked at the water together, I could see the different roads in life again intertwining but also going in different directions.

As I stood there next to the old man, I heard the voice of "I Am" say, "I am sending him to show you what road to take in your life." Then the dream ended.

When I awoke the following morning, I felt different; brand new and starting all over again in life. I felt like a newborn baby starting out in the world again fresh, as if everything bad from the past had been washed away.

I also noticed that when I went to the supermarket that afternoon, as I stood in line to pay for my groceries, there was a man standing in front of me with a 12-pack of Budweiser beer in his hand. I knew somehow that this man was going to go home, sit on the sofa, turn on the television set to the ball game and start drinking those beers. And after he had finished that 12-pack, he was going to slap his wife around a little bit, which I thought is the same as abusing and beating up your wife.

He was also prone to get into the occasional bar fight if he was shit-faced enough. I could also tell something was wrong with him emotionally that made him drink and lash out physically at his wife. It had something to do with childhood physical abuse he had suffered from his father, being told repeatedly what a worthless piece of shit he was, while getting his butt kicked at least three times a week by his drunken father.

This totally cemented his future of inflicting pain on women. In fact, he had purposely chosen a woman with a submissive personality; one who reminded him of his mother who was no stranger to his father's fist.

I realized as I stood there that all of this was a bitter pill to swallow as a child and I immediately understood why this man was the way he was at that very moment and felt compassion for him.

It was revealed to me that if he joined Alcoholics Anonymous, along with weekly visits to a good psychiatrist, that he might have a decent chance of becoming a different person. Otherwise, he was going to continue working in construction, coming home to the trailer park, opening a beer in front of the television set, watching NASCAR, while treating his wife badly to boost his own self-esteem.

All this information ran through my mind in a matter of seconds. It was as if I were seeing this man through "I Am's'" eyes. I saw the way he truly was deep down inside, and what he would do that afternoon and why.

I also saw the path he could take to get free from his negative behavior patterns.

This experience, the one with the little boy, and the one where I was in the presence of "I Am," was strange and extraordinary. I wondered if I had lost my mind. There were plenty of crazy people in the world who really believed that they saw "I Am," when in fact, it was a sign of mental illness.

I truly wondered if I were in the beginning stages of schizophrenia or something. I mean, who the hell sees the Army of God fighting demons in real life?

That is the type of stuff you see in movies and not real life. At that thought, I became slightly concerned about my mental state. The only thing that held me in check was the fact that the little boys showed up at my doorstep with a police officer who told us that whole situation was real.

I was not ready to go insane at my age, and I looked up toward the sky and told "I Am" that.

Meanwhile, at the grocery store, I paid for my items and was driving home, when I decided that I had to find a minister or someone with knowledge of these things to explain to me what was going on and why it was happening to me.

I had questions and needed answers. I really needed to understand why I was with "I Am" at Phil's house. The only people whom I had ever heard of this happening to were in Bible stories I had heard in Sunday school as a child, or people who had died and come back.

But the thing that struck me were my memories of the "Ten Commandments" movie by Cecile B. DeMille. Especially the part where Moses climbs the mountain and "I Am" talks to him from the burning bush, and he comes down from the mountain a different man. And Abraham came to mind, as just some normal man going about his business and starts hearing "I Am's" voice, Noah who was told to build the Ark, as well as Adam and Eve who heard the voice of "I Am," whom I saw in the movie theater with my father and sisters as a child.

In the movie, "I Am" talked to these people and walked with them in spirit while they lived naked in the Garden of Eden. I tried to tell myself that even though this happened to people who lived a long time ago, that it had happened to someone else besides me.

Also, it had happened to more than one person, so that made me feel slightly less insane.

I decided that I did not want cult members knowing where I lived after seeing demons attempting to step through my living room wall, and strange people walking past my house who seemed to be possessed.

I knew that the Archangel Michael and his Army had fought for us, but I decided it was time to find another place to live.

CHAPTER 174

A t this point I figured our little duplex held a bad memory and I wanted out.

I began looking for another place for us to live and within weeks I found a two-story house with three bedrooms that had been built at the turn of the century. I just loved Victorian homes and I was excited because this place was not only huge with a big backyard and full basement, but it was also affordable.

It had three floors: the main floor had a living room, dining room, bathroom and kitchen. By the front door was a beautiful old antique wooden staircase that led to the three bedrooms upstairs. There was also a giant-sized front porch.

Lots of kids were running around in the neighborhood playing ball or riding bicycles. The neighborhood looked very family-oriented.

Happily, we moved into this house that had a wonderful landlord, an older black woman named Miss Tisdale who owned the house for over 25 years and had once lived in it with her deceased husband and three children.

Unfortunately, there was also a biker house next-door and that was the only thing I was unhappy about because I figured that bikers engaged in, parties, drugs, drinking and noise.

And I was right. During our first week living there, the bikers had at least four parties. Through the window you could see there was a bar set up instead of furniture in the living room.

There was an older black lady named Margie who lived across the street from us with her husband and mother. I liked talking with them while I watched my kids playing outside.

One Saturday afternoon I told Margie about the little boy who had been kidnapped, the angels, and my experience of being in the presence of "I Am" and remembering who I was.

I asked her if she had any knowledge about that kind of stuff?

She suggested that I see Pastor Rainey. She told me that he was the minister of Ebenezer Baptist Church and that he could explain everything to me.

She said, "Pastor Rainey knows that bible inside and out and he can explain to you why you were seeing angels and give you some insight into what happened to you."

Ms. Margie wrote down the address of the church and told me to show up there at 9 the next morning which was Sunday.

The following morning, I got up, put on a dress out of respect for the church and drove there. When I saw the building, I was surprised. It was just a tiny little white building that looked like a business from the outside. The only thing that let you know that it was really a church was it had a sign with big broad letters on the front of the building that read, "Ebenezer Baptist Church."

I parked, walked to the church, opened the door and was shocked even further. Instead of there being a big congregation, the place looked like an empty room filled with chairs. I saw maybe 11 people sitting in that church including the minister.

As I stood there the minister looked at me and said, "welcome to Ebenezer Baptist Church, please have a seat."

I sat down thinking to myself, "What the hell have I gotten myself into?"

As I sat there, I felt like I was a little girl again back at my grandfather's church in South Central Los Angeles. Instead of an older black guy beating slowly on a drum, there was a young black guy sitting at the organ. In fact, everyone in the church was black. I also felt underdressed in my white mini skirt suit.

I totally thought I was the shit when I put it on that morning because my suit had shoulder pads like Joan Collins on the Dynasty TV show. Everyone else in the place was dressed extremely conservatively.

As I sat there and watched the minister as he spoke, I realized that this minister was the same man I had dreamt about: the man at the well in the dream when "I Am" told me it was sending this man to show me which road to take in life.

I sat there amazed and thought to myself, that dream was real and not random; it really was a message from "I Am." I thought, I am supposed to be here with this old man listening to him preaching about being faithful to God in your heart and how you will be rewarded afterwards with something called the crown of life.

He preached a good sermon, and even though his church was little and only had 11 members beside myself sitting in there, he reminded me of Grandfather Johnson who had died five years earlier of a diabetes-related heart attack and I missed him.

After Pastor Rainey finished preaching, everyone picked up a hymn book which was sitting next to each seat. We were instructed to turn to page 148 and sing a song called, "In the Garden." I sang along reading the words from the hymnal remembering the song from when I was a little girl in my grandfather's church.

After singing the song, we all bowed our heads in prayer and then the service was over. Immediately everyone approached me happy and excited to meet me.

I thought to myself "It's not shocking that they're happy and excited to meet me because I'm the only unknown person who walked through those doors today."

I quickly found out that three of the people greeting me were the pastor's family: his wife and two sons. They quickly introduced themselves, welcomed me to the church and gave me a hug. One of his sons Paul seemed to be mentally disabled, I did not know what was wrong with him, but it did not matter. I just accepted him immediately for the happy outgoing guy that he was. He was also the one who played the keyboards during the church service, and he reminded me of Stevie Wonder because anyone who heard him play could tell that he was a musical genius, even if he was disabled.

The preacher introduced himself as Pastor Sam Rainey and asked how I heard about his church.

I told him that my neighbor across the street suggested that I come see him because of some experiences I had.

"I have questions," I told him. "And she said that you're the man with the answers."

He led me over to a chair and told me to sit down as he took a seat next to me, "Start from the beginning." He said.

"Well, first, I had a dream about you and I'm positive it was you in the dream. You were a minister in my dream, and I heard the voice of "I Am" tell me that you will help me choose the correct direction in life." I told him.

Pastor Rainey looked at me and started laughing, more like chuckling to himself, and asked, "God told you that?"

"Yeah" I said.

"And how do you know it was God talking to you?" He asked amused.

"Because I recognize the voice and I was in the presence of "I Am" not too long ago," I said. "That's what I wanted to talk to you about, weird stuff has been happening since I was in the presence of "I Am.""

"Well, tell me what's been happening," he said.

I told him about dinner at Pete's house and how the lady played a prayer flute for me over the telephone; how I had fallen onto my knees and left my body in front of my husband and two children. I told him everything that I saw, everything that had happened, I even told him about the little boy and the police showing up at my back door. I also told him about seeing the angels with my son.

"The Army of 'I Am' is something to behold." I added.

And then I told him about how after I had been in the presence of "I Am" I could tell what people were thinking, and I knew what was wrong with them inside.

"Not everyone, just some people. I'm kind of learning how to control it by not concentrating on the people around me."

I told Pastor Rainey everything that I could think of; before I knew it an hour had passed and everyone in his family was sitting in a chair patiently waiting for us to finish.

"I'm going to pray for you, and I want you to come back next Sunday, so we can talk some more about it then," Pastor Rainey said.

I agreed and then he took my hands in his, closed his eyes and began praying for me. He asked God to protect me and my entire family and give me peace of mind, insight and understanding of all the things I was experiencing. He also asked "I Am" to cover me, and my entire household and my finances with the precious blood of Jesus.

I had never heard anyone pray the way that Pastor Rainey did. Before leaving I told everyone in his family goodbye with a promise to return the following Sunday.

As I drove home that afternoon, I thought to myself how Pastor Rainey was the most usual man I had ever met.

After I had returned home and changed my clothes, I told Jake about the church and about Pastor Rainey and the dream I had before I ever met him.

Jake was a little blown away by the whole thing. The little boy, me being in the presence of "I Am," and now dreaming about an old man who is supposed to show me what direction to go in life and then meeting him.

It was kind of a jaw-dropping situation for us both, but I felt good about it. I felt as if I were truly supposed to meet this man who would teach me things, but what things I did not know. What I did know was I had to get answers to my questions, and I certainly had many questions, and Pastor Rainey was going to give me the answers.

I returned to the church the following Sunday morning, and as I listened to Pastor Rainey preach from an old wooden pulpit, I began to realize that what he was talking about made a lot of sense.

It was not a boring dry lecture about the Bible; this man was preaching about cleaning out your soul and being the best person that you could be which he called, "shining with the light of God," and how putting all your trust in the power of God was one of the most powerful things that you could do in the world.

After the service, I approached Pastor Rainey and asked him if he had prayed and asked 'I Am" what was going on with me. He took me into a little room in the back of the church that he called his prayer and counseling room. He sat me down and told me that I had the devil running after me. "And you have had a spiritual awakening." "Some people call it being born again." He said.

"Why me? What the hell have I ever done to the devil?" "And why would I be chosen for a spiritual awakening?"

Pastor Rainey told me that when I prayed for the little boy, I brought light into the situation which made the darkness follow the source of that light.

"What you did was pray an intercessory prayer for that boy." He informed me.

"What's an intercessory prayer?" I asked.

He told me that intercessory prayer was when you prayed for someone when they were unable to pray for themselves. That you were standing in the gap for them before God.

"When I prayed for you, the answer I got was that you have a gift to intercede for other souls by praying for them." He told me.

"Oh, that's funny" I said, "Because I really don't pray, I thought you had to be a really religious person and pray every day and attend church on a regular basis to do something like that?" "I just talk to "I Am" every day I am not a religious person."

That is when Pastor Rainey looked at me and said, "God is no respecter of persons."

"What does that mean?" I asked.

"It means that God chooses who he wants to choose, and sometimes it's not the person that you would expect it to be." Pastor Rainey explained that when I prayed for that little boy to be protected from the cult by calling on the Saint, that the devil turned around and traced it back to me. "Now you're a threat to the kingdom of hell, and the enemy will do anything to stop you from praying for other people." He finished.

None of this mess sounded good to me and I still did not understand why "I Am" would choose me to pray for someone. I mean who the hell was I? I cussed like a sailor, and I had a long list of personality defects that I was working on.

"You and your son saw the Archangel Michael riding in on his horse along with his Army to protect you and your home that night." God himself showed you that he had this. I am here to teach you the truth and how to use it to protect yourself every single day of your life." He told me.

"Protect myself how?" I asked.

"I'm going to teach you the word and how to fight for yourself and how to master spiritual warfare."

"What's spiritual warfare?" I asked.

That is when he picked up his Bible and turned to a page and began reading out loud.

"Ephesians 6:12 thru 6:13. 'For we wrestle not against flesh and blood, but against principalities, against powers, against the rulers the darkness of this world, against spiritual wickedness in high places. Wherefore take unto you the whole armor of God, that ye may be able to withstand in the evil day, and having done all, to stand.'" He quoted.

Pastor Rainey put the Bible down and looked at me.

I looked back at him and asked, "What's a principality?"

"It's a higher-level demon, an angel gone bad, and it will do anything to stop you from helping other people. It's time for you to realize that God is real, and you have a decision to make on which side you're going to be fighting on."

Then he proceeded to tell me what a bright future I had ahead of me and how I was going to help other people find their way in life.

I told him that was insane, "Dude, how am I going to help other people when I can barely help myself?" I depend on "I Am" for everything, so how am I going to help other people?

"That's why I'm here, to teach you how." He said.

"Okay, what do I have to do first?" I asked.

"Well, you can start out by showing up at choir rehearsal tomorrow night." He said.

"But I'm not in the choir and you only have 11 people in your church." I said.

"Don't you worry about that; if you count yourself that makes it 12 choir members. That is why we need you in the choir. Besides, it is therapeutic to the soul to sing to God. Also, on Friday nights, I want you to attend Bible study at my home with me and my family." He told me.

"I don't even own a Bible," I said.

That is when he reached over to the side of him where he had a box filled with Bibles and handed one to me. "Well, you've got one now." He said.

I drove home that night thinking to myself damn, I have to sing in the choir and go to Bible study? I was thinking to myself I do not mind showing up at the church on Sunday mornings, but choir rehearsal and Bible study every week, that was going to cut into my schedule at home with Jake and the kids.

And what if it was boring? I hated being bored. Then a voice inside me told me to stop complaining and go.

The following night I showed up at Ebenezer Baptist Church for my first choir rehearsal. The songs were not so bad, and one of the songs I really liked a lot was called "In the Garden" I liked it because the lyrics said, "I come to the garden alone, while the dew is still on the roses, and He walks with me and He talks with me, and He tells me I am His own."

For some reason, that really hit home with me, because that was the relationship I had always had with "I Am." I asked "I Am" for everything under the sun even my underwear. I talked to it like a normal person, like I was talking to a friend or my dad. Sometimes I got an answer and sometimes I did not.

Friday night I showed up. I was pissed off that it was raining, and I had to drive in it.

As I walked into Pastor Rainey's home, I found it to be nice and comfortable. His wife April, who preferred to be called "Mother Rainey," had coffee and cookies set up at the table for us to eat and drink while we had Bible Study.

When Pastor Randy said we are going to start at the very beginning of the New Testament, I felt that he was doing this just for me. Because I knew everyone in that room knew the Bible inside and out except me.

As the months passed, I went to church, Bible study, choir rehearsal and sang with the choir on Sunday mornings in that tiny church. I began to grow closer to Pastor Rainey and his family as he taught me spiritual lessons. Paul, their son who played the piano, was one of the coolest people I have ever met. Every time I talked with him, I felt as if I were speaking with an innocent 14-year-old child. Except the child was a grown man and a total prodigy on the piano and organ. He may have been handicapped but he had a big happy jolly soul. I would watch Paul play and think to myself, I bet this boy played in heaven.

There was also Pastor Rainey's other son Carlo, who was closer to my age and became my friend. Pastor Rainey had appointed him the duty of being the church choir director. Carlo and his mother both had beautiful singing voices.

Soon Pastor Rainey not only had me attending his church but also his home church, Mount Tabor Baptist Church. The church had a huge choir with at least 200 choir members. Mother Rainey and Carlo were members of that choir as well, and Paul played the organ for that church too.

So at least four nights a week I was involved in church activities. I had not shown this much dedication since I was a kid going to the Church of Religious Science with Daddy.

It was not so bad since I had never studied the Bible before, and Pastor Rainey was a good teacher. He taught me things such as every time I prayed with faith mountains moved. And that my lifelong habit of talking to "I Am" was a form of prayer.

I started applying the knowledge he was feeding me to my life and the paranormal activity happening in my life. No more moving objects or strange dreams, I was rebuking and verbally applying the blood of Jesus against any dark forces that could possibly be around me. And I started playing the Christian radio station as background music 24 hours a day in my home. I figured I could chase whatever it was that had moved objects in my home away with the music.

Within a month I knew how to protect my home and my family from any negative forces coming into it. And all negative activity stopped.

Three months later Pastor Rainey had my children in church with me and in Bible study. And he baptized both of them. He also got me involved with the March for Jesus organization which was a fun experience because I had a job helping with the Port-a-Potties. And marching through the streets of Seattle with hundreds of Christians from different religious faiths and churches was a great experience.

The only thing we all had in common was we all believed in Jesus Christ. We all sang as one choir as we marched together through the streets of Seattle. I could see the light of "I Am" that day as we all marched. I also knew that the angels were there marching and singing with us.

Within six months, since Jake refused to go to church, Pastor Rainey had somehow managed to become friends with him outside of church. Every time he showed up to pick me up with the kids, he would come early enough to spend time talking to Jake, next thing I knew the two of them were fishing together on a regular basis.

I asked Pastor Randy why he was fishing with Jake all the time. That is when he told me with a grin "I'm just fishing for souls to save the best way I can."

I soon realized that Pastor Rainey was helping Jake overcome his inner anger over his military disabilities.

Jake was getting out of the military and had been classified as a disabled veteran because he had so much shrapnel in his ankles that he was now walking with a limp in constant pain. He could no longer run 25 miles with the rucksack on his back and that pissed him off. Also, because of both the amount of shrapnel and how it was scattered, surgery could not remove it.

I knew that it bothered him all the time now, but he never complained or allowed it to take over his life. He also had PTSD in the form of a problem with his vocal cords that affected his speech. Instead of acting out in a negative sense, the PTSD affected his vocal cords.

Sad thing was, he refused to speak about any of the missions he had been on. He kept saying that he signed paperwork that required him not to speak about the missions. Jake had been assigned to the supply room for his last few months in the military, working as the supply sergeant for his unit.

The first sergeant of his company was a black guy who was pissed off at him for being married to a black woman. He made it a point to treat Jake badly every day at work because he did not believe in inter-racial marriages.

"People are crazy" I told him, "Don't pay any attention to the guy. You are getting out of the Army soon, so you will not have to deal with his crazy butt anymore. You'll be looking for a civilian job and getting ready to go to college," I told him.

Jake had veteran's benefits which made him eligible to attend college for free it was called the Vocational Rehabilitation Program.

We decided to move out of our big old house and into a place with cheaper rent to prepare for any extra college expenses that Jake might incur.

There was a beautiful antique two-bedroom apartment across the street from a huge park near downtown Tacoma. As a teenager, I had wanted to live in an old brownstone apartment building, so this was a dream come true.

I also planned on getting a job to help out financially now that Lucy was in school full time. Jake and I had everything planned out. I would work him through school and when he graduated, he would make tons of money designing video games and doing 3-D modeling with his new multimedia degree. That was our plan.

He had decided to go to a college called the Seattle Art Institute in downtown Seattle. I did not want him to go to the Art Institute; instead, I wanted him to go to the University of Washington. Even though I knew the Seattle Art Institute was a good school, I knew somehow that getting a degree from Washington State University would work out better for Jake in the long run.

Jake did not listen to me and chose to go to the Art Institute.

After we settled into our new apartment, I got permission from the owners to begin fixing it up by sanding down the hardwood floors myself and putting a fresh coat of polyurethane on them. I also put a coat of fresh paint on the walls and the ceiling, which had water stains on it.

And the best part was I talked the owners into deducting the money I spent on supplies off my rent since I was improving their real estate investment.

Then I began looking for a job in the newspaper. I found an ad for a law clerk in Seattle which was only a 20-minute ride from Tacoma on the freeway.

I called the number and made an appointment for an interview the following week.

When I arrived at the law firm the receptionist offered me a cup of coffee and motioned me to sit down on the sofa in the reception area.

As I sat there, I heard "I Am's" voice saying, "this is the job I'm giving you." It was profound because I knew without a doubt that it was "I Am" speaking to me. So, in thought I replied, "thank you."

Shortly after, Marlene a 30-something year old blonde-haired woman invited me into her office. She had an attractive office overlooking the Puget Sound with immense windows and perfect ocean views.

Marlene asked many questions about the law firm I had worked for in Los Angeles and was happy that I had gained mail room knowledge at my last firm.

After I answered all her questions, she told me that she was going to take a chance on me and hire me even if my resume did not have tons of legal experience. She told me that I was skilled enough to do the job I was applying for which was assisting the paralegals and the attorneys, along with taking care of the mail room and filing new legal documents into their case folders.

The salary was high with full medical benefits for me and my family.

I liked Marlene and could tell that she liked me too. She told me how she was a single mother struggling to raise two daughters by herself, and how impressed she was that I was honest enough to tell her that I wanted the job so that I could support my husband and children while my husband was in college full-time.

After my interview I walked out of that building on cloud 9. I could not believe I had just been hired by Barnard Jamison and Barnard, Attorneys at Law. I may have been hired to do office back-up work and run the mail room, but it was a decent high-paying job with health insurance, and I could support my family. I could hardly wait to tell Pastor Rainey the good news.

I looked up at the sky as I stood there at the bus stop and thanked "I Am" for giving me a decent job. "I Am" really had my back; not only did I feel it, but I knew it.

Only thing was, I often wondered why me? What was so different or special about me that "I Am" would pay attention to me and help me? I thought about that all the way back to the Tacoma Park and ride on the bus ride.

The state of Washington was a very environmentally conscious state. There was no trash or graffiti on the streets of Seattle, and just about everyone who lived there did their part to keep it that way. I once attempted to leave a soda pop can on the side of a building in downtown Seattle when a woman from across the street yelled at me to pick it up.

"There's a trashcan on the corner. We must have respect for the planet and take care of it," she yelled.

That was the last time I ever did that because I knew she was right. Because of this attitude a lot of people commuted by bus or carpooled.

By the time I got to my car at the park-and-ride I could hardly wait to get home and tell Jake and the kids about my new job.

We had a few things to celebrate, Jakes parents called us on the phone apologizing for not supporting our relationship and now wanted a relationship with us and their grandchildren. I was going to make a big pot of spaghetti to celebrate that and my new job. But the kids were not interested. They only cared about playing Super Mario Brothers on television and fighting if the other one did not die fast enough.

Jake and I made the spaghetti together in the kitchen while listening to Elton John. We talked about how everything was working out for us. How we loved our little two-bedroom apartment with the affordable rent that overlooked a lush green park across the street with a duck pond and running path.

It also had a swimming area with a little cafeteria attached to it for the kids, as well as lots of swings and slides in different sizes. All my kids had to do was run across the street and they were right there at the park. Jake and I liked that. I also liked the fact that I could run two miles a day on the running path near the duck pond.

Jake had just started school and liked it. He seemed happy about school and enjoyed the Seattle Art Institute where he was making lots of friends who shared his love of art, photography and 3-D modeling.

When we received our tax refund, we decided to buy a used BMW 200i so Jake could drive to Seattle every day. Because our Pontiac now had high mileage, I felt it was going to start breaking down.

Jake trusted me to pick out the car. I did my homework and found out that this series BMW was very solid mechanically. You could really rack up some miles on the engine. I looked at a few of them and used my gift of sight to see just how mechanically sound each car was. I found one with a perfect body that needed a tune up, oil change and brakes and only had 65,000 miles on the engine.

Still, I learned the owner lied and said nothing had to be done to the car except for the paint job. And it drove like a dream on the highway. The guy was asking $850, but when I opened the car hood and looked at the engine, I told him about the needed repairs and negotiated the price to $650.

I figured a $1000 investment, which would include the new paint job, would make the car like new again. That would leave us money to add to our savings.

It was important that Jake drive to Seattle for school because he had to be back in time to get the kids from Darlene across the hall who would baby sit while I worked. She would get the kids from school and take them to her apartment.

A few months later after getting our BMW completely restored, we felt like we had a new car.

One morning Jake left the car running outside in the parking lot of our apartment building because he had forgotten a textbook in the house and ran back into the apartment to get it. When he returned to the parking lot our car was gone. Jake came back into the apartment extremely upset telling me that he had to call the police because our car was gone, and how stupid he felt for leaving it running with the keys in it in the first place.

When the police showed up my hopes for any type of justice were quickly dashed when the police officers told us that we would probably never see our car again. If we did, it would probably be destroyed.

They also told us that they did not spend too much time looking for stolen cars since there were higher priority crimes.

After the police left, Jake caught the bus to the park and Ride and went to school anyway.

Then I sat on the sofa in the living room wondering what the hell we were going to do with two kids and no car. Since the car was paid for and Jake was in college full-time, we had decided not to purchase full coverage on our car insurance and only had liability. I regretted that decision now.

I was supposed to start work in a few days. I struggled to deal with the situation and got the kids to school.

Then I spent the morning in the apartment depressed because our car had been stolen. Finally, around one in the afternoon I was washing dishes in the kitchen when suddenly I heard a voice from within me telling me to go across the hall and borrow Darlene's station wagon and drive to Sixth Avenue to the furniture store.

I did not pay attention to the voice and thought it was my imagination playing tricks on me because I was so upset about being without our car. Why would I go down the hall to borrow Darlene's car I asked myself?

But for the next 30 minutes I continued to hear the voice come from within me saying go borrow Darlene's car and drive down to Sixth Avenue where the antique furniture store is.

By then Lucy was home from school, so I took her by the hand and together we went down the hall and I borrowed Darlene's station wagon.

I began to drive down Sixth Avenue which was three short blocks away from my apartment building and drove west toward the antique furniture store. Minutes later before I had even reached the store, I could see my car parked across the street from the furniture store, and there was a guy standing next to the driver's side.

I pulled up next to the furniture store and parked. I looked at Lucy sitting in the passenger seat and told her to stay in the car and not to get out.

Then I ran across the street and confronted the thief standing next to my car by saying, "What the hell are you doing with my car? This is my car that you stole this morning from my apartment building!"

That is when he told me that he had just gotten out of prison a few days prior and begged me not to call the police. I looked and saw that the guy was selling what I assumed were stolen golf clubs out of the back of my car. I just could not believe it; I told him that I was going to go inside the liquor store to call the police.

I cautioned him not to go anywhere, but as I walked into the liquor store, I realized that there was no way this guy was going to wait around for the police to show up. I quickly turned around and saw him running away. I called the police anyway because I knew that his fingerprints were all over my car and the cops could use his fingerprints to pick him up and get his car stealing butt off the streets of Tacoma.

When the police arrived, they were even more disinterested than they had been that morning. The police told me to take my car home.

I looked at them and asked "Well, are you going to take my car down to the station for fingerprinting and evidence for a court trial? And are you guys going to go out and look for this guy and pick him up and put him back in prison where he belongs? He should not be on the streets because he's out here selling stolen golf clubs on a street corner and stealing cars, and he's only been out of prison for a few days according to him."

Once again, the Tacoma Police Department told me that they had cases that were a higher priority, and how I should feel grateful that I got my stolen car back in one piece.

"What a bunch of butt holes!" I looked the cop in the eye and said, "no wonder 'God' had to intervene in this disgusting situation, because if I had not heard the voice of 'God' telling me to borrow my neighbor's car and drive down Sixth Avenue I wouldn't even have my car right now."

I took a breath and continued, "Since 'God' told me where to find my car, then that means He also knows that you and your police department did nothing to find my car or the shit hole who stole it in the first place. That's something you're going to have to answer for when you die."

Then the officer got mad and told me once again that the Tacoma Police Department had cases that were a higher priority. Like murder, he said sarcastically.

The police just left me there on the street corner with two cars to drive home by myself.

I called Darlene from a nearby phone booth and told her what happened. She got Ken the owner of the apartment building we lived in to drive her down there to pick up her station wagon so I could drive my car home.

Super excited I could hardly wait to tell Jake when he got home from school that evening and Pastor Rainey. They were going to be shocked!

I looked up at the sky and thanked "I am" for caring about my family enough to give us our car back. Because I knew that it was "I Am's" voice that told me where my stolen car was, and then supplied me with a vehicle to go get it back.

When Jake came home from school that evening, he was not only surprised, but shocked and could not believe that "I Am" found the car with the thief selling stolen golf clubs out of it.

I kept telling Jake about the voice I heard telling me to borrow Darlene's station wagon and drive down Sixth Avenue near the furniture store.

Jake said it did not matter if it was God or if it was me who found the car, he was just glad that we had our car back.

CHAPTER 175

The following Monday morning, dressed in my office work attire, I went to work at the law firm, knowing that a presence that I could not see had given me my job and my stolen car back.

Marlene had Betty, the receptionist, explain my daily job responsibilities. Once Betty and I were alone, she wasted no time telling me that she had applied for my job and wasn't selected.

"I just don't understand it," she said, "I have a master's degree and you don't."

"Well, I don't understand it either, but I sure am glad to be here," I told her with a big smile on my face.

It must have been hard for her seeing me in a position that she wanted, as well as introducing me to all the lawyers and paralegals in the office. I felt sorry for her.

I was to be on call for anything these people needed assistance with. The job was easy: all I had to do was retrieve the mail, sort it and distribute it to the correct people. I also had to pick up all the informational paperwork from legal cases and file them back into their case folders after the attorneys and paralegals were finished using them. In addition, I was also in charge of mailing checks out to clients, along with getting birthday cakes. Basically, I was the office gopher, but it did not matter because I was well paid and had a family to support.

As time passed, I caught on quickly at the office and got along well with the attorneys, secretaries and paralegals. The firm was quite prestigious and had an impressive client list that worked on high-profile oil litigation, among other cases.

I worked closely with an attorney named Dan Jones whom I suspected was a partier because when I came to work every morning, he was in his office cat napping. Most times he was even hung over, and on occasion still smelled like alcohol from the night before.

One of my duties was providing cups of hot coffee to get him going for the day before other attorneys saw how hungover he was.

To my surprise, one night he called me at home and confessed that he had a cocaine problem and did not know what to do about it. I talked to him for hours on the phone at night, and at one point he even broke down crying. He told me that he had been raised Mormon and that he was ashamed of himself because he knew better than to get hooked on coke.

I prayed for him, and I urged him to go to an AA meeting or check himself into rehab before he lost his job over his addiction. Then we prayed together over the phone.

A week later he was fired. I guess no matter how hard I tried to cover for him in the office by giving him coffee and V-8 juice to drink, obviously somebody else realized what was going on with him. Or maybe his work was suffering. I never knew for sure; all I know is a week later he was gone. I prayed for "I Am" to help him.

He continued to call me on the telephone for advice, then two months later he packed up his things and moved back home to Utah. He said that his family had arranged for him to check into a rehab hospital there and that he was returning to the church and his faith. The prayer worked.

I was happy for him, and proud of him for being man enough to realize that he had a problem with cocaine to begin with and the balls to get the help he needed.

After Dan had gone, he was quickly replaced with another attorney, and life at the office went on as if nothing had ever happened.

I had no idea why people liked to tell me such personal details of their life. Once Dan left, Betty quickly took his place. She would be late coming back from lunch and asked me to cover for her at the receptionist desk. She took long lunches with her ex-boyfriend to have sex in his car while she was engaged to somebody else. Every time her current boyfriend called the office while she was on one of her little lunch dates, I would tell him that she was on a long lunch.

One day I asked her why she was even engaged to begin with if she still felt the need to sleep with her ex-boyfriend behind her fiancé's back. She said that her fiancé was the type of guy you married, and her ex-boyfriend was the guy that you slept with on the side.

Wow, I thought. This girl is going to marry someone then keep a lover on the side. I felt sorry for the guy she was about to marry because Betty was a real snake.

Shortly after that I started noticing that some of the secretaries were giving Betty my work instead of giving it to me. I thought it was strange and I asked a few of the secretaries about it. They told me that Betty did not have enough work to do between phone calls and appointments at the receptionist desk, and they were only throwing her work to help her fill up her time.

I suspected that Betty was trying to take my job. I figured if Betty was slimy enough to accept an engagement ring from her fiancé while having sex with her ex-boyfriend in the car on her lunch break, then she was capable of anything.

Another reason I did not trust her was she made a comment once that her father was prejudiced against black people and Mexicans and basically anyone who was not white. She had to hide the fact that she even had a working relationship with me when she got home from work. I thought to myself what kind of a grown woman hides her real life? Besides, something in my gut just told me that smile on her face where I was concerned was not to be trusted under any circumstances.

As time went on, I noticed that even more of my work was being channeled her way by the secretaries. I suspected that they were all in cahoots with one another for Betty to get my job. They thought that I should be the receptionist and Betty should be assisting the attorneys, paralegals and secretaries.

None of them had a clue that I could tell what they were thinking and knew what they were doing. I did not know what to do about it except to pray and talk with Marlene, my office manager, whom I considered my friend.

After speaking with Marlene, I felt a little better because she told me that she knew what was going on as well. She already knew that those secretaries were attempting to make it look like I was unable to do the work they gave me and that they had been forced to pass it on to Betty. Marlene told me that she knew I was competent. She told me not to worry about it; that she was going to solve the problem by speaking to the secretaries and Betty herself.

As I walked to the bus stop that evening after work, I thought to myself who knew that there was this type of dirty dealing going on in a law firm. As I stood there waiting for my bus, I silently told "I Am" that I did not want to be around people like that on a regular basis. I especially did not want to go to work and have to fight to do the work I was assigned. I could tell that Marlene knew that Betty was untrustworthy before I was hired. Perhaps that was why she hired me for the position instead of her. No wonder Marlene told me during my interview that the law firm needed some fresh blood around the office.

My instincts told me that not only did Marlene know about Betty, but purposely kept her there at the receptionist desk because of her attitude.

I looked up towards the sky and asked "I Am" to give me another way to make money because I did not want to go to work five days a week playing games with somebody where my job was concerned. It was not that I could not take a little competition, I could. But I had two children and a husband to think about, and at this point in my life I really felt the need to be happy during the day while I was at work.

I did not want to work with vipers like Betty and the secretaries. They even gossiped about the head of the firm despite his invitation to everyone at work to visit his beach house where he personally grilled fresh salmon for us.

The secretaries claimed that Mr. Jamison was an alcoholic. As I got to know him better, I realized that he did not want to be a lawyer. His heart's desire was to be a glassblower, just like the glass blowers in Italy. He even traveled to Venice to learn special techniques from the Italians.

I looked at some of his pieces when he invited us to his home and thought that they were exquisite. What a shame that this poor man thought he needed to go to law school and become a lawyer all for the sake of money, instead of the true artist he was. He should have had enough confidence to realize that he was good enough to make a living at it. But I never saw any evidence of Mr. Jamison being an alcoholic.

The secretaries also thought he was a little eccentric and strange, which was stupid to me because the only thing strange about Mr. Jamison was the fact that he continued to show up at that damn law firm every day instead of getting on a plane to Venice and living out his artistic dreams.

This was one of those rare moments when I wished I were a stay-at-home mom. Then I thought to myself there was no value to that financially. Staying home with your kids and raising them did not pay to keep the lights on.

Then I heard "I Am's" voice say: raising your two children is the most important job you could have in the world. The voice was so profound that I stopped thinking and my mind fell silent because this was the same voice that told me where my stolen car was. I stood there contemplating it for a moment. It made sense to me; raising a child was probably the most important job in the world because you were molding the life of another human being.

It was at that very moment I felt honored that "I Am" had entrusted Lucy and Jack to my care.

Time passed and I began to hate my job at the law firm more because I was being constantly undermined by Betty. She had the secretaries giving her my work even more now than before since Marlene was on a three-week vacation. It did not matter that she had instructed all of them to stop. I wanted to say something about it to the attorney in charge, but I was trying not to cause drama in the office. So, I kept silent and endured because I knew that "I Am" had given me my job.

I was relieved and thankful when Jake graduated from college at the top of his class with a degree in multimedia and 3-D modeling. I had managed to make it through two years at the firm, which felt like a lifetime. I now had the option of quitting because Jake had a job with a company called RealTime before he even graduated.

RealTime was a multimedia start-up company, and its goal was to make interactive computer game software. They were hiring Jake to do 3-D models and textures. Plus, they were contracting Jake out to the United States government to do something called flight simulation. It made Jake angry because his boss was getting $50 an hour, and he was not seeing any of that money, yet he was the one doing the work.

The office where he worked was attractive and overlooked the water in downtown Seattle. Everyone came to work in blue jeans, tee-shirts and walked around the office barefoot. They also had a refrigerator stocked with expensive beer, bottled water and a large variety of soft drinks.

When I gave my two-week's notice at the law firm I was so happy. I had certainly missed being around my children during the day, feeding them and dropping them off at school and then picking them up again. I had not realized how lucky I had it until I started working at BJ & B, but it did not take me long to get back into the routine of being a housewife and mother.

CHAPTER 176

This time I tried to be more grateful that I had two children to raise and was lucky enough to have that option of working or staying at home.

I made sure that before I quit working at the law firm, I purchased my first dream car: a 1968 automatic stick shift Volkswagen convertible bug with a cloth top, that was Coca-Cola red. I had been fantasizing about this car since sixth grade and knew that "I Am" had given it to me. How did I know? Because after dreaming about the car for years I saw one for sale but was broke at the time and the seller told me that he would save the car for me for six months so I could save the $2000 necessary to purchase it.

At this point we also purchased a Volkswagen van since Jake wanted something with a lot of space for the kids and our dogs. We had moved up to Seattle into a small rural community called Skyway Renton where we rented a lovely house sitting on 2 acres of land in a wooded area. I commuted on the freeway for church.

Jake had purchased a wolf dog for me that we named John Henry and we also had a black lab named Zoe after Fremont died of old age.

Jake also got himself a mynah bird and named him Pink Floyd after the rock group. Jake trained that bird to talk trash to people and attack on command. We found Zoe because I decided to visit the dog pound one afternoon and could not leave without taking one of those poor animals' home with me.

We also had a colorful Koi Pond that Jake and Lucy built together in our backyard. Lucy loved animals and over the years Jake had bought her fish, hamsters and snakes for her to keep in her bedroom. She enjoyed fishing and crabbing and reminded me of Ellie Mae Clampett on the Beverly Hillbillies.

Lucy was determined to move to Texas when she grew up where she claimed that she was going to buy herself a pick-up truck. She was usually running around in a pair of cut off shorts, a T-shirt and a pair of cowboy boots that she refused to remove from her feet unless it was time for bed or bath.

Unfortunately, she had outgrown the cowboy boots and, when we offered to buy a new pair, she refused. She wanted to keep the pair that she had.

Many nights I went into her room and thought, these boots are too small for her.

Finally, one day the side of the boot split open because her feet were too wide for them. It was a sad day for Lucy when she was forced to throw those boots away.

Lucy was my beautiful little girl who looked like her father with his complexion, little freckles on her face, and long blonde, wavy hair that reached the middle of her back. She was such a tomboy that I kept her hair in ponytails or braids just to keep her somewhat neat and tidy looking.

She enjoyed riding with me in my convertible bug. I remember the day I first caught a glimpse of the "girly girl" in Lucy. As we drove to Bellevue, WA. I was excited because this was our first girl's trip to the department store together.

As we were driving on the freeway "Born to be Wild" began to play on the radio. Lucy loved that song and we both began singing it together. Suddenly, as I was going 55 miles an hour on the freeway, Lucy stood up in the car on her seat in her little cut-off shorts with her new cowboy boots and began singing waving her head and arms in the air. I thought how lucky she was to be completely free just to be a kid without the adult responsibility I had when I was her age.

I vowed to make sure that she remained a child who would never have to endure the things that I had experienced and suffered.

Lucy was nine years old and today we were going to get her first tube of ruby red lipstick that she had requested! It was a good day that day, because it was just the two of us together: mother and daughter buying lipstick. Just us girls on our first official girl's day out no animals, or people, just us.

Our lives happily unfolded this way for a while with our family, hybrid wolf, black lab, Lucy's hamsters, cat, fish, rooster and snakes.

Then one day at all ended.

CHAPTER 177

I went to pick Jake up from work and was given the bad news that his boss had decided to sell the company to Sony.

As we drove home that evening both of us were in shock because it was so unexpected that his company would be bought out by somebody. His boss kept the whole thing quietly to himself.

The only thing Jake would be leaving with was $9,000 worth of stock.

Immediately he began to look for another job and as the months went by, he was unable to find one. We suspected it had something to do with his voice. At this point words were missing from sentences and his voice sounded raspy. He was always hoping that the fact he had PTSD, along with bad ankles, could remain a secret from future employers.

People often got nervous when you mentioned PTSD.

One day as I was washing dishes in my kitchen I begin talking to "I Am" asking it to give us a means of support. Then I heard a voice say Jesus was a carpenter.

Now, I have a habit of doubting everything. I am one of those people who need concrete proof, otherwise something is just a crazy thought. But as the day went on, I continued to hear the voice.

By late afternoon I thought to myself what is the significance of Jesus being a carpenter? Then I thought to myself it means he built stuff. That is when I had a vision: I can build furniture to support my family while Jake finds another job. Only problem was I did not know how to build furniture.

Another idea was to go to a thrift store buy a used piece of furniture and fix it up. Then I could take it to the Fremont open market that was held every Saturday and Sunday by the waterfront near downtown Seattle. I was thinking there would be lots of people there.

Every time Jake and I walked through there with the kids there was always a large crowd of people every weekend. So, I would have customers without advertising.

I quickly went to find Jake who was on the computer looking for another job. I told him about my idea and how "I Am's" voice told me to do it. He thought the idea was ridiculous, but I figured we had nothing to lose. We had our savings to live on, but savings only lasted so long.

Besides, I knew that I did not want to leave my children to go to work at a bank or something worse. To me that was like spending eight hours a day in hell on Earth. I figured what did I have to lose?

I decided to go for it and prove Jake wrong.

That afternoon I went to the local thrift store and bought a 1950s era wooden four, drawer dresser, that could be used in a child's room. It was selling for only eight dollars, so I bought it, put the top down in my Volkswagen and was able to fit it in the backseat.

At the paint store I asked the clerk if they had any cans of paint that had been returned. Then I went to a pawnshop and purchased a palm sander for $10; used of course. Sanding paper in different grades came with it.

I did not know what the hell I was doing, I was just following that voice that came from within me because it had not failed me yet.

When I returned home, I got everything out of my car by myself, opened the garage door and put everything inside. I plugged in the palm sander and began sanding off the old, cracked paint on the dresser. The color of the chest of drawers was a pale yellow so I decided to sand some of the paint off and put a coat of white paint on top of that color. After it dried, I sanded it again so hints of the yellow would show through the white paint. Then I created a patina on the finish by applying some light brown wax I found in the garage.

The whole thing only took me an hour and a half and looked beautiful. My plan was to sell it for the wholesale price of $65, that would allow me to make my investment money back, plus a nice profit.

I went into the house to get Jake, who had no idea what I was doing in the garage. I wanted to show him my masterpiece just to prove to him that we could make money this way.

As I expected, Jake saw my chest of drawers and was impressed.

"It looks like an antique." He said.

"It looked like a piece of junk when I first brought it home," I explained enthusiastically.

"I can actually build a chest of drawers like this in a couple hours," Jake said.

"What! I had no idea you knew how to build furniture."

"My dad taught me and my brothers when I was a kid, and we had that relative who built furniture for that Mormon guy I told you about named Brigham Young so it's in my blood. Jake told me.

"Wow, I'm impressed. I'll find some more used furniture, fix it up and sell it at the Fremont open market this coming weekend." I said enthusiastically.

By the end of that week, I had six pieces of furniture to sell: two chest of drawers, two wooden nightstands and a wooden bench. Jake and I loaded the furniture into our Volkswagen van, paid $25 to get a booth at the Fremont open market and we were set.

We started selling the furniture at 8 a.m. when the market opened and by noon were sold out. I had invested $60 buying beat up old furniture and had just earned $325.

My profit margin was fat, and I felt just like my grandfather with his used furniture store. I thought to myself grandfather must be looking down on me proudly as I carried on a family tradition.

I went home and immediately reinvested, and this time I bought 12 pieces of furniture for five and 10 bucks apiece at the thrift store. Nobody wanted the stuff because it had a wobbly leg, or the wooden finish needed to be redone so I purposely looked for pieces of furniture that needed a hammer and a nail put to it.

By the second weekend at the flea market, I came home with $900 after a $150 investment. This time I decided to go further and bought a copy of Country Living Magazine which was doing a spread on Martha Stewart. I totally made everything in that week's collection look: shabby chic. Everything was white with a pale green undertone and on a few of the pieces Jake painted little vines on them.

The third week I had a hard time finding pieces of furniture that were $10 and under, so Jake and I had the brilliant idea of tearing down an old shed that was on our property for wood. That week, for the first time, we made our own furniture. Instead of using nails, Jake decided to peg the wood together. Jake enjoyed making what he called Shaker Furniture.

We invested another $100 to buy more tools at the pawnshop and began making Shaker side tables with drawers, Shaker nightstands with a drawer or two, as well as a long narrow dining table, like the kind they used in the 15th century with matching benches and church pews. We decided that everything we made would be an antique reproduction.

Jake was so good he could just see a photo of a piece of furniture and duplicate it.

Each week we were so successful at the flea market that store owners bought our stuff and began reselling it in their stores.

After four months of this we started getting custom orders from customers as well as store owners. Jake would draw the piece of furniture out on paper for the customer including the finish and get the customer's approval. We would then take a deposit of half the price upfront for the materials, then fill the order.

It got to the point where we had so much work that we were working seven days a week, sometimes until 3 and 4 a.m. in our garage. I did not even have time to attend church now, but I still checked in regularly with Pastor Rainey by phone, which became a lifelong habit for me.

We decided to call our little home-based business, "Lone Wolf Designs."

I even identified a permanent source for pine wood. I got the idea to go to a big wood company in our Volkswagen van and purposely took my children. I walked into the building and asked for the man in charge.

When he came out and invited me into his office I sat down and explained that my husband was a disabled veteran who was having a hard time finding a job, and how we had started our own furniture business to support our family. I asked if he would mind helping us out and selling us wood at a low-cost.

And to my amazement, he told me that he had pine boards that had markings on them that he always put in the scrap bin.

"You're welcome to have that for free, and if you want to buy other wood, I can help you out with a little discount."

I drove away from Weyerhaeuser Wood Company that day with so much free wood in my Volkswagen van that I had to put both children upfront in the same seat to drive home. And the beauty of it was we either painted or stained our furniture so the wood marking did not show. I thanked "I Am" on the way home because I knew that what just happened was a miracle.

So, each week I would show up at Weyerhaeuser and fill my Volkswagen van up with as much wood as I could fit into it. Sometimes I even went back for a second trip there was so much wood for me to take home and I soon had wood piles in my garage.

At this point, we were adding onto our collection: Shaker blanket stands and entertainment centers, TV stands; in fact, anything that a person could use at home.

Within six months, we were making more money from our furniture business than we ever had with both of us working full time. Not only were we making enough money to pay our monthly living expenses for the family, but we had tons left over for savings.

I thought about what a genius "I Am" was to give me this idea and was grateful that it loved me enough to make sure I could support my family with my husband. It was amazing; I never would have guessed that my idea of a good time would be using a scroll saw in my garage.

For the next three years we worked our butts off building a name for ourselves around the Seattle area supplying stores and custom making furniture for clients. I still did the market every weekend just to keep the flow going. After all, the flea market was where I had gotten my start.

By then I had sold my Volkswagen convertible and was driving a 1961 cream color Volvo 122S series two-door with a cast-iron engine. I had to have my own stereo system installed into the car and I got myself a 1950s car coat and some antique slacks to wear with it.

Every time I drove my car, I thought about Lucille Ball in the I love Lucy Show. Plus, the best thing about driving the Volvo was it never broke down and used diesel fuel instead of gasoline. And when you started the car there was no key, you just pushed the start button. I could often be found listening to *Frank Sinatra's Greatest Hits* or Doris Day while driving my antique car around town.

After three years of furniture prosperity, sales began to slow down because Boeing had laid off a bunch of workers which cut our monthly profit in half. It made us reconsider being in the furniture business. We started thinking that since we had children to support that we needed to have more dependable income. We had plenty of savings, but figured it was time for a change and to move on.

CHAPTER 178

That is when Jake and I decided to get regular jobs again. I found one working for our landlord and her real estate office. She had her own business buying and selling foreclosed homes. She wanted me to run her office while she was out in the field and list real estate properties for her on the computer. There was no health insurance provided, but the pay was excellent.

Jake worked with our friend Michael making and installing expensive bars for places in the Seattle area while looking for a new computer job that never came.

Six months later we decided to move to Utah where his family was so the kids could get to know their relatives on Jake's side of the family. Since the initial apology Jake's parents had been calling to speak with their grandchildren on a regular basis. Besides, Jake wanted to go to college all over again. This time he wanted an environmental studies degree.

So, we packed up everything we had into a large U-Haul truck, got a tow device from U-Haul to pull the Volvo with, packed the animals and the kids into the Volkswagen van, which I drove, and we were off.

When we arrived in Utah, we stayed with Jake's parents for the first few months until we found jobs. I was shocked when his parents allowed us to put a coffee machine in the kitchen. Mormons do not allow caffeine in their systems.

His parents and I became fast friends. And they accepted the fact that Jake and I would never be Mormons. They even allowed us to keep our wolf dog and lab at the house.

I thought their meals were a little bland. So, for Christmas I cooked a dinner the Los Angeles soul food way. I make a turkey with gravy and basted it in butter. I made brown sugar ham with baked stuffing along with Mac and cheese. I also made some candied yams and a pot of greens. The entire family went crazy for my soul food. They even enjoyed my Christmas music of Nat King Cole and other Christmas songs.

Soon after, Jake enrolled in college with the VA paying for it again with a living allowance every month while he was in school.

We found a rental house in the University of Utah area across the street from a private school called Judge Memorial Catholic school.

Jake worked part-time for the Veterans Administration on Fort Douglas as a VA counselor in a work-study program. I worked for a woman artist named Amelia who owned a business called "The Design House." She designed pillows, and quilts; anything that a person could need for a home. She also sold designer fabric that was $200 dollars a yard and lower. Amelia was the best in town and knew it.

She reminded me of the actress Barbara Stanwyck whom I used to watch on a TV show called The Big Valley. Amelia was as strong as steel and I looked up to her as a role model, because this woman came from nothing and started out with nothing. Now she was living in a large luxurious home worth millions of dollars in Park City that was featured in a magazine. She owned the building where her business operated and every designer in Salt Lake City and Park City came to her for their fabric and design needs.

Her husband was named Charlie and owned an auto repair shop called "Charlie and Mick's."

Whenever I looked at Amelia, I saw the possibilities of what I myself could be achieving in my own life; she was such an example to women everywhere. I loved working for Amelia because she was fabulous in every way. She even designed her own clothing and had them made by her head seamstress. And at age 65 she drove a top-of-the-line convertible Porsche to work every morning unless it was snowing, or the roads were bad. Then, she was forced to drive her Mercedes-Benz SUV.

I waited on the best interior designers from Park City to Salt Lake City and I loved it. I worked for Amelia for a few years then I moved on to the bank for a few years which bored me senseless, so I quit and took a job at a local record store. This job I loved because I could listen to records all day long. I realized that the record store job was a dream come true from high school. I had wanted to work at Aaron's records across the street from my high school, but there was never a job opening since the job was too cool for people to quit.

While I was working at the record store Jake graduated from college and obtained a job working for the Federal Government as a computer engineer.

That is when we decided to start looking for a house to buy. Only problem was all the houses we liked were seriously out of our price range. Then one day Jake and I were taking the dogs for a hike in Red Butte Gardens when we saw an exquisite home with a For Sale and Open House sign in front of it.

Jake insisted that we stop and look, but I told him that he was crazy because the house looked way out of our price range.

"Let us go look anyway. It doesn't cost anything to look," he said as we parked the car and went in.

There were a few other people inside looking at the house as well. The owner approached us and introduced himself as Bob Smith, then shook Jake's hand.

"Take a look around and let me know if you have any questions," he said as he handed Jake a fact sheet about the house.

We fell in love with the house the moment we stepped into it. It was over 90 years old and had been built in 1906. The bright red door led you inside where you entered the home and stepped onto hardwood floors. The entryway was big enough for a hall tree and coat rack. The spacious well-designed living room had three large windows and plenty of light.

The dining room also had hardwood floors, three windows and a fireplace with colorful tile surround. In addition, there was a pantry that led into a medium-sized kitchen with new wooden cabinets and a dishwasher. There was a back door in the kitchen that led out to a large wooden deck and a generous backyard with a few trees.

There was also a lovely hallway that led to two bedrooms, and a bathroom with a tub/ shower. Then there was a door that led down to a basement that had two bedrooms and the laundry room that also had its own entry door from the backyard.

Finally, there was the staircase that led up to an attic area which had a bathroom with a tub, a closet, a main bedroom area with a huge window as well as two other bedrooms. The house was huge, old and beautiful, and most likely out of our price range. We looked on the fact sheet and saw the asking price was $50,000 more than we were preapproved for by our credit union.

The owner approached us again and asked us what we thought of the house. We told him that we loved it, but it was a little out of our price range.

"I'm going to take your number anyway, I have a good feeling about the two of you," he said. Jake and I left for a hike never expecting to hear from the guy again. Then three weeks later we got a phone call from him asking us to meet him at the house that afternoon.

When we showed up, he told us that he had gotten no offers on the house and since we seemed to love the house so much, he decided to offer us a "rent to own" program for a short period of time.

"I will charge you rent each month then an additional $250 a month to go toward your closing costs when you buy the house. This way you will have plenty of time to increase your income."

Thrilled, Jake and I accepted.

We went home, told Jack and Lucy the good news then we celebrated by going out for dinner.

A month later the last dream that I had asked for came true: we moved into our amazing new home with our two kids and wolf dogs. At this point our lab had died and we took in a wolf coyote husky mix dog.

Immediately Lucy and Jack began fighting over the basement apartment. Jake and I settled it by telling them they could both stay down there since there were two bedrooms. We really did not want either of them sleeping down there because of the entry door. We did not want them sneaking out in the middle of the night past curfew.

The wolf dogs loved their big backyard, while Jake and I were excited to start our very own vegetable garden for the first time together.

For the first time we were living in our dream home, and we would never have to move out until we were ready because it was all ours.

All my childhood dreams had now come true: The Little Boy on The Moon loved and adored me more than anything in the world, we had two beautiful children, a family of pets and the perfect home which we eventually brought and lived in for over twenty years. And I owned a beautiful red convertible sports car among many others. And for me each car started as a dream then became a reality.

Some people dream of having wealth, power, success in the material world. For me, all I ever wanted was for the "Little Boy on the Moon" to find me.

That invisible power had not failed me; instead, it led me to this moment of fulfillment, and I knew that without a doubt.

My message to you is no matter what religion you are something made you, it makes breath come out of your nostrils 24 hours a day. Most people call it God, but it goes by many names. I choose to call it "I Am." I figured if it had the power to create the solar systems and other life forms then it had the power to make my dreams come true.

It will do the same for you if you just ask, talk and listen to it. Believe that all obstacles can be overcome and shine as bright as the sun itself because your dreams can come true too.

THE END